SINGLED
OUT

SINGLED
OUT

How Singles Are Stereotyped,
Stigmatized, and Ignored,
and Still Live Happily Ever After

BELLA DEPAULO, PH.D.

St. Martin's Press
New York

www.stmartins.com

Excerpt from "The Disappearance of Elaine Coleman" by Steven Millhauser. Reprinted by permission of International Creative Management, Inc. Copyright © 1999 by Steven Millhauser. Originally published in *The New Yorker*.

Excerpt from "The Hill Bachelors" by William Trevor. Reprinted by permission of Sll/sterling Lord Literistic, Inc. Copyright © 2000 by William Trevor. Originally published in *The New Yorker*.

Excerpt from "Select All" by Christopher Caldwell. Reprinted by permission of Christopher Caldwell. Originally published in *The New Yorker*, March 1, 2004.

Excerpt from "Let's Get Married." From Frontline and WGBH Educational Foundation Copyright @ 2002 WGBH/Boston.

Excerpt from Amazon.com about the stereotyping of singles in the medical profession. Reprinted by permission of Cathy Goodwin.

Excerpt from *Elle*. Reprinted by permission of Rachael Combe.

Excerpt from "When Valentine's Day Doesn't Go Your Way." Permission was granted by David Borgenicht, author of *The Worst Case Scenario Survival Handbook: Dating and Sex*.

Excerpt from "Alone. Ahh. Sigh," reprinted as "Living Alone" in *Off Ramp* (2004, Henry Holt). Copyright © 2004 by Hank Stuever, reprinted by permission of Hank Stuever.

(continued on page 325)

Design by Susan Walsh

Library of Congress Cataloging-in-Publication Data

DePaulo, Bella M.
    Singled out : how singles are stereotyped, stigmatized, and ignored, and still live happily ever after / Bella DePaulo. — 1st ed.
        p. cm.
    Includes bibliographical references.
    ISBN-13: 978-0-312-34081-0
    ISBN-10: 0-312-34081-8
    1. Single people. I. Title.

HQ800.D47 2006
306.81'5—dc22   2006012816

First Edition: November 2006

10   9   8   7   6   5   4   3   2   1

To Susan Hurt
an extraordinary friend

And to single people everywhere, living happily ever after

CONTENTS

SINGLED OUT

CHAPTER ONE

Singlism: The Twenty-First-Century Problem That Has No Name

I think married people should be treated fairly. They should not be stereotyped, stigmatized, discriminated against, or ignored. They deserve every bit as much respect as single people do.

I can imagine a world in which married people were not treated appropriately, and if that world ever materialized, I would protest. Here are a few examples of what I would find offensive:

- When you tell people you are married, they tilt their heads and say things like "Aaaawww" or "Don't worry, honey, your turn to divorce will come."
- When you browse the bookstores, you see shelves bursting with titles such as *If I'm So Wonderful, Why Am I Still Married* and *How to Ditch Your Husband After Age 35 Using What I Learned at Harvard Business School.*
- Every time you get married, you feel obligated to give expensive presents to single people.
- When you travel with your spouse, you each have to pay more than when you travel alone.
- At work, the single people just assume that you can cover the holidays and all the other inconvenient assignments; they figure that as a married person, you don't have anything better to do.
- Single employees can add another adult to their health-care plan; you can't.
- When your single coworkers die, they can leave their Social Security benefits to the person who is most important to them; you are

not allowed to leave yours to anyone—they just go back into the
system.

☐ Candidates for public office boast about how much they value single
people. Some even propose spending more than a billion dollars in
federal funding to persuade people to stay single, or to get divorced if
they already made the mistake of marrying.

☐ Moreover, no one thinks there is anything wrong with any of this.

Married people do not have any of these experiences, of course, but single people do. People who do not have a serious coupled relationship (my
definition, for now, of single people) are stereotyped, discriminated against,
and treated dismissively. This stigmatizing of people who are single—
whether divorced, widowed, or ever single—is the twenty-first-century
problem that has no name. I'll call it *singlism*.

To be stereotyped is to be prejudged. Tell new acquaintances that you are
single and often they think they already know quite a lot about you. They
understand your emotions: You are miserable and lonely and envious of
couples. They know what motivates you: More than anything else in the
world, you want to become coupled. If you are a single person of a certain
age, they also know why you are not coupled: You are commitment-phobic,
or too picky, or have baggage. Or maybe they figure you are gay and they
think that's a problem, too.

They also believe they know something about your psychological development and your psyche: You are just not as mature as the other people
your age who are coupled. And at heart, you are basically selfish.

From knowing nothing more about you than your status as a single person, other people sometimes think they already know all about your family:
You don't have one. They also know about the important person or persons
in your life: You don't have anyone. In fact, they know all about your life:
You don't have a life.

Because you don't have anyone and you don't have a life, you can be
asked to stay late at work or do all the traveling over the holidays. When
you are a guest in other people's homes, they will know where you can
sleep: on the couch in the living room rather than in a bedroom with a door
that shuts.

They know how your life will unfold: You will grow old alone. Then you will die alone.

Are you a single person who does not recognize yourself in many of these descriptions? So am I. I am happy, I have a life, and there is no way I will grow old alone (a matter that has little to do with having a serious coupled relationship or even living by yourself). That's just for starters. But it is also exactly the point: The conventional wisdom about people who are single is a mythology, a gloss. It is not an accurate description of the textured and varied lives of real people who are single.

I would like to clarify what I mean by "single," but I cannot do so without first explaining what it means to have a serious partner. That, too, is part of the problem: Single people are defined negatively, in terms of what they do not have—a serious partner. They are labeled as "unmarried." But it is singlehood that comes first and then is undone—if it is undone—by marriage. So why aren't married people called "unsingle"?

Back to the serious coupled relationship. Marriage is the gold standard. If you are married, you have your serious partner. It does not matter if you are happy or miserable, faithful or philandering, whether you live in the same home as your partner or on different continents. If you have the certificate, and you are not in the process of tearing it up, you are official.

Official marriage matters. Only the legal version of marriage comes with the guaranteed treasure trove of perks, privileges, rewards, and responsibilities. Access to another adult's Social Security benefits, health-care plan, hospital room, and decisions about a life-sustaining feeding tube can all turn on whether you are legally married. When the Census Bureau counts married people, it is counting the official kind. *Legally single* people, then, are adults who are not officially married. They include people who are divorced and widowed as well as people who have always been single.

More important to the texture of your everyday life is whether or not you are *socially single* or socially coupled. Once again, if you are married, you automatically count as coupled. Beyond that, the criteria are more slippery. People try to discern your coupled status from a hodgepodge of clues. Do you seem to be in a romantic relationship with another person? How long have you been with that person? Do you seem to expect to stay together? Are you living together? One question that does not matter much to the social-coupling criterion is whether your pair consists of one man and one woman. Straights, gays, bisexuals, and transsexuals all count as socially coupled if they are in a certain kind of relationship with another person.

Sex is the component that conventionally distinguishes the coupled relationship from every other close relationship, even if that component has not yet been realized or if its practice is a vague and distant memory. (Of course, sex alone is not sufficient. A one-night stand is not a coupled relationship—it is just a fling.)

In trying to discern who really is socially coupled, we are less likely to wonder about the couple's practice of sex than about their approximation to an image, a romantic ideal. The image is two people looking lovingly into each other's eyes, no one else in the picture, the background gauzy and ethereal. In song, the notion is captured by the titles that all sound so similar, such as Nat "King" Cole's "You're My Everything," Elvis Presley's "There Goes My Everything," or Andy Gibb's "I Just Want to Be Your Everything." In lyrics, the romantic ideal is LeAnn Rimes asking "How do I live without you? . . . You're my world, my heart, my soul."

Serious partners, in our current cultural fantasy, are the twosomes who look to each other for companionship, intimacy, caring, friendship, advice, the sharing of the tasks and finances of household and family, and just about everything else. They are the repositories for each other's hopes and dreams. They are each other's soulmates and sole mates. They are Sex and Everything Else Partners.

Now I can explain what *single* means: You don't have a serious partner. The simple distinction—you either have a serious partner or you don't—maps onto the golden rule of singlism, the way of thinking that has become the conventional wisdom of our time: You have a serious partner, or you lose. If you are single, then you lose by definition. No matter what you can point to on your own behalf—spectacular accomplishments, a lifelong and caring convoy of relatives and friends, extraordinary altruism—none of it redeems you if you have no soulmate. Others will forever be scratching their heads and wondering what's wrong with you and comparing notes (he's always been a bit strange; she's so neurotic; I think he's gay). It is like having a gymnastics routine lacking a key element to qualify for a perfect score; no matter how skillfully and gracefully you perform your routine, it will always be judged as deficient.

Serious partner or no serious partner must sound awfully simplistic. Surely the many significant distinctions must matter somehow. Among those without a serious partner, for example, there are single men and single women (always a distinction worth pondering); people who have always been single and those who are divorced or separated or widowed; young singles and old singles; rich singles and poor singles; singles who have children and singles who do not; singles who live in the city and singles who live in the suburbs or the countryside; coastal singles and Midwestern singles; singles living alone and singles living with others; smug singles and singles pining for partners; and singles of different races, ethnicities, and religions, to name just a few. These kinds of distinctions do matter. Some singles are stigmatized more relentlessly and unforgivingly than others.

The many varieties of singlehood, rather than creating hopeless complexity, can actually be sorted out with two simple rules. First, all the existing prejudices remain in place. For example, since men still typically trump women, feminism notwithstanding, single men will have an easier time of it than will single women. Similarly, rich singles will sail more smoothly through singlehood than will poor singles. Second, everyone else curries favor to the degree that they honor soulmate values. Did you ever have a serious partner? If so, then you are better than all those people who never had one. (So, divorced and widowed singles are better than people who have always been single.) Is your soulmate no longer with you through no fault of your own? If so, then you get some credit, too. (So, widows are in some ways better than divorced people.) If you don't have a serious partner, are you at least trying to find one? That's good, too.

When I say that some singles are better than others, I mean better in the public eye. Better mythologically. The lives of the "better" singles seem to make more sense and seem worthy of greater respect than the lives of the "lesser" singles. With regard to how different kinds of singles are actually doing, though—now, that's a whole different story.

Singlism is not something that only coupled people practice. If you are single, you have a role in sustaining the lofty place of couples. You support couples emotionally—cheering them on as they announce the first engagement and wedding, and then the next, and then the one after that—and, of course, financially, with all the gifts. You support them with your time and your flexibility as you take the off-hour assignments and the travel that no one else wants. You support their sense of entitlement as they choose the conditions, the time, and the nature of any get-togethers. You support their presumptuousness as they ask when you are going to settle down, while you politely refrain from asking when they last had sex. You subsidize couples when they pay less per person for vacation packages and memberships in clubs, while you pay full price.

Some components of singlism are built right into American laws and institutions, which means that neither coupled nor single people have any say about sustaining them. Take Social Security, for example. If you are a married person covered by Social Security and you die, your spouse can receive your benefits. But if you are a single person who worked side by side with that married person at the same job for the same number of years and you die, no other adult can receive your benefits. Your money goes back into the system.

Our cherished American notions about all people being created equal and deserving of the same basic civil rights and dignities—they apply mostly to married people. If you are single, even your dead body is deemed less valuable. The eligible spouse of a married person receives a small amount of money from Social Security to cover funeral expenses. No such allowance is available for single people. I suppose the reasoning is that since single people don't have anyone, their dead bodies can simply be tossed into a ditch by the first stranger who discovers them (probably in an empty apartment where they are rotting away or being nibbled at by their starving cats).

The lesser value of single people is institutionalized in other ways, too. For example, the mission of the U.S. Commission on Civil Rights is to ensure equal protection under the law regardless of "race, color, religion, sex, age, disability, or national origin." The U.S. Equal Employment Opportunity Commission is tasked with the same kinds of protections in the workplace. Where's marital status?

When I first became interested in the beliefs and practices I would later construe as singlism, I knew nothing about the big issues, such as the differences in Social Security benefits between me and my married colleagues. I was also oblivious to the demographic revolution that was changing the face of the nation.

When I first accepted an assistant professorship at a university, I would have sworn that just about everyone there and everywhere else was married, or on the cusp of marrying. I did not see it coming that by the year 2003 there would be nearly 52 million Americans, ages eighteen on up, who had been single their entire lives. Nearly 22 million more would be divorced, and 14 million more widowed. So even without counting the nearly 5 million Americans who were separated in 2003, there were more than 87 million adults who were some sort of official single person comprising more than 40 percent of all the adults in the country. (Even subtracting the 11 million who were cohabiting left an impressive 76 million.)

I also did not realize that the household consisting of a married couple and their young children would be in the minority by the turn of the twenty-first century, eclipsed in numbers (though surely not in sentimentality) by households composed of a single person living alone. (And most single people don't live alone.) I still find it remarkable that Americans today will, on the average, spend more years of their adult life single than married.

At first, I didn't think about the potential economic, social, or political power of people who are single. In the opening years of the twenty-first century, single people made up about 40 percent of the workforce, purchased more than 40 percent of all homes, and contributed about $1.6 trillion to the economy. If they had shown up in full force at the polls in the presidential election of 2000 or 2004, they could have knocked soccer moms, security moms, NASCAR dads, or just about any other voting bloc du jour right off the menu.

It wasn't the demographics or the economics or the politics that first tapped me on the shoulder and told me to listen up. For me, the growing awareness that there was something wrong with the place of singles in contemporary society started with the little things, the personal experiences that seemed hardly worth mentioning at the time. The experiences piled up most noticeably when I moved from graduate school, where most of my friends were single, to my first university position at the age of twenty-six.

Here's an example. During one of my first weekends on the job, I had been invited to an out-of-town event with some of my friends from home. I decided not to go. I did not want to miss any opportunities to get to know my new colleagues, who were among the people I expected to be my friends. One of them, a married man, did indeed plan a social event that weekend. He and his wife invited the other person who was hired the same time I was, together with his partner, to go out to dinner. I, however, was not invited.

I wasn't always excluded by the couples, though. For example, one woman I'll call Joanna was single when I first met her, and we became friends. Later, when she found her soulmate, the two of them did include me occasionally. Here is my memory of one such event.

JOANNA: Want to have dinner some night with me and Pat?
ME: Sure. How about this weekend?
JOANNA: We were thinking about Wednesday.
ME: Well, I have some work that I need to finish up on Wednesday night, so that's not the best for me, but I guess I can fit it in.

On Wednesday the three of us began to discuss where to go.

PAT: So what are you in the mood for?
ME: How about the new Thai place? Or maybe Duner's?
JOANNA: We were thinking about Rococo's.

Rococo's was an Italian restaurant and I was happy to have some pasta, so I said fine. When we got there, though, I learned that Joanna and Pat had a different plan.

JOANNA: We thought we'd order a pizza and we could all share.

It was not what I had in mind, but Rococo's did have some interesting toppings, so I agreed. I was ready with my suggestions. The waitress arrived before we had discussed our preferences, but no matter: Pat was ready, too, and recited the four choices that had apparently been agreed upon beforehand with Joanna. The waitress scrawled them down, pivoted, and left. Moments later, though, she returned, saying that regrettably two of the toppings were not available that evening. Finally, I had my chance. My mouth was open, but before I could get the words out, Pat had already announced "our" substitutions.

There were some memorable moments in the workplace as well. Once, I was asked to teach in the evening because "it is harder for the men who have a wife at home to come back in at night." The friend of a colleague, whom I was meeting for the first time, had a suggestion for me upon learning that I was single: She thought I should volunteer to be the leader of her daughter's Girl Scout troop. Then there was the annual department picnic, organized in different ways over the years. My favorites were the ones in which each faculty member contributed the same amount, then each of us could bring everyone in our family. So on the same dime, I went by myself, and my senior colleague brought his wife and four kids.

I am cringing as I describe these instances. Why did I even notice them, much less remember them decades later? That's one of the secrets to the persistence of singlism. It often manifests itself in the minutiae of everyday life. Am I really going to write a book about not getting pepperoni on my pizza? (No. I wanted anchovies.)

Another reason that singlism persists, usually unacknowledged, is that it is so hard to tie the bad behaviors directly and unambiguously to a person's marital status. Perhaps my colleagues excluded me from their weekend plans when I first arrived in town not because I was single but because they found me annoying and wanted to spend as little time with me as possible. Perhaps Joanna and Pat made all the decisions not because they are a couple and I am single but because they are bossy, self-centered, and obnoxious. Or maybe they are smart, as in wise enough not to let anyone speak up who might suggest anchovies. Maybe the person I just met asked me to serve as leader of her daughter's Girl Scout troop not because she thought that as a single person I had lots of free time but because she sensed my inherent leadership qualities in that first instant of our acquaintance.

I was also deterred from acknowledging the prejudices and exclusions by my fantasy of societal redemption. I nurtured the delusion that one day I would wake up and find a whole new world. I would walk into the department and a colleague would say, "Wow, was that ever dim-witted of us to organize the picnic in a way that made the single people subsidize their coworkers who were married with children. We won't do *that* again!" I would open my *New Yorker* and find that the column of restaurant reviews was no longer titled "Tables for Two." I would turn on the TV and hear a candidate boasting that because she was single and had no children, she would devote more time and energy to the concerns of her constituents than would any of her competitors.

I'm still waiting.

There was another deterrent, too. This set of myths and misbehaviors toward singles had no name. There was nothing to tie them together and show how weighty and meaningful and interconnected the whole collection had become. Motorists who are pulled over for driving while black seethe not just because of the inconvenience or the one-time insult but because the indignity suggests an entire constellation of prejudices, stereotypes, and acts of discrimination that is widely recognized as racism. Single people, in contrast, often interpret their experiences of discrimination or stereotyping or exclusion as personal and individual, with no bigger implications for the place of singles as a group in contemporary American society.

It is in the spirit of consciousness-raising that I have coined the term *singlism*. Over the course of this book, I collect the myths about single people, tie them all together, and then throw them out with the rest of the trash.

The term *singlism* points directly at single people and the ways in which they are marginalized and stigmatized. That's only half the racket, though. The other half is the glorifying of marriage and coupling, especially the "You're My Everything" variety. I'll call that matrimania.

Whenever I mention singlism in the same context as racism or sexism or heterosexism or any of the other noxious isms, a slew of protests are hurled my way. I deserve them. In many important ways, singles are simply not in the same category as the most brutally stigmatized groups. As far as I know, no persons have ever been dragged to their death at the back of a pickup truck simply because they were single. There are no "marrieds only" drinking fountains, and there never were. The pity that singles put up with is just not in the same league as the outright hatred conveyed to blacks by shameless racists or the unbridled disgust heaped upon gay men or lesbians by homophobes.

There is another objection I hear a lot. My timing is all wrong. How can I claim that singles are in a difficult position when in fact contemporary singles have newfound freedoms of staggering significance? That's an important point, too.

Financial freedom—women's, in particular—is high on the list of social changes that have empowered many single people. Although women are still paid less than men for comparable work and far too many women and men live in poverty, there are currently sizable numbers of women who earn enough money on their own to support themselves, and maybe even some kids. They are no longer tethered to husbands for economic life support. Neither men nor women need a spouse to have sex without stigma or shame. Children born to single mothers now have the same legal rights as those born to married mothers. With the advent of birth control and legalized abortion, and with progress in medical reproductive technology, women can have sex without having children, and children without having sex.

When sex, parenting, and economic viability were all wound up together in the tight knot that was marriage, the difference between single life and married life was profound. Consider, for example, the Americans who were newly wedded in 1956. No Americans on record married at a younger age than they did, before or since. Half the 1956 grooms had not yet reached the age of 22.5, and half the brides were 20 or younger. The young couples were setting up a household for the first time and saving to buy their first home. In so many deeply significant ways, marriage really was a transition to adulthood. It was a big bold bright line keeping singles on one side and married people on the other.

Now, about half a century later, the institution of marriage remains ensconced in our laws, our politics, our religions, and our cultural imagination. But it is of little true significance as a meaningful life transition. Today a twenty-seven-year-old man is just about as likely to be single as married, and men and women have often cycled through multiple schools and jobs and residences and relationships before they ever marry—if they ever do.

As all the components of marriage that were once tied together have come undone, the number of possible life paths has multiplied. The promise offered by this brave new world is a nearly limitless array of imaginable life stories. Individual Americans can design individualized lives.

But the promise is also the threat. Opportunities can be exciting, but they can also be frightening. Sometimes familiarity, predictability, and simplicity are far more appealing. I know this from my experiences with technology. Just as I am becoming comfortable with the latest e-mail program, it is knocked off my desktop by the next best version, complete with its dazzling scroll of ever more options that I don't understand and don't want. I want my familiarity, predictability, and simplicity. I liked my old e-mail program. I knew how to use it and think about it. I want technological progress to stop.

That's how a lot of people feel about the changes that have shaken the world of marriage and family. That's also why I can claim that singles are in a difficult position when in so many ways they have never been in a better place. The freedom to be single, to create a path through life that does not look like everyone else's, can be unsettling to people who feel more secure with fewer choices.

The technology analogy is not entirely apt. My clinging to my old and familiar e-mail program says little about my deepest values, my moral center, or the meaning of my life. My resistance to the latest upgrades does not double as a judgment of other people who embrace the new innovations. Decisions about how to lead a life, though, are fraught with significance.

In our minds, there was a golden American era, the 1950s, when marriage was at the center of our lives, its place sacred and uncontested. It suffused life with meaning and predictability. As we imagine it, that time was safe, warm, comforting, and morally unambiguous (even if the realities were not nearly so serene). The more complicated, unsettled, and contentious our current American lives and American values seem to be, and the more these complexities seem threatening rather than freeing, the more we yearn for the way we believe things used to be.

I think that many people would like to restore the place that marriage once had in our lives. They would like to be able to predict the broad outlines of a life well lived: Stay at home with Mom, Dad, and sibs through late adolescence or early adulthood; perhaps work or go to school for a while, or just proceed directly to marriage; continue working if you are a man; buy a home, have kids, stay married, have grandkids. Live happily ever after, with the esteem and respect and moral approbation of your community and your nation. No arguments about the components of a good and worthy life in the culture at large or in our own individual families.

What could Americans do if they wanted to bring back marriage as they once knew it (or thought they did)? How could they persuade single people to continue to yearn for marriage when so much of what marriage used to bring is now available outside of it? The legal, medical, and societal transformations that stripped marriage bare of what had made it so special are not likely to be reversed. Birth control is not about to be outlawed, and abortions would not disappear even if they were recriminalized. The forward march of reproductive science will not be stopped in its tracks. Women will not ever be legislated out of the workplace. Children born to single parents will not have "illegitimate" stamped on their birth certificates ever again. How, then, can that big bold line be restored when it has already been all but erased?

There is a way. It is the most powerful way of them all. It can leap over legislation, step on science, and turn its back on the most sparkling opportunities in public and professional life. It is called mental blanketing. It is like mind control, only without the conspiratorial undertones.

At a time when marriage is so inessential, mental blanketing aims to instill in an entire populace the unshakable belief that marriage is exactly what it is not: utterly and uniquely transformational. Marriage, according to the mythology generated by mental blanketing, transforms the immature single person into a mature spouse. It creates a sense of commitment, sacrifice, and selflessness where there was none before. It is the one true place where intimacy and loyalty can be nurtured and sustained. It transforms a serious sexual partnership from a tryout to the real thing. Before, you hoped you were each other's everything; now you really are. Marriage delivers as its ultimate reward the most sought-after American prize: happiness. Not just garden-variety happiness, but deep and meaningful well-being. A sense of fulfillment that a single person cannot even fathom. Marry, the mythology promises, and you will never be lonely again.

The mythology is fueled by fear and yearning. Yearning for the riches that await you on the other side of the marital divide; fear of what will become of you if you never get there. Fear and yearning, singlism and matrimania, singles and marrieds. There are always two sides, a push and a pull. That's what makes the mythology so powerful.

The mythology faces a daunting challenge, though: It is pure poppycock. Every inch of it is either grossly exaggerated or just plain wrong. The science is wrong, the public policy is wrong, our beliefs are woefully wrong. Mental blanketing needs to work relentlessly to keep such inconvenient truths under wraps. Both sides of the scam need constant attention. On the side of singlism, every sliver of the single life that might prove validating or rewarding must be diminished or dismissed. On the side of matrimania, marriage must be unstintingly extolled so that it maintains its mythical place as a magical and transforming experience.

Mental blanketing trivializes the lives of singles by providing ready-made rebuttals for any claims that singles might make for the value of their lives. Do singles have close friends who are deeply important to them? They are "just" friends. Do they have a sex life? Then they are sluts or horn dogs. But what about the singles who obviously are not promiscuous? Tsk, tsk. What a shame that they aren't getting any. Are singles devoted to their jobs? They are just compensating for not having a spouse, the only object of devotion that is meaningful and real. Do singles have lots of interests? Actually, they don't. All they are interested in is just one thing. As soon as they snag their soulmate, they will quit the ski club. Are singles happy? They just think they are. Without a soulmate, they could never know true happiness.

Still not convinced? Fine. Singles can have their so-called happiness and friends and relationships and career and passions and peace and solitude, and maybe they can even be selfless and loyal and mature. They will still die alone.

Singlism is absolutist, contradictory, and utterly unforgiving. By blanketing the entirety of a person's life until everything is snuffed out, singlism is worse than some of the other isms. Take sexism, for example. Some women really do believe that a woman's place is in the home and that her highest calling is to her husband and children. For those women and all the other men and women who hold such a worldview, women can earn full faith and credit for their lives. They can be attentive and devoted wives, loving and giving mothers, selfless keepers of the hearth and home. They can feel complete, fulfilled, and worthy, and they can be recognized as such by all who believe as they do.

Singlism holds out no such place for people who are single. Short of becoming the pope or one of his minions, there is no way to be a good or worthy single person—and there will not be until all of the pernicious myths are busted. In the meantime, to be valued, you have to be married.

The other side of mental blanketing—the buffing and puffing up of marriage to keep it seeming shiny and magical—is up against a formidable fact. Statistically speaking, the act of marrying is banal. Even though many Americans wait longer than ever to marry, and often do not stay long in the marriages they do enter, most Americans—close to 90 percent—still do marry at some point in their lives. Some try it over and over again. Marrying, then, does not make people special; it makes them conventional.

How can something so ordinary be made to appear extraordinary? Turn on the television and watch show after show just pile it on. Start with the obvious—the reality programs such as *The Bachelor, The Bachelorette, Joe Millionaire, Average Joe,* and all the increasingly smarmy sequels. With castles and hot tubs, champagne and limousines, they put lipstick on the pig of public humiliation. What's a little groveling when the prize is a shot at marriage?

In other genres such as dramas and comedies, characters and plot lines twist and turn through one season after another until they all finally come together, in the denouement, at the altar. It is as if the creative community can imagine no more thrilling way to end a series than with a wedding.

Some shows seem to promise an absorbing alternative to matrimania, but ultimately they, too, give it up for marriage. In *Friends,* the show that was supposed to be about, well, friends, all but one of the stars had landed a soulmate by the finale. Even *Sex and the City,* the blockbuster hit that began with four smart, sassy singles taking the city of New York (and much of the rest of the country) by storm, ended with four cooing couples.

The funny pages, at their best, should be able to stand back and mock all this fetishizing of marriage and coupling with wry humor. But instead, they have leapt aboard. Cathy, the decades-long singleton, has married dorky, clueless Irving, the pathetic punch line of years of bad jokes. Now, though, creator Cathy Guisewite paints the couple as hopelessly in love, the pride of all their parents and pets. Asked by *Newsweek* why she married off her protagonist, Guisewite paid tribute to her own soulmate: "I've been married for six years, and I can't write about dating without feeling like I'm cheating on my husband."

Book publishers, too, are waving the white veil. One reporter who looked into the contemporary publishing scene concluded that "dating advice books just keep coming to the shelves. [They] do not have to be written by experts, they don't have to contain any new information—and the advice doesn't have to work!"

In the advertising world, blushing brides have been used to sell cereal and soft drinks; ice cream, chocolate, and cheese; dentistry, headache medication, eye drops, and body lotion; cars, clothes, shoes, credit cards, and lottery tickets; beer, cigarettes, and wine coolers; hotels, real estate, life insurance, and financial institutions. These were not celebrity brides, but the ordinary variety. All brides, it seems, are magical, and a sprinkle of their fairy dust is sufficient to seal the good fate of just about any product.

The possibilities of the single life have opened up for men and women over the past decades, but they have widened more for women. It is women who have marched into the workplace in swelling numbers, it is women who are more liberated by birth control and legalized abortion, and it is women whose parental possibilities are more likely to be multiplied by progress in reproductive science. That is one reason why mental blanketing is directed so overwhelmingly at them. If marriage is to be restored to an undisputed place of honor and privilege, then women especially need to be convinced that it is marriage, above all else, that they should wish for, work for, and yearn for.

Sure, women are warned, they can pursue their fancy jobs, but those jobs will not love them back. They might think they can put off childbearing, but if they wait too long, even the best medicine in the world may not be able to revive their dried-up eggs.

To keep this drumroll of fear and yearning beating, beating, beating—and beating especially loudly in the hearts of women—popular culture must do its part. And so it does. True, there are reality shows in which the prize is a bachelorette, but they are greatly outnumbered by the ones in which hordes of women compete for the affections of just one man. Magazine racks are brimming with *Modern Bride,* but *Modern Groom* is nowhere to be found. Little girls sink their fantasies in Wedding Barbie, but little boys do not dream of dressing their favorite Rescue Hero in a coordinating tux.

It is not that single men get a free ride. All singles need to be nudged toward marriage. So men are cautioned that without the civilizing hand of a woman, they will run amok with slovenliness, horniness, and criminality. (And if they do not seem at all sloppy or out of control, well then, they are fastidious, frivolous, and gay.) Still, compared with women, men get a break. They can turn on *Monday Night Football* in full confidence that the game will not end with a wedding.

In the television show *Judging Amy,* Amy is a divorced woman living with her widowed mom and raising her young daughter. At work, she is a brilliant, witty, and wise judge in the juvenile justice system. As the 2003 season was drawing to a close, another attorney named Stu proposes to Amy. On the CBS website, viewers were invited to weigh in with their advice to Amy. In response to the question "Should Amy accept Stu's marriage proposal?" they could vote for one of three alternatives: (1) Yes! They're a perfect match; (2) No! I don't think Stu is the one for Amy; or (3) Not sure.

Superficially, the CBS poll fetishizes marriage in much the same way as all the other television shows that climax with a wedding, all the mate-bait books that provide how-to tips on reeling in the perfect catch, and all the advertisements that light up their products with the glow of a lustrous bride. But there is another more subtle, and perhaps more insidious, element to the chirpy quiz. It is difficult to see it, because it is nowhere on the screen. It is the universe of answers that no one gets to choose.

No one gets to say that Amy's life seems fine just the way it is, that her love for her mom and her daughter and her passion for her work fill her soul, or that adult humans need not come in matched sets. No one gets to say that Amy tried marriage once, which was quite enough, thank you very much.

The moral of the CBS poll is that you have only these options: Marry Bachelor Number 1, marry some other bachelor, or think about it some more and then pick your bachelor. If CBS and the rest of society can slip that one by us, then singles are toast.

It already worked once, in one of the most infamous and frenzied bouts of matrimania ever to hit the mainstream press. In 1986 a reporter looking to pen the annual Valentine's Day story for her local newspaper put in a call to the Yale sociology department. She learned about some preliminary findings from a Harvard-Yale study suggesting that women who put education and career ahead of marriage could face vanishingly small chances of ever becoming a Mrs. The news leapt from the front page of the town newspaper to the Associated Press wires to the talk-show circuit to the cover of *Newsweek*. An off-the-cuff quip soon morphed into the sound bite heard round the world—that a forty-year-old college-educated woman who had always been single had a greater chance of getting hit by a terrorist than of ever getting married.

The scare story was not true, but that's not my point. The story could never have become scary, or even very interesting, unless a much more fundamental and pernicious myth were in place: that life without marriage is hardly worth living.

When scare stories are shouted from the headlines, they serve themselves up for scrutiny. We can address them head-on, contesting the statistics and the methods, the motives and the agendas. More often, though, the favoring of marriage and coupling settles so softly and quietly into the habits of our everyday lives that we barely even notice its presence or its power.

Here are a few of the snippets I have collected over the past several years:

- In *Time* magazine I notice a story about a new website offering advice on preparing a will. The basic package, I learn, "can cost anywhere from $300 to $500 per couple."
- Here in Southern California, where housing prices rise at record-setting speeds, a home is raffled off every year. In the local paper I read that I can buy a raffle ticket "for the price of a dinner-date at Citronelle."
- My Magellan's catalog tries to tempt me to buy a colorful luggage strap with the promise of solving that pesky problem, "Which bag is ours?"
- A travel writer for a newspaper e-mailed me to describe her most recent assignment. Come up with half a dozen day trips, she was told; half should appeal to couples and the other half to families.
- The Bon Appetit section of *Westways* magazine features restaurant reviews. Each review is prefaced by a description of the location, service, best dishes, and the price of a dinner for two.
- A colleague who is single asks a salesman at Lowe's home-improvement center a question about two different approaches to a repair. He responds with his own question: "Is your husband good with tools?"
- Vanguard would like me to sink my retirement funds into its coffers. It mails me a promotional brochure describing a new way to build retirement assets. On the cover is a picture of an elderly man and woman holding hands on the beach, with the waves kissing their bare feet.
- When I look for a sympathy card, I often have few choices left after I have skipped over all the ones that express "our" condolences.
- The television news program *Nightline* broadcasts a show about seriously wounded soldiers "who may not be able to do any of the things they did before. And that means that the lives of their spouses are changed forever too."
- Robert Putnam, author of *Bowling Alone,* wants to encourage more community participation. He suggests to a hypothetical Bob and Rosemary that they try starting a Parent-Teacher Association at their child's school. Even if the turnout is disappointing, he notes, "at the very

least, Bob and Rosemary will have [met] another couple or two with whom they can catch a movie on Friday nights."

Each of these examples is based on the presumption of coupling. Each assumes that adults come packaged in sexual partnerships or that adults who come in such conventional pairings are the only ones who truly count. Only they are worthy of luggage tags or dinner on the town or the sympathy and concern of the *Nightline* staff.

What grabs me about so many of these examples is that the privileging of couples actually undermines the whole point. Singles make up a huge chunk of the target audiences. Magellan's, for example, wants to sell luggage tags; why talk past all the solo flyers and the groups of vacationing friends and the business travelers and even the couples who have enough confidence in their relationship to pack separate suitcases? *Nightline* prides itself on the seriousness and accuracy of its reporting; how did it miss the fact that at least half of all service members are single? Putnam would like to see Americans renew and strengthen their ties with one another, and he knows that close to one in three children live in single-parent households. So why does he address his suggestion only to couples? Why does he envision those couples as reaching out only to other couples? Surely he would never have said that "at the very least, Bob and Rosemary will meet some other white people with whom they can catch a movie on Friday nights."

The practices are akin to the unthinking sexism that prevailed before the dawn of women's consciousness-raising in the 1960s. Back then, *he* could be used to refer to all of humankind, medical textbooks could show mostly male bodies, and millions of dollars in federal funding could be allotted for studies of heart disease that included only men as participants. That's just the way it was.

Even if you accept everything I've said so far about singlism and matrimania, you may still come to the conclusion: So what? Can't single people just roll their eyes and continue to live their lives joyfully, productively, and undeterred?

They can and they do. Some, such as lifelong singles Condoleezza Rice and Ralph Nader, reach great heights or do spectacular things. Many divorced people, such as Barbara Walters, do the same. But they are still on the wrong side of the marital line, and that makes them fair game.

"She has no personal life," journalist Bob Woodward flatly declared. He was talking about Condoleezza Rice on CNN's *Larry King Live*. Over at MSNBC, political talk-show host Chris Matthews was badgering guest Ralph Nader, insisting that Nader just had to be less responsible and less mature than George W. Bush, because Bush was married and Nader was not. On ABC, *Nightline*'s venerable anchor, Ted Koppel, hosted a show celebrating the great career of colleague Barbara Walters. "Do you ever sometimes lie in bed at night and say, 'You know, maybe if I'd given up the job and focused on the family, that would have been worth it'?" he asked. Congratulations, Barbara!

A few years ago I showed an earlier version of this chapter to a single woman I'll call Jennifer. She was not impressed. "I had a lot of trouble reading your draft," she said, "because I believe, as I think 99.9 percent of the people on the planet do, that it is human nature to find another person. There is an emotional and physical intimacy that one will never find as a single person."

I think Jennifer was describing two deeply significant beliefs: (1) Physical and emotional intimacy has always and everywhere been the foundation for marriage, and (2) people who do not find such intimacy in marriage do not find it anywhere. These are powerful statements—and, among those who internalize them, quite damning of single people. Jennifer seemed to regard the sentiments as universal and timeless truths—facts of human nature. I think many other people do, too. That makes the set of beliefs even more formidable.

But are our contemporary ideas about relationships and intimacy really so timeless? Let's start by looking at love.

"For most of Western history until the eighteenth-century," the authors of *Love and Sex* attest, "love was not expected to end well." Instead, "passion was assumed to end in shame, humiliation, dishonor, suicide, and ruin in almost every early society." Added social historian Stephanie Coontz, in *Marriage, a History,* "Certainly, people fell in love during those thousands of years, sometimes even with their own spouses. But marriage was not fundamentally about love." If you wanted to build something that would last, like a marriage, you would know better than to try to base it on romantic love.

Here, again from Coontz, are a few of the considerations that served as grounds for marriage throughout the ages, when love was not the answer:

- In the Stone Age, "marriage spoke to the needs of the larger group. It converted strangers into relatives and extended cooperative relations beyond the immediate family or small band by creating far-flung networks of in-laws."
- In civilizations that had become more stratified, "propertied families consolidated wealth, merged resources, forged political alliances, and concluded peace treaties by strategically marrying off their sons and daughters."
- "The concerns of commoners were more immediate: 'Can I marry someone whose fields are next to mine?'; 'Will my prospective mate meet the approval of the neighbors and relatives on whom I depend?'; 'Would these particular in-laws be a help to our family or a hindrance?' "

Once a couple came together on the basis of considerations that were important to people of their time and place and social standing, it was still unlikely that they waxed quite so rhapsodically about sex as we often do today. The eminent social historian Lawrence Stone, in describing the Early Modern period, explained why he thought sexual experiences were far less plentiful and pleasurable back then. Personal hygiene was one likely deterrent: "Most people, even in the highest social stratum, hardly ever washed anything, except their faces, necks, hands, and feet." Disease was rampant, and adults "often suffered from disorders which made sex painful to them or unpleasant to their partners." Many poor people were malnourished and utterly exhausted by their work in the fields. Adults who did summon the stamina for sex then faced "the ever-present risk of venereal disease." For women who became pregnant, the specter of a painful and dangerous childbirth loomed ominously before them.

Gradually, advances in medicine and hygiene washed away some of the barriers to bountiful sex. Even so, for a long time, taking great pleasure in sex was regarded as unseemly or worse. Up to the sixteenth century, Catholicism deemed sex for any purpose other than baby-making to be a mortal sin and grounds for rotting in hell. I don't think Saint Jerome wanted even procreative sex to be any fun. Said the saint, "He who too ardently loves his own wife is an adulterer."

The Protestants who left Europe to form the colonies in America were a bit less rigid. Though spouses might regard sex as a duty they owed each other for the purpose of producing children, they were not discouraged from actually enjoying it.

By the late eighteenth century, our pet theory about marriage—that it should be based on love—was beginning to take hold. At first the practice of marrying for love seemed radical, and too unbridled an interest in sex seemed tawdry. But by the time Freud made his mark on the American psyche in the 1900s, it seemed more shameful to have sexual inhibitions than to not have them.

Still, any zest for sex among couples marrying for love was initially tempered by some unnerving practical considerations. Most notably, it was a long time until birth control was widely available, highly reliable, and stigma-free. In fact, the Food and Drug Administration did not approve the pill as a safe form of birth control until 1960.

To Americans today, it seems self-evident that sex is at the heart of marriage, that it brings fulfillment to the marriage and to life, and that it opens the door to a kind of intimacy that, as Jennifer said, "one will never find as a single person." These bedrock beliefs, though, far from having grown out of the stuff of human nature, are in fact rather contemporary points of view.

None of this means that Westerners for centuries led emotionally empty lives. Humans have probably always nurtured close ties with other humans. What has changed over the course of history is the place of the spouse as the object of an adult's intense and exclusive affections.

In medieval through early modern times, to describe the love for a spouse as the greatest love of all would have been sacrilegious. The most special place in anyone's heart was supposed to be reserved for God. Over the years many kinds of people and entities have been deemed deserving of love and affection. They have included spiritual figures and ancestors, immediate and extended family, friends and community.

Even when the love for a spouse was compared only with feelings for other mere mortals, it did not always come out ahead of all the rest. As Coontz notes, during the 1800s Westerners believed that "love developed slowly out of admiration, respect, and appreciation"; therefore, "the love one felt for a sweetheart was not seen as qualitatively different from the feeling one might have for a sister, a friend, or even an idea."

Intense feelings did develop sometimes—often between two men. I'm talking about American men here, including men with wives. Until the turn of the twentieth century, many men spent vast amounts of time in men's clubs and fraternal organizations, and married men often shared closer bonds with their best friends than with their wives. Men with wives and children typically spent more time during weekends with their male friends than with family, and they even vacationed with other men. None of this was stigmatized.

Women did the same. They traveled and vacationed with other women. The feelings of married women for their sisters and friends, and for their children, were often deeper than their affection for their husbands.

This all-too-brief romp through bits and pieces of the past few centuries in Europe and America suggests that people can get their needs for emotional intimacy met outside of marriage and coupling. For most of history they probably have.

By the 1920s big changes were afoot. This period spirited in the initial rumblings of the tyranny of twos. Not just any twos, but one particular variety—the heterosexual couple. This was the era when young men and women began for the first time to get together without any chaperones and without necessarily intending to marry. Dating, they called it. It was enabled by the appearance on the scene of the automobile, which carried courtship out of the parlor, and out from under the family gaze, and into the commercialized playspaces of movie theaters and amusement parks. Familiar and comfortable customs began to change in ways that glorified the couple and demeaned and dismissed everyone else. Take dancing, for example. Before, it often took the form of a group activity; now it was more often a union of one man and one woman. Valentine's Day was once a community celebration of wide-ranging bonds of affection; now it was shrunk to the fetishizing of just one slender stalk of romantic love.

To the new kind of married couple that emerged in the twentieth century, no other feelings seemed as shiny or bright as the love they felt for each other. The fondness married people once nurtured for all sorts of other people who were important to them—well, that now seemed a bit dull in comparison, and maybe not really worth the effort.

Friendships got a demotion. Women still maintained ties with other women, but now they were more likely to enjoy those friendships than to cherish them. The screws were turned even more tightly on the close friendships between men. Those relationships were not just downgraded in importance, they were stigmatized as homosexual and pathological. Bonds with siblings lost some of their luster, too.

Aging parents were thrown out the door of the family home and into institutions. The older generation had once been welcomed into a couple's home. Now experts warned wives that opening their hearths to needy parents was old-fashioned and might even be a sign of insufficient devotion to their husbands.

Even motherhood took a hit. In *Love in America,* Francesca Cancian notes that less than a century before the married couple and their feelings for each other had become so glorified, "intimacy and sexual relations between spouses were not central and both spouses had important ties with relatives and friends of their own sex. The key relation was an intense, emotional tie between mothers and children." But as the decades of the twentieth century ticked by, that was no longer so. For the first time, there was room in the culture for "popular advice books [that] suggested that having children might weaken a family." Children were still important, and the home that wrapped its arms around Mom, Dad, and the kids continued to be sentimentalized. That bond between husband and wife, though—nothing else compared.

Today, the exalted place of the insular couple continues to be encouraged and trumpeted. Once you "find another person" (in Jennifer's words), that person becomes the center of your life. Everyone and everything else becomes secondary.

Consider, for example, the advice doled out by sociologist Pepper Schwartz. She is the author of a stack of books and was coauthor for many years of the "Sex and Health" column for *Glamour* magazine. In her book *Peer Marriage,* Schwartz describes what she believes to be the ideal form of contemporary coupling. Partners in a peer marriage, she notes, "give priority to their relationship over their work and over all other relationships. . . . Their interdependence becomes so deep . . . they have to be careful not to make their own children feel excluded."

Schwartz proudly describes Jerry and Donna, an exemplary peer couple. Says Jerry, "I don't like to do things with other people. We just like being together. We do Siskel and Ebert when we're at the movies. We do the Frugal Gourmet when we cook. We are just our own show." The "only danger" Schwartz sees to this intense togetherness is that "the couple's isolation inhibits their ability to get good advice about their relationship." Therefore, they should socialize occasionally with "other like-minded couples."

Sociologist Linda Waite and columnist Maggie Gallagher put it this way: "A wife should spend weekends with the family, not friends." Also: "A man or a woman should put his [sic] spouse first before the demands of parents, friends, or other family members."

Some experts tell soulmate seekers that they do not need to wait until they are actually married to dispose of the other people in their life. Another good time to do so is when you are still single but have finally decided to get with the Program. Rachel Greenwald's program, to be exact, as described in her mate-seeking manual: *Find a Husband After 35 Using What I Learned at Harvard Business School.* If you are serious about finding a husband, cautions Greenwald, there is something important you must do: "Stop interacting with people who are not supportive of your quest for a mate, people who facilitate your single status."

There is much more to the story of the glorification of the couple, of course. I hope I have conveyed enough to make the point that the way coupling is envisioned in contemporary American society is not universal, it is not timeless, and it is not human nature. Instead, the reigning American worldview may well represent one of the narrowest construals of intimacy ever imagined. Where once the tendrils of love and affection reached out to family, friends, and community, reached back to ancestors, and reached up to the heavens, now they surround and squeeze just one other person— sometimes to the point of asphyxiation.

My ideas can be misconstrued and mischaracterized in many ways. So I want to end this chapter by anticipating and clarifying some of the most likely confusions.

First, I'm not against coupling. Some of my best friends are coupled. Coupling itself—in contrast to the fetishized way we practice it now—is in fact timeless. Before the advent of reproductive technology (which in evolutionary time is very recent indeed), coupling really was the only direct route to the continuation of the species. The kind of interest that people have in coupling—interest in getting coupled, in knowing who else is coupled and to whom—cannot be manufactured from whole cloth the way a sudden intense desire for a Cabbage Patch doll can be. It is based on something real. So, my problem is not with our current interest in coupling or our valuing it, but in our overvaluing it and our undervaluing so many other important relationships and life pursuits. We seem to have lost all perspective on the many ways to lead a good and meaningful life.

Many people who practice marriage and coupling have sensed their special status and gotten greedy. Couples expect their love to be the only love that matters, and their goals and values to be the standards against which all other lives are measured. I don't see why we can't value coupling in a mature way, as one possible component of a life worth living rather than as a mandatory requirement imposed on all.

Second, parenting is a separate issue from coupling. That little ditty about love coming first, then marriage, then the baby carriage—it's history. Over the past few decades more and more single people have been having children, and more and more married couples have not been. When I talk about the ways in which a single person does or does not differ from a married person, I am usually talking about instances in which both have children or neither do. Whether marriage will transform you is a whole different question from whether parenting will. Single people who have children are their own special category of singles, different in important ways from singles who do not, and I give them their own chapter.

Third, am I talking about marriage or coupling? In the practice of singlism and matrimania, marriage always matters. Marriage is the epitome of privilege. There are no special rewards enjoyed by people who are coupled (but not officially married) that are not also bestowed upon people who are married. When government gets involved—especially the federal government—only official marriage matters. Coupled unmarried people do not have access to each other's Social Security benefits: no exceptions. Most often in everyday life, though, marriage and serious coupling are indistinguishable. Whether you get the singles treatment depends much more on whether you are intensely coupled than on whether you are officially married.

Fourth, I do not think that everyone buys into the mythology of marriage and singlehood. Not everyone believes that marriage transforms miserable and immature single people into paragons of maturity and bliss. Not all couples want their partners to be their everything. Plenty of them continue to value deeply other people and other life pursuits. Not all single people have taken seriously the silly things they have heard about themselves. All these exceptional people can feel smug as they read through this book, having known all along what it took me a lifetime to figure out.

Finally, this is not a book about the "plight" of singles as victims but about their resilience. Obviously, I'm going to moan about the many ways that singles are viewed and treated unfairly. I've already started. But I will not end with the predictable "woe is us." Instead, I will express pride at how well so many singles do despite all the singlism and the matrimania. Singles, by definition, do not have that one special Sex and Everything Else Partner who is supposed to fill up all their empty spaces with happiness, maturity, and meaning. Yet, as we shall see, the singles who actually are miserable and immature and who believe their lives have no meaning are the exceptions. How can this be? And if married people so obviously have so much going for them, why do they need swarms of scientists, pundits, politicians, experts, authors, reporters, and entertainers making their case for them?

Science and the Single Person

Marriage is good for everyone." That's what sociologist Linda Waite told *The New York Times* in 1998. "This is definitely a public health issue," she maintained. "People need to know the facts so they can make good decisions." A year later she told *USA Today* that "marriage improves the health and longevity of men and women." Then in 2000 she and Maggie Gallagher published their book, *The Case for Marriage: Why Married People Are Happier, Healthier, and Better Off Financially.* The case they made was soon to become the received wisdom of the times, accepted as fact by the media, the public, and much of the scientific community.

The Wall Street Journal said that Waite and Gallagher had provided "impressive evidence showing that married people are healthier." The *Journal* also thought that the authors had served up "a hard truth: that the real road to happiness lies not in the direct pursuit of personal fulfillment but in love of, compromise with and commitment to another."

Over at *The New York Times,* on the op-ed page, Jonathan Rauch echoed the same conclusions that were bouncing off all the media walls: "Social science research has established beyond reasonable doubt that marriage, on average, makes people healthier, happier, and financially better off." If marriage is so powerful, he continued, then shouldn't gay men and lesbians have legal access to it?

In the *Journal of Marriage and Family,* perhaps the most esteemed scientific venue for research on marriage, *The Case for Marriage* was featured in the book review section. Although the reviewer complained that the tone of the book "oozes with disrespect for those who deviate from lifelong marriage," he never disputes the authors' fundamental claim that marriage makes people happier and healthier.

By 2005 the claim was written into a history book. In *Marriage, a History,* author Stephanie Coontz maintains that "today married people in Western Europe and North America are generally happier [and] healthier," compared with people "in any other living arrangement." She acknowledges the possibility that people who marry may already be happier or healthier—even before they wed—than people who stay single. But she does not believe that any such initial differences can fully account for the supposedly superior health and well-being of people who marry. "Marriage itself adds something extra," she explains.

The university students I have queried seem convinced. My colleague Wendy Morris and I asked 760 undergraduates to answer these two questions: (1) How happy would you be in your life if you married? and (2) How happy would you be in your life if you stayed single? The students anticipated hugely different outcomes. On a scale ranging from 0 to 10, with 0 indicating the least happiness and 10 the most, their answers indicated that they expected, on average, a life happiness level of 8.4 if they married, as opposed to 3.2 if they stayed single.

The results were for just one group, though, and they were all undergraduates. More telling are the results of nationwide surveys, such as the one in which 1,300 American adults of all ages were asked about their agreement with the statement "Married people are generally happier than unmarried people." Fewer than one in five disagreed.

I think that all these people—the students and the authors and the scholars and the editorial writers—have swallowed whole a set of claims that should have been chewed over rather carefully. In so doing, they have helped perpetuate—often unwittingly—a mythology of marital superiority. In this chapter I take aim most insistently at the Waite and Gallagher book, *The Case for Marriage.* Lots of social scientists, essayists, and pundits have waved their pom-poms in praise of people who have married, but few have fired up the fans as successfully as Waite and Gallagher.

When Waite and Gallagher declare that "marriage for most people is the means to health, happiness, wealth, sex, and long life," they are extolling the rewards that adults reap from marriage. To many, though—Waite and

Gallagher included—what is perhaps even more important about marriage is its value to children. I will address that issue in the chapter on single parents.

Getting Married and Getting Happy

I begin by stepping outside the shoutfest about marriage momentarily, to illustrate how research should be conducted and interpreted. I describe a drug study that is flawed and fictitious. But the implications for understanding research on marriage are real.

Imagine that a team of scientists working for a pharmaceutical corporation is testing a new drug called Shamster, designed to increase people's health and well-being. Unlike most drugs, this one is not meant to remedy some illness; it is supposed to make your life better, whether you are sick or not.

The scientists are optimistic about the drug, but it is still experimental. They put out the word to physicians that Shamster is available to patients who would like to try it. Circumstances permitting, the patients get to decide whether they want to try it, and once on it, whether they want to continue. Over the course of the study, the people who were offered the drug end up in one of four different groups.

Some patients sign up for Shamster and stay on the drug for the entire course of the study. Scientists call this first group the *drug* group.

Some people never do take Shamster. Maybe they have some condition that disqualifies them from the study, or maybe they just don't want to try it—they are happy with their lives and are not looking for any magic bullets. The scientists call this second group the *no-drug* group.

Nearly half the people who sign up for Shamster change their minds after they have been taking it for a while. The drug is not what they had hoped or expected. They just don't like it, and they are not going to take it anymore. Scientists name this third set of people the *no drug—intolerable* group.

In the last group are the people who started taking Shamster but had it taken away from them. Maybe their prescribing doctor retired and they could not find another doctor with access to it. Or maybe there were distribution problems in their area of the country. One way or another, through no choice of their own, the people who wanted to take Shamster and had already been taking it could no longer continue to do so. This fourth group is called the *no drug—withdrawn* group.

A total of 2,200 Americans from forty-eight different states participate in the study. They all answer the question "Taking all things together, how happy would you say you are these days?" People who say they are "very happy" get a happiness score of 4; those who are "pretty happy" get a score of 3; people who are "not too happy" are assigned a 2; and people who say they are "not at all happy" are scored as 1. Here are the average scores for each group.

Drug	3.3
No drug	3.2
No drug—intolerable	2.9
No drug—withdrawn	2.9

The scientists and the drug company want to celebrate. They notify the media that people in the drug condition are happier than people in any of the no-drug conditions. "See how wonderful our drug is," they boast. "If only more people would take our drug, they would feel so much better."

As a sophisticated consumer, you can see right through this. Sure, the so-called drug group looks better than the other groups, but that is because the sleazy drug company has classified all the people who found the drug intolerable as a no-drug group. But they did take the drug! They stopped taking it because it made them miserable. The company did the same thing with the other group that did not fare so well—the people who had the drug withdrawn. That group was also labeled as a no-drug group and set aside. Then the pharmaceutical company had the audacity to use the bad outcomes of the people who could not tolerate the drug and those who had it withdrawn as evidence of the drug's effectiveness! "See," they said, "people who are currently taking Shamster are doing better than people who are not currently taking Shamster."

You can see what a fair conclusion would be, and it is not at all what the drug company says it is. What really happened is this: Of those who took Shamster, close to half of them could not tolerate it, stopped taking it, and ended up worse off than people who never took Shamster at all. The people who started on Shamster and had it withdrawn against their wishes also ended up doing worse than the people who never took Shamster. In fact, if you average the scores of the three groups of people who did take Shamster, at least for a while, you get the number 3.0. That is lower than the score of the group of people who spent their whole life Shamster-free, 3.2.

You simply cannot say that Shamster "makes" people happier. You cannot ethically suggest that if only more people took Shamster, they would feel so much better—and the Food and Drug Administration would never allow any company to make such a claim. Close to half the people who start taking the drug feel so much worse that they just will not continue with it. The others who start on the drug and then cannot continue with it also end up worse than if they had never taken the Shamster at all.

Suppose, though, you think that you will tolerate the drug. You have confidence that if you sign up for Shamster, you will stick with it, and no one will take it away from you. You have no real scientific basis for your optimism, and you have no control over whether the drug will be taken away from you. Still, you have a good feeling about your future on Shamster, so you go ahead and take it. Suppose you do end up in the best group: That's the group of people who start on Shamster and stay on it. They have an average happiness score of 3.3. Compare that with the score of those who never do take Shamster: 3.2. Statistically speaking, you are in the group that did better. But realistically, on the basis of a difference of one-tenth of a point on a four-point scale, would you really say that Shamster transformed your life? If you had to pick just one label (out of the four original choices) to describe the happiness of the people in each of the four groups, it would be the same each time. The average score of every group is closer to the "pretty happy" label than to any other.

Even if the difference between the drug group and the no-drug group had been sizable, you still could not confidently give credit to Shamster for making the people in the drug group happier. That's because the people who signed up for Shamster were different people from the ones who declined the drug. Maybe the Shamster takers were happier than the Shamster-free people even before the drug was offered to anyone, and taking the drug did not add to their joy. If so, then Shamster did not "make" them happier—they were already happier.

If the study were better designed, people would have been assigned at random to take the drug or not. They wouldn't get to choose. That way, the two groups would, on the average, have the same initial scores on happiness and everything else. That's one of the hallmarks of respectable experimental research. A more rigorous study would also have assigned pills that looked the same to all the participants. No one would know until after the study was over whether they had actually taken Shamster or a placebo that just looked like Shamster. That's important. If the drug company had blanketed the media with ads about the wonders of Shamster, people taking it might report greater happiness just because they knew that Shamster was supposed to make them feel that way.

In my hypothetical example, though, the scientists do make their bold and reckless claim. What's more, many other teams of scientists develop an interest in Shamster and conduct the same sort of flawed study. Not all the teams get results identical to the first team's, but often the patterning is similar. Eventually, there are so many Shamster studies out there that you could write a book about it. So, of course, some people do. Among them are one of the scientists who conducted Shamster studies and a columnist who always did like the idea of Shamster. Together, they review a number of the studies that, in their opinion, made Shamster look good. They call their book *The Case for Shamster: Why People Taking Shamster Are Happier and Healthier.*

If the study I just described really had been a drug study, no respectable medical journal would ever publish it. No scientists worth their salt would want their names associated with it. Authors of a book with such a shameless and misleading title could kiss their credibility good-bye.

Yet this is just what much of the research on married and single people looks like. The study I described is one that actually has been conducted, much as I detailed it—2,200 participants from forty-eight states. I call it the One-Time Happiness Study. The numbers in the table really are the results from the 2,200 participants who answered exactly the question about their happiness that I described earlier. (The actual scientists, though, were more appropriately cautious about their conclusions.)

In the hypothetical study, I changed the names of the four groups. Here again is the same table, this time with the actual group names:

Drug Group (fictitious)	Marital Status (real)	Happiness (1=not at all happy; 4=very happy)
Drug	Currently married	3.3
No drug	Always single	3.2
No drug—intolerable	Divorced	2.9
No drug—withdrawn	Widowed	2.9

When you hear claims about the latest study showing that married people are better off than unmarried people, you are probably dealing with a study like this one. There would be nothing wrong with saying, on the basis of the data in the table above, that people who are currently married are, on average, happier than people who are currently unmarried—as long as you also made it clear that the biggest difference was between the currently married and the previously married, and that on a four-point scale, the always-single group differed by just a tenth of a point from the currently married group. That would be a descriptive statement and accurate as far as it goes.

The enterprise becomes problematic when descriptive statements get recast as claims about the transformative power of marriage. When Linda Waite and Maggie Gallagher summarize a book full of results such as the ones in the table and trumpet to the media the conclusion that marriage "makes" people happy or "improves" their lives or "is good for everyone," they are flat-out wrong. Marriage was not good for the many people who could not stand it and divorced. In the end, perhaps it was not so good for the people who outlived their spouse. Even the married people who were skimmed off the top (the ones who never experienced divorce or the death of a spouse) ended up just a tad happier than people who had always been single.

To be fair, it is impossible to conduct perfectly rigorous scientific research on marriage. That's because it is impossible and unethical to assign people at random to be married or to stay single. It is also impossible to keep people unaware of whether they got the marriage drug or not. If you are married, you know it; and if you are single, you know that—there is no placebo comparison group.

It is possible, though, to be clear and accurate in conveying the conclusions that can be supported scientifically by these studies. That's where the objectivity breaks down. The unsubstantiated claims are overwhelmingly ones that make marriage look better than it really is, and singlehood look worse.

I am not accusing Waite or Gallagher—or anyone else whose writings I criticize in this book—of scientific fraud. But scientific accounts do vary in rigor and even-handedness, and Waite and Gallagher's account, in my opinion, does not meet the highest standards.

In the One-Time Happiness Study, as in most studies of the differences between married and single people, the participants are surveyed at just one point in time. They report their marital status and answer the other questions. The results tell you how, for example, people who are widowed feel at the moment but not how they felt year after year before they married, then after they married, and then after they were widowed. In their contribution to our understanding of the link between marital status and happiness, studies in which the lives of individuals are followed over the course of many years are vast improvements over the studies that survey people only once.

More than thirty thousand Germans have been participating in a study every year for as many as eighteen years (and counting). I call it the Lifelines of Happiness Study. Households were selected at random from many locations within the country, and everyone sixteen years or older was invited to participate. Every year, participants have indicated how satisfied they were with their life in general by selecting one of eleven numbers ranging from 0, "totally unhappy," to 10, "totally happy."

The director of the study, Richard Lucas, has looked separately at the lifelines of happiness for people who (1) got married and stayed that way over the course of the study, (2) stayed single, (3) married and then divorced, and (4) married and then were widowed. The results for the first three groups are shown in the three bold lines in the first graph, which I call the Marriage Graph.

The Marriage Graph:
Happiness Before and After Marriage, and During Singlehood

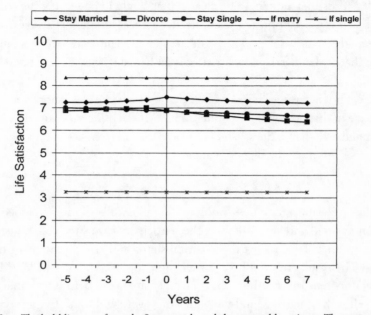

Note: The bold lines are from the Lucas study and show actual happiness. The top and bottom lines are from data collected by Bella DePaulo and Wendy L. Morris and show expected happiness. The vertical line (0 years) indicates the year of marriage for those people who did marry.

The first thing to notice is that all three groups were reasonably happy. The scale midpoint is 5.00. Every year, every group reported an average happiness score of at least 6.4. These results are similar to the findings from the One-Time Happiness Study, in which all groups reported that they were, on the average, pretty happy.

The top bold line of the graph shows the happiness of people who got married and stayed married throughout the study. Notice what happens to their happiness as they approached the day of their wedding and in the years that follow. In the year surrounding their wedding date, people who married show a tiny blip in happiness. On average, they were about a quarter of a scale point happier around the time of their wedding than they had been about five years before. Notice also, though, that within a few years that small puff of happiness disappeared; the continuously married people were then, on average, no happier than they were when they were single.

In general, then, marriage did not "make" people happy. Typically, people who got married enjoyed a brief honeymoon effect, then went back to being about as happy or as unhappy as they were before they married. The fact that marriage did nothing for people's happiness is especially noteworthy because the analysis was selective. Only the people who got married and stayed married were included in the top bold line of the graph. Those who were widowed or divorced (and whose happiness could be expected to decrease) were temporarily set aside.

The next line on the graph (the one with the circles) shows the happiness of people who stayed single throughout the study. As in the previous study, their average happiness is slightly lower than the happiness of people who married and stayed married. Importantly, the people who would eventually marry and stay married were already a bit happier than the people who would stay single, years before they married (7.2 versus 7.0). So it was not marriage that "made" them happier than single people; they were already happier. Over the course of the study, the happiness of the people who stayed single declined about four-tenths of a point, ending up at 6.6.

The group that started out with the lowest average happiness scores consisted of people who did get married but eventually divorced. So, years before anyone married, the people who would eventually divorce were already less happy than the people who would stay married (and they were slightly less happy than those who would stay single, 6.9 as opposed to 7.0). In fact, in the year before the marriage, when the happiness of the people who would stay married began to enter the honeymoon phase, the happiness of the people who would eventually divorce was already beginning to slip. Then it continued to slide some more. For most of the years shown on the graph, the people who stayed single were a little bit happier than the people who married and then divorced.

The two lighter lines in the graph—the highest line and the lowest—show the predictions made by the 760 college students about how happy they would be if they married (the top line) and how happy they would be if they stayed single (the bottom line). The college students expected married life to be happier for them than it was for the people in the Lifelines of Happiness Study who actually did get married and stayed married. The students also anticipated a less happy singlehood—much less happy—than the people in the study who actually did stay single the whole time. I think that when consumers of popularized science hear claims that married people are happier than single people, they envision the enormous differences that the college students described. They do not imagine a set of lines snuggled up next to each other.

The Marriage Graph does not show one of the significant trends in the lives of the people who would eventually divorce—the level of happiness or unhappiness they experienced as the year of their divorce drew near and then was passed. That is shown in the second graph, which I will call the Divorce Graph. As these married people were approaching the year of their divorce, their happiness dropped to a low of 6.2 in the year just before the official divorce date. (That's about four-tenths of a point lower than the lowest average happiness score of the people who stayed single.) After that, they began to regain their happiness but, on average, never did become as happy as they were when they were single.

The Divorce Graph:
Happiness Before and After Divorce

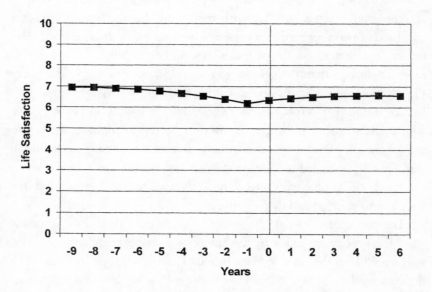

Note: The vertical line (0 years) indicates the year of divorce.

Unsurprisingly, the married people who became widowed also experienced a decline in happiness. The third graph (the Widowhood Graph) shows the lifeline of happiness for those people, beginning five years before they became widowed. Their happiness declined steadily, particularly in the year before the death, when their partner may have been sick and dying. The year of the death marked the low point of 6.0. (That's about six-tenths of a point lower than the lowest average happiness score of the people who stayed single.) Little by little, in the following years, their happiness rebounded, though it never quite reached the prewidowhood high.

The Widowhood Graph: Happiness Before and After Widowhood

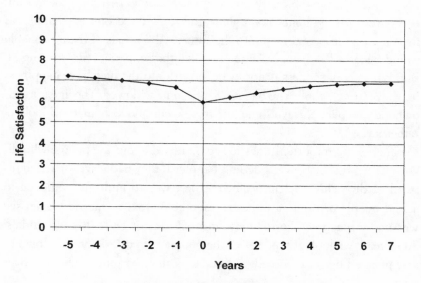

Note: The vertical line (0 years) indicates the year of widowhood.

The results of this study—and in fact, any scientific study—are just averages. The results for individual people could differ. Take, for example, the finding that people who stayed single were generally a little less happy than people who eventually married, before anyone had married. That result does not mean that every person who stayed single was less happy than every person who eventually married. Similarly, just because married people typically went back to their premarriage level of happiness does not mean that every married person did. Some became happier and stayed that way. But those whose happiness continued to grow were balanced by others who became less and less happy as their marriages progressed.

Sometimes the results of subgroups of people also differ from the overall averages. For example, among the group of people who married and then divorced, men's happiness dropped further and more quickly than did women's as the year of the divorce drew nearer.

Looking back over the results of the graphs, we see that the people who married and stayed married look the happiest. Again, though, marriage did not "make" them happier; they were already happier than the others. And, except for the brief honeymoon phase, they did not become any happier as their married life continued into the future. About half of them probably would become less happy eventually, when they experienced widowhood. But that time of sadness is not incorporated into the lifeline of happiness for the married people who had not yet become widowed. The line for widowhood is separate, leaving the line for the continuously married looking rather flat.

There is an important question to be raised about the people who divorced: Would they have ended up happier if they had stayed married instead of divorcing? Scientifically, the best way to find out would be to assign people at random either to divorce or to stay married, then see who ends up happier. Fortunately, scientists do not get to do such studies. So instead, we look at the lives of the people who decide on their own to stay married or get divorced, and see how their happiness changes over time.

The people who married and then divorced were the least happy at the outset. Maybe they were especially likely to look to marriage as their ticket to greater joy. But that is not what they got. On the average, people who start out less happy and then get married continue to feel less and less happy, and ultimately they divorce.

Maybe Linda Waite was right after all when she said that "people need to know the facts so they can make good decisions." On the basis of the Lifelines of Happiness Study, the facts seem to be as follows: If you are not already a happy person, don't count on marriage to transform you into one. If you are already happy, don't expect marriage to make you even happier. Chances are, it won't. Finally, if you are single and happy, do not fret that you will descend into despair if you dare to stay single. That's not likely, either.

Now I'm going to speculate, so be forewarned. I wonder about the differences between the people who married and then divorced and the people who stayed single. Could it be that at least some of the people who went through with the marriage, even though they were becoming less and less happy as the wedding day approached, were marrying not out of love but because of goading or obligation or some unanalyzed sense that getting married is what everyone "should" do? If the pro-marriage movement keeps prodding people to marry, will we end up with more divorces rather than fewer? Could differences in pressures to marry explain different divorce rates in different parts of the country? It has often seemed a bit of a paradox that some of the most religious states also have some of the highest divorce rates. Maybe moral pressure can coax people into marrying, but it cannot make a bad marriage good.

It is worth returning to Waite and Gallagher's signature claim that married people are happier. Here it is, in its most sweeping rendition:

> Virtually every study of happiness that has ever been done has found that married men and women are happier than singles. The happiness advantage of married people is very large . . . and appears in every country on which we have information.

When authors make pronouncements like that, I like to look up all the studies upon which the conclusions are based to see what the original authors really did report. I will spare you a detailed critique of every source of Waite and Gallagher's misleading statements, and go straight to the study purportedly showing that married people are happier "in every country."

That study was based on happiness reports from seventeen industrialized nations (mostly Western). As in the One-Time Happiness Study, the survey was taken at one point in time. So, the people who were currently married were different people from the ones who were divorced, were widowed, or had always been single.

To see whether marriage was linked to happiness, the authors used a cheater technique. They set aside all the people who married and then divorced or became widowed, and counted as married only the remaining married people. They then compared the happiness described by the currently married people with the happiness described by the people who had always been single. That's the comparison that showed that married people are happier "in every country." (Actually, that isn't true, either; in one country married people were not any happier than single people even when the formerly married were taken out of the equation.)

So, here is what that study actually shows: When you disregard all the people who married but then divorced, and when you also disregard the people who were once married and are then widowed, you can say that married people were, in sixteen of seventeen nations, happier than the people who had always been single.

Now here are a few findings from that seventeen-nation study that Waite and Gallagher never do mention. First, the people who had always been single were happier than the people who did get married but later were separated, divorced, or widowed.

Second, the married, divorced, separated, widowed, and always-single people were all different people. They may have had different happiness levels even before anyone ever married. As in the Lifelines of Happiness Study, getting married may not have "made" any group of people in any country happier.

Third, even when only the currently married (and not the previously married) were included in the calculations of the purported benefits of marriage, it still was not marriage that provided the largest advantage in happiness or even the second largest. When other life factors were considered, the people who were happiest were those who were most satisfied with their household finances, and the next happiest were those who had good health. Marriage came in third.

Waite and Gallagher's message to anyone who will listen is not just to get married but to stay that way. The high rate of divorce, they claim, is one of the factors that "threaten the health, wealth, and well-being of adults." It is curious, then, that they did not mention another finding from the seventeen-nation study. In nations with lower rates of divorce, married people had lower levels of happiness. Perhaps those citizens were staying in miserable marriages, and their reluctance to let go was the real threat to their well-being.

Getting Married and Getting Healthy

According to the mythology, happiness is just one of the supposed riches that marriage brings. Another is good health. Scholars have been studying and debating the physical and mental health implications of marriage for decades. The results of one of the most recent large-scale studies were released by the Centers for Disease Control and Prevention (CDC) in December 2004. The study was based on one-time interviews with a representative national sample of 127,545 Americans who were eighteen or older. The questions covered both physical and mental health.

CDC Report on Marital Status and Health

Health Measure (%)	Group 5	Group 4	Group 3	Group 2	Group 1
Fair or poor health	20	17	14	13	11
Serious psychological distress	7	6	4	3	2
Overweight or obese	57	58	56	51	60
Lower back pain	30	32	34	25	28
Headaches	20	19	19	14	15
Activity limitation	26	23	16	19	12
Current smoker	30	35	38	24	19
Heavy drinker	5	6	8	5	4

Rank Ordering
(1 = best off; 5 = worst off)

	Group 5	Group 4	Group 3	Group 2	Group 1
Fair or poor health	5	4	3	2	1
Serious psychological distress	5	4	3	2	1
Overweight or obese	3	4	2	1	5
Lower back pain	3	4	5	1	2
Headaches	5	3.5	3.5	1	2
Activity limitation	5	4	2	3	1
Current smoker	3	4	5	2	1
Heavy drinker	2.5	4	5	2.5	1

The CDC provided a brief press release as well as links to an online source in which the results were presented in great detail. The CDC should have no particular dog in the marriage fight, so I thought it might be especially interesting to see how its presumably objective analysts described scientific findings on marriage and singlehood.

The study includes results for the same four categories we have been considering so far—currently married, always single, divorced (or separated), and widowed—plus one more, cohabiting. The results of the five groups are on page 43. For now, I've simply labeled the categories Group 1 through Group 5. That's so you can study the numbers and draw your own conclusions before you know which groups are the cohabitors or the currently married or the widowed or the divorced or the singles.

The table shows the results of eight different aspects of health. Two are indicators of problematic physical heath (fair or poor health) or mental health (serious psychological distress). Obesity is also included, as are several more specific components of health (lower back pain, headaches, and limited activity). Two bad habits, smoking and heavy drinking, round out the list.

The tabulations provided by the CDC are far more detailed than those I have presented in the table. For example, the CDC presents separate results for a number of different kinds of activity limitations (e.g., leisure activity, work activity); for simplicity, I present just the overall measure. Also, the CDC reports separate results for a number of different subgroups, such as men and women, and people of different ages, races, and income levels. For starters, I think that the five different marital status groupings and the eight different health measures provide plenty to mull over.

The CDC reports percentages for each health measure. For example, the top row of the table shows that the percentage of people reporting fair or poor health ranged from 20 percent in Group 5 to 11 percent in Group 1. To make the results a little easier to digest, I've converted the percentages into rank orderings. They are listed at the bottom of the table. The group that has a 1 on any given measure has the best health on that measure, and the group that has a 5 has the worst. The difference between any two rankings is not necessarily a big or statistically meaningful one; a quick glance at the top of the table shows the actual differences.

If you were going to write a brief press release about these results, what would it say? What would be your one-sentence summary of the groups that have the best and the worst health?

A first glance at the rank orderings offers no clear answer as to who is the healthiest. There is no one group that is always ranked first on every measure. Group 1 has the most first-place finishes (five), but it also comes in last in obesity. So Group 1 is the healthiest in a lot of ways, but it is also the fattest. Group 2 is next best in first-place finishes, with three, and it never finishes last or even second-to-last in any one category.

On the other end of the health scale, Group 4 consistently comes in around fourth. Group 5 is a bit more variable but overall looks about the same. Group 3 does a little better than Groups 4 and 5, but not much.

To provide an even rougher estimate of how the groups compare in health, I've averaged the eight rank orderings. Groups 1 and 2 come out the best, with average scores of 1.8, Groups 4 and 5 have average scores of 3.9, and Group 3 averages 3.6.

There are other ways to look at the results. For example, you could argue that one of the health measures is more important than the others, and should count more. Or you could point out that for some of the measures, the differences among some of the groups are so small that they hardly seem meaningful.

My own conclusion would be that, overall, Groups 1 and 2 are the healthiest and Groups 4 and 5 are the least healthy. Group 3 is closer to Groups 4 and 5. That conclusion corresponds to the averaged rank orderings. It also corresponds closely with the results of the two most global measures (fair or poor health, serious psychological distress) and is inconsistent only with the results for obesity.

Here are the actual group labels:

Group 1	Currently married
Group 2	Always single
Group 3	Cohabiting
Group 4	Divorced or separated
Group 5	Widowed

The title of my press release would be "Adults Who Are Currently Married or Have Always Been Single Are the Healthiest." (I would be tempted but would refrain from saying that "currently married adults are the fattest.") The actual title of the CDC press release was "Married Adults Are Healthiest, New CDC Report Shows." That title was followed by a one-sentence summary: "A new report from the Centers for Disease Control and Prevention suggests that married adults are healthier than divorced, widowed, or never-married adults."

The CDC summary sentence gives the impression that adults who have always been single are just like people who are widowed and divorced, all of whom are less healthy than people who are currently married.

There are at least two important take-home messages from this study. One is that the pattern of the results for this one-time survey of health is very similar to the pattern of the results of the One-Time Happiness Study. In both studies adults who were currently married or had always been single fared similarly, and better than people who were previously married.

The second point is that even when results are described by presumably nonpartisan statisticians, people who are currently married are made to appear better than they really are, and people who have always been single are made to appear worse.

Even if the currently married people had been healthier than the people in all the other groups, as the CDC misleadingly suggests, the study of health at just one point in time could not show definitively that it was marriage that caused the greater health. Marriage clearly did not do much for the health of people whose marriages ended. And as the CDC did acknowledge, it is possible that the currently married people who looked healthier than others were already healthier even before they married. That's why in the study of health, as in the study of happiness, it is important to study lives over time.

As far as I know, there is no study of health that is comparable to Richard Lucas's Lifelines of Happiness Study, in which the same adults are asked about their well-being every year for almost two decades. However, there is published research comparing the health of the same people at two different points in their lives, and that is still better than asking them how they feel at just one point in time.

In a study conducted by sociologists Kristi Williams and Debra Umberson, a nationally representative sample of several thousand Americans, ages twenty-four to ninety-eight, were asked the question "How would you rate your health at the present time?" They responded with one of five numbers,

1 meaning that their health was poor and 5 meaning that it was excellent. They were also asked the same question about four years later.

Williams and Umberson compared the health of people of different marital statuses when they first signed up for the study. The results were similar to what the CDC found. For example, divorced people reported worse health than the married and single people. But again, when the study first started, the divorced, married, and single people were all different people. What the scientists really wanted to know was how the same person's health would change over time, depending on what the person's marital status was at the beginning of the study and whether it changed or stayed the same.

In the four-year interval between the two times that they were surveyed, some of the people started out single and got married. How, if at all, did their health change? Remember that when Lucas asked about happiness, he found a honeymoon effect: People who got married and stayed married did report a small increase in their happiness about the time of their wedding. Williams and Umberson found the same effect for health—but only for men. Women's health did not change as they made the transition from single to married.

In the Lifelines of Happiness Study the happiness of the married people dropped back over time to where it was before they married. The people who stayed single showed a slight drop in happiness over time, but they still ended up squarely on the happy end of the scale. In the Williams and Umberson study, the most comparable groups would be those who were continuously married and those who were continuously single. Whose health was more likely to improve (or deteriorate) over that four-year interval? No one's. The health of the people who had settled into their marriage looked no different from the health of people who had settled into their singlehood.

Lucas found that when people became widowed, they also became less happy. Williams and Umberson found the same dip in health—but only for men, and only if they had become widowed within the past year. Although recently widowed women became less happy than they were years before the death of their spouse, they did not typically become any less healthy.

After about a year the people who had been widowed and stayed that way generally looked similar to the other people who stayed in their marital status over the course of the study. On the average, changes in health from the first year of the study to the fourth were no different for people who had been widowed the whole time than they were for people who had been married or single the whole time.

In the Lifelines of Happiness Study divorce did make a dent in people's happiness. Over the years the happiness of divorced people made a comeback, but it never did make it all the way back to the level it was before they married.

So what about health? No problem. Married people who had gotten divorced by the second time the survey researchers contacted them were no less healthy than they were four years earlier. In fact, on the average, they had become healthier. Not everyone did, of course, but those who became less healthy in the first few years after their divorce were in the minority.

There was also no evidence that divorced people did any worse than anyone else, healthwise, as they settled into their divorced status. On the average, people who had been divorced at both the first and the fourth year of the study were no more or less likely to report improvements in their health than were people who were married at both times, single at both times, or widowed at both times.

In all these findings, was there any evidence to support a claim that marriage makes people healthier? Yes, for men—when they first married. But they got over it.

Any evidence that becoming single after having been married is bad for your health? Again, yes—but only for men who became widowed and only in the first year of widowhood. Even becoming divorced did not do men in, with regard to health.

As for the women, the stability of their health was rather remarkable. Basically, nothing fazed them. Regardless of whether they got married, got unmarried, stayed married, or stayed single, women (on average) noticed no real changes in their health.

Waite and Gallagher would like you to think that the results of scientific studies on marriage and health could be summarized in a fortune cookie: "Get married, be healthy." That fortune has about as much validity as a horoscope.

Getting Married and Getting to Live Longer

Waite and Gallagher's discussion of life and death opens with a bang. "How much can getting married do for you?" they ask. "Sometimes, it can literally save your life."

In case that was too subtle, the authors proceed to pile it on. People who are divorced, widowed, or have always been single, they declare, "are far more likely to die from all causes." If you are a man, you may fear heart disease, but actually, they reassure you, being unmarried is far worse. Heart disease will cost you six years of your life; being unmarried will cost you ten. As for women, being single is a fate worse than cancer or impoverishment: Being unmarried, they claim, will reduce a woman's longevity "by more years than would being married and having cancer and living in poverty." No scientific studies are referenced in support of the claims about heart disease, cancer, or poverty.

Here's another claim that Waite and Gallagher quote approvingly: "Being unmarried is one of the greatest risks that people voluntarily subject themselves to." That was published in *Health Physics: The Radiation Safety Journal*.

I know you've heard enough by now, but I just have to include one last source of Waite and Gallagher's pronouncements, because it includes an important code word. The assertion comes from the author of *RealAge: Are You as Young as You Can Be?* The author, according to Waite and Gallagher, figures that "for men, being happily married is the equivalent of being one and a half years younger than chronological age." He believes that happily married women are six months younger than their chronological age.

The code word is *happily*. When authors make claims that "happily" married people are superior to others in this way or that, it means that they have gone beyond the cheater method. The ordinary cheater way to back up the claim that getting married "can literally save your life" is to act as if the only people who ever got married are the people who are currently married. Adding "happily" means that the claims are based on even more selective (and misleading) evidence. The only people included in the married group are the currently married people who are happily married.

The first few times I saw such "happily" statements, I thought they were just sloppy writing errors. Scholar E. Mavis Hetherington and her coauthor, John Kelly, for example, noted that "happily married couples are healthier, happier, wealthier, and sexier than are singles, especially single men." Did they really mean to say that married people are happier than single people, as long as you include among the married people only those who are happy? Well, actually, they did. Some married people stay married even though they are unhappy. When you compare unhappiness levels across groups, no one matches the unhappily married in misery—not divorced people, not widowed people, and not people who have always been single.

But back to issues of life and death. There actually are serious scientific studies of the links between marriage and mortality. Waite and Gallagher refer readers to a review of some of those studies, and they also present a reanalysis of a published study that Waite coauthored.

I checked out the recommended review article. It points to three studies of marriage and mortality, so I tracked them down. One compares the mortality rates of married people who stayed married with those who became widowed over the course of an eleven-year interval. That means the study is irrelevant to Waite and Gallagher's trumpeting of the livesaving value of getting married: All the people in the study had gotten married. Still, for the record, the women who were widowed did not die at any greater rate than women who stayed married, and remarriage was not linked to higher or lower mortality rates, either. The men who were widowed did die at a higher rate than the men who remained married, and remarriage did lower their death rate.

The other two studies both compare the death rates of people who were currently married with those of all unmarried people combined (the divorced, the widowed, and the people who had always been single). So these studies also fail to address the claim that getting married saves lives, because even in the "unmarried" group, most of the people had in fact gotten married. The studies show that currently married men lived longer than unmarried men, but currently married women had less of an advantage or no advantage at all over unmarried women.

That leaves just Waite and Gallagher's reanalysis of data that Waite had already analyzed and published. Waite and Gallagher introduced the new analyses with a thought experiment. We, the readers, are to imagine a group of forty-eight-year-old men and women who are exactly the same in every quantifiable way except one—their marital status. How many would live to be at least sixty-five years old?

What is interesting about the hypothetical question is that the original study addresses it, only without restricting the group to the forty-eight-year-olds. A national sample of more than 11,000 people, from age ten on up, was followed for seventeen years as they stayed single, married, separated, divorced, became widowed, or remarried. When the people who stayed married were compared with everyone else, the now-familiar results emerged: Among the women, those who stayed married had death rates that were not measurably different from those of the other women. The men who stayed married did live longer than the other men.

As always, none of the comparisons addressed Waite and Gallagher's bold claim that getting married saves lives. That would require comparing all of the people who had ever married (the currently married, separated, divorced, and widowed) with the people who had stayed single. In the original study, though, the death rates of the separated, divorced, and widowed people were compared with those of the people who had stayed single. For men, the rates were not different. For women, comparisons with the continuously single showed that the separated women had higher death rates and the widowed women had lower rates.

Waite and Gallagher do not describe the original comprehensive results but only report the results of their analyses of the forty-eight-year-olds. They claim that "almost nine out of ten married men alive at forty-eight would still be alive at sixty-five," but only about six out of ten unmarried men would. They then conclude that "three out of ten single, widowed, or divorced middle-aged men can expect to lose their lives when they lose their wives." Never mind that the single men had no wives to lose; the rhyme was more important than accuracy.

Not that the description was accurate, even for the select sample of forty-eight-year-olds. The authors tucked the actual percentages into an endnote. Eighty-eight percent of the married forty-eight-year-old men and 66 percent of the unmarried men were alive at sixty-five. So they rounded 88 up to 90, and they rounded 66 down to 60 and got their statistic about three out of ten men losing their lives when they lost their wives.

All the special analyses, though, could not doom the unmarried women. Waite and Gallagher were stuck admitting that marriage mattered less to women's longevity—even using the cheater method of comparison—and that just as many widowed forty-eight-year-olds as married ones made it to sixty-five.

Here's a quick recap:

□ For women, getting married does not seem to have any remarkable implications for longevity. Even women who get married and stay that way do not seem to live longer than other women.

□ Married men do live longer than unmarried men if you use the cheater method. So, you can say that getting married saves men's lives if you pretend that the men who divorced or became widowed did not actually get married. Call it a statistical annulment.

But what if the more scientifically respectable comparisons were made? Interesting question. Waite and Gallagher do not mention all the longevity studies that were available to them at the time they published their book. They skip over what is probably the longest-running study ever conducted— the Terman Life-Cycle Study. It started in 1921, with 1,528 eleven-year-olds. Scientists kept track of the participants for as long as they lived. The people who lived the longest were those who stayed single and those who married and stayed married. People who divorced, or who divorced and remarried, had shorter lives. What mattered was consistency, not marriage. The results were the same for the men and the women.

Getting Married and Getting Sex

I bet you can anticipate the bottom line of Waite and Gallagher's chapter on sex. Married couples have more sex and better sex.

There is only one problem with that conclusion: It is not exactly true. Married people do not have the most sex—cohabiting people do.

If I were in Waite and Gallagher's place and wanted to defend married people's second-place finish in the sexual frequency sweepstakes, I'd say that raw frequency means nothing apart from desired frequency. So what if cohabitors are having the most sex if one partner wants even more and the other wishes there were a whole lot less? Maybe married people are more likely to get the amount of sex that they want.

Waite and Gallagher try to shrug off the more active sex lives of cohabitors in a different way. Cohabiting relationships, they say, are more likely than marriages to be "built around sex." In Waite and Gallagher's view, married people who are not having sex still consider themselves married, but cohabiting people who are not having sex just consider themselves roommates.

Does that sound unconvincing? That's okay. Waite and Gallagher are ready with another way to diminish the people who are having more sex than married people: "They don't seem to enjoy it quite as much." In support of their conclusion that married people have more extremely satisfying sex than other people do, Waite and Gallagher cite a lot of percentages. Those numbers are listed in the first column of data in the following table. In the adjacent column are the actual numbers from the original source, the National Sex Survey.

What Percentage of People Are Extremely Emotionally Satisfied with Their Sex Lives?		
Waite and Gallagher's Categories	Waite and Gallagher's Numbers	Actual Numbers from the National Sex Survey
MEN		
Married	48	48.9
Cohabiting	37	35.2 for single cohabitors
		52.6 for divorced or separated cohabitors
WOMEN		
Married	42	42.1
Single with sexual partner	31	31.4 for not cohabiting
		44.1 for cohabiting
Divorced with sexual partner	27	27.4 for not cohabiting
		36.5 for cohabiting

Waite and Gallagher are reasonably accurate when they describe the satisfaction of married people. When you compare the percentages they report for the married men and married women to the actual percentages from the National Sex Survey, the two sets are similar. But Waite and Gallagher really do a number on everyone else.

Take, for example, their claim that for men, being married "beats shacking up by a wide margin: 48 percent of husbands say sex with their partner is extremely satisfying emotionally, compared to just 37 percent of cohabiting men." Now look at the second row of numbers in the table (the one corresponding to the cohabiting men). Yes, 37 percent is close enough to the actual number of single cohabiting men who describe their sex as extremely emotionally satisfying. But Waite and Gallagher do not happen to mention that for divorced men who are cohabiting, the number is 52.6 percent. That amounts to more sexually satisfied cohabiting divorced men than married men. And that is not the case that Waite and Gallagher are trying to make.

To make the married women look good, they take a different tack. They compare the sexual satisfaction of married women with that of the single and divorced women who are not cohabiting. That's convenient, because, as you can see from the table, it is the cohabiting women who usually report the more satisfying sex lives.

The National Sex Survey was full of information about rates of sexual problems. Waite and Gallagher do not have much to say on that topic. Here's some of what they skip over. With regard to some of the problems men might have, such as an inability to maintain an erection, climaxing too early, or experiencing pain during sex, currently married men have nothing over men who have always been single. When there's a difference, it is the married men who are more likely to be having difficulties. Men who have always been single also report fewer sexual problems than do divorced men.

Among the women, the group most likely to be problem-free is not the currently married women. Rather, it is the widowed women who are less likely than all the others (married, divorced, separated, or always single) to complain that they do not find sex pleasurable, that they cannot reach orgasm or reach it too early, or that they experience anxiety or pain during sex.

Waite and Gallagher wrap up their chapter on the sexual advantages of marriage by describing the results of one last survey. This one, sponsored by the Family Research Council, describes all the people who could lay claim to the most satisfying sex. Married people, of course, top the list, but some married people are even better off sexually than others. Among them are those who attend church weekly, who believe that out-of-wedlock sex is wrong, who have three or more children, who live in one-earner households, and "who see sex as a sacred union, exclusive to marriage." There is an endnote corresponding to the description of these results. It says that the Family Research Council "is an activist not a scholarly organization." Indeed. According to its website, the council "champions marriage and family as the foundation of civilization, the seedbed of virtue, and the wellspring of society." Also, it "promotes the Judeo-Christian worldview as the basis for a just, free, and stable society."

In all this research, people were surveyed about their sexual behavior at one point in time. As always, that means any differences between people may have had nothing whatsoever to do with getting married. The sexual behavior of the married people, for example, may have been the same even before they married. As far as I know, there are no published studies on sex in which the same people are studied over time, as their marital status changes or remains the same.

Getting Married and Getting Scammed

It is time now to evaluate Waite and Gallagher's claims about getting married—claims that have been accepted and repeated by so many others—in light of the actual findings from scientific research. Waite and Gallagher promise at the outset of their book to show that "marriage for most people is the means to health, happiness, wealth, and long life." At the end, they declare the benefits of marriage to be "profound."

If the benefits of marriage are in fact profound, then there should be big bold differences between single and married people. And if there were such huge differences, then no one would need to write a book to make the case for marriage. The case would be obvious.

I do not think any of the scientific findings indicate that the experience of marriage is transformative. That purported power is mythical. As we have seen, there is nothing profound about the changes that have been scientifically documented.

In fact, of all the changes into and out of various marital statuses that have been studied by scientists, the one least likely to make a lasting difference to adults' health and well-being is the transition into marriage. When people first get married, they get a small blip in happiness, which soon dissipates. Small as that blip is, not everyone enjoys it. People who get married but eventually divorce are already becoming less happy—not more—as they approach their wedding day.

Health does not improve when women first get married, though men do seem to show some early benefits. A few years down the marital road, though, those men do not become any more or less healthy than men who have settled into other marital statuses.

So just getting married does not much matter, but getting married and then getting unmarried may not be quite as benign. People who divorce do become less happy than they were before they married, and may not live as long as people who stay single or who marry and stay married.

The marriage movement would have you believe that the implications of those results are clear: Married people should stay married. But it is not at all apparent that staying married would provide a happy ending for those contemplating divorce. The Lifelines of Happiness Study shows that people who eventually divorce are less happy than people who stay married even before anyone marries, that they are already becoming less happy even before they marry, and that the slide continues until the year before the divorce becomes official. This does not look like a pattern that could be stopped in its tracks by a decision to stay married.

Moreover, it may be the anticipation of a finalized divorce that begins to reverse the descent into lower happiness. Although divorced people do not seem to recapture the level of happiness they enjoyed when they were single, they do eventually feel better than they did when their marriages were crumbling.

Even the finding that people who divorce have shorter life spans does not come prepackaged with a moral. Maybe if they stayed in the marriages that they found so troubling, their lives would have been shorter still. And maybe if they had never married at all, they would have lived longer. We just don't know.

The same is true for all the findings about divorce that might seem to offer bragging rights. For example, just because divorced men who are cohabiting report the most intensely satisfying sexual experiences does not mean that they are having great sex because they are divorced or because they are cohabiting. Maybe the particular men who divorce and then cohabit would have fabulous sex lives no matter what.

I say all this not to encourage or discourage divorce but to urge more honest interpretation and reporting of the science of marriage and singlehood. It is, I believe, ethically reckless to lead people to believe that getting married and staying married is the means to health, happiness, and a long life, when the science does not unambiguously support any such claim. It would be equally reckless to suggest that staying single or divorcing is a magical elixir, when the science does not clearly support those claims, either.

———

What, then, counts as good science, when the question of interest is the relative health or well-being of people in different marital statuses? Here are a few questions to keep in mind as you try to evaluate claims based on the latest research:

1. How credible is the study?

- Scientific claims should be based on scientific research, not on the work of partisan advocacy groups.
- Studies based on large, nationally representative samples are better than those in which smaller numbers of participants are recruited more haphazardly. This is especially so when people cannot be assigned at random to participate in the different experiences (such as marriage, divorce, widowhood, and singlehood).
- Studies in which the same people are followed over time are usually more informative than studies in which people are surveyed only once.

Even the very best studies can be described in ways that are misleading or just plain wrong. That is the real story behind the conventional wisdom—shaped in no small part by Waite and Gallagher—about the "benefits" of marriage. Much of the research is of reasonably high quality, considering the constraints of doing this sort of science. (Most important, people get to choose for themselves whether to stay single, marry, or divorce.) The problem is what is said about the results.

2. Who got counted as married and unmarried? The typical headline from a study of marital status is that married people are better. Here are some questions to think about:

- What married people? Usually the answer is "currently married people." Any study that counts as married only those people who are currently married cannot provide a complete answer to the question of the implications of getting married, because people who did get married but later divorced or became widowed are not included.
- Better than whom? If the answer is "unmarried people," you should wonder about that, too. All unmarried people combined (divorced and widowed people, and people who have always been single)? Just the previously married? Just the people who have always been single? The implications of getting married cannot be determined by comparing

the currently married with the previously married, because the previously married got married, too.

☐ Do the groups make sense? Consider, for example, the category of people who are widowed. If the headline claims that getting married is linked with, say, greater happiness or better health, why are widows included at all? If widows feel sad after their partners die, does that mean they never should have married? (Waite and Gallagher play it both ways. When widows fare worse than married people, then the authors say, See, it is better to be married. But when widows do just fine, Waite and Gallagher do not then conclude that perhaps being unmarried is not so bad after all. Instead, they say that marriage is so amazing that its protective powers continue long after a spouse has died.)

3. How different are the groups? When you hear that married people (or any other group of people) are better, you should also ask how much better. In presenting the results of the Lifelines of Happiness Study, for example, it would have been easy to make the differences between the continuously married people and everyone else appear huge. Look back at the first graph. The average happiness scores for the three groups (the bold lines) all ranged between 6.4 and 7.5. So I could have selected just that part of the graph and blown it up so that it expanded to take up the whole page. Doing so would not be dishonest—I would not be changing any of the numbers. But I would be leaving it to the reader to keep in mind that the survey participants could have chosen numbers ranging all the way from 0 to 10 to describe their happiness, and that the numbers they did choose, on the average, were all on the happy end of the scale.

4. Is the advice really justified by the study? Scientists and reporters can compare any groups of people they choose—what is important is the conclusions they draw. When you hear a claim such as "the latest study shows that married people are happier, and therefore you should marry so you will be happier, too," turn on your cheater detector. Remember the Shamster study. If a drug company tried to convince you to take Shamster by pointing only to the people who are still taking the drug, you would think you were being scammed. Especially if you knew that nearly half the people who tried Shamster found it intolerable. You would be even more outraged if you learned that the drug company tried to use the ill feelings of the people who could not tolerate the drug, or who had it withdrawn, to bolster its case for the powers of the drug. If a pharmaceutical company said to you, "Look—people who go off Shamster feel worse; if only they had stayed on it, they would feel so much better," you would turn and walk away.

If you want to make the case for getting married—which is exactly the case that Waite and Gallagher were trying to make—then you should include in the married group all the people who have ever gotten married. That means people who are currently married and people who are separated or divorced. If you insist on including widowed people in your study, then they have to be part of the group that got married, too. How does the happiness of all those people who got married, taken together, compare with the happiness of people who have always been single? That's a comparison I have never seen made, even though I believe it is the most relevant one.

I think the marriage mafia would have a quick comeback. Oh, we didn't mean "just get married," we meant "get married and stay that way." That's how they justify counting only the currently married in the married group. (I guess widowed people are supposed to remarry instantly.) Still, there is an obvious fallacy. They want you to believe that the people who divorced would have had the same happiness scores as the people who stayed married, if only they had stayed married, too.

Suppose all the people who had ever gotten married really were compared with people who had always been single, and the married group was happier. Would that mean that marriage made them joyful? Not necessarily. If the people were surveyed at just one point in time, then the married and single people were different people. The people who got married may have been happier than the single people even before they married.

If the same people became noticeably happier after they married than they had been before, and if that happiness continued or even intensified over time (rather than returning to its premarriage level, or declining), then I might conclude that marriage made those people happy. I would still want to ask one other question: What about the people who stayed single at the same time—were they also becoming happier? If all people were becoming happier, regardless of their marital status, then again, marriage probably had nothing to do with it. (Maybe something changed in the world that made everyone happier.) I am not being impossible, though I know it must seem that way. If all the people who ever married became happier after they married and stayed happier, when the people who stayed single at the same time did not become happier, then I would conclude that marriage made those people happier. Really.

I know of no such data.

If I were to make the claim that staying single makes people happier, I would hold myself to the same high standards. I am making no such claim. I know of no findings that convincingly establish that.

Here's what I do think. People who have gotten married and people who have stayed single are more similar than they are different. In some studies, in some ways, some singles will look better than some marrieds; in other studies, in other ways, some marrieds will look better than some singles.

If this sounds annoyingly wishy-washy, that's because it is. I think the research is a wash. And that is a radically different claim than the one trumpeted by people who say that marriage brings profound benefits. It is also wildly different from the marriage mythology that has permeated the land.

I think we need to go back and reexamine our initial assumptions. Why was it again that we thought people who got married would be so much happier and healthier than people who stayed single?

Actually, there are some sound reasons to place our bets on marriage. As I will explain in greater detail in Chapter 12, married people have financial advantages over single people. They have those advantages not because they earn them by working longer or harder but because American society favors them and discriminates against singles. In part because of the greater economic resources they consequently enjoy—and because of other forms of discrimination, too—married people also have greater access to health care. Finally, married people have greater social status. Many people really do believe that marriage elevates humans to a higher place, from which they can legitimately look down on beings who remain mere singletons.

All the ways in which married people are advantaged over singles only make the scientific findings all the more baffling. If married people have so much going for them, then why doesn't the experience of getting married transform people into much happier and healthier humans?

If you buy into the mythology, then the similar health and happiness of single and married people should be even more perplexing. Here's why.

People who have married, according to the mythology, have learned to be responsible to another person. They have learned to compromise and to act selflessly instead of selfishly. Married people protect each other from bad things. Wives nag husbands until they drink less and drive more carefully; husbands protect wives from financial disaster. Finally, married people—for as long as they remain married—"have someone." Single people, mythologically speaking, "don't have anyone."

The Wall Street Journal's "hard truth" that I quote at the beginning of the chapter succinctly sums up much of the same marital mythology: "the real road to happiness lies not in the direct pursuit of personal fulfillment but in love of, compromise with and commitment to another." The *Journal* seems to believe that singles pursue personal fulfillment and married people do not; that married people love others, compromise with others, and commit to others and single people do not; and that such differences explain why getting married makes people happier. Only it doesn't.

There's something wrong with the set of "truths" we hold to be self-evident. The mythology of marriage and singlehood does not square with the actual lives of people who are married and people who are single. Over the next ten chapters, I take on each of the myths of marital superiority, one by one, and show why they are wrong.

CHAPTER THREE

Myth #1 The Wonder of Couples

Marrieds Know Best

Soon after John F. Kennedy Jr. died in a plane crash, *New York* magazine published a collection of reminiscences contributed by his colleagues, neighbors, and friends. John once worked as a district attorney. Owen, his officemate from those days, described a time when he and his aunt were at a wedding that John was attending, too. Owen asked John if he would say hello to his aunt. John, he noted, "went right over. He talked to her the way one of my best friends from college would have talked to her." The designer Kenneth Cole told a story of inviting John to one of his shows, offering to send a car. John declined the car. "The morning of the show, my people were waiting for him outside, and suddenly, right before the show, they see this guy, all dressed up, pedaling over on a bicycle. It was John. He got on his knees, locked his bike to a post, and just walked in." A neighbor recounted seeing a man in front of her at a small café. She made a friendly remark about his bicycle chain, then was mortified when he turned around and she realized who it was. John, though, continued the conversation on that day and on others as well. "We ended up meeting often there, locking our bikes to the same pole, getting the same blueberry muffins."

Such are the stories that are told about celebrities, sometimes even by people who are themselves celebrities. John F. Kennedy Jr., son of a beloved president, talks nicely to people who have no claim to fame. He rides a bicycle and even lets his knees touch the ground as he locks it to a post. He eats the very same blueberry muffins as his neighbor, who is just another New Yorker. These tales of the awesome celebrity and little old me are told with fondness, awe, and gratitude.

I mention this because I think that couples are accorded a whiff of the same celebrity in their interactions with people who are single. I don't mean just celebrity couples. Even the most ordinary couples elicit gratitude for the most unextraordinary gestures when the recipients of their non-largesse are adults who are single.

Consider, for example, author Carol Shields's description of Tom Avery, a thrice-divorced character she created for her novel *The Republic of Love*: "Luckily, he has a few married friends, but he's noticed that he's seldom included anymore in their dinner parties. Instead, he's more likely to be asked to brunch, joining the family around the table for waffles." Tom's contributions to these get-togethers have also changed: "He feels obliged now to earn his invitations with gifts of fresh flowers or bottles of expensive wine. He admires his friends' babies and dutifully bounces them on his knee. . . . In return, these married friends dispense well-meaning advice, and occasionally fix him up with single women."

Like so many real single people, Tom has been demoted from dinner with the grown-ups to brunch with the kids. Without a serious partner, Tom is no longer the equal of the couples. They give him waffles; he gives them expensive wine. He fawns over the kids, admiring them just the way they are; the couples, apparently seeing him as broken, try to fix him up.

All of that interested me, but what really grabbed me was one word: *luckily*. Tom owes more than fine wine for the adults and emotional subsidies for the kids; he is also expected to feel grateful for the mere fact that he still has a few married friends.

The feeling is not just found in fiction. I have heard the same sentiment expressed by real-live humans, including single people. One time when I was traveling, I struck up a conversation with a woman who was recently widowed. I asked her if she saw her coupled friends any more or less than she had before her husband died. She said she was "really lucky" because her coupled friends still included her.

It seems to me that therapists should be attuned to intimations that their single clients are selling themselves short in the dignity department in their interactions with couples. So it was with great interest that I read a book by two clinicians, *Being Single in a Couple's World*. I was especially intrigued by the story they told about Adam, a client who had recently divorced.

Adam and his ex-wife had a cabin they rented for a month every year, and two other couples always joined them for the last week and split the cost. There were only two bedrooms, so each night one of the couples slept in the living room. The first year after his divorce, Adam decided he would rent the cabin again and continue the tradition of inviting the same couples to join him for a week.

On the day his friends were due to arrive, Adam had gone to work and got back to the cabin after his friends had settled in. Adam was delighted to see his friends. He was a little less thrilled, though, when he noticed the neat pile of clothes in a corner of the living room. They were his. The couples had moved them from his bedroom, figuring that "since Adam was alone he wouldn't need his own bedroom and could sleep in the living room. This would give the two couples more privacy."

Adam told his friends how he felt: He was dismayed at finding that his friends had decided to move him to the living room without asking him what he thought of the idea. (Marrieds know best.) Sheepishly, his friends headed to the pile of clothes to begin to move them back to Adam's room. (Marrieds still know best.) Adam stopped them, explaining that what he wanted was to be included in the decision process. Finally, they talked it through and Adam ended up expressing his willingness to stay in the living room.

That could have been the happy ending—Adam got to express his opinion just like the other adults. But there was more. At the end of the week, the couples asked Adam what he thought of the idea of splitting the expenses five ways, instead of continuing the three-way split that had been their tradition when Adam was coupled, too. Adam happily agreed. As Adam recounted the story in therapy, his last line was a proud one, "You gotta love friends like that!" In describing that ending, the therapists seemed proud, too.

By now it may not surprise you that I am going to reprise my role as the skunk at the garden party. (And I wonder why I'm not always invited to these parties.) "You gotta love friends like that"? Huh? Why is Adam giving his friends extra credit for not treating him unfairly? He sounds to me like the woman I met in my travels who felt lucky that her lifelong friends did not ostracize her after her husband died. And why didn't the therapists, who were writing a book on singles in a coupled world, recognize that by feeling grateful for being treated fairly, Adam was perpetuating the cult of the couple? It was as if Adam agreed that his coupled friends were more special and more worthy than he, simply because they were coupled and he was not.

I don't mean to single out Adam, or even his therapist. The notion that couples are entitled, just because they are coupled, has settled into the habits of our minds. It seems so natural that we rarely recognize how bizarre it really is.

At an auto repair shop as I stood in line to pay my bill, the person at the register said that he was going to ring up the other customer's bill first. The customer's wife was at home waiting for him, the clerk told me, and it was her birthday.

Couples idolatry becomes even more preposterous when people who have relevant achievements to flaunt are overlooked while couples are applauded. Sometimes literally. A singleton and scholar told me about a welcoming event he attended at a university he had just joined. The new faculty members were there to meet one another and learn more about the school. It was an excellent university, so the new faculty brought with them many outstanding intellectual accomplishments. Those were not named or acknowledged. However, the new faculty who were married had been invited to bring their spouses. Those partners were asked to step forward to be recognized, which is when the room filled with applause.

Consider also an e-mail I received from a professional society. The group is composed of academic researchers who study relationships, and the e-mails are usually filled with society business and announcements about new books or upcoming conferences. On the day in question, the e-mail included a link to a story in *The New York Times*—about the wedding of one of the society members. This is an organization that includes many eminent scientists. In the interim between one e-mail and the next, any number of members have had their professional work described in prestigious newspapers and magazines. But only the story about the wedding was mentioned.

Washington, D.C., is not a place where consensus comes easily, but as to the prize for the best-kept secret in contemporary American politics, there is widespread agreement. That secret was the identity of the person known for more than three decades only as Deep Throat. "Throat," as the cool people called him for short, was the man who stood in a darkened parking garage and passed along to journalists Bob Woodward and Carl Bernstein the devastating revelations that would ultimately bring down the Nixon presidency. Amazingly, during all that time, in a town where so many secrets are spilled, Woodward and Bernstein kept their promise of confidentiality to Mark Felt (Deep Throat). They told only the one person they were obligated to tell—Ben Bradlee, their editor at *The Washington Post*.

That's the legend. But it is not the truth. Someone else knew for twenty-three of the thirty-three years. Woodward had told his wife, Elsa Walsh. In so doing, Woodward betrayed Felt's trust. Faced with a choice between indulging in pillow talk and upholding the integrity of the profession of journalism, Woodward chose the pillow.

What I find almost as appalling as the breach of ethics was Woodward's attitude, which I learned about in an essay by Sally Quinn (who neither asked nor was told about the identity of Deep Throat by her husband, Ben Bradlee): "Every time we were together and the subject of Deep Throat came up, Bob would grin mischievously and say something provocative like, 'There are no secrets between Elsa and me.' "

In the years leading up to 2005, when Felt's identity was revealed, the mainstream media were relentlessly scrutinized, criticized, and forced to eat crow. *The New York Times* apologized for printing stories fabricated by reporter Jayson Blair and also expressed regret for its overly credulous reporting of the run-up to the war in Iraq. On network television, CBS and its star anchor, Dan Rather, acknowledged that they were too quick to air an election-year exposé. Over at Fox News, unfair and unbalanced stories were produced in such abundance that legions of critics were moved to write essays and books with titles such as *Lies and the Lying Liars Who Tell Them*. Journalists such as Woodward, icons of the profession, were now accused of trading intrepid investigative reporting for the kind of access that comes with more sympathetic portrayals of the people in power. Yet in this atmosphere of relentless suspicion and doubt, no one—with the possible exception of Sally Quinn—seemed to think that there was anything wrong with Woodward's divulging to his wife such a sacrosanct secret. Woodward was presumptuous in carving out a special place of privilege for his spouse, and our entire society was complicit.

Contemporary couples are tightly linked twosomes. To their friends, Dick and Jane are probably DickAndJane. And when couples socialize, it is typically with other couples. Singles are not included.

To some degree, this is unremarkable. People who have something important in common often seek one another's company, and in contemporary American society, being coupled is very important indeed. Social scientists who study these matters systematically have found this clustering by common life paths in every place they have looked for it. Widows gravitate to other widows; parents seek out other parents; older students on college campuses find and befriend one another. All enjoy one another's company, and for good reason. They compare notes, reassure one another, and talk ardently about matters that others might find soporific.

So, what seems noteworthy is not that socializing in couples occurs but that it occurs so often and so exclusively. Many couples do not just add other couples to their social rosters, they also ditch their single friends. Or relegate them to a lesser status.

I usually got the lesser status. My coupled friends on the East Coast routinely invited me to their kids' birthday parties. When they made plans for Saturday night, though (sometimes in the hallway right outside my office door), I was not included.

I think it may have mattered that when I first met many of those friends, they were already coupled. We differed on that dimension right from the start. Often, though, a group of people start out in the same boat, singles all; then, as some become coupled, the remaining singles get tossed off the ark. That, to me, seems even more curious.

An anecdote told by a person I'll call Sandy is an apt example of many similar stories that single people have shared with me over the years. Sandy had become quite close to two other single women, Valerie and Haley. For years they were friends and confidantes. Eventually, Valerie and Haley married, then had kids. Along the way, Sandy listened to the sagas of the ups and downs of the relationships and the pregnancies. If Valerie and Haley seemed a bit less interested in the stories from her life, Sandy didn't mention it. At the time of the wedding showers and the weddings and the baby showers, Sandy really did not mind that all the talk was about those events. She was there for her friends with her time and her resources. She was generous in planning, hosting, and attending bridal showers, then baby showers. Her contributions to those celebratory events were warmly welcomed.

However, after the weddings Sandy saw less and less of her coupled friends, and contact grew even more infrequent after they had children. Sandy of course recognized that parents might have less time for socializing than do nonparents, but that was not her issue. It was, instead, that the two friends and their husbands would socialize with one another, and later, when they had kids, with their families. Sandy was not invited, not to the dinner parties and not to the backyard barbecues.

Sandy was plucky, so she did something few others dare: She asked Valerie why she had been excluded. Valerie said she didn't know if Sandy would like it that the other people at the dinners were all couples. As for the events with the families, "I honestly didn't know if you would feel comfortable with just couples and babies." Rather than asking Sandy about her feelings and preferences, as she did with Haley when planning the time that the couples would spend with one another, Valerie simply assumed she already knew how Sandy felt. Marrieds know best.

If singles passively wait at home for their coupled friends to call and then sulk when they do not, maybe they deserve all the exclusion they get. Singles who want to maintain their relationships with friends who have become coupled need to take some of the initiative. Myself included.

Sometimes it works just fine. Your coupled friends are happy to hear from you and eager to get together for dinner or a movie or just about anything else.

There is a risk, though. I learned that from my own experiences and from the stories related to me by other singles. The risk is that you will be told, in one way or another, that you are not worth it. You are not worth a weekend night. You are not worth a babysitter. You are not worth a trip from an out-of-town couple. You are not worth the money. You are not worth the time.

I do not mean to imply that these are necessarily just lame excuses, crafted specially to elude those annoying single friends. People who have kids, for example, really do have claims on their time that people without kids do not. And they do need to pay to play: They need to hire babysitters, and people without children do not. So those reasons are fine. Except when the same couples have no problem finding the time or the money for a sitter when they want to socialize with other couples.

I am also not saying that couples and singles should continue to see one another when they really have grown apart in their interests or their affections. One of the true joys of friendship, in its ideal form, is that it is voluntary. It is based on fondness, not on obligation. Maybe in Sandy's case, and in others like hers that evolve over time, sentiments really did shift. Sandy wasn't excluded because she was single while her friends became coupled but because feelings of closeness waned, as can happen among any friends, regardless of anyone's status as single or coupled.

The exclusion of singles seems more suspect when it happens suddenly. Consider, for example, this story about Kim. She and her longtime partner had socialized with two other couples every weekend for years. When Kim and her partner broke up in midweek, she called a woman from one of the other couples and had a long and tearful conversation. As Kim expected, her friend wanted to hear all the details and conveyed lots of kindness and compassion. What Kim had not anticipated was her friend's final words before the call ended: "I'm so sorry to hear all this. We were looking forward to seeing you this weekend."

Kim's so-called friend was not the least bit embarrassed to uninvite Kim once she was suddenly single. To her, it seemed self-evident that couples socialize with other couples, and so if you are no longer coupled, you are no longer welcome.

The assumption that couples are special and singles are second-class explains why couples can plan couples-only events or vacation trips right in front of their single friends and think nothing of it. It also accounts for the rule that was once in place in a Canadian hiking club for seniors: If you become widowed, you need to leave the club by the end of the calendar year.

Were the friends of Sandy, Kim, and all the others just a bunch of ignoramuses? I doubt it. Maybe they read too many advice columns.

Suppose they went searching on the Web for suggestions on maintaining their friendships with their single friends. On the MSN website, The Knot, Valerie and others like her could have found just what they were looking for—a column titled "Friends: Keeping Them After You Tie the Knot." Here are some choice excerpts:

> Now that you are married . . . married friends may joyfully add you to their roster of couples to dine and vacation with, while your union may remind single friends of their lack of success in the relationship department.
>
> You may have trouble staying close to single friends after marriage. They may seem distant and jealous. . . . Don't take friends' negative reactions personally; they're likely feeling a bit deserted. If you want to maintain the friendship, call your hurt friend and ask him or her out for coffee or a drink.
>
> Your friendship may die a natural death. Don't feel guilty; this happens sometimes.

Most married couples gravitate toward other married couples. It makes for a nice, even number and lets you see how other couples handle their relationships.

The lesson here to Valerie about dealing with Sandy and her other single friends is clear: Just dump them. And don't feel bad about it, either. They are jealous and hurt because you are such a stunning success at relationships and they are all dismal failures. If you insist on spending time with them, make it a quick get-together for coffee or a drink. Dinners and vacations are for couples only. Really, you should just hang out with other couples. It makes for a nice, even number.

Maybe Valerie also consulted one of the first issues of *2: The Magazine for Couples.* In the "Instructions for Living" section, she would have found an essay explaining "How to Break Up (with a Single Friend)." Every time your single friend calls to suggest a get-together, *2* recommends, "tell him or her that you have plans with your partner (something absolutely cancelable, like watching the umpteenth showing of *The Prince of Tides*)." If you are planning your own social event, it is fine to invite the singleton: "Just make sure to subtly point out that the rest of the guest list comprises couples." Then, as a last resort, push your single friend to get coupled. "Nothing says 'for God's sake get hooked up, already' like frequent setups and blind-date offers."

The Knot and *2* paint the single friend as a throwaway and a failure. By their reckoning, single people have problems, and the problems are their own.

There is a more sobering cautionary tale for the happy couple, though: The single friend, desperate to score a success in the relationship department, may just try to steal your spouse. That's the warning issued by Shirley Glass's book, *NOT "Just Friends."* Watch out if your spouse claims to be "just friends" with a coworker: You may soon find yourself picking up the pieces of infidelity. Glass dispenses counsel for avoiding that sad fate. For example, *do not* "lunch or take private coffee breaks with the same person all the time." *Do* "surround yourself with friends who are happily married." New fear factor, same bottom line: Ditch your single friends.

CHAPTER
FOUR

Myth #2 Single-Minded

You Are Interested in Just One Thing—Getting Coupled

I love food. I love everything from the very simplest culinary delights, like a perfectly ripe strawberry, to the most complex. I like to think about food, read about it, and figure out how to present it. I love entertaining. And I have never hesitated to prepare something fabulous because I was cooking "only" for myself.

So, when I first learned in early 2002 that there was a website called Single Gourmet, I expected it to become an instant favorite. Here, I thought, would be the website that would speak to me. It would acknowledge that you do not need to be a couple or a family, or striving to become one, in order to savor fine food.

That's not what the Single Gourmet was about at all. The first hint came from the four pictures that were on the home page at the time—all were of couples. One couple was slow dancing on a deserted beach. Another was nestled together on a park bench, with luscious greenery behind them. A third twosome embraced each other, foreheads touching, in still another verdant setting. The fourth couple was cheek to cheek and suffused with a warm orange-tinged glow.

On the website called Single Gourmet there was no food anywhere in sight. Instead, the site declared itself the "Answer for Singles." "Are you single?" the text begins. "Do you love the pleasures of fine dining, exciting travel and fun-filled events in a relaxed atmosphere? . . . . What are you waiting for? Sign up today through the *Single Gourmet* Web Site. For only $100.00 per year, and with your first event free, you could be on your way to meeting the love of your life."

The Single Gourmet was not for single people interested in gourmet food—it was just another gateway to becoming unsingle. A singles bar will hand you a glass, and the Single Gourmet will supply the knife and fork; at either place, though, there is only one item on the menu.

In what I call the "just one thing" myth, single people are seen as single-mindedly seeking coupledom. Depictions of singles, interpretations of their motives and emotions, and conversations with them are driven by the assumption that for single people, the quest to become unsingle dominates their lives.

Author Penny Kaganoff noticed this after she got divorced. In *Women on Divorce: A Bedside Companion,* she describes her new social life as an unmarried woman: "I am tired of these affairs, where no one asks what books I've read, only a handful of relatives are interested in how I'm advancing at my job, and everyone quizzes me about my dating life."

Kaganoff did something risky by expressing her exasperation. She invited emotional caricaturing. She had to know that some people would refuse to believe that she was frustrated by having her richly textured life flattened; instead, they would be sure that she was just bitter about being single.

Single women, according to the "just one thing" myth, are preoccupied with the talismans that promise to deliver them from singlehood. Lingerie, skin treatments, hairstyling, and the latest diet, they hope, will make them more attractive. Glossy magazines and books of rules will steer them in the right direction. And a crammed social calendar will afford them ample opportunities to put all the lotions and potions to good use.

The "just one thing" mythology is the most predictable guide to advertising. Regardless of whether marketers are hawking drinkable yogurt, vacation travel, lip balm, or real estate, what they are really selling the single woman is a better chance at a spouse.

Mythologically speaking, single men are not quite as obsessed with becoming coupled as are single women. Still, married men seem to delight in egging on their single male friends. Wedding receptions are among the most popular venues for such prodding. Author Warren St. John mused about the phenomenon after several of his single male friends returned from wedding festivities with similar stories. In his essay "Bob, Meet Jane. And Give Me the Details," St. John notes, "There's nothing like having a single friend to turn married people into the matchmaking equivalent of

Wall Street traders—frenetic go-betweens in the romantic marketplace."
What was striking to each bachelor was that his married friends seemed far
more interested in seeing him coupled than he was himself.

Although the lives of single people are routinely reduced to a narrow-
minded obsession with coupling, the lives of married people are rarely so
readily diminished or dismissed. The multidimensionality of their interests
and concerns is touted and respected. Homes, for example, are sold to
couples as havens for indulging their love of relaxing, working, cooking, gar-
dening, nurturing, and entertaining. Singles, mythologically, are so single-
minded that they may not even need a real home as long as they remain
uncoupled. Occasionally, in the annals of advertising or in the cultural
conversation, someone slips and reveals the belief that singles are so insub-
stantial that they do not even count as real people.

It took me a while to recognize the full extent of the "just one thing"
mythology. I know how dumb this is going to sound, but I'm going to admit it anyway. Even after my Single Gourmet experience, I ordered a book
called *Single's Guide to Cruise Vacations,* thinking I might find descriptions
of cruises where single people would feel comfortable simply enjoying the
cruise. On the cover? Pictures of five couples.

Maybe I should just accept that "for singles" is code for becoming unsingle and move on. It is an annoying practice but hardly consequential. I'll
admit as much for now. But I still have a beef with Coldwell Banker.

Coldwell Banker is in the real-estate business. In 2004 it ran a television
ad over and over and over again. The narrator said the following, in a dewy
sort of "isn't this so cute" tone of voice: "When Sylvia Maxwell was single
again, she came to me at Coldwell Banker to find a new home. I searched
high and low and when I found one she loved, she made a proposal to buy
it. Larry was a single professor who lived next door, until one day he made
a proposal of another kind. Gives a whole new meaning to 'love thy neighbor.' For almost a century, Coldwell Banker has known that real estate is
only part of the story."

Visually, the ad introduces us to Sylvia and Larry. By the end, the two of
them are holding hands, skipping, and frolicking through the yards of their
homes, she in full bridal attire and he in his groomwear. The bridesmaids
and groomsmen follow gleefully behind them.

You probably think I'm going to make fun of the wedding theme, but I'm not going to bother. That is dopey enough on the face of it. The object of my objections this time is the part about how Coldwell Banker has known for almost a century that real estate is only part of the story. I, a single woman, might go to a Coldwell Banker agent in search of a home. The agent, though, will just know that what I really want is a husband.

Singles may be trolling for mates, but the rest of America, it seems, really does want a house. A really, really big house. Preferably one fashioned by a team of architects and interior designers. *Time* magazine documented this contemporary obsession in a 2002 feature story, "Inside the New American Home." As if to illustrate the supersizing of homes, the story went on for eleven pages. Let me take you on a brief tour of the highlights.

The kitchen shown in the opening photo is so cavernous that it sprawls from one full page onto the next. With its breakfast nook, island, industrial appliances, dual dishwashers, triple sinks, built-in espresso maker, television, and work area, the kitchen, says *Time*, is "a family magnet" and "family HQ."

Visually, contemporary kitchens extend through glass doors onto decks or patios "outfitted with a killer barbecue and outdoor fireplace." There may be an outdoor shower as well.

Look the other way, and a huge family room beckons. The plasma screen approaching movie theater size is visible from each of the several sofas, alcoves, and window seats.

One of the rooms does have actual walls. It is the parents' master suite. The king-size bed is just one place to rest your eyes in a yawning vista that may include "sitting areas, breakfast bars, exercise rooms, computer rooms and his-and-hers walk-in closets." The master bath is a suite in itself, with the walk-in steam shower, oversize tub, and, of course, the his-and-hers sinks. For even more space, Mom and Dad can step outside their bedroom bonanza into their own private garden.

Two other rooms are also important—the home offices. "Dad and Mom often have one each." The only rooms that are shrinking are the children's bedrooms.

At last, the story ends. "Family" has been mentioned twenty-four times. All the peopled pictures show a wife, husband, or kids, alone or in various combinations.

But wait—there is one more part to the feature story. It is a box at the very end, about the spate of TV shows featuring homes and home design. In the last paragraph of this last page of the eleven-page story, there is finally a mention of single people without children. "On the blind-date home show *Love by Design*," *Time* notes, "one single visits a stranger's pad for a surprise home renovation and, just maybe, a little somethin'-somethin' afterward."

The moral of the *Time* story is not subtle. Houses are for couples and families. Couples and families have lots of different interests and lead multidimensional lives. They are successful people who unabashedly celebrate themselves by hiring professionals to turn their homes into their own personal resorts.

Single people, in contrast, are of little significance. They live in "pads." For company, they invite people they don't know for televised foreplay and for help with home design. No need to hire actual design professionals. The renovation is a pretext. What singles really want from the strangers they meet is sex. Subsequently, perhaps they, too, will become coupled and can look for a real home.

The couples and families in the *Time* story appropriate not only all the attention and respect but even the terminology. In a great example of word creep, what was once a "living room," suggesting that any living person might hang out there, has become a "family room." There are no more spare rooms or guest rooms; they are now Dad's home office and Mom's. Closets and bathroom sinks now come in pairs labeled "his and hers."

A year later *Newsweek* also published a feature story about American houses. Contemporary homes, *Newsweek* contends, can be "effortlessly cool," as in the shelter magazines, yet still be "inhabited by actual humans."

"Actual humans," of course, consist of Mom, Dad, and the kids. They are the sole stars of the story. Again, though, after the feature story ends, there is a shorter piece. The very last line of that story, wedged between pictures of two stylistically different homes, is the question "Which would a cool Gen Y couple prefer?" In the *Newsweek* story, singletons do not even rate a condescending little somethin'-somethin'.

There is an irony to the extolling of the homes of marrieds-with-children and the vaporizing of the homes of people who are living single. By the numbers, *Time* and *Newsweek* have it exactly wrong. More households consist of single people living alone than of Mom, Dad, and the kids.

The millions of single people in contemporary American society include more than just the very young singles who may not yet have the financial resources to buy a home and the older singles who may not want to care for one. As of 2004, 39.8 million people who were divorced, were widowed, or had always been single were between the ages of thirty and sixty-four.

And they are not hiding in apartments or pads. Singles are one of the fastest-growing group of people buying homes. They account for more than 40 percent of first-time buyers, and nearly 30 percent of repeat buyers. Increasingly, they are renovating homes and even buying second homes.

No matter. Even when a single person can obviously afford a great home, that will not be the story line. Take, for example, a series of episodes of the television show *Judging Amy*. Series star Amy Gray, a single mom, is a lawyer with an Ivy League degree who rose quickly through the ranks to become a judge. Throughout most of the series, she and her daughter live with Amy's mother in the New England home Amy grew up in.

Amy seems to have no major expenses. She does not take exotic trips, she rarely goes to dinner at expensive restaurants, and her daughter is not in child care. Nonetheless, when Amy and her daughter move out of the family home, they end up in a cramped, noisy, ratty apartment. Amy is shown banging on the walls in the vain hope that her neighbor will turn down the music. Amy and her daughter are both miserable, and eventually they return to live with Mom and Amy's other siblings who periodically return to the family hearth.

One thing does change, though, if only for an evening. Typically it is Amy's mother who serves dinner to her children and grandchildren gathered around the dining-room table. One night Amy takes a turn in the kitchen and comes out serving coq au vin. As her relatives raise their eyebrows, Amy explains that she learned to make the recipe while she was living in the apartment because there was nothing else to do.

Here's what I want to know. Why can't Amy become absorbed in the process of finding or even building exactly the home that she has always dreamed of owning? Why can't she fall in love with the process of renovating and furnishing her new home, assembling all sorts of new skills, knowledge, and experiences in the process? Why can't she move into her new home and learn to cook because she loves it and fits it into her life even though as a judge, mother, daughter, sister, friend, and homeowner, she always has more to do than any human could fit into a day? Maybe because then she would seem too much like an actual human—a married one, that is.

Later in the series Amy reveals that there is a home nearby that she has always loved. She tells this to the man with whom she has become pregnant. He is delighted and surprises her by putting a down payment on the home. But then Amy miscarries, the relationship fizzles, and the down payment is forsaken. No marriage? Then no home, either.

When I was in Virginia and looking for a home, I went only to the open houses in my price range. I had been living in a town house flooded with sunlight that warmed my heart. But I was renting when I wanted to own, my place was too small, and I didn't want to live in a town house anymore. When the real-estate agents discovered that I was buying "just" for myself, they sometimes tried to steer me to a lesser housing solution. One, for example, urged me to take a look at a town house down the road.

A newly hired single woman in her thirties arrived in town ready to buy a modest two-bedroom home she liked. When she described it to her colleagues, they demurred. Wouldn't it be "too much house" for her? they asked.

Another single friend wanted to buy a roomy home that she and her daughter could enjoy. Her agent showed her one tiny home after another. Finally she insisted that he show her the priciest home available. Only then was she shown the kinds of homes she originally asked to see.

I am not just describing idiosyncratic experiences of me and my quirky friends. These sorts of instructions are in the books. Take, for example, the book *Buying a Home When You're Single*. The section titled "Location, Location, Location" asks whether you want to live near other single adults. If so, the author advises, one of the "obvious" choices would be "developments that specialize in studio or one-bedroom units." At the time the book went to press, nearly 60 percent of single women owned their own homes.

I can't say I was surprised to find that the author of *Buying a Home When You're Single* dedicated the book to her husband and daughter. Not that I think you have to be single to write about singles. I just thought that a single person—especially a successful one—might be more likely to suggest that singles need not congregate in one-bedroom enclaves.

So I went to *The Road to Wealth,* written by the singleton and fabulously successful financial guru Suze Orman. I skipped to the section on home ownership and started to smile. "If you are a single person, a one-bedroom condo may seem ideal now," she begins. Yes! I could finish the sentence for her: "but you will soon discover how much you will enjoy and value more space; if you can afford it, go for it!" Only that isn't how Suze completes her sentence. She says, "But if you hope to get married and start a family in the next few years, you'll need more space pretty quickly."

When real-estate agents lead their single clients to smaller and cheaper places than the clients are seeking, they are doing something extraordinarily rare in the business world—working against their own self-interest. If the agent had persuaded me to buy the town house down the road, rather than the home he was showing that actually did interest me, he would have made a whole lot less money.

It would be hard to think of a group of people more interested in the bottom line than entrepreneurs, but there may be one. Politicians. The bottom line for them is, of course, the vote.

The results of the 2000 American presidential election set in motion a subsequent scampering for votes like nothing ever seen before. In the 2000 contest the candidate with the most popular votes, Al Gore, did not ascend to the White House. That prize went to George W. Bush, who claimed an electoral college victory after the state of Florida went his way by a mere several hundred disputed votes. By 2004, both sides were gunning for a good demographic to help them secure the presidency.

They found it. It was a demographic that tilted left, so Democrats especially stood to gain. This new "it" group in the world of politics was single women. In the 2000 election about two-thirds voted for Gore, compared with the less than one-third for Bush. Married women, in contrast, voted in roughly equal numbers for Gore and Bush. Gore should have, could have, would have won if only those single women had shown up at the polls at the same rate as married women. But they didn't. Only a little over half the women who were divorced, widowed, or ever single and were eligible to vote actually did so. About two-thirds of the eligible married women made their voices heard.

For the media, the new demographic was great fun. The frenzy over a cute and condescending name began instantly. They were the *Sex and the City* types, the lipstick liberals, the new swingers. These women were not seen as citizens of all ages and backgrounds with many layers of interests and concerns who needed to be persuaded to vote for a particular set of policies. Rather, they were portrayed as shallow and salacious young things who needed to be "wooed" into embracing one special man.

Reasonably enough, one of the first questions asked was why single women had not voted in greater numbers in 2000. Unreasonably, it was all too rare for reporters or critics to ask single women to provide their own answers to the question. I guess they already "knew" that single women were interested in just one thing. Republican pundit Kellyanne Conway, for example, offered singletons this piece of election-day advice. "Pretend it's a hair appointment we would not miss," said she, adding a flirtatious little wink at the end. John Tierney at *The New York Times* had the same general idea. Single women, he said, "could have put Al Gore in the White House if they had found time in their social schedules to get to the polls." A CNN reporter threw in her own special dash of dismissiveness as she tracked down a single woman she described as successful and asked her, "Is it scary to think about politics?" (No, it wasn't.)

With the problem squarely in focus, the solution became obvious. Appeal to single women not with scary policy pronouncements, but with parties, panties, beauty products, and other mate-bait accoutrements. The group called Axis of Eve posted links to PantyWare Party Kits on its website. The tiny panties sported big bold slogans such as "Expose Bush," "My Cherry for Kerry," and "Give Bush the Finger." Another group, Running in Heels, organized cocktail parties and "Wine Against Bush" and "Wax Away Bush" events, designed to attract "fun, fashionable, fed-up women whose bras are too attractive to burn." The grassroots group Code Pink offered pink lingerie with the message, "Give Bush the Pink Slip." Slogan-inscribed nail files were passed out at beauty parlors and nail salons across the land.

The Wall Street Journal reported on the efforts by the nonpartisan dating service Match.com to get singles to the polls. The campaign was called "Every Single Vote Counts" and the company said that increasing turnout was a good thing to do. The *Journal,* though, understood "the real reasons" for the effort: Showing up at the polls, with all those other potential partners milling around, "could help customers reach their ultimate goal—marriage."

There was near consensus: Single women were interested in just one thing. To get them to the polls, harp on that one thing. By now, you know I'm going to make fun of all this. But I must confess to something first: I think the slogans are hilarious. So, I do not totally object, especially if the campaigns are effective. But I do cringe at the single-mindedness of the focus on sex, partying, and soulmate seeking.

Even if I did not care about the caricaturing of single women, I'd still find much amiss in the Get Out the Single Vote campaigns of 2004. The statistics from the 2000 campaign documenting the disappointing turnout of single women were based on all single women of voting age. So, why speak to just that small sliver of single women who savor racy thongs? Not even all young single women want to be quite so exposed.

Appeals to single women who can afford cocktail parties, body waxing, and new pink lingerie fly right by women who can barely afford the money for groceries or the time to go shopping for them. The diversity of ages, incomes, backgrounds, and interests of women who are single is, to some critics, exactly the problem. What do they have in common that could be the basis of a coherent political appeal? Oddly, the same thing is rarely asked of the constituency called women. That group, because it includes as a subset women who are single, is by definition the more diverse of the two.

Here's what single women have in common: They are single and they are women. They get by on their own dime, and often their dimes are not as big or as shiny as the coins earned by men. Put simply, single women care about getting paid a decent and fair wage. They care about health care—it is not as if in a pinch they can coast along on their husband's plan. They care about affordable housing; about 60 percent already own their own homes, but even more would like to see prices they can reach out and touch. They care about education and day care and after-school programs. The many single women who have kids welcome all the help they can get in keeping their jobs and their kids in one piece. Other singles do not necessarily need kids of their own to empathize.

Oh, and one other thing: Single women care about international issues, too. Remember the CNN reporter who asked the successful single woman if she found it too scary to think about politics? By the end of the segment, she finally let the woman supply her own answer. The singleton had a very strong opinion about the war in Iraq, and she was going to get to the polls to let it be known.

Single voters, like married voters and voters from every other bloc, would like to be recognized as the multidimensional people they are. I've already discussed the multidimensional part. That just leaves the part about being regarded as real people. Here is an example of how not to accomplish that. It was posted on the website of Arizona Republican governor Jane Dee Hull in 1999: "Wife, parent, grandparent—isn't it nice to have a real person running Arizona?"

Single people are lulled to sleep, if not to tears, by candidates' mantra-like repetition of such words as *marriage* and *family*. Most singles are not antifamily. They would just like to be reassured that the candidate of their choice is capable of pronouncing the word *single* in public without pairing it with words like *sex* or *illegitimacy* or including it on lists of things that no adult should be.

One last note on the disappointing voting record of single women, which started the whole foray into the underwear of single women voters. Actually, it was not single women who had the lowest rate of voting in 2000—it was single men.

Two prospective authors were looking for single people to participate in a survey. The survey results, they hoped, would provide the content for their book on singles. The two people contacted the executive director of the American Association for Single People (AASP), the singles-rights advocacy group, to request that he post a link to their website so that AASP members could take the survey online. The director forwarded their request to me.

The book had a working title, *The Single Syndrome*. So, of course, already I did not like it. Tourette's is a syndrome. So is fetal alcoholism and sudden infant death. Singlehood is not.

The authors protested that the syndrome idea was just what they were challenging, and forwarded this synopsis of their book: "The business of love is big business . . . singles are presented with a mind-boggling array of ways to find the One." But what about the fundamental question at the core of any business proposition: "What is my return on my investment? . . . Would I be better off pursuing the things I love rather than chasing love itself?"

Now, that's a question I can get behind. So I proceeded to the website to take a look at the survey.

Except for the bold heading, *The Single Syndrome,* and the picture of a heart with nails stuck in it, the home page seemed promising at first. It posed these questions:

☐ Do you feel that single people are constantly being told by others, rather than speaking for themselves?

☐ That the media is creating a vision of the single life that doesn't exist?

☐ Had enough?

Now is your chance to have a voice and tell us what you're really thinking!

Here are some of the questions I was invited to answer as part of the survey:

☐ Is it really true that blonde highlights will help you catch a man?

☐ Is your resolve to go it alone disintegrating?

☐ Do you think people should consider themselves as failures if they re-main single?

☐ Do you think it is OK for a "career" to take the place of a relationship?

Over the course of the next dozen or so pages, the survey listed just about every imaginable way of landing the One—as long as it involved fix-ing myself. Had I ever hired relationship experts such as psychiatrists, life coaches, or professional matchmakers? Had I read books, signed up for seminars, or arranged for personal sessions on mate-seeking? Which of the following eight varieties of cosmetic surgery had I tried? The survey also asked how much I had spent on each of the strategies I had attempted and whether I had traveled to some other land to pursue any of them.

Next, I was asked about the qualities that most attract me to a potential partner. How important was each of the following: looks, eyes, hair, height, weight, race, intelligence, sense of humor, sporting ability, and financial stability?

There was also a statement I was supposed to answer by checking either yes or no. It was: "I have a checklist of items that constitute my perfect partner." Next came the request "Please list your items; i.e., blue eyes, tall, slim, financially secure, etc." Finally, there was more of the same.

I thought I was supposed to get a chance to tell the authors what I was thinking. Instead, they told me what they were thinking and asked me to confirm it. They said they were interested in whether I would "be better off pursuing the things I love rather than chasing love itself." But nowhere in the survey did I get to express an interest in anything other than how to find a mate. Never did I get a chance to say that I like to read and think and write and walk the beach and have long talks with friends and sample some of the world's most wonderful offerings at the farmers' market.

Oh, wait, there was that question about career: "Do you think it is OK for a 'career' to take the place of a relationship?" So, here we are in the new millennium and I'm still supposed to choose either a career or a relationship. What's more, there is no parallel question, "Do you think it is OK for a relationship to take the place of a career?"

And if the authors want to ask whether "people should consider themselves as failures if they remain single," then I think they should also ask whether people should consider themselves conventional and boring if they marry.

The entire survey seems to be predicated on the assumption that since I'm a single person, I am obsessed with finding a partner and have already spent fistfuls of money on that futile pursuit. There was no opportunity for me to claim anything else. Consider, for example, that simple question about whether I have a checklist of items that constitute my perfect partner. For my answer, I got to choose between yes and no. What I wanted to say is that I am not looking for a partner, perfect or otherwise, and that I am living my single life happily and contentedly. But that was not an option.

Suppose, though, that I *were* looking for a partner. The survey researchers had already decided on the ten qualities I am most likely to be seeking. They offered me more than half a dozen opportunities to claim to be an utterly superficial person. I didn't get to say that I want someone who is thoughtful, curious, open-minded, who shares my values. I didn't even get to wish for someone who is kind or warm. Moreover, all the qualities on the list are characteristics inherent in the potential partner. But suppose I want someone who clicks with me, someone who delights me not because of what he or she is but because of what we are together? Someone who has always wanted kids and would feel deprived without them? Someone who will be there for me even when I'm insufferable and any other reasonable person would just walk away? Someone who does not want me to be his or her everything and who does not want to be everything to me? That was not an option, either.

It is true that there was an opportunity in the next question to describe my own list. But in case I was tempted to say something that is not shallow or predictable, the survey prompted me with an example of the kind of response I might want to give: "blue eyes, tall, slim, financially secure."

Eventually the authors will publicize their results. They will say that singles have tried relationship coaches and psychiatrists, rhinoplasty and Botox; that they have spent money hand over fist, and have even crossed international borders, but that they still have not landed the Tall, Slim, Blue-Eyed Dreamboat who is the object of their pursuit. What they will not say is that they gave singles hardly any opportunity to say anything else. They will not admit that there is no way a single person could have completed their survey and not come across as completely superficial and pathetically preoccupied with just one thing.

There is an important postscript to the *Single Syndrome* project—and indeed to all the industries, such as matchmaking services, online dating sites, and mate-bait book publishing, that have been built on the premise that singles are interested in just one thing. It turns out that, in far bigger numbers than even I had imagined, single people say that they are not "looking" at all.

In the last few months of 2005, the Pew Internet & American Life Project surveyed more than three thousand American adults of all ages and marital statuses. They asked those who were single (divorced, widowed, or always single) whether they were in a committed relationship. Twenty-six percent said that they were. The biggest group of singles, 55 percent, said that they were not in a committed relationship *and* that they were not looking for a partner. Only 16 percent of single people said that they were not in a committed relationship but were looking. (Three percent did not answer.) Even when the younger singles, ages eighteen to twenty-nine, were analyzed separately, the number who said that they were not in a committed relationship and were looking for a partner increased to only 22 percent.

After years of wading through the slop of the *Single Syndrome,* the little somethin'-somethin', the panty parties for single women voters, and all the rest, I had a craving. Or maybe it was a revenge fantasy. I wanted those caricatures of single people—you know, the one-dimensional stick figures—to be stomped out by stories about real-life, full-bodied contemporary American single people who had brains and jobs and friends and relatives and interests and passions. I wanted the stories to be written in single-speak, or in just about any language other than the tired old tongue of the kissing couple. And for one splendid moment, I thought I had found it.

It was a book called *Urban Tribes: A Generation Redefines Friendship, Family, and Commitment.* Author Ethan Watters was part of a generation of Americans whose first marriages were occurring later in life than they ever had before—if indeed they occurred at all. What were these singletons doing with the years or even decades of their adulthood that had once been filled with marriage and family?

The story of Watters's singleton years began after he finished college, when he and a childhood friend set out for San Francisco, where they knew exactly one person. Years later Watters was embedded in a community of several dozen friends. Some lived together, some worked together, and all of them socialized together. They met for dinner at least once a week, and they often spent weekends and holidays together. In between, they kept up with one another's day-to-day lives with e-mails and phone calls. Watters called his group, and the many others like it across the country, an urban tribe. His book builds on the stories he collected from hundreds of tribe members in America and beyond.

I judged *Urban Tribes* by its cover. Unlike the 2002 home page of Single Gourmet or the cover of the *Single's Guide to Cruise Vacations,* the *Tribes* dust jacket was not a numbing blur of dewy-eyed couples. Instead, there were pictures of hikers and boaters and swimmers, people eating and singing and strumming and traveling, or just hanging out. It was a lot like a family photo album—lots of fun, and no pictures from the office. It wasn't just one family, though, but lots of different ones, and none were composed solely of Mom, Dad, and the kids. Here, it seemed, were singles who were not just about becoming coupled. The pictures on the jacket, along with the book's subtitle, said to me: Caricatures not invited. Do not look inside these pages for tips on snagging a mate. And thankfully, there were none.

The inside cover sets the tone for the book. There we learn that to Watters, time spent in the tribe represents not so much "a failure to mate" as "a stage of personal development that makes later partnerhood that much more mature and successful." The chapter titles also provide hints of what is to come: "Confessions of a Yet-to-Be-Married," "On Friendship and Risk," "Men and the Marriage Delay (My Hunt for a Good Excuse)," "Love Versus the Tribe."

The story of Watters's singlehood opens with the tribe of twenty-five friends heading out to Black Rock Desert for their annual five-day outing to Burning Man, a quirky art festival. This is the tribe's tradition; they have been heading out there for years.

Missing from the group is Julia, Watters's girlfriend. She is back in her hometown of Athens, Georgia, attending her best friend's wedding and presumably still fuming that Watters is not with her. That he could even consider opting for Burning Man over her friend's wedding is, to her, "jaw-droppingly bizarre." The two of them argued repeatedly and heatedly, but to no avail. In the end, they went their separate ways.

Julia had gotten under Watters's skin. He could not seem to stop obsessing over her charge that his life was Seinfeldian—it was about nothing. How else could he explain his "carrying on" with a group of two dozen friends?

Watters believed that he and his friends were happy most of the time, but Julia got to him on that count, too. So what if he was happy?

Several chapters later, Watters is sitting around a conference table with several staff members and volunteers for the singles-rights advocacy group, the American Association for Single People. He tells us about the work of the group, the stereotypes it is challenging, and the legal issues that motivate its quest for social change. The chapter ends with Watters's description of one of the volunteers. Cliff, whom Watters describes as overweight, talked "in that compulsive way that suggested that he hadn't had the chance to talk to other people in some time." In response to Watters's question of how he came to volunteer for the organization, Cliff says he found the organization in the Yellow Pages. But, Watters adds, Cliff does not indicate "whether he was looking for something else at the time or simply reading from page to page looking for something to do."

Fast-forward to the last chapter. There you do not find Ethan Watters flipping through the Yellow Pages to find something to do. He has found his Rebecca. He realizes that this could be an important development for the tribe: "If things worked out with Rebecca, I would have to ask all my many roommates to find new homes."

Things do indeed work out, and his friends fall in line. Hearing about the upcoming nuptials, they all convey their best wishes. One friend after another offers not just to attend the wedding, but to play music, be the mistress of ceremonies, decorate, and officiate.

Watters muses about his future relationship with the tribe. He isn't sure how that will unfold. But there is one thing he can say with certainty: "I would not have grown into the man that Rebecca wanted to marry without them."

He continues to ponder the fate of his group of friends. He describes his "sincere hope that things work out for all the yet-to-be-marrieds." He is optimistic, for sociologists have shown that the vast majority of people do indeed marry eventually. And what of those who do not? "I have faith that these forever-singles will find happiness and satisfaction in their lives."

Watters, it seems, has found his own happiness. He is on his way to Hawaii with his wife. By choosing such a clichéd destination for his honeymoon, he thinks, everyone in the hotels and restaurants will recognize that he and Rebecca were newlyweds—and that is exactly what he wants.

Apparently, he got that recognition, right from the moment he stepped onboard the plane. Lovingly, Watters describes the two dozen or more newlyweds who shared the flight to Kauai. They were all so different in their hairstyles and attire, their ages and origins. Yet they were similar, too. They were self-conscious about their rings, and affectionate with each other. Each couple seemed proud to be in the company of so many other couples, offering toasts all the way from the mainland to the island.

Watters is about to bring his tale to a close, but before he does, he takes one last look back at the tribe years. "Having spent so many years living single, I have an unavoidable 'bias' to discover that those years were not wasted." Bias notwithstanding, though, Watters remains convinced that the tribe years are not wasted years.

Finally, it is time to wrap up. Here are Watters's closing words:

> The "us" in my world has shrunk to Rebecca and me, but we intend to find
> a way to use the energy that still exists from my tribe years. . . . I suspect

there will be more [tribe] betrothals within the year. I imagine there will be years when we all focus on our young marriages and then children. [Eventually] we'll gravitate together again. I could go on about this fantasy future, but why imagine future joy when your life is full of happiness in the present? Right now the sun is shining, I can hear the ocean crashing about, and my new wife awaits.

There is lots not to like about *Urban Tribes,* but I want to start with something I did like. In one strong section, Watters delivers. It is the answer to Julia's question of what those tribe years add up to. Watters considers the whole range of experiences that fill the lives of the tribe members. On one extreme are all the silly projects, such as home-brewing beers and collecting clunky computers left in the dust of an ever-advancing technology. On the other end are the serious pursuits—caring for one another in times of illness, networking for the person who was fresh out of work, tracking down the best medical care in the country for an ailing relative in a small Midwestern town, and being there for one another at the worst of times, such as the final services for parents. Most of the tribe time, though, is spent somewhere in between those extremes. Day-to-day life is a matter of sharing time together, sharing meals, and sharing a caring and concern for one another that can be tracked in a continual stream of phone calls and e-mails. Mate seeking is part of the lives of many tribe members, but it does not seem to define their lives. All told, Watters concludes, living single in an urban tribe provide a sense "of belonging to an intensely loyal community of people."

Julia was not convinced by that rendering, and Watters realizes that others would also be unmoved. And yet, he points out, the same kinds of experiences, when shared within a traditional family rather than an urban tribe, are of unquestioned value. A spouse or parent gets credit for living the good life simply by preparing meals, attending games, and showing care and support in all these unextraordinary ways. Yet "the act of cooking for one's single friends did not carry the same weight."

Watters does not pursue the issue in the depth I may have liked. He does not ask, for example, whether the same small acts of caring, such as cooking dinner or showing an interest in the minutiae of another person's life, have the same moral import among couples who have no children, or whether it is raising the next generation that gives the attentiveness of everyday life its significance. Still, the question Watters does ask is profound. What makes a life valuable, worthwhile, moral? He knows the conventional wisdom but offers it up as only one possible answer. He gives other answers a chance. I only wish he had maintained that attitude throughout *Urban Tribes*.

Here is my bottom-line disappointment with Ethan Watters: In the end, all he was interested in was just one thing.

Even that succinct characterization is not quite right. If all Ethan Watters cared about personally was finding a spouse, that would have been uninteresting and unimaginative, but ultimately his prerogative. My objection is that he characterizes the lives of tribe members everywhere in that presumptuous and stifling way. And he is not equally presumptuous when characterizing the lives of people who are married.

Watters calls people who are single "yet-to-be-married." He does not call married people "yet-to-be-divorced," aspiring writers "yet-to-be-published," or old people "yet-to-be-dead." I think that in so dubbing single people, Watters means to flatter them. He is expressing his confidence that they, too, will eventually be married like him. Married people: good. Single people: bad.

Does that sound too harsh or too simplistic? Probably not to Cliff (the volunteer at the singles' organization). Basically, Watters paints him as a big fat loser. Compare that sketch with the fawning portrait of the dozens of honeymooners on their way to Hawaii. Chances are, if you collected dozens of Americans of any variety, at least one of them would be turn out to be fat. But if that were true of any of the Kauai-bound newlyweds, Watters does not mention it. Watters wonders whether Cliff is just looking for something to do with his time, but he does not wonder whether any of the newlyweds are just looking for something to do with their lives. Married people: good. Single people: bad.

Throughout *Urban Tribes*, Watters wrestles with the question of whether the tribe years were "wasted." In the end, he claims to have come to the conclusion that they were not. But what does it mean that he accepts the premise of the question, that the tribe years may have been a big waste, without ever wondering whether years spent married may also be "wasted"? Why does this man—who claims to speak for his generation in a redefining way—quip that his chapter on men and the marriage delay is actually his "search for a good excuse" without offering any excuse at all for his utterly conventional decision to marry?

The reason Watters musters for valuing the tribe years is also telling. As the dust jacket forewarns, those years, to Watters, "represent less a failure to mate . . . than a stage of personal development that makes later partnerhood that much more mature and successful." Or, as Watters says of the debt he owes his tribe mates: "I would not have grown into the man that Rebecca wanted to marry without them."

The tribe years, for Watters, were grooming for grooms.

Suppose Watters really does value his tribe years, if only for the demeaning reason that they made him better husband material. Suppose he truly appreciates the friends who were so loyal to him for more than a decade, who tracked down the best medical care in the country when his father so desperately needed it, who showed up at his wedding and subsidized it with their efforts, their gifts, and their goodwill. Let's accept that he and Rebecca really do "intend to find a way to use the energy that still exists" from the time that Watters spent with those friends. What, then, do Ethan and Rebecca plan to give in return?

Nothing. As a couple, apparently they are entitled to be the recipients of single people's largesse. Hail to the couple.

Am I doing it again—attributing to Watters a condescending attitude toward single people that is just not there? Maybe. I admit that when I first read his comment about life singles—"I have faith that these forever-singles will find happiness and satisfaction in their lives"—I swore I could feel his hand reaching out from the pages and patronizingly patting me on the head. I can also reread that sentiment and acknowledge that there may be nothing wrong with it at all.

Here's why I still want to remove Watters's hand from my head. Consider once again the very last paragraph of his book, where he describes his fantasized future: "I imagine there will be years when we all focus on our young marriages and then children. [Eventually] we'll gravitate together again." Where are his longtime friends who stay single? In his mind, he has already ditched them.

Frankly, though, Watters's married friends do not fare all that well, either. They are back-burnered for decades while Ethan and Rebecca focus on their marriage and children and assume all their friends are blithely doing the same. When Watters notes that "the 'us' in my world has shrunk to Rebecca and me," he does so without apology or embarrassment. In fact, he seems rather proud. In his world, intensive coupling is a good thing.

Watters seems to be planning, once he and Rebecca have kids, to shut all the windows and doors of his family home until the kids are grown, then emerge to pick up the pieces of his former friendships. He probably thinks that such an intensive focus on just the one little unit of Mom, Dad, and the kids will be good for the kids, who will feel doted on and cared for. I wish he had at least considered something brighter and more expansive for his children. Why not plan to include his friends not only in his own life but also in the lives of his children? Why not envision the possible friendships that his kids might forge with the kids of his friends? They could become like the bevy of cousins that children once enjoyed when families were bigger and aunts and uncles and other family members were closer to one another emotionally and geographically.

If Watters truly wanted to "redefine friendship, family, and commitment," he might have started by imagining love, friendship, loyalty, and marriage as potentially compatible (and not because the love, friendship, and loyalty all reside exclusively within the marriage). His chapter titled "On Friendship and Risk" could have been replaced or complemented by one called "On Friendship and Lifelong Loyalty." His chapter on "Love Versus the Tribe" could have been reframed as "Love and the Tribe."

I'm not suggesting that Watters should have shoved under the rug all the genuine conflicts that can potentially occur as friendships and mateships compete for limited time and emotional energy. What I am suggesting is a sense of balance. If, in fact, friendships and sexual partnerships can sometimes be at odds with each other, isn't it also true that they can be mutually enriching? And if Watters wants to consider whether having such good friends may have been (in his mind) costly in the sense of making it easier to delay marriage, then I think he should also consider the possibility that marriage comes with costs of its own.

Watters had another opportunity to redefine friendship, family, and commitment when he describes the argument he had with Julia over attending her best friend's wedding. He seems to have conveyed Julia's position on the issue: Her best friend's wedding should trump his annual outing with his friends, and it is bizarre that he even consider choosing the outing over the wedding. Moreover, his carrying-on with dozens of friends adds up to a life that is about nothing. What Watters does not do in the book is stand up for his own point of view, or question Julia's. She tries to put him on the defensive, and he complies.

Watters's single years, by his own accounting, add up to an experience "of belonging to an intensely loyal community of people." Julia wants to dismiss those years of friendship, loyalty, and community as "nothing." Why shouldn't she be the one to feel defensive?

Here's what else Watters could have asked Julia. Why should the wedding of two people who are strangers to him take priority over an outing planned years in advance with friends he has known and cared about for more than a decade? Why was it so important to Julia to have Ethan at her side? Was she afraid to attend a social event alone? Was she concerned that people might think she had no partner? Or was she worried that the people who knew about her relationship with Ethan would think she had exaggerated its significance? Or that they would think that Ethan was not such a great catch after all? Why didn't she tell anyone who asked about Ethan that he was at an event that he attended every year with dozens of people with whom he had been friends for more than a decade? Why not add that this was one of the things she loved about him, that he was so loyal to his friends and they to him? That it underscored her own faith in his fundamental goodness and decency that so many other people seemed to think as highly of him as she did? That anyone who would pack up and head out to a wacky desert art festival once a year is someone who does not take himself too seriously, and that's a good quality in a human? That she loved Ethan because he was a real-live many-splendored person with friends and interests and talents and passions rather than some stick figure interested in just one thing?

I am not denying that Julia's point of view deserves just as much consideration as Watters's. It does. My point is that Julia's point is obvious. It is the conventional wisdom. I want the redefinition I was promised, or at least some serious rethinking.

Here's something else I wanted Watters to question—his assumption that "if things worked out with Rebecca, [he] would have to ask all [his] many roommates to find new homes." My question is simple: Why?

Is that question, as Julia might say, "jaw-droppingly bizarre"? Personally, I find the mere thought of living with a house full of people cringeworthy. I do not want to live with even one other person. But I signed up for a redefinition of friendship, family, and commitment when I bought the book, and that's what I want. Where is Watters's commitment to his friendships? If he really cannot rethink the customs of contemporary American society, can't he at least offer a nod toward history? Maybe mention to his readers that there were times and places where households were not so narrowly construed as ours are—when apprentices and workers and grandparents all lived under the same roof as Mom, Dad, and the kids, and all were considered family.

In and of itself, there is nothing remarkable about becoming a matrimaniac. And I'm not picking on Watters because I was bored by his book. I wasn't. I found it wholly engaging. I'm giving Ethan Watters a hard time because he promised something more. He promised to tell the untold story of a generation that was staying single longer than any had before. Hundreds, if not thousands, of tribe members entrusted him with their stories of singlehood. In turn, he dedicated his book not to all of those tribes or tribe members, nor even to his own tribe, but to Rebecca. The book that promised so much devolves into a dime-store romance. In the last line of the book, Watters's new wife is waiting for him, drenched in sunshine and clichés.

I want my money back.

CHAPTER FIVE

Myth #3 The Dark Aura of Singlehood

You Are Miserable and Lonely and Your Life Is Tragic

As a child growing up in a Catholic community, I spent a chunk of each Sunday in church. Now that I'm an adult in Southern California, I've adopted the native religion. I often spend Sundays looking at open houses.

During the summer when Coldwell Banker seemed to have the Sylvia Maxwell television ad (about the woman who went to a real-estate agent to find a home, but the agent just knew that what she really wanted was a husband) on an endless loop, I happened into a Coldwell Banker home. For the moment there was no one else looking at the home, so I figured it was my chance to tell the real-estate agent that I liked the house she was showing and I liked being single, and that if I came to Coldwell Banker, I would like to be sold a house and not a husband. First I asked if she had seen the ad. Her face brightened as she told me how much she loved it.

Undeterred, I started in on my take on the ad: "Well, I'm single. . . ."

That's as far as I got. She interrupted, tilting her head and assuming the tone of a grown-up consoling a small child. "Aaaawwww," she cooed.

Once the real-estate agent learned that I was single, she knew all that she needed to. As a singleton, my life was tragic. So, of course, pity was the appropriate response. Moreover, it was probably my own fault that I was leading such a sad single life. I was BLAME-worthy: bitter, loveless, alone, miserable, and envious of couples. That much the agent had already established. All that was left to discern was the specific reason for my lamentable life. What was my tragic flaw? Was I too neurotic? Too picky? Those are the hackneyed attributes mindlessly ascribed to single women. If I were a single man, I'd probably be considered a commitment phobe. Or if it seemed from my age that I had "waited too long," I might be said to be "set in my ways."

I think that BLAME is an apt acronym because it suggests that something unwanted is being pinned on a person who may not deserve it. To pin BLAME on singles is to suggest that there are big differences between single people, who are pitiful, and married people, who are not. In fact, just knowing that a person is single at an age when many others are married is reason enough to summon a full measure of pity.

That assumption is, of course, nonsense. As shown in Chapter 2, psychological and emotional differences between single people and married people are often small, inconsistent, and unreliable and do not always favor married people.

The question, then, is why the BLAME sticks to singles and eludes married people.

Consider this essay by Hank Stuever about one variety of singletons, those who are living alone. It was published in *The Washington Post* in May of 2001. The occasion was the recent Census Bureau report showing that the number of Americans living alone—27 million—was greater than ever before. Says Stuever:

> That's a lot of bowls of cereal eaten over the sink around 1 in the morning. That's quite a few people who lost the love of their life, which meant that they sold the house they thought was too big for just one person, and moved into a condo, and sometimes drive around the complex wondering which condo, exactly, is theirs.

Stuever goes on to describe how solo dwellers spend their time: "You alphabetize your CDs. You congratulate yourself for owning the greatest albums of all time, and set about listening to them all over again, so that you can rearrange them by genre."

He acknowledges the worst of the popular images of singles: "Woe to the solo: Wicked queens live alone in castles, waiting to eat children. Pedophiles, Unabombers, civics teachers, the fat and the unloved."

"But," he immediately amends, "these are cheap jokes. Living alone is also a joy. No one is pandering to your vote."

He also notes that "everything you always suspected about the secret pleasures of living by yourself—it's all true. The whole ugly mess."

Because the solo dweller has the sole say over what's tacked on the fridge and what is stored only in a mental bin, "it's a clean life."

Quickly, though, he reconsiders: "It's clean unless you die, alone, and then maybe it's a mess. Fingernail clippings. Curly hairs on the rim of the tub . . ."

At the end, Stuever imagines singletons responding to a knock on the door: "When they opened the refrigerator door to get the census worker a cool drink . . . there would be eight kinds of beer, or there would be nothing but a swallow and a half of sour 2-percent."

In one brief essay, Stuever puts on the table for well over half a million subscribers to read just about every miserable stereotype of people who are single. They have no love in their life. They have no life, so they need to think up useless and pathetic things to do, like endlessly rearranging their CDs. They also have no house, just a condo, and are so inept that they cannot even figure out which condo is theirs. In their refrigerators are sour milk and no food. In their bathtubs are disgusting hairs. They die alone, in their mess.

Stuever seems to be building, at times, to an acknowledgment of the satisfactions of the single life. But his gestures toward the positives of being single are just setups to mock singlehood still again.

When Stuever suggests that "living alone is also a joy," I sighed in relief, looking forward, at last, to hearing about others who experience the same delights of living alone that I do. His "joy," though, is that "no one is pandering" for the singleton's vote. I agree, but I find that a source of exasperation.

Here he goes again: "Everything you always expected about the secret pleasures of living by yourself—it's all true." My hope builds. Only to be punctured by the punch line: "The whole ugly mess."

And still another: "It's a clean life." This would not be at the top of my list of the joys of living alone, but I'll take it. The author, though, is taking it away: "It is clean unless you die, alone, and then maybe it's a mess."

The BLAME is sticking. Readers vaguely remember that the essayist promised to touch on both the good and the bad of living solo, but now that they think about it, all that comes to mind is bleakness.

But what about Stuever's point? Are there really any single people who live like this?

Of course. If there are 27 million people living alone, some will fit this dreary description. Indeed, Stuever may even be one of them. So, I'll concede to him the narrow point. But I protest the sly insinuation that it is not just his own life he is discussing but the lives of millions of solo dwellers.

I have three more objections. First, Stuever is summoning a panoply of BLAME-worthy attributes and pinning them exclusively on people who live alone. The attributes are all pathetic, and they can all be found among people of just about every type of living arrangement and every marital status. (For example, although I don't know any people who endlessly sort and re-sort their CDs, I do know a woman who spent her days arranging the clothes in her closet by color, then starting all over and rearranging them by length. She was married.)

Second, if Stuever is going to write a riff on people living alone and take up valuable real estate on the pages of *The Washington Post,* he should at least say something fresh and new. If I were to ask random undergraduates to list the thoughts that pop into their minds when they think about single people, they might list the same dopey and predictable qualities printed in the *Post.* In fact, my colleague Wendy Morris and I did ask undergraduates to list their thoughts about single people, and they spouted all the same worn-out stereotypes.

Why not write instead about the dazzling diversity of styles that can be found in the spaces created by people whose abodes are their own? That's what journalist and photographer Adrienne Salinger did in her book *Living Solo.* I ordered the book as soon as I saw the first review of it, and it was already sold out. Or why not consider this: Never before in history have so many people lived alone, not only in the United States but in most other Western nations as well. Is this really a tale of worldwide woe, or is there a hint, in this "stunning explosion of solitary living," that a good many grown-ups actually prefer to live on their own?

Finally, I wish Stuever had shown some self-consciousness about his singles bashing. Imagine his editor's response if his proposed essay had instead included the following: "The newly released 2001 census showed that there are still millions of households consisting of a breadwinning husband and a stay-at-home wife. That's a lot of women arranging the clothes in their closets by color, then mucking them up so they can then rearrange them by length."

It would not happen. You would never read such a story in the *Post.* But you did read the equally defamatory story about singles. The message is that there is nothing wrong with slamming singles. That's one of the reasons why the BLAME sticks. No one is questioning it.

To me, what the *Post* essay conveys is relentless dreariness. As I added to my collection of singles notes and stories over the years, I began noticing the recurrence of a darkness motif. The title of this chapter was adapted from an observation penned by author Daphne Merkin in an essay on divorce. Merkin noticed that the divorced woman seems to unnerve other people with "the dark aura of her singleness." Author Carol Shields, who was married, mused about her social circle—all married couples who had never been divorced—and why they seemed to have separated themselves from others. She suggested that "the divorced and separated know, as we can't possibly know, that dark zone that surrounds the cessation of love."

Unmarried people are finally credited with knowing something that married people do not, and it turns out to be the cessation of love.

When people get started on the theme of singles and darkness, they seem to lose all good sense. See if you notice what is wrong with this opening sentence of the story "All I Want for Christmas," because the editors of *Newsweek,* where it was printed, obviously did not:

> It's the most wonderful time of the year—unless you're single. The weather gets colder, the sky gets darker and there's one holiday after another to remind you that you're all alone.

Get it? The weather is getting colder and the sky is getting darker only if you are single. Married people look up at the same sky and see something warm and wonderful. (Yes, the part about single equaling "all alone" is pathetic, too—I'll get to that later. And the "All I Want for Christmas" title would have been a fitting addition to the chapter on how singles are interested in only one thing.)

The darkness that gets hung around the necks of people who are single comes in different varieties. Single people who are strong and unapologetic, and who show a little attitude, get pinned with the darkness that is menacing on the outside and insecure on the inside. They are called bitter, ballsy, difficult, angry, and scary. And all that is cast as just a show, a brittle cover for their true selves, troubled and scared, lurking pathologically beneath the bravado.

Single people who show some vulnerability are deemed as fragile through and through. They are sad and hurt and deserving of pity. And lonely. Always lonely. Coupled people try valiantly to cheer them up. They offer tips to the sad singles about how to eke out a dollop of happiness to tide them over until they are safely coupled.

The darkness and the BLAME that gets pinned on single people is easiest to track in the lives of celebrities. Their status as singletons, and their transitions in and out of marriage and coupledom, provide inexhaustible grounds for snide speculation. Much of the sniping gets recorded in print.

Take, for example, singer-songwriter Sheryl Crow, a singleton in 2002. She knew how she was viewed. To *Newsweek* she explained, "I carry that label of being difficult, angry, sardonic. I don't know why that is. I think part of it is that I'm single, strong and famous. People perceive me to be all about balls."

A year later Crow was still single and told this story about herself: "I ran into someone pretty well-known recently, who said to me, 'Oh my God, I was just thinking about you the other day! I was thinking, she's such a great girl, why doesn't she get married and have kids?'" Crow was flabbergasted. "I felt like the breath rushed out of my body. I couldn't believe somebody was actually voicing what most of America probably thinks of me. I know it seems odd to people—if you're not married by a certain age you're either gay, asexual, or a freak who can't get along with anybody. And I know people wonder." Crow's anecdote appeared in *The Week,* in a story titled "Why Crow Is Alone."

Now on to the vulnerable singles. Apparently, that's how actress Sarah Jessica Parker views her friends. For years Parker played one of the most famous singletons on TV, star Carrie Bradshaw of *Sex and the City*. In real life Parker was married. *Time* magazine observed that Parker "regales her single friends with tales of how boring married life is and how much luckier they are to have freedom and fun." Asked whether she really believed what she had just said, Parker showed just how condescending she could be. "Well, no," she said. "It's just a fun thing to say to make single people feel better."

Author Barbara Dafoe Whitehead, who has made a name for herself tut-

tutting about divorce and single parenting, also thinks she knows a thing or two about single women. She told *Elle* magazine that the increasing amount of time women are spending single, going in and out of relationships, is leaving "a residue of mistrust and hurt." The residue, she added, "is like plaque on teeth."

The comparison with married people is left unstated but is easy to imagine. Married couples never bicker and never stray. They are always available to each other for picking up the groceries and the dry cleaning, for heart-to-hearts and passionate sex. No plaque on their teeth!

Something odd happens when people notice someone who is (or who may be) single or when they think about an adult who may be alone, even temporarily. Their mind seems to leap immediately to notions of loneliness. *Single* can jump straight to *lonely*, or it can stop at *alone* along the way. In fact, *alone* is often used as a stand-in for *lonely* or even for *single*—no further hop, skip, or jump is required. Links between singleness and loneliness, like the ones between singleness and bitterness, are unfree associations.

One sunny beach-day afternoon I was in one of my "life does not get any better than this" trances. I was sacked out on a chaise longue, paperback in hand, and close enough to the ocean for the waves to lick my feet. There was an empty beach chair next to me. A fellow sunbather—part of a group looking for another chair—wondered if anyone was using it. He could have asked me that question. But instead he inquired, "Are you here all by your lonesome?"

Time prints a "Numbers" feature in the front of the magazine. It is composed of several sets of related statistics—for example, the total number of pages on the Web, and the number accessible using the most powerful search engine. In 1999 one set started with the number by which single men outnumbered single women in a California county. The next statistic in the set was the number by which single women outnumbered single men in New York City. The third was the number of miles separating the two locations. Okay, I got the point. But *Time* wasn't finished. One final number was added to complete the set: "1, The loneliest number."

In 2001 an editorialist for the *Honolulu Star-Bulletin* had just learned about the lobbying efforts of the American Association for Single People, and pondered whether the cause was a worthy one. Maybe. "Their status as singles, that lonely number one, masks in many cases their true identities: unmarried couples who feel they need not legally validate their relationships, gays and lesbians, widowed people who remain unmarried for fear of losing pensions, college students, young adults just starting out their careers, single parents, and older divorced men and women." Never mind the snarky implication that only those singles who have a good reason for being single (a reason that honors soulmate values) are worthy of fair treatment in taxation, health insurance, employment policies, or anything else. What interested me was the inclusion of the phrase "that lonely number one." It was totally gratuitous.

Here's a fill-in-the-blank challenge. It comes from a description of a group of people who stay single after divorcing, as related by the award-winning psychologist E. Mavis Hetherington and coauthor John Kelly: "Well-adjusted, self-sufficient, and socially skilled, [such a person] often has a gratifying career, an active social life, and a wide range of hobbies and interests. [They] have everything they need to make their life a happy and fulfilling one."

If I were to describe people with active social lives, happiness, and fulfillment, I might call them wildly successful. Hetherington and Kelly call them "competent loners." The moniker is not only grudging—it is also wrong. A loner is not a person with an active social life; a loner is someone who prefers to be alone.

The misfitting label, I think, functions as an undoing ritual. Hetherington and Kelly describe single people's success and fulfillment in one important life domain after another; then they take it all back with their loopy label. What might stick in the mind of the reader who flipped casually through the book or the student who took notes on the main points, such as the names of the various categories of divorced people? Not the notion of impressive success, but the label of the competent loner.

On the eightieth anniversary of *Time*, the magazine celebrated with a special section titled "80 Days that Changed the World." Each day was described in just a few paragraphs. Some featured individual people, such as Martin Luther King for his "I have a dream" speech. The personal profiles often included an interesting or quirky detail. For example, it was mentioned in the King account that when President Kennedy met with the leader to discuss civil rights legislation, Kennedy quipped, "I have a dream."

One of *Time*'s eighty days was May 9, 1960, when the Food and Drug Administration declared the pill a safe form of birth control. It was Margaret Sanger who since 1914 "had battled ridicule and rigid laws, even gone to jail, all in pursuit of a simple, inexpensive contraceptive that would change women's lives—and save some as well." At the time, Sanger was eighty and had divorced her first husband and outlived her second. The brief story recounted that no one from the drug companies, the medical community, the government, or anyone else had bothered to call Sanger personally to tell her the news. Her son and granddaughter saw the story in the newspaper and dropped by her home to show her. She asked them to stay to celebrate, but they had to get to work. Sanger, we are told in the last sentence, "celebrated her victory alone."

There is a better way to applaud the lives of single people who have made their mark on the world, and one example appeared in the pages of the same magazine. After Eudora Welty died in 2001, the author Richard Ford described her in *Time*. Welty, he said, "produced 20 or so extraordinary books, a world of adoring readers, a house full of prizes, and a life lived solely, though not alone, and utterly to her own measure."

The Democratic presidential primary season of 2004 was packed with candidates, but Dennis Kucinich was the sole bachelor vying to represent his party. In one of the debates the hopefuls were asked to describe the role they envisioned for their spouse, should they win the White House. Kucinich replied that "as a bachelor, I get a chance to fantasize about my first lady." He then went on to describe the kind of dynamic, outspoken, fearless woman he would love to meet.

CNN was on the story. Its website noted that "bachelor Dennis Kucinich could soon be king of the lonely hearts." "Lonely," though, was not one of the characteristics on Kucinich's list. The candidate had not in any way suggested that women who are looking for a partner are by definition lonely. CNN did that. Kucinich, I think, was describing the kind of woman who would approach a romantic relationship from a position of strength because she could be happily coupled but could be happily single as well.

When CNN, *Time,* social scientists, or men on the beach make the leaps from "single" to "alone" to "lonely" and imply that coupling will provide the magical cure, they are closing their eyes to reams of evidence to the contrary. The dissenting opinions come from memoirs, essays, advice columns, and scientific research. Loneliness is not about being alone or being single, it is about feeling alone. To quote Daphne Merkin again, "I, for instance, married a man who left me feeling lonely not because he wasn't home but because he was."

There is a big problem with trying to tar all singles with bitterness, lovelessness, aloneness, misery, and envy: For many singles, those descriptors just do not fit. What is singlism to do with affluent and attractive singles, fabulously successful singles, or singles with remarkable interpersonal talents, such as a great gift for friendship?

No problem.

Consider, for example, the story of Neil, as told in a book written by two academics. Neil was a forty-something-year-old always-single architect who fell in love with Joanne and got engaged. Just before the wedding "Neil insisted on a punitive prenuptial arrangement." It drove Joanne away. "From the outside, many men might envy Neil," say the authors. "He's affluent and attractive, and he's not tied down. But those close to him see a lonely, troubled man who sabotages his chances for happiness."

Like so many stories about single people, the anecdote about Neil comes with a moral. Even if a single man appears to be anything but miserable, do not trust your impressions. Do not even trust his own reports of his life. Listen to those close to him. They will tell you that in fact he is bitter, loveless, alone, miserable, and envious of couples. And his tragic life is his own fault. He sabotages his chances for happiness.

Here is an example from the world of celebrity superstars, brought to us courtesy of *People* magazine. Actress Julia Roberts was "walking the red carpet for the L.A. premiere of *America's Sweethearts*. While cameras flashed, Mrs. Michael Douglas leaned in for a second's girl talk. 'How are you?' she whispered. Roberts pulled back, grinned, and quietly responded, 'I'm great.' But Zeta-Jones wasn't having it. 'No—how are you?' she persisted. Roberts looked at her again, apparently just getting the question behind the question: How are you now that your it-all-seemed-so-perfect four-year romance with Benjamin Bratt just collapsed in smoke and ashes?"

Never mind that the writer is salivating with glee as she relates the tale of the married celebrity twisting the verbal knife into the gut of the newly single superstar, and at just that moment when Roberts should have been basking in her movie star glory. Even if the exchange were reported with professional disinterest, it is an award-winner. Single people, see, cannot be "great." Not even if they are outrageously famous, wealthy, and successful; not even at the very moment they are publicly and glitzily recognized for their stardom. Marrieds will insist on a real answer. They know best.

Truth and Beauty: A Friendship is a book written by Ann Patchett about her friendship with Lucy Grealy. In a brief review *The New Yorker* credits Grealy with being a wonderful friend. There is a qualifier, though: "But Grealy's tremendous gift for friendship signaled a deep neediness and an inability to be alone." Well, maybe it did and maybe it didn't. But how often do you see a tremendous gift for marriage interpreted as indicative of a deep neediness and an inability to be alone?

In the wake of all the perceived neediness, loneliness, and despair of people who are single, experts of many stripes are rushing in to help. They offer books with titles such as *Being Single in a Couple's World: How to Be Happily Single While Looking for Love*. Readers already learn, before even turning to page one, that singles have no love and are just marking time while they look for some and that singles need instructions on how to be happy, whereas marriage brings immediate and lasting bliss.

If you want to see fools rush in to provide well-meaning advice to hapless single people, buy a ticket for Valentine's Day. One of my favorite examples appeared in *USA Weekend* in 2003, under the title "How to Survive Valentine's Day Without a Sweetie." Here's what it said.

> Valentine's Day alone need not be depressing or embarrassing; you can survive and even thrive without a lover if you plan accordingly. These tips come from dating guru Jennifer Frye:

1. **Don't just sit at home and mope.** Keep your spirits high by getting together with other single friends. Make dinner, watch empowering movies (*The War of the Roses* is a good one) and talk trash about love.

2. **If you have no single friends, take the day for yourself.** Do something fun: Take yourself shopping, go for a nice lunch, go to a museum. No errands today!

3. **Avoid romantic restaurants and bars.** The scene will just remind you of your loneliness.

4. **For a little end-of-the-day affection, kiss your pets, if you have any.**

The guru is so smart that she knows without asking that if you have arrived at Valentine's Day without a sweetie then you are miserable. Moreover, you are also stupid and cannot figure out how to survive this tragedy without professional help.

Your first option, if you have some friends who are also losers, is to hide at home with them and cook your own dinner. I would not make fun of the suggestion to watch an empowering movie if the example of a "good one" involved strong, successful, happy singles. Instead, the guru expects singles to be empowered by a story in which a husband runs over his wife's cat and his wife cooks his dog for dinner, just to spite each other.

If you don't have a sweetie and you don't have any single friends, either, then you will have to play more than one role so you can pretend you are not alone. You get to be the grown-up who "takes" the kid out for a really special day, and you also get to be the pathetic single person patted on the head by the indulgent adult.

Even without a sweetie or a single friend, you may still be salvageable. Perhaps you have some pets. If so, then you can kiss them.

If you have no sweetie, no single friends, and no pets, the guru is apparently stumped. She's out of advice.

In fairness, I will admit that *USA Weekend* did also offer Valentine's Day instructions for people who do have sweeties. Even coupled people need advice if their sweeties turn out to be imperfect. Take, for example, the problem of the "good guy who's a lousy kisser." To "handle" him, you can "stop the kiss as soon as it turns bad" and "without being obvious, use thumbs to clean up after a wet kisser."

Frankly, I think the advice given to people drowning in their sweeties' kisses should parallel the advice given to singles. Here are some suggestions:

- ☐ Keep your spirits high by fantasizing about getting back to your own home where no grown adults will be slobbering all over you.
- ☐ Avoid romantic restaurants and bars. They will only remind you of all of the other drooling kissers.
- ☐ For a really good kiss, look to your dogs. They are neater.

CHAPTER SIX

Myth #4 It Is All About You

Like a Child, You Are Self-Centered and Immature and Your Time Isn't Worth Anything Since You Have Nothing to Do but Play

I f you are a couple in love, the Sandals resort beckons. A Sandals vacation will take you to the Caribbean, to some of "the most romantic beachfront resorts on earth." Opt for a select suite and your room will come with your own personal butler, "who will attend to your every whim," from "bringing your favorite drink and a selection of imported cheeses to drawing a bath scented with rose petals." Dining at Sandals is not just gourmet, it is "ultra gourmet," with an ambience that is "a unique blend of sophistication and opulence that defines the height of elegance." Of course, there are water sports and land sports; spas, saunas, and misting pools; and entertainment in the evenings—so don't forget to pack your most elegant attire. No children are allowed at Sandals resorts, "because we wanted to make your vacation as romantic and relaxing as possible."

When people pity the presumed plight of the poor single person, perhaps they have in mind the exclusion of single people from the boastful decadence of resorts like Sandals. Maybe that's what singles are missing; that's why their lives are so sad.

Enter Japan's new generation of singles. The women among them have garnered the most attention. They have jobs and are marrying later than Japanese women ever have before. In the meantime, they live at home and maintain close ties with their parents, as so many Japanese women have done before them. A story in *The Washington Post* noted that these new single women also nurture and value their friendships with one another. As one woman told the reporter, "In Japan we treat our girlfriends well. Boyfriends come and go, but girlfriends are your sustenance, your life."

Groups of Japanese single women dine together regularly, and at some

of the upscale restaurants the tables of single women outnumber the tables
of couples. They often travel together, too. The Sheraton Grande Tokyo
Bay Hotel offers them a popular Cinderella package, complete with a
sumptuous room and an invitation to the pool, sauna, and some aro-
matherapy. Some of the women drive luxury cars and buy themselves pricey
presents for special occasions.

There is no dark aura enveloping these Japanese singletons. They have
close ties with friends and family, and social lives to rival those of any American couples at Sandals. Surveys suggest that "they are the most contented
demographic group in Japan." The *Post* story, then, together with all the
other media attention lavished on these single women, must have been a
celebration of the joy of singlehood in a forward-looking Japanese society.

Well, not exactly. Japanese singles were in the spotlight in the year 2000
because a Japanese sociologist, Masahiro Yamada, had put them there with
his new and much-hyped book about them. This new demographic, he
thought, was bad news. Because these singletons were still living with their
parents, they were hurting the economy by not buying enough durable consumer goods. They were also driving down the birth rate with their late marriages. They seemed at risk for never really maturing. Plus, they had an
attitude problem; since they were not paying for housing or supporting families, they felt free to reject jobs they did not like. Yamada's bottom line was
this: These new singletons, both men and women, "cast a shadow on the
health of society in the future." (Oops, there's that dark aura again.) He gave
them a name, "parasite singles." These twenty- and thirty-something-year-
old singles, who had jobs but still lived at home, were sucking resources out
of their parents.

Not everyone agreed with Yamada. Critics noted that although the
"parasite singles" were not buying durable goods, they were keeping the
economy humming with their other purchases. The age of first marriage
was indeed increasing, and the birth rate decreasing, but these trends
were not unique to Japan; in fact, they were characteristic of many other
nations. "Parasite singles" were not blithely rejecting good job offers—
there were fewer good jobs to be had. They lived with their parents not
just to mooch off them but because the cost of housing had slipped beyond reach. Moreover, parents often liked the arrangement. The extended
time that children spent at home afforded those offspring more opportunities to pursue higher education and to get a financial head start. Parents

anticipated that their adult children would care for them when they grew older and needier.

Others, of course, disagreed with the critics of Yamada, and the discussion continued. Years later, though, when people scratch their heads and try to recall something they once read about the new singles in Japan, they will probably recall just one phrase: "parasite singles."

On second thought, they may remember one other thing. Those parasite singles? They were women.

In fact, though, they were no more likely to be women than men. It was the press who pinned the parasite tag primarily on women. When Japanese women did marry, many would set aside any further educational or career aspirations and tend to the home, the children, and the care and feeding of their husbands. However, no one has yet referred to the indulged Japanese men as "parasite marrieds."

What seemed to bother Yamada most about the singles he studied is that they lived at home. Meanwhile, in England the demographic trend that was drawing notice was the growing number of single people who lived on their own. British singles had their own jobs, their own housing, and their own lives. No "parasite singles" there. Were they to be applauded?

Not by Princess Anne. "Most people would call it independence," she conceded. She, however, believed that living on your own was "just plain selfish." Living by yourself "means that you don't understand the impact of your life on other people's lives, and how you depend on other people all the time. It's no good."

Princess Anne is hardly alone in her insistence that singles are selfish. By itself, her remark is unremarkable. The meaning comes from the juxtaposition of Yamada's criticism of single people for living with their parents with Princess Anne's criticism of single people who are not living with their parents. The real problem for both critics, I think, is that too many contemporary singletons refuse to wallow in misery. Dr. Yamada and Princess Anne are exasperated by single people who will not stay in their self-pitying place.

The Japanese singles living fully and unabashedly are indeed troublemakers. They make a mockery of the notion that single people are miserable and lonely and that their lives are tragic. That's why another myth has to scurry to the rescue. The "it's all about you" myth cautions singles that if they refuse to acknowledge the wretchedness of their uncoupled lives, they will be dismissed as selfish, immature, irresponsible, and insignificant. In short, as long as they remain outside the gates of the Married Couples Club, single people are just oversized children and deserve to be treated as such.

I've already mentioned a number of stories that struck me as suspiciously suggestive of the "singles as great big children" theme. Remember Tom Avery? He is the Carol Shields character who used to be invited to dinner parties with other grown-ups when he was married. Once divorced, though, he was demoted to the family brunch, where he could play with the kids. Remember Adam? When he divorced, his still-coupled friends let him know that he had been reassigned to sleep in the living room of his cabin— by depositing his clothes there. Perhaps they assumed that single people, like children, need no privacy. And in assuming rather than asking, they again took the role of the knowing adults tending to the immature child in need of guidance.

Remember the professionals who told their thirty-something-year-old single colleague that the modest town house she was about to purchase seemed like "too much house" for her? Or the authors of the real-estate guides who suggested that a studio apartment may be the ideal living arrangement for a single person? Did they think they were making recommendations to a person whose last residence was a Fisher-Price fun house, complete with an Easy Bake oven?

And what about the married people who planned their couples dinners and gushed about the wonderful trips they took with other couples in the presence of their single friends who were not invited? They did so unselfconsciously, in the same way that adults make plans with one another to go to the theater while their kids play quietly within earshot.

Sometimes couples do include singles but make all the decisions. They are still playing the part of the grown-ups, who are the only ones whose preferences count. I am not going to say one word about a pizza.

The gifts given to singles can also be infantalizing. Edie is a university professor who has always been single. She likes hiking and fine wine and has a passion for politics. When she turned thirty, one married friend gave her a T-shirt adorned with a picture of a teddy bear and another gave her face paints.

I opened this chapter by riffing on the Sandals resorts that are open only to couples. However, the same travel professionals that sponsor Sandals vacations also offer another set of packages called Beaches—their "paradise for families." The website promises a great time for everyone from "the smallest child to the youngest-at-heart grandparent." It also boasts that you can "meet your favorite Sesame Street characters at all Beaches Resorts." Apparently, single people can come, too. The site doesn't say so explicitly. But it does note that if you are traveling with friends, the Beaches professionals will always do their best to accommodate you—though not to the point of guaranteeing adjacent rooms.

Even the language used to talk about singletons can be childlike. I first noticed that in the office on a Monday morning as my colleagues and I engaged in our ritualistic "so what did you do this weekend" exchanges. A coupled colleague told another coupled colleague that she and her husband "took" me to a wine festival. By my reckoning, you "take" a five-year-old places; you "go with" other adults. (It was not as if they had paid my way.) Over the years I would hear many tales from the same colleague of weekends spent "going with" other couples to dinners, movies, concerts, and plays.

Baby talk about singles was also part of the punditry in the 2004 presidential campaign, when survey research revealed that in the previous presidential race, single women were highly likely to vote Democratic when they did vote but rather unlikely to get to the polls. Much discussion ensued as to what it would take to "woo" the single-woman vote. Pollster Kellyanne Conway opined that "the government is a partner or safety net when you are going it alone. For women without husbands, Uncle Sam and Big Brother are the greatest protectors." Another commentator added that "single women welcome the presence of a nurturing Uncle Sam in their lives."

Their point is not wrong. Single women can survive a spell of unemployment less readily than married women who can take cover under the umbrella of a husband's paycheck. At retirement time, an always-single woman has only her own benefits to draw from. In contrast, a wife who never worked for pay but married a man who did can tap into his plan. Yet when single women are characterized as needing nurturing uncles and protective big brothers, they are being cast as indulged children—children who perhaps should jump into the arms of the goodly men, smother them with kisses, and yelp with joy in ecstatic gratitude for their largesse.

The benefits that single women seek from the government are not profligate splurges. They are the basics of human dignity—for example, access to affordable heath care and the means to live decently after a lifetime in the workforce. Senators and Representatives award themselves these benefits as a matter of course. In doing so, they see themselves not as patted on the head but as duly compensated.

Reams of legislation that could, in theory, be described in the language of protectiveness pass through congressional offices each year. For example, about the time of the 2000 discussion of single-women voters, a bill came up for consideration that would disallow lawsuits against restaurants for making people fat. In the halls of Congress and in the public discourse, the restaurant owners were not described as in need of nurturing.

Among the most ludicrous portrayals of singletons as great big children are those that paint singles as endearingly inept, hopelessly naive about the ways of the world, or just plain dumb. Even singles with Ph.D.'s are not exempt from being presumed stupid. I noticed that when the chair of a graduate program was asked whether the new faculty hire had been at all dissuaded by the price of housing. The chair shrieked in dismay, "He never asked!" adding, "He's single—he's stupid!" (Note just a few of the possibilities that were not entertained: The candidate had no other job offers. He was independently wealthy or had saved enough money to get a foot in the door. He had looked into the housing market on his own; if he were going to raise the topic, it would not be with the department chair.)

Singles can be depicted as particularly moronic in dramas that unfold over time, as in the movies or on TV. One of my favorite examples is an episode from the television show *Judging Amy*. Amy's mother, Maxine, a social worker, is called to the scene when a tiny human skeleton is unearthed in the garden of three elderly sisters. The three, all of whom are lifelong singles and have lived together in the same home all their lives, come out to talk to Maxine. They recall in great detail stories about the men who worked in the yard forty years ago, but they claim to know nothing about the skeleton.

An autopsy shows that the skeleton is that of a preterm baby. After much coaxing by Maxine, the sisters finally reveal to one another what they have never before discussed with one another or anyone else. Decades ago one of the sisters miscarried late in a pregnancy. She did not know what to do with the fetus, so she left it in the attic. Several days later another sister found it. She did not know what to do with it, either, or even where it came from, so she buried it in the yard.

Viewers were supposed to find it plausible that one sister sharing a home with two others could become pregnant without anyone noticing. They were also supposed to buy that the sister who miscarried would simply leave the remains in the attic and never look back. (Apparently, no one would notice a strange smell, either.) Later, another sister would find the fetus, shrug in puzzlement, and bury it in the garden—then never say a word about it for forty years.

It may seem odd that a television show starring two single women who are brilliant, wise, likable, and successful would so debase itself in its portrayal of three other single women. The stars, though, could lord it over the other singles because they had already earned their badge of marriage: Maxine was widowed and Amy was divorced. There is a hierarchy of single people, and older singles who never "achieved" marriage are at the very bottom. They are the most infantile singles of them all.

Sometimes married people get babied, too. On more than one occasion I have heard Sarah Jessica Parker boast about the childlike treatment she bestows upon another adult. In 2000 Parker told *Time* magazine that sometimes, as she works on the set of *Sex and the City,* she worries. "I know he doesn't have his laundry done, that he hasn't had a hot meal in days. That stuff weighs on my mind." Three years later, on *60 Minutes,* she said, "I take care of him. I pack for him, I shop for him, I get his groceries. He's taken care of."

Who is this man who is attended to so assiduously by Sarah Jessica Parker? Is it her father or the father of her husband, movie star Matthew Broderick? Actually, it is neither. It is Matthew Broderick himself, in theory a fully grown, able-bodied adult—and a wealthy one at that. Perhaps he could master the challenge of tossing clothes into a washing machine or boiling water. Short of that, maybe he could figure out how to dial the number of a dry cleaner or a restaurant with take-out service. Who knows, maybe he could even find his way to a restaurant, with the help, say, of a cab?

Parker, though, is not telling these stories with any embarrassment. She seems to think of Broderick not as a big baby who ought to grow up but as an adorable husband. *Time* and *60 Minutes* apparently agree. No one ever asks Parker why it is that she is still married to this man (or why she married him in the first place). No one insinuates that Broderick is selfish and childish, as they surely would if he were single and his mother were still doing his laundry. For people who are married, even the most infantile behavior can be reconstrued as simply endearing.

If single people really were immature and self-centered, what would their behavior look like? In considering this question, I tried to come up with a situation involving actual children in which self-centeredness would be very much on display. A birthday party seemed to be just the thing. Many children are endlessly indulged on their birthdays. They are the special person, and it is their special day. They get their favorite cake, sometimes grandly decorated, along with all sorts of other tasty treats. Lots of friends and relatives come and bring them presents. The birthday kid will often dress up for the occasion, and the other kids who come to the party might dress up, too. Occasionally one of the special friends cannot make it, and the birthday child might pout. That's allowed. It is a special day. Others may try to comfort and cheer the child. Some kids like to go someplace special on their birthdays, and that wish, too, is often granted.

How, I ask you, is this scenario any different from a wedding?

Okay, that is unfair. To the children and their parties. In the race to ever more staggering displays of self-celebration, weddings beat birthday parties hands down. Couples planning their nuptials can be far more self-indulgent, self-centered, and self-promoting than most children could ever get away with. In extravagance, newlyweds also leave "parasite singles" in the dust. But they are rarely called on it. Their splurges are deemed not selfish but romantic.

I realize that weddings do not have to be garish. In theory, they can be tasteful, meaningful, and sweet. Two adults come together in a simple and soulful ceremony. Friends and family offer modest gifts to the newly wedded couple (or perhaps to a favorite cause, if the couple prefers). The two are grateful for the presents but even more grateful to have people who are important to them and who will continue to have a cherished place in their lives from that day forward.

The weddings I just described really do have a place in the contemporary cultural landscape. I've even been invited to a few. But they are not the ceremonies that bridal magazines glorify or celebrities boast of, and they are not the ones that television networks stage during sweeps weeks. They are not even the everyday weddings of the boy or girl next door.

The first hint of the nature of the typical turn-of-the-twenty-first-century wedding is the price tag. In 2002 the median income for an American adult was $22,794. In the same year the average cost of a wedding was $22,360—honeymoon not included. For that, a Baltimore newspaper noted, a person could pay for three years of in-state tuition and fees at the University of Maryland.

Instead, couples treat themselves to a day of music, flowers, photography, videography, a reception, a limo, and costumes that would be preposterous in any other setting—and indeed are never worn again. Those are some of the components of the basic wedding package. Many couples want much more. More days, more uniqueness, more drama.

In 2004 *USA Weekend* magazine described some of its favorite ways in which "brides- and grooms-to-be are upping the wow factor at their nuptials." Rent special-effects equipment, the magazine suggests, so you can have fog, mist, haze, or wind at your ceremony, or even snow in the summer. Have your initials "projected in lights on the dance floor." Go to City Hall, get a special-event permit for your wedding, and close down a street. Get in touch with a talent agency and book its most stunningly beautiful clients to file into your ceremony as if they were your attendants. "Your guests' jaws will drop as these gorgeous men and women walk down the aisle." Then your real wedding party can enter.

The indulgences that couples bestow upon themselves are not the only offerings they will receive in commemoration of their special day. In 1997 newlyweds received an average of 171 wedding gifts. By 2004 the average total that an individual guest (not a couple) spent on a wedding and shower gift was approaching two hundred dollars.

That's the tab for the ordinary wedding guest who lives in town. For those with a special role in the ceremony, it can be just the beginning. For example, the *Wedding Gazette* suggested in 2005 that bridesmaids set aside up to nine hundred dollars for gifts, showers, parties, dress-up clothes, and travel.

On top of the presents and parties, couples sometimes get kickbacks from the stores where they are registered. At Macy's, for example, guests who select gifts from a wedding registry pay full price, then the couple gets a 5 percent reward back from the store.

As newly wedded couples receive more and more from their guests, their appreciation does not always grow accordingly. Something more akin to entitlement seems to have sprouted. The gift registries were just a baby step in that direction. Now couples want more than bed linens. One guest complained to *Newsweek* about the wedding invitation she received that included a request for help with the expenses of the honeymoon: "They're basically saying, 'Pay for us to go have sex in a really nice spot.'" A bridesmaid unloaded on "Dear Abby" about the bride who called her several times on her wedding night "demanding a gift of money!" This was after the bridesmaid had already spent four weeks doing alterations for free. Such stories have become so commonplace that when a new reality TV show called *Bridezillas* was launched, no one needed an explanation for what the neologism meant.

It wasn't always this way. We like to think of the white wedding as "traditional," but in fact it is not. In Europe and North America just a few centuries ago, wedding ceremonies looked very different. There were different versions at different places and times, but none approximated the spectacles that are showcased today.

Histories of courtship and marriage often highlight the differences in the relationship between the two people who are marrying. Was the pairing arranged, or freely chosen? How well did the two know each other before the wedding? What was the nature of their courtship? Did they marry within or across the lines of class, religion, or race? And now, of course, we ask whether a wedding ceremony marks only the coming together of a man and a woman or whether two men, or two women, can marry, too.

An equally important change, I think, is the relationship between the couple and their friends, family, and community. Before the nineteenth century the ceremonies marking a marriage were more likely to underscore the links between the couple and the other people in their lives than the specialness of the couple apart from everyone else.

That the newlyweds were part of a social network and a community, rather than above it, was evident even from their attire. The newlyweds did dress up for their wedding, but sometimes no more so than their guests.

The customs of gift giving were even more telling. People in the community contributed what they could afford so the new couple—especially if they were of modest means—could have what they needed to start a new household and thereby take their place within the community. Historian John Gillis has noted that in Wales "each gift would be noted and paid back in due time." At first, it was only among the wealthy that wedding presents took the form of glittering luxury items with little practical value.

The china, the crystal, and the silver tea sets would be set on display atop a white woven tablecloth in a special room. The baubles spoke for the couple. "We do not need the community to help us," they said. Most newlyweds, though, did need the help of the people in the community who were in a position to offer it.

The honeymoon, too, was once a time for underscoring the reciprocal ties between the couple and the important people in their lives. It was commonplace for the couple to visit friends and family who lived some distance away and who were not expected to make a special trip to attend the wedding. The couple's closest companions often joined them in these travels. The trip was not a time for the couple to be alone.

Once the couple arrived back in town, they would take their place among their neighbors. It did take a village to maintain the village, structurally and interpersonally; and couples, singles, and children were all part of it.

The historical perspective helps us cut through the mist of the contemporary lavish wedding to recognize what a profoundly self-centered and self-celebratory ritual it has become, especially at the hands of its most out-of-control practitioners.

First, the attire. Today no one could mistake the bride for a random guest.

Second, the gifts. All guests are expected to make offerings, and substantial ones at that, no matter what their own personal circumstances may be. These contributions to the couple are especially remarkable at a time when the bride and groom are at such a different place in their lives from where newlyweds were in the past. The age at which adults first wed is trending ever upward. The two people who are coming together often have their own jobs and a household that they share. Their joint household may well have been created from the merging of their own previous individual households, already well stocked with linens and demitasse cups.

Some observers have acknowledged that showering gifts on well-off recipients does not always sit well with guests, but they do not find that troublesome. The authors of *Cinderella Dreams* explain that "the most dissatisfied guests seem to be nontraditional women." In contrast, "the satisfied guests are recent or future brides who recognize the reciprocal nature of gift-giving and understand that when it is their turn they will also 'pick up the loot' from all of the brides whose showers they had attended."

What the authors do not mention is that the "dissatisfied guests" (translation: the bad ones—the women who are single and intend to stay that way) do not "recognize the reciprocal nature of gift-giving" for a reason. For them, it doesn't exist. For lifelong singles—especially those who live alone or with dependents—showers and weddings are occasions for the redistribution of resources from those who have one paycheck to cover one set of household expenses to those who have the same one set of household expenses but two paychecks to cover them. When the bride and groom are serial remarriers, the inequities are greater still.

Discussions of gift giving at showers and weddings tend to focus on presents and cash. But couples receive far more. They also enjoy the gift of their guests' attention, time, and validation. For no other event in a person's lifetime do so many people show up at your side at the appointed time and place, regardless of whatever else may be happening in their own lives.

The guests who come from near and far to attend a wedding have a new role to play at the ceremony. In the past wedding guests welcomed the new couple as part of the community. They would all be neighbors and friends. Now guests at weddings serve as fans who look up to the couple as the stars of their own show. They subsidize the twosome emotionally as they ooh and aah at the choreographed spectacle.

In one of the ways of upping "the wow factor" that *USA Weekend* so admired, the people closest to the bride and groom—the members of their wedding party—are literally hidden away so that more stunningly beautiful actors and actresses can play their roles for them and give the guests a greater thrill. In one of the other wow factors, community members with no relationship whatsoever to the couple are inconvenienced for the sake of the couple's show. That's the one in which the newlyweds are encouraged to get a permit to shut down a city street. In the orgy of self-celebration that some contemporary weddings have become, no gesture is a bridge too far in setting the couple above everyone else in their lives and above so many others who should not have to go out of their way, literally, to accommodate the wedding of a pair of strangers.

The glorification of the newlyweds that begins at the wedding ceremony kicks up a notch at the reception. There, the distinction between the awesome wedded couple and everyone else is relentlessly telegraphed. Singles especially are singled out. In his essay "It's a Paired, Paired, Paired, Paired World," Paul Jamieson described the singles table. It is "all the way in the back, right by the door to the kitchen" and "farthest away from the head table." In theory, a place near the kitchen door could mean super service, but that does not happen, either; "the guests at the Singles Table are invariably the last to get their Chilean sea bass with mango salsa." Single women are treated to an additional indignity when they are asked to gather round for the bouquet toss. They are presumed to want to catch the wilted flowers, and feel fortunate if they do. That's because, in the marriage mythology, the bouquet is a talisman signaling their imminent escape from the singles table to the place of honor. With both practices—seating the singles with one another, so that they, too, might meet someone and become coupled, and tossing the bouquet—the newlyweds say the same thing to their single guests: "We know you want to become married and special, just like us."

On to the honeymoon. The contemporary version could hardly be more different from what it was in the past. Today's honeymooners travel far away from all the other people in their lives, to celebrate and seal an intense emotional and physical connection only to each other. They re-create, as if on cue, the cloying romantic ideal: "just the two of us."

Back from their wedding trip, the newlyweds retreat into their own home. They are still apart from everyone else. They will emerge now and then, as a pair, often to socialize with other look-alike pairs. Then to their own place they will again return, "just the two of us."

Think back to the singles I described at the beginning of this chapter—the ones who were castigated as selfish "parasite singles". Their gatherings—dinners out, travel adventures, shopping trips—really are communal. Whole groups of women participate as equals. No one woman, and no pair, is singled out as special and above all the rest. The bonds they cherish as lasting are with each of the other women. These women are not narrowly linking themselves to just one other person.

The women who live with their parents are nurturing interpersonal bonds as well. The parents and their daughters all anticipate reciprocity down the road, when the parents need help and their daughters will graciously provide it.

It is true that the single women described by Yamada buy themselves pricey handbags and clothes. Unlike bridal wedding wear, however, the adornments purchased by singles are worn over and over again.

How is it, then, that singles are so readily presumed to be selfish and self-centered while the far more self-indulgent newlyweds are instead deemed romantic?

First, some clarifications. I realize that lots of people love over-the-top weddings and do not at all mind being demoted from friend to fan. So, I am not saying that couples should never throw wild wedding parties for themselves. What I am saying is that we should recognize extravagant weddings for what they are: self-centered, self-celebratory, and self-congratulatory ceremonies that declare the couple as more special than anyone else, and as especially superior to people who are single.

I am not suggesting that singles should compete with newlyweds in a race toward wretched excess. I just think we should use the same standards for evaluating singles as we do couples. So, couples who spend tens of thousands of dollars on their wedding cannot fault singles for being selfish until the singles, in their dinners and travels with their friends, have spent that much money, too—and also extracted 171 gifts from their friends and family. Even then couples can begin dissing singles only if, after their wedding and honeymoon, they never again indulge themselves with fancy dinners, pricey purchases, or nice vacations.

For all the debauchery of so many weddings, though, perhaps the celebration is simply a one-time splurge—or one time for each marriage. Afterward, the newly married couple can be expected to settle into a lifetime of altruism and selflessness.

Some people really believe this. One of them is sociologist Steven Nock. To answer the question of whether married people are more selfless than singletons, you first need to decide what counts as selflessness. Nock looked at one of the most straightforward measures: giving money. He had access to nationally representative survey data from thousands of Americans who were questioned in 1987 or 1988, then again five years later. The participants were asked to name all the people to whom they had given at least two hundred dollars in the past year and to categorize those people as friends or relatives. How did patterns of giving change, Nock wondered, for people who had transitioned in or out of marriage in that five-year interval? Nock's specific interest was in the role of marriage in the lives of men, so he described only the answers given by the men.

Recognize at the outset that this is a setup. First, as I discuss in Chapter 12, single men are paid less than married men, even when they have the same level of seniority and the same accomplishments. So, on the average, two hundred dollars is a greater proportion of a single man's income than a married man's. Second, as Nock acknowledges, gifts from married men are often gifts from the couple, not just the man. For working men who are married to working women (which is most of them) and putting two salaries toward the expenses of one household (as almost all of them do), two hundred dollars is part of a much larger pot than that of the single man whose one salary covers all the expenses of one household. Finally, the money given by a married man may not have anything at all to do with his own personal spirit of generosity. Nock frames that argument this way: "Might it be that any change in men's giving associated with marriage is because wives make such decisions? The stingy bachelor may not change at all once he gets married. Perhaps he parts with his (their) money only because his wife insists."

Now that I have lined up all my reasons for why married men might give two-hundred-dollar gifts more often than single men even if they really are not any more generous, I can tell you the results. Men who married were not any more generous than they were before. The frequency with which married men gave such sums to relatives was no different from the frequency with which single men did so. That similarity is remarkable in light of all the additional relatives married men have that single men do not (obviously, all the wife's relatives).

There was a marked difference, though, in generosity to people who were not relatives. Men who married gave an average of $1,875 *less* to friends than they had when they were single. The reverse was true for men who had divorced: They gave an average of $1,275 more to friends than they had when they were married. Men who remarried went back to being less generous to their friends (by $1,050) than they had been when they were divorced.

In sum, men who are single give no less to relatives than men who are married, despite drawing from one (rather than two) incomes and getting paid less to boot. And they give more to friends than married men do. Still, Nock calls the single man a "stingy bachelor."

Regardless of their financial means, men of all civil statuses can be generous with other resources, such as their time and their work outside of work—for example, housework. Stereotypically, single men are slobs. Maybe when they marry, they give their wives the gift of the housework that they never did as bachelors. Nock looked into that, but it is not what he found. Men who married spent an average of 1.4 hours less on housework each week than they had when they were single. If they divorced, they spent 3.8 hours more than they had when they were married; and if they re-married, they spent 4.7 hours per week less than they had when they were divorced.

One of the clichés about marriage is that it takes self-centered singles and turns them into concerned citizens. By marrying, the story goes, adults begin to feel that they have a stake in the fate of the nation, which they did not have as self-absorbed singles. If this were true, then married people might be expected to put their time where their values are. They may, for example, devote more time to just those organizations billed as providing service to the community and to society. They might also become more in-volved in political groups. Nock looked into these possibilities, too. But he found no difference. Men who married spent no more time in service clubs, political groups, or fraternal organizations than they had when they were single.

Nock believes that marriage motivates men to work harder and more responsibly. As he notes in his chapter on adult achievement, "Marriage is also the engine that fuels greater effort and dedication to the goal of doing well." Workers who care about the good of their fellow workers and about their occupation or profession should put in the time to back up that dedi-cation. Married men could, for example, evince their greater responsibility to the workplace by participating more often in groups such as farm orga-nizations, unions, or professional societies. Only they don't. In fact, ac-cording to Nock's own reporting, men who married spent less time at such work-related activities than they had when they were single. They did, though, work 2.2 weeks more per year than they had before. That's the kind of work that pays—them, but not anyone else. Even this one marriage in-centive fizzles for men who remarry; they worked 7.4 weeks less than they had when they were divorced.

Of all of the types of organizations the men were asked about in the survey, there was only one to which men devoted more of their time once they married—church groups. There was little indication, then, that men who married became more generous with their money or their time than they had been before they wed, and some indications they were less so. Yet when Nock gets to the last few sentences of the last page of his book on marriage in men's lives, he offers this conclusion:

> Husbands will be changed by their marriages. They will earn more and achieve more. They will become members of organizations devoted to improving communities. They will be generous to their relatives. These are things our society values. Those who engage in them earn our respect and thanks. Collectively, we value and depend on such people. When men marry, they are more likely to make such contributions. They become better men.

Nock did not gather all the studies that had ever been published on the differences between married and single men in gift giving, service, or housekeeping. He selected one set of survey data to analyze. That means he was selective in what he presented right from the start. What is striking about his conclusion is that it does not even represent accurately the data he did choose to present. It is as if Nock decided at the outset that single men were "stingy bachelors" and was not about to let the data dissuade him.

Nock is not the only scholar with reams of data on marital transitions and opinions to accompany them. Another is E. Mavis Hetherington, who devoted her career to the study of both men and women who had divorced. She followed more than a hundred people for decades as they stayed single or transitioned in and out of remarriages. At the twenty-year mark she recorded her observations of the people she had gotten to know so well. I smiled as I read her description (written with coauthor John Kelly) of one particular subgroup: "Our single women accompanied one another to important medical appointments, did volunteer work for charity organizations, devoted time to their children and parents." At last, I thought, singles' selflessness is recognized and applauded.

Silly me. That was not Hetherington's conclusion at all: "Helping others gave many women a way to feel good about themselves."

There is one category of helping that Nock never acknowledges and Hetherington mentions only in passing: long-term intensive help for ailing elderly parents. Such caretaking is emotionally daunting and often entails sacrifices at work, which can translate into lost pay and slowed opportunities for promotion. It also takes its toll on the social and personal lives of the caregivers. This most selfless of acts is often provided by women and singles. It is more likely to be provided by single daughters than by married daughters. Men who marry sometimes add more to their lives than a wife; they also get a caretaker for their own parents. Yet Nock still blithely praises married men for their generosity to their relatives. And Hetherington dismisses the altruism of single women as just a way of making them feel better about their supposedly pathetic lives.

In the mythology of marriage, spouses are supposed to care for each other in every imaginable way. And they are supposed to long for each other when they are away, or even when they anticipate being away. Couples believe the songs that say of lovers, "you are my heart, my life, my soul," "you are my everything," and "you're nobody till somebody loves you." When coupled people experience the pain of separation, it is, to them, evidence that they are indeed somebody.

Here, for example, are scenes from three marriages.

Scene 1. Author Cheryl Jarvis craved time away from her marriage and family—not just hours, but weeks or even months. She got it. For three months she would go, alone, to the destinations of her dreams. She also found fifty-five other wives with the same yearning for a "marriage sabbatical." Then she got a book contract to write about it. Jarvis wanted to go to writers' colonies. She did. After the first two, she became intrigued with the idea of living on a ranch in Montana. So she canceled her reservation with the third writers' group and headed west. By the tenth week of her sabbatical, Jarvis wished her husband were right there with her. "In tears, I reach for the phone and call him. For an hour and a half, he listens and soothes."

Scene 2. During the many months when *New York Times* reporter Jodi Wilgoren was covering the 2004 presidential campaign of John Kerry, she was also planning her wedding. The hardest part, she said in a personal essay printed in the *Times,* was "all those nights in all those hotel rooms, crying into the telephone, not about which videographer to hire, but about being apart."

Scene 3. Soon after former president Ronald Reagan died, the cover of *Newsweek* promised to tell readers all about "Nancy's Story." The featured report was filled with "tender" tales of her marriage. For example, "back in 1981, the night before she flew to England alone to attend the wedding of Prince Charles and Diana Spencer, Nancy had wept at the thought of being away from Ronnie for even a few days."

Here's my question: What are these married people crying about? Cheryl Jarvis is taking the sabbatical of a lifetime. She is going exactly where she wanted to go, doing exactly what she wanted to do. On a whim she can change her plans and go somewhere else. What's more, she is getting paid for it all. Still, she is crying and needs an hour and a half of her husband's soothing.

Jodi Wilgoren has one of the plum journalistic assignments of the year 2004. She is covering the Democratic candidate in one of the most impassioned presidential elections in recent U.S. history. Moreover, she is doing so for one of the most prestigious newspapers in the world. But she's crying, too.

Why is Nancy Reagan crying? She is a fifty-nine-year-old who for just a few days is going to be away from her husband (whom one imagines was occasionally busy with the work of the presidency and so not solely attentive to her in any event). As First Lady, it is unlikely that she would be left to her own devices to find fine dining or accommodations once she got to England. Moreover, it is not as if she were headed to a funeral or the opening of a sewage-treatment plant in some godforsaken land. She was on her way to the social event of the century.

All three stories are described without embarrassment—indeed, with pride. To the tellers of the tales, these are love stories. The characters in them are true romantics.

I think they are immature whiners. They all got their way, then cried anyway. That's what babies do. Plus they expect sympathy. So, to the author with her long, leisurely sabbatical and book contract, to the *New York Times* reporter with one of the best professional gigs in the land, and to the First Lady with her tickets to the social event to die for, I say this: It's your party. You can cry if you want to. But what you can't do is claim that you are fully grown and mature adults simply by dint of your marriage. Nor can you ever again say or even imply that single people are the sole repositories of adult immaturity.

Democrat John Kerry and Republican George W. Bush were not the only two candidates in the presidential campaign of 2004. Another potentially strong contender was Ralph Nader, a man who had always been single and who was running as an independent. To some, Nader had played the role of the spoiler in the 2000 election, skimming just enough votes from Al Gore in key states to tip the balance of the electoral count to Bush. There was much concern among Democrats, and giddiness among Republicans, that Nader might do the same in 2004. In short, the Nader candidacy was serious business.

In policy, in political philosophy, in just about every issue facing the American electorate in 2004, Nader differed dramatically from Bush. Is it more important to decrease windfalls from lawsuits or to increase the minimum wage? Is green stuff what citizens should have more of in their pockets by means of permanent tax cuts, or what citizens should see when they look out their windows? Is the quality of American life more seriously threatened by gay people having access to marriage or by poor and even middle-class people lacking access to health care? And is war in Iraq keeping the country safe from terrorism, or making the nation more vulnerable than ever?

Nader's and Bush's political biographies were also very different. At the time, the White House website proclaimed that President George W. Bush had an undergraduate degree from Yale and an MBA from Harvard, that he had been a fighter pilot in the National Guard and a managing general partner of the Texas Rangers baseball team, that he had had a career in the energy industry and a role in his father's presidential campaign, and that he was a two-term governor of Texas.

Nader, of course, had no White House website. He was, however, widely known as the number one advocate for citizens' rights and protections in the face of government malfeasance and corporate corruption. Because of Nader, water is cleaner, food is more nutritious, and workplaces are safer than they were before. Ralph Nader was an investigative journalist before that style of reporting had became fashionable, and a proponent of renewable energy when the need seemed less critical than it does now. He inspired sunshine laws and the Freedom of Information Act, the Environmental Protection Agency, and public-interest research groups. The routine reporting of the energy efficiency of appliances, the side effects of prescription drugs, the nicotine levels of cigarettes, and the results of automobile crash tests can be traced directly to the efforts of Ralph Nader and the generations of citizen advocates he inspired. By his contributions to auto safety alone, Nader has probably saved millions of lives.

The personal life paths that led Bush and Nader to political prominence also had little in common. The God-praising, alcohol-abstaining persona that the public saw in Bush at the turn of the twenty-first century was of relatively recent vintage. Of his years before the age of forty, Bush quipped, "When I was young and irresponsible, I was young and irresponsible." Nader, in contrast, had already read the writings of the early muckrakers such as Upton Sinclair by the time he was fourteen. He read the *Congressional Record,* too.

Chris Matthews, host of the political TV program *Hardball,* knew all this and much more about the presidential candidates when he invited Ralph Nader to appear on his show in February of 2004. He asked Nader point-blank whether Bush, intellectually, was up to the job he already held.

Nader pounced. Bush, he noted, did not exactly have a long personal history of reading and thinking. Then, recalling what Bush once said about himself, Nader added, "Until he was forty, he was young and irresponsible."

Here was the ever-single Ralph Nader calling the married George Bush irresponsible. Matthews was not going to stand for it. "Why do you say he's irresponsible? He's raised two daughters; he's had a happy marriage. Isn't he more mature in his lifestyle than you are?"

Nader answered that he was using Bush's own words and that, by Bush's account, it was wife Laura who set him on the righteous path.

"But you've never even gotten married and settled down and had kids," Matthews countered. "How can you hold it against a guy who's been a good family man?"

"I'm not saying he's a bad family man."

"You said he's immature," noted Matthews, apparently still smarting from the mere suggestion that a man who was married could be anything but a paragon of maturity. Then he launched into a mini-lecture: "You're an ascetic guy. You go to movie night and maybe have dinner with some pals. I like you personally. But you haven't exactly grown up and had a family and raised them and seen them off to college. . . . He's had a happy marriage. Isn't that a sign of maturity that you haven't demonstrated?"

Nader replied that he had contributed to the health and safety of children nationwide.

Then Matthews asked Nader if he had a car. When Nader replied that he could get by with walking, taking public transportation, or hailing cabs, Matthews counted that as another strike against the man. Most Americans do own cars, he said.

Nader described the virtues of not owning a car when you do not need one and also reminded Matthews of all he had done throughout his lifetime to make cars safer and less polluting.

Matthews turned next to home ownership. He pointed out that if Nader became president, he would live in the White House, and that would be the first house he had lived in since childhood. Then, putting together the pieces of his argument—Nader had no house, no car, and no marriage—Matthews delivered his conclusion: "You live a life that's about as responsible as what's on the movies tonight."

By the time the segment had drawn to a close, Matthews had stated five times that Bush was married or Nader was not, and another five times claimed that Bush was mature or responsible and Nader was not. Exasperated, Nader finally exclaimed, "Chris, no wonder they parody you on *Saturday Night Live!*" But it was no use. Matthews's mind was in lockdown. Married meant mature, single meant immature. No amount of scholarship or public service on the one side, or debauchery on the other, could pry the equation apart, or open Matthews's mind.

There are people who have read everything I've said so far in this chapter, got the point of all of the examples, laughed at all the jokes, yet still ended up uncomfortably unconvinced. It still seemed to them, in ways they could not articulate, that married people really are more mature, more responsible, and more selfless than people who are single.

I've puzzled over this for a long time, wondering whether there actually might be some logic to it that I simply had not yet discerned. I now think that there is, and it goes something like this: Married people are obligated to be there for each other. Regardless of their own personal whims and wishes, if a time comes when their spouse really does need them, they really need to be there. Jonathan Rauch, in arguing for the importance and meaning of marriage, has put it this way. Imagine, he suggests, that

Mrs. Smith is diagnosed with a brain tumor. She will need treatment and care. Mr. Smith, an able-bodied adult with no history of mental illness, responds by leaving town. Now and then he calls her, chats for a few minutes as a friend might do, and then goes about his business. He leaves Mrs. Smith in the hands of her sister, who has to fly in from Spokane. When the doctors call, he lets the answering machine take a message. "She can sign on our bank account," he says. "Let her hire help."

Rauch declares that no person would behave like Mr. Smith and still call himself married. A spouse can get away with lots of bad behaviors, but abandonment is not among them.

So that's the difference and that's why married people are deemed ultimately more mature and responsible and less selfish than single people. If a married couple splurges on a Sandals vacation and one of them gets seriously ill, they both throw in the beach towel. In contrast, Ralph Nader really could spend every evening at the movies if he so desired. Single women may well help one another (in the ways Hetherington describes), but then again, they can just as easily decide not to.

I don't buy it. I think that the generosity that married couples show each other is less impressive exactly because it is obligatory and reciprocal. Suppose Mr. Smith acted in a manner more appropriate to a husband and cared for his wife throughout her illness. Suppose further that Mrs. Smith fully recovered. She would then be available to care for Mr. Smith, should he fall seriously ill.

Now suppose that Mrs. Smith's sister is single and spends years of her life caring for her ailing elderly parents. All three peers in this picture (Mr. and Mrs. Smith and Mrs. Smith's sister) are doing caring and loving work. All deserve moral accolades. But it is the single person's work that is the most selfless. The care she gives her parents is not likely ever to be reciprocated, at least not in kind.

In the same way, Ralph Nader's devotion of so many days of his life to the good of his fellow citizens and of the nation is all the more impressive because he did not need to be so selfless. If he had gone to the movies every night instead, all it would have cost him is the charge of being immature and irresponsible—which Chris Matthews laid on him anyway. Nader's counterpart, George W. Bush, did shape up eventually, but it took him until he was forty years old and he did so not from a wellspring of maturity and selflessness but because his wife was on his case.

The example Rauch describes is important for another reason. Rauch needlessly embellishes the caring that married couples give each other by demeaning the caring that comes from friends and relatives. A close friend would not, as Rauch suggests, "chat for a few minutes" with Mrs. Smith, then go on about her business. She would talk for as long as Mrs. Smith wanted to, quite possibly listening more empathically than Mr. Smith. She would not hang up and return to her routine with the same emotional vapidity as if she had just had a conversation about a bad hair day instead of a brain tumor. Same for Mrs. Smith's sister. If she and Mrs. Smith were close, she would not "have to" fly in from Spokane; she would insist on it. She would want to be there for Mrs. Smith even if Mr. Smith had not become an absentee spouse.

It is true, and it is significant, that Mrs. Smith should feel more secure in her expectation that Mr. Smith will be there for her than that her close friends or her sister will. She and Mr. Smith have a pact called marriage, which at its best functions like an insurance policy against catastrophic events. But contemporary marriage is akin to the contemporary insurance policies that turn out to have staggering gaps in coverage. A spouse really can walk out at a partner's time of greatest need. Former congressman Newt Gingrich, for example, did it twice. Gingrich was the Republican who in 1994 led his party to sweeping midterm victories in Congress on the promise and allure of his "Contract with America." But he did not bother to honor his own personal contracts. He divorced his first wife while she was hospitalized with cancer. His second wife was diagnosed with a neurological condition that could be a forerunner to multiple sclerosis. She was visiting her mother on her birthday when Newt gave her the news that he was leaving.

Gingrich, reassuringly, is the exception. Not in divorcing—that's commonplace. Not in divorcing in a mean-spirited way, either; that's also all too common. He did, though, seem to take heartlessness and cruelty to a new level. He took the Rauch hypothetical example of the most unthinkable thing a spouse could do and then did it. Twice.

Again, though, most married people do not have a Newt-like figure as a spouse. They can expect a specific other person to be there for them in a way that a single person typically cannot. Does that make married people more mature than single people? Or in terms of pure, raw maturity, don't you have to hand it to the people who can live their lives fully, joyfully, and fearlessly without the crutch of a signed and sworn statement of support to have and to hold?

Married people are on training wheels. Singles are riding the bikes for grown-ups.

Within the best marriages and families, people really are there for each other and enjoy great comfort and security as a consequence. They are proud of themselves for their devotion to each other, within and across generations, and rightly so. In the conventional wisdom, they have earned their claim to selflessness.

When cultural critics worry that the rising tide of single people bodes ill for our sense of community and suggest that marriage and family are antidotes to the threat of rampant individualism, they have in mind the marriages and families that are exemplary. So, it is instructive to look at the link between the caring that takes place within loving marriages and families and the caring that extends beyond a family's own picket fence.

I found one married woman's story in a "My Turn" essay in the pages of *Newsweek*. Beyond the picket fence of Angela, the writer, was her elderly neighbor of twenty years, Claire. Over the years, Angela reported, she and Claire "made small talk while we raked leaves, shared vegetables from our gardens and took a few walks together. . . . Three years ago Claire was among the first to read one of my published essays. She was full of praise, telling me not to give up."

Then, about a year before Angela wrote her *Newsweek* essay, things started to change. Claire would show up at Angela's door but would not remember Angela's name. She would repeat the same thing over and over again. She would drive around and around the neighborhood, forgetting where it was she had wanted to go. Angela knew what these and so many other strange behaviors portended: Claire was "exhibiting all the classic symptoms of Alzheimer's disease."

Angela worried about Claire, and so did the others who lived nearby. As Angela noted, "The entire neighborhood shared in the drama." For example, on one particularly hot summer day, Claire passed out in her front yard and Angela, her husband, and one of the neighbors all showed up to help. Angela talked to a policeman, but he said that it was up to Claire, not Angela, to decide whether to go to the emergency room. Claire did have a son, but he was rarely around except on Christmas.

"As Claire's neighbors," Angela noted, "we had no legal rights, and the truth is, we really didn't want any. We had handled the decline and loss of our parents and grandparents. We had our own families and jobs. Whose job was she?

"We'd try to help, to listen, to be patient, but we could not totally smother our resentment toward Claire's absent, mysterious son." He should have been the answer to Claire's problems. In the serene setting where Angela lived, there were laws against "cutting down trees too close to the lake, but nothing about abandoning the desperately ill. Where was Claire's family?"

In the end, though, Angela realized that love within families would not always suffice; some people outlive all their kin. "I'm praying I don't die last in my family," she conceded. "In 'A Streetcar Named Desire,' Blanche says, 'I have always depended on the kindness of strangers.' Surely, in America, there is a better way."

I take Angela at her word that within her own family she is caring and devoted. But I think she has drawn a line around her family and called it the outer bounds of her generosity. The kindness she practiced within her family is not a personality trait. Angela does not look with warmth and empathy toward all of humanity, nor even toward the woman she has known as a neighbor for two decades. When Angela asks, "Whose job is she?" the "job" she is referring to is a person.

When Claire took the time to read Angela's work and to offer praise and encouragement to Angela as she pursued her writing career, Angela was happy to accept it. She was still the bride at her own wedding, merrily collecting all the gifts that her guests had offered.

Then she would write her thank-you notes, and that would be the end of the place of those guests in her life. When Claire needed help, Angela saw herself not as a friend or even as a neighbor; she was, instead, a stranger.

I don't need to tell Angela that what goes around comes around. I don't need to remind her that marrying, or even having children, is no guarantee against being the last kin standing. She is already praying that she does not outlive all the people who reside within her family lines and are thereby obligated to care for her.

Angela is absolutely right when she says that we in America should do better than this. No one should have to count on divine intervention to save them from wandering lost and aimless in their own hometown. What interests me here is Angela's attitude. To me, it seems stone-cold. I have no idea whether this heartlessness is representative of the majority of married people. It seems telling, though, that Angela is unashamed of it. In fact, she acts put-upon. How dare Claire develop Alzheimer's and become a burden? Where's Claire's son?

I don't think Angela sees herself as uncaring. She made sure we knew that she "handled" her own parents, grandparents, and family. I think she assumes that since she discharged her obligations to her kin, she is covered. She has shown all the caring that is needed to get credit for being a selfless, mature, and responsible person. Any further caring that crosses the line of marriage and kinship is a job. Angela might do that job now and then, but she will let us know how much she resents it.

Angela's thinking illustrates an unintended consequence of setting marriage and family too far above every other human relationship. Angela, and so many others who nodded in agreement as they read her essay, is dividing humanity into a group worth caring for and a group that can be dismissed as mere strangers. People in the worthy group can feel good about themselves if they care for one another and need not fret about any other caring that remains undone.

By the same logic, the caring that goes on within marriages and families is the only caring that truly counts. This is how single people are deemed selfish. Any contributions made by single, childless people to current and future generations fall short by definition. No matter what they do, it is not important and it does not count. Even this sleazy logic works only if we all close our eyes to older generations, to which single women give more than their share of care.

The biological-kin cliques are not just precarious for the individuals within them who worry about whether they will be the last in their circle to die. They are just as precarious for society. The cliques ultimately leave too many people on the outside looking in. They encourage all of us to keep our empathy in check. Why can't we value our common humanity instead?

I am not arguing against the special valuing of the people who are most important to us. No one can be the care provider to the world. What I am saying is that we have taken a small set of relationships that deserve to be treasured, and turned them into the only relationships worth valuing at all. That's what I find troublesome.

CHAPTER
SEVEN

Myth #5 Attention, Single Women

Your Work Won't Love You Back and Your Eggs
Will Dry Up. Also, You Don't Get Any and You're
Promiscuous.

A revolution in higher education has created the most professionally accomplished and independent generation of young women in history." That was the tease for a new book in the online catalog for Random House in 2003. But the author of the book, Barbara Dafoe Whitehead, was not celebrating these talented young women of the new millennium. She was bemoaning their "plight." In *Why There Are No Good Men Left: The Romantic Plight of the New Single Woman,* Whitehead declares that far too many of these supposedly successful women have failed to find husbands.

Here, for example, is Whitehead's account of a woman from New York:

> This 42-year-old professional woman had lived together happily with her boyfriend for eight years. She had grown up in a warm, happy household and wanted to get married, but he had been scarred by his parents' divorce, and was skittish about marriage.... One night, as the couple was sitting on the couch eating mango sorbet, she turned to her guy and asked, "Bob, why won't you just marry me?"... He put his head on her lap and didn't answer.... The next day she went off as usual to her job as director of research at Fiduciary Trust Company in Tower Two of the World Trade Center, and that was the last time he saw her.

So, there you have it. Back in 1986, long before Americans could even fathom the possibility that terrorists might knock down the tallest towers in the land, college-educated women were being warned that if they did not marry by age forty, they were more likely to be killed by a terrorist than to find a husband. By the time of the actual September 11, 2001, attack, the cautionary tale turned deadly. The forty-something-year-old singleton who could not persuade her boyfriend to marry her actually was incinerated in a terrorist inferno.

Death by staying single is the explosive ending of Whitehead's morality play. But notice also all the little sparks she sets off along the way. The heroine had been raised in "a warm, happy household." She "wanted to get married." She was good. So were her parents. The guy, though, had parents who divorced. He was "scarred" by the experience and "skittish about marriage." He was bad. His parents were, too.

Think the mango sorbet was just a throw-in, to add a little color? Maybe it was another warning sign. The two singletons were career-oriented effete Easterners; blue staters, both. You cohabit and eat mango sorbet, you die. Should have gotten married and picked up half a gallon of chocolate chip at Safeway.

When a book offers to explain *Why There Are No Good Men Left,* you might expect to learn something about what's wrong with men. You do. But what's wrong with them turns out to be largely the fault of single women. Here's how Whitehead puts it:

> Today, single men don't have as much need for advice on how to get a college girl into bed. They can count on a pool of attractive peer women who are willing to sleep with them, compete over them, take care of them, spend money on them, and make no big demands on them.

Yes, Whitehead really is invoking that old adage about the cow that the single guy need not buy since the single gal is already letting him milk her for all she is worth. So, it is the single woman who is undisciplined and bad for letting the guy lap up all he wants without offering to be her bull forevermore.

Online, the publisher has lobbed a few more grenades of blame:

> . . . the exacting standards of educated women are leading them to stay single longer—and to find the search for a mate even harder when the time is right. From the frontlines of colleges, where dating is dead, to the trenches of corporate solitude, Whitehead reports on a wholesale shift that has stacked the marriage deck against the best and the brightest women.

The best and the brightest single women, by this account, are not showing good judgment, wisdom, or discretion in their search for a life partner;
instead, they are trotting out their "exacting standards" (more commonly
known as pickiness). They are not gleefully and triumphantly crashing
through the glass ceiling but slogging through "the trenches of corporate
solitude."

But Whitehead insists that she is not blaming individual single women,
even if she does seem to regard some of them as corporate drudges and others as bovine sluts. In her book even the good girls have not been rewarded
with their just desserts. For example, she notes that

> there are plenty of sexually conservative women who "aren't giving away
> the milk for free," but are just as discouraged by their search for a suitable
> man to marry as the women who are behaving like sexual dairy queens.

So, what's the problem?

Whitehead thinks there are two. First, there has been "an upheaval in
the mating system." The "epidemic of cohabitation," as the publisher calls
it, is part of it. (Notice the intimation of pestilence and scourge.)

The second problem is "the new life pattern" of today's single woman.
"She completes a four-year degree. She then goes on to graduate or professional school or enters the world of work, possibly to return to school a few
years later. If she is marriage-minded, she doesn't begin to focus on marriage until she reaches her late 20s." By then she may find that there are no
good men left; many have already been snagged by younger, more shapely
and seductive women.

So, should women go back to getting married when they are much
younger and only later attend to their education and careers? Whitehead
concedes that this is unlikely and even acknowledges that the early-to-wed
are more likely to divorce than those who wait. Instead, she says that it is
the system for meeting life partners that needs to be redesigned. Funny,
though, her book is not titled *Why the System for Meeting Life Partners
Needs to Be Redesigned*.

When single women with fabulous educations and sterling careers are being chased by the likes of Barbara Dafoe Whitehead, wagging her finger

and warning that in the man department they are going to end up empty-handed, you know the threat of an empty womb cannot be far behind. At the dawn of the millennium, Sylvia Ann Hewlett was on the scene with *Creating a Life: Professional Women and the Quest for Children*. Look no further than the dust jacket and you will learn that most professional women

> yearn for a child and are prepared to go to the ends of the earth to find a baby, often expending huge amounts of time, money and energy. But in the end, the age-old business of having babies eludes many. Modern women can be playwrights, politicians, and chief executives, but increasingly, they cannot be mothers.

In fact, "the more a woman succeeds in her career, the less likely it is that she will have a partner or a baby."

Unlike Whitehead, Hewlett does not even pretend to be evenhanded about the appropriate life paths of women who want careers and kids. "Give urgent priority to finding a partner," she warns. This is a project for your twenties, not later. Then start having kids right away. If you wait too long, you are setting yourself up for failure and "enormous regret." There is a "drastic fall-off in fertility," Hewlett warns, because as women age, they "run out of eggs." One more thing: Women who want to be moms should consider "avoiding professions with rigid career trajectories."

Armed with her warning that professionally successful women are at risk for ending up three eggs short of an omelet, Hewlett made the rounds. From the *Today* show in the morning through *The Oprah Winfrey Show* in the afternoon and on to *60 Minutes* and *NBC Nightly News* in the evening, her dirge filled the air. *Time* magazine even made it a cover story, "Babies vs. Career."

The only problem with Hewlett's thesis is that it is completely wrong. Economist Heather Boushey tested Hewlett's ideas using U.S. survey data from more than 33 million working women (compared with the 520 women in Hewlett's study). Importantly, Boushey also made the appropriate comparisons. Remember, Hewlett's claim is that "the more a woman succeeds in her career, the less likely it is that she will have a partner or a baby." The right way to test that claim is to compare high-achieving working women to other women working full-time rather than comparing them only with men (which is what Hewlett did). The results showed that high-achieving women are not any less likely to have married by age forty than are other women working full-time. Further, once married, high-achieving women are exactly as likely to have had children by age forty as other married women who work full-time. Single women in high-powered jobs are less likely to have children than other single women, but Hewlett is wrong even about them. Often they have no children by choice, not because they traveled to the ends of the earth in search of a baby and still couldn't find one.

Anyone who was alive and reading in 1991, and anyone who had taken a women's studies course any year thereafter, must have experienced a vague sense of familiarity as they felt the somber warnings of man shortages and barren wombs fall heavily upon them. We've been there before. We've heard all the horrible things that can happen to women who dare make their way in the world of work—especially those who have the audacity to go there and succeed brilliantly. They will be spouseless and childless unless they make a sharp turn and head right back home and into the arms of a man—where, let's face it, they truly belong. The person who debunked all such myths so brilliantly was Susan Faludi. Her book was called *Backlash: The Undeclared War Against American Women.* The title of Chapter 2 was "Man Shortages and Barren Wombs: The Myths of the Backlash." Whitehead and Hewlett are recycling the same old tired tales, and the take-home messages are just as excremental now as they were in 1991. Just because the media stepped right into it again does not mean that it doesn't stink.

Maybe because of Faludi's consciousness-raising, there were some glimmers of awareness this time around. Some people really do recognize a turd when they see one. Take, for example, Rachael Combe of *Elle* magazine. She opens her review of the Whitehead book like this:

> Before I say anything else about Barbara Dafoe Whitehead's new book, *Why There Are No Good Men Left: The Romantic Plight of the New Single Woman,* let me say this to every "new single woman" (which by Whitehead's definition is an unmarried, well-educated, successful woman in her twenties or thirties): They're just trying to scare you. Don't you dare panic, and don't you dare buy this book, because that would be falling right into their evil trap.

Hewlett was treated to an even higher-profile lampooning. She became the butt of a skit on *Saturday Night Live*.

As delicious as these come-uppances were (at least to me), they were not nearly enough to stem the rising tide of retribution meted out to single women who had succeeded. Read on for a sampling of the long line of single women taken to task for their achievements in this, the twenty-first century.

In 2001 Nicole Kidman, Meg Ryan, and Julia Roberts had a lot in common. They were all fabulously successful movie stars. Their success, however, is not what *People* magazine underscored in its screaming bold headline. EVERYTHING BUT LOVE, *People* panted. "Sure, they're rich and gorgeous. But that doesn't make it any easier to find a love that lasts."

Is the moral of the story not yet clear? Then continue reading inside the magazine. "They seem to have it all, but Julia Roberts, Meg Ryan, and Nicole Kidman struggle to find the right script for romance."

Well, so what? It is *People's* role to report breathlessly that behind the surface glitter of fame and fortune lies darkness and despair. That's what the magazine does. *Newsweek,* though, should be a bit less histrionic. There, perhaps, successful single women will be honored and recognized for their achievements.

The lead-in to the feature story is promising. "Black women," *Newsweek* claims, "are making historic strides on campuses and in the workplace." The story lists the accomplishments—more black women in college than ever before, more getting promoted in the workplace, names showing up on lists of officers of Fortune 500 companies. A photograph spread across two pages illustrates another success story: There were seven black women in the lab of just one veterinary school. "Today a black woman can be anything from an astronaut to a talk show host, run anything from a corporation to an Ivy League university."

How do single black women feel about their lives at this time of such inspiring successes? Author Ellis Cose wanted to know. He talked to a group of single black women who got together every Friday night. There was a big picture of them, too—four women (three of whom had downcast eyes and sullen expressions) and a cat. "The weekly gathering," Cose notes, "could easily be dubbed 'the black, beautiful, accomplished but can't find a mate club.'" He also talked to a single mom who "warns her daughters that they may end up on their own," and to a professor and advice columnist who worried that she "will die in a room all by myself."

Cose first repeats that the professional progress of black women has indeed been impressive. "Long confined to menial jobs, black women are advancing faster than black men—and many whites—in education, income, and careers." However, Cose continues, the new black woman is looking "not only for recognition but for 'models of happiness.'"

Will she find her happiness? "Is this new black woman finally crashing through the double ceiling of race and gender? Or is she leaping into treacherous waters that will leave her stranded, unfulfilled, childless, and alone? Can she thrive if her brother does not, if the black man succumbs, as hundreds of thousands already have, to the hopelessness of prison and the streets? Can she—dare she—thrive *without* the black man, finding happiness across the racial aisle? Or will she, out of compassion, loneliness or racial loyalty 'settle' for men who—educationally, economically, professionally—are several steps beneath her?"

Cose ends his story with a projection of two possible futures for the new black women. In the bleak vision, "more and more black women will lead lives of success but also isolation." In what he calls the more optimistic version, "black women are weathering a period of transition, after which they will find a way to balance happiness and success."

Ellis Cose is a serious, respected, and award-winning author and editor who has written book-length treatments on topics such as race in America. But in asking whether the new black woman is "leaping into treacherous waters that will leave her stranded, unfulfilled, childless, and alone," his rhetoric is about as hyperbolic as anything to leap out of *People* magazine. In fact, his moniker "the black, beautiful, accomplished but can't find a mate club" differs hardly at all from *People's* "Sure, they're rich and gorgeous. But that doesn't make it any easier to find a love that lasts."

Consider the choices Cose ascribes to the women of such great accomplishment. What are their alternatives to ending up stranded and unfulfilled? There is the guilt option: Maybe they can thrive, but meanwhile untold numbers of their black brothers are on the streets or in prison.

There is also the rescue possibility: Out of compassion, they can lower themselves to marry those poor brothers. Then there is the setup. We are led to believe that a free-spirited alternative is about to be unveiled—"Can she—dare she—thrive *without* the black man"—only to be let down. The thought is completed not with the possibility that successful black women can lead rich and full and happy lives without marrying, but instead with the option of "finding happiness across the racial aisle."

Think, too, about Cose's two visions. In one, black women end up successful but isolated. In the other, they end up balancing happiness and success. There is only one story here, and it is a familiar morality tale. Women's success in the workplace cannot bring happiness but needs to be "balanced" by happiness. Success is isolating. Happiness comes only from finding the One and then creating a family. Without marriage or family, the black woman (indeed, any woman) will, as the advice columnist feared, "die in a room all by [herself]."

There were other stories that could have been told, but they were hidden in plain view. There was, for example, the story of the four women who got together every Friday night. Cose describes them as lamenting the relationships they do not have. He does not seem to notice the relationships they do have. He does not seem to appreciate that even if these women do wed, their friendships with one another are more likely to endure than are their marriages. These women are not isolated and they are not alone. He does not know, nor do they, that hardly anyone is less likely to be lonely in old age than women who have always been single.

It is also telling that even though it is the single black men who are on the streets and in the prisons and failing to keep up educationally or professionally with the single black women, the hand-wringing in *Newsweek* is about the women. It is them whom we need to think about and wonder about.

Meanwhile, *Time* magazine was also having its say about women and work, and it was none too subtle, either. "Wedded to Work: A new book warns the career obsessed that their jobs won't love them back." That was the invitation that *Time* extended to its 4 million readers to partake of this modern-day version of a tired old morality tale. The author of *Married to the Job,* Ilene Philipson, is a psychotherapist who had treated nearly two hundred patients who were overcommitted to their jobs. Her patients spent long hours at work during the week, stayed productive and in touch electronically over the weekends, and developed intense loyalties to their bosses and coworkers, whom they often regarded as family.

Their jobs, however, were not always so loyal in return. Workers who had dedicated their lives to their jobs, sometimes even skipping vacations, were shocked to find themselves transferred, laid off, or shrugged off, even in the wake of work-related injuries. The malady, Philipson believes, is experienced primarily by women. As she told *Time,* "A lot of women I've seen have traded the anticipation of having security emotionally and economically through marriage to having security through work."

In closing, *Time* asked Philipson about her own life. She used to work fifty-five hours a week, she confessed. But now she is down to twenty-six. So does that mean she is happier? *Time* asked. "I'm getting married soon," she replied, "to a man, rather than my job."

Take one successful professional woman, subtract work, add husband, live happily ever after.

Larry King nailed it. Martha Stewart had just been sentenced to five months of jail time three days before, and now she was giving her first and only live interview since then on his show. It was not yet clear whether Stewart would let the appeal run its course and hope for victory and vindication, or begin serving time, the sooner to put prison behind her.

It was a sobering moment. Though hardly a universally beloved figure, Martha Stewart had become one of the most widely recognized public personas, and one of the most wildly successful businesswomen, in contemporary American society. She had a magazine with a circulation of over a million. She had a consulting and advertising contract with Kmart for several million dollars. She produced briskly selling books, videotapes, and CDs. Martha had appeared regularly on the *Today* show and launched her own syndicated show, recognized with many Daytime Emmy Awards. At the summit of Martha's success, Martha Stewart Living Omnimedia was a multimillion-dollar public enterprise. She was on everyone's top lists of most powerful this or most influential that. And now it could all come tumbling down. There was a lot to talk about.

Talk they did. Larry asked her about her feelings of fear and shame and regret. He asked her about the perverse delight that Americans seem to take in the wreckage of the rich and the famous. He wondered what she had learned during this difficult episode in her life, and what kept her going through it all. ("My work. My ideas. My family. My friends.") Callers wanted to know how hurt she was by the made-for-TV mocumetary of her life and how her eighty-nine-year-old mother was able to deal with it all.

Then there was this exchange:

LARRY KING: You once said business is your life.

MARTHA STEWART: My life is my business and my business is my life.

LARRY KING: Isn't that kind of sad in a way? I mean I know you love it and everything but . . .

MARTHA STEWART: Sad?

LARRY KING: Your life is your business?

MARTHA STEWART: Well, my business encompasses a lot of things that I do. I mean, all the things I love is what my business is all about. So that's not sad.

That snippet of the hour-long interview became its defining moment. Later that evening, on CNN's *NewsNight with Aaron Brown,* that exchange was the tease for the segment on the sentencing of Martha Stewart. Then the excerpt was shown on CNN Headline News, over and over again.

So that's what it all came down to. Not a stunningly successful career or the threat of its unraveling. Not the fear of prison, the ridicule in the press, or the lick of injustice in the juxtaposition of Martha Stewart in shackles and far more sinister scoundrels roaming free. No, what mattered is that a woman could love her work enough to call it her life. Now that was sad.

Next up, Barbara Walters.

Like Martha Stewart, Walters was a trailblazer and a cultural icon. She broke into broadcast journalism when women stayed behind the scenes, writing the words that men read on the air. But by the time she was interviewed on *Nightline* in September 2004, she had been the first television journalist to command a million-dollar salary. She had also interviewed Iraqi president Saddam Hussein, Russian presidents Boris Yeltsin and Vladimir Putin, Chinese premier Jiang Zemin, many Western leaders, and every American president since Richard Nixon. She coaxed Israeli prime minister Menachem Begin and Egyptian president Anwar Sadat into their first joint interview, and her historical hour-long interview with Cuban president Fidel Castro was broadcast around the world.

As fellow journalist Lesley Stahl has noted, Walters is also the one "who brought serious magazine journalism up against sitcoms and dramas and made it succeed." In 2004, after about four decades in the business, Barbara Walters was stepping down from just one of her posts—her role as anchor of the television newsmagazine *20/20*. To mark the occasion, Ted Koppel interviewed her as part of a *Nightline* program called "The Art of Conversation: Celebrating Barbara Walters."

At the top of the show, other icons from the world of broadcast journalism saluted Walters. Tom Brokaw, Diane Sawyer, Peter Jennings, Lesley Stahl, Morley Safer, Jane Pauley, and Sam Donaldson—they all had their say. *Nightline* was just a half-hour show, so that did not leave much time for the heart of the show, which was Koppel's one-on-one with his friend of twenty-five years.

Koppel asked whether journalism had gotten softer, now that movie stars seemed to be bigger "gets" than heads of state. He invited Walters to comment on her on-air longevity in a career in which women over fifty were once considered "dog meat." He encouraged her to reflect on the difficulties for women trying to break into serious television journalism so many years ago. Then Ted Koppel was ready to dig in and insist that Barbara Walters answer the question he seemed to care about most.

"Imagine," Koppel suggested, "someone is softly humming in the background 'Is That All There Is?' Was it worth it?"

Walters responded without hesitation. "Oh, yes. I never thought I'd have this kind of a life."

Koppel then brought up a brief time early in her career when Walters was in public relations. She was fired.

Still, Barbara Walters was not about to whine. "I've had an extraordinary life." Then, addressing what Koppel was obviously trying to get at, she added, "I have a very strong personal life. And I want some time to enjoy it."

Koppel reminded her that she had been married twice and divorced twice. "Was it the job?" he asked. "If it had not been for the job, would you still be married to one of those two men?"

Walters said she wasn't sure. But she had her daughter, and "she is absolutely wonderful."

Wrong answer. Koppel tried again. "Do you ever sometimes lie in bed at night and say, 'You know, maybe if I'd given up the job and focused on the family, that would have been—that would have been worth it'?"

No, she didn't.

Ted Koppel is a skillful and persistent interviewer. At the time of the broadcast, he had already won thirty-seven Emmy Awards and six Peabody Awards. But he could not get Barbara Walters to concede tearfully that her fancy job did not love her back and that she should have devoted herself to a husband instead of chasing down interviews with the most powerful leaders in the world.

He did, though, get his lead. As the show was about to begin, and ABC had just a few seconds to try to tempt viewers away from Jay Leno and David Letterman, it rolled the tape of just this one question: "If it had not been for the job, would you still be married to one of those two men?"

Single women who might like to have a husband and some children as well as pursue excellence in their careers or their passions are easy targets. To keep them in their place, simply dangle the threat that their achievements outside of the home may well undermine their chances of having their own family to gather around the hearth inside of a home.

But what about the single women who skate right past any such threats with utter aplomb? What's a singlistic society to do about them?

Let's consider a sparkling moment in the life of Svetlana Khorkina. The year was 2004. Svetlana was an internationally renowned athlete, at the show-case event for the best athletes in the world, the Olympics. Plus she was competing in women's gymnastics, the sport that has about as much prestige and showstopping drama as any.

Svetlana was intense. She had been practicing her grueling craft for about twenty of her twenty-five years and had a raft of medals to show for it. She was older than most of the other Olympic gymnasts, and taller, too—both impediments to gymnastic success. They must have seemed like trivial obstacles relative to the cruel fate that tripped her up at the Olympic Games four years earlier. Astonishingly, the vault had been set at the wrong height. Svetlana fell, was unnerved more than she was hurt, and never did win the gold in the all-round competition that just moments before seemed to be hers for the taking.

When 2004 rolled around, she was psyched. So, too, were the broadcasters assigned to cover women's gymnastics. With their day-to-day close-ness to the athletes and the thrill of a sporting extravaganza, they of all peo-ple should get it about what a gold medal means to athletes like Svetlana.

So, when one broadcaster proclaimed, in promoting an upcoming seg-ment, "You won't believe what she [Svetlana] has to say about how much she wants to win," I was indeed curious. The sense of astonishment in his voice suggested that the interview to come would offer more than the usual prepackaged blather.

"I want to win a gold medal as much as I want to mother my own child."

That's what Svetlana said. That's what sent the NBC sports reporter over the edge.

Why was he so upset? More than that, why was he even surprised? Svet-lana had trained for the gold—yearned for the gold—for decades. If the broadcaster had any familiarity with contemporary demographics, he would have known that many women do not want children at all—and not because they want Olympic medals more.

They are a threat, though—these women who do not want children. They are beyond the reach of the horror stories peddled by Sylvia Ann Hewlett and her ilk. If you don't want kids, you are not frightened by the prospect of losing eggs as you age. But you are plenty disturbing to those who would like to think that there is nothing a woman should ever crave more than mothering.

The NBC sportscaster did not even try to talk Svetlana into a more sen-timental position. But he did make his own position clear. Caring no more about mothering than about becoming the most accomplished person in the world in a sport that you adore—that's just shocking.

Single women who perform superbly at their jobs or their avocations are prime targets for singlism. But they are not the only targets. Just about any single woman can be turned into an object of pity.

Consider, for example, some musings by Cheryl Jarvis. She penned them while enjoying the marriage sabbatical that would become the topic and title of her book:

> I think of the many conversations I've had with single friends over the years, who moaned about the lack of sexual intimacy in their lives, maybe

for one year, maybe for three. These confidences always intrigued me because they were so removed from my own experience, where the opportunity to make love was almost always an arm's-length away.

Pity the poor single women don't get any. How intriguing. Especially when compared with married women, who at any moment can simply roll over and dig in.

Jarvis is not just smug, though. She is also worried. Or at least she would be if she had scheduled her sabbatical during warmer weather. "I was glad," she writes, "that I'd be away during the winter when the beautiful single woman in the neighborhood wouldn't be outside in her shorts."

The sexy, scantily clad singleton is not so easy to dismiss as pitiful. She can, though, be cast as a dangerous, promiscuous predator. Jarvis is simply spouting stereotypes. Single women are either sniveling about their celibacy or recklessly pursuing sex in all the wrong places. Apparently there is little room in the mythology of singlehood for women who are getting exactly the amount and kind of sex that they desire—including, for some single women, no sex at all.

Most single women do not achieve the pinnacle of success of a Svetlana Khorkina, Martha Stewart, or Barbara Walters. Many would not, when outside in their shorts, be alluring bait for the husband whose usual source of sexual indulgence is away on sabbatical in Montana. So, what about the single women who are not seeking sex, success, celebrity, husbands, or babies? Can they get credit for a pure and simple life, which they may in fact find completely satisfying?

I found a portrait of one such woman in a short story, "The Disappearance of Elaine Coleman," by Steven Millhauser. It appeared in *The New Yorker* in November 1999.

Elaine Coleman is a single woman who rents two rooms on the second floor of a home in a small New England town. She always pays her rent on time, never has visitors, and never misses a day of work. One day she seems to disappear without a trace. Her key chain with the silver kitten is left on the kitchen table, as is her wallet with her money. Her coat is on the back of the chair.

Local reporters try to find people who know Elaine. Former coworkers can suggest only that she is "a quiet woman, polite, a good worker. She seemed to have no close friends." Her mother, who has moved to California, says that "she didn't have a mean bone in her body." Her father, who has moved on alone from California to Oregon, is not quoted.

The narrator thinks he may have been in the same English class in high school with Elaine, but neither he nor his classmates can summon any distinct memories. "She had joined no clubs, played no sports, belonged to nothing." He keeps thinking about Elaine and trying to remember her. He recalls a time when he was at a movie with a woman he was dating and another couple, and thinks that a woman in dark clothes in the far aisle may have been Elaine. A dream reminds him of a party he attended as a teenager, in which a girl with her hands in her lap may have been Elaine. He remembers vividly "the dazzling knees of Lorraine Palermo in sheer stockings," but he has no image of the face of Elaine. The narrator also describes a time when he was advising his friend Roger on strategies for attracting the girl with whom he was infatuated. On their walk the boys passed a girl who was playing basketball by herself; perhaps that was Elaine.

The police, along with just about all the town citizens, try to come up with solutions to the mystery of Elaine's disappearance, but none fit the facts. A sentimental favorite is that Elaine, "alone, friendless, restless, unhappy, and nearing her thirtieth birthday . . . had at last overcome some inner constriction and surrendered herself to the lure of adventure." Ultimately, however, the narrator comes to believe that "Elaine Coleman did not disappear suddenly, as the police believed, but gradually, over the course of time . . . the quiet, unremarkable girl whom no one noticed must at times have felt herself growing vague, as if she were gradually being erased by the world's inattention." On her last night, "she turned on the lamp and tried to read. Her eyes, heavy-lidded, began to close. . . . The next day there was nothing but a nightgown and a paperback on a bed."

The narrator brings the story to a close with these thoughts:

> She is not alone. On street corners at dusk, in the corridors of dark movie theatres, behind the windows of cars in parking lots at melancholy shopping centers . . . you sometimes see them, the Elaine Colemans of this world. They lower their eyes, they turn away, they vanish into shadowy places. . . . And perhaps the police, who suspected foul play, were not in the end mistaken. For we are no longer innocent, we who do not see and

do not remember, we incurious ones, we conspirators in disappearance. I too murdered Elaine Coleman. Let this account be entered in the record.

Onto the fictional Elaine Coleman was affixed just about every stereotype of women who are single. She was suffused in darkness—dark movie theaters, melancholy shopping centers, dusky street corners, shadowy corridors. She even wore dark clothes. She had the pathologies that come with the dark aura—the unhappiness, the restlessness, the "inner constriction." But she was also unbearably light and insignificant—so light, in fact, that she vanished into thin air.

Elaine was, of course, alone. Improbably so. She had gone to a small college and had worked at a restaurant, a post office, a local paper, and a coffee shop. She may have been in the same high school English class as the narrator, every day for a year. Yet somehow she is friendless. Actually, she is beyond friendless: Most people cannot even picture her face. Her mother does not rush back to the East Coast upon learning of her daughter's mysterious disappearance, but instead simply comments that Elaine didn't have a mean bone in her body.

The narrator, in contrast, is coupled and self-important. At the movie theater he is with a date, and the two of them are with another couple. When he is strolling with his friend Roger past the house that may have been Elaine's, he is instructing Roger on how to lure the woman who intrigues him. The narrator can vividly recall the "dazzling knees" of a girl who once interested him, but he cannot picture Elaine's face. He even assigns himself blame for Elaine's murder, as he counts himself as among those "who do not see and do not remember" the Elaine Colemans of the world. If only he had blessed Elaine with the most insignificant of his attentions—looking at her and actually seeing her, for example—he could have been her savior. The single woman, insignificant though she was, could have been alive today.

CHAPTER EIGHT

Myth #6 Attention, Single Men

You Are Horny, Slovenly, and Irresponsible, and You Are the Scary Criminals. Or, You Are Sexy, Fastidious, Frivolous, and Gay.

Have you heard the one about the single man and the married man? The single man asks his married friend, "Do you think there is anything in the theory that married men live longer than unmarried ones?" The married man thinks for a moment and says, "Oh, I don't know—seems longer."

The quip is an enduring one, having been printed and reprinted for more than a century. It captures a distinctly male mythology of marriage and singlehood. It is men, not women, who make snide remarks about being snagged, trapped, and hounded into marrying.

Even in the days when single women were more often tarred as spinsters and old maids than they are now, there were no comparably derogatory terms for single men. They were bachelors. Still are. In the same year that *People* magazine headlined its special issue on single women movie stars EVERYTHING BUT LOVE, it splashed a rather different banner on the cover when the featured celebrities were single men: SEXY, SINGLE, SIZZLING.

Single men are rarely warned that their jobs won't love them back or that their sperm will dry up if they do not hurry up and get married. The cover of *Time* magazine has never taunted them with the dilemma of "Babies vs. Career." And I've never read a short story about a single man that ended with him mysteriously ceasing to exist.

And yet the image of the single man is hardly unblemished. He is ridiculed, too, just as single women are, but for different reasons.

It was July of 2003 and movie star Johnny Depp was on the cover of *USA Weekend* magazine. Depp was the star of the soon-to-be-released *Pirates of the Caribbean.* Disney had dibs on Depp to steer the movie into the cool summer theaters and make off with all the hot ticket sales.

Depp already had some quirky successes under his sash, having starred "in a series of strong, offbeat movie roles" such as in *Edward Scissorhands* and *What's Eating Gilbert Grape.* The mainstream liked him. In *The New York Times,* Janet Maslin wrote that Depp brings "soulfulness and strength" to his roles. *Salon* observed that "from his earliest performances, he showed a depth beyond his years." *Salon* also observed that "his girlfriends, most notably Winona Ryder and Kate Moss, have been fairly long-term." Depp did not seem to fit the caricature of the flighty, superficial celebrity—nor of the immature bachelor sowing his wild oats, for that matter.

USA Weekend told the Depp story a different way:

> The early line on his career held that he was bound for self-destruction. He was expected to date one too many supermodels, develop a drinking or drug problem, destroy too many hotel rooms, attack too many paparazzi, alienate one too many producers and end up as a better-looking version of Mickey Rourke, unable to find meaningful work.
>
> Instead he fell in love.

Now Depp is "a doting dad playing Barbies on the floor with his four-year-old daughter while he gives his baby boy a bottle early on a Sunday morning." The three of them, plus mom Vanessa Paradis, actress and singer, live in a tiny village in the south of France. When Hollywood producers have feature roles to offer Depp, they go to him. Depp especially liked the idea of a pirate movie because his kids, he said, "should get a kick out of it."

Depp, we are told, "occasionally orders $18,000 bottles of wine in restaurants." In a sidebar, we also learn that "Depp has a habit he can't shake: reading. He reads four or five books at a time." Mostly, though, he is "smitten with his children."

Depp was also smitten with the life he had created for himself once Vanessa and the kids became a part of it. Referring to the earlier years when he was earning respect for his strong performances in smaller films, Depp said that, without a family, they amounted to "a total waste of time." He added, "I literally feel as though I didn't have a life."

The Depp story stretched to fill up two pages only with the help of five pictures and a sidebar. Yet it conveyed nearly every key element of the reigning morality tale about men who are single. First, we learn what is wrong with single men. They are irresponsible and their lives are chaotic. They need to settle down. Next, a quick lesson on how to make that happen: Find love, have kids. Then some advice on how to think about the "before" and "after" versions of the man and his life. Everything that came before love and kids can be demeaned and dismissed. Once a bachelor has been transformed by a soulmate and some kids, then his new and improved life is all about them.

Note how the magazine describes the "before" version of Depp in a way that creates the starkest of contrasts with what is to come. The prefamily Depp was painted as a drunken, drug-abusing, paparazzi-pounding lout, more likely to end up donning mouse ears at Disney's theme parks than a pirate hat as the leading man in the movie division. Louthood was *USA Weekend*'s projection of where Johnny Depp was headed, had he not been saved by a family.

Depp himself joined in the fun. *The New York Times* may have been taken by the soulfulness of his earlier acting, and *Salon* may have been impressed with his "depth beyond his years," but to Depp, all that was "a total waste of time." Now that he had Vanessa and the kids, he finally had a life—an "after" life.

The family-focused "after" version of Depp, though, is an artfully edited construction. We get to see the touching tableau of Depp on the floor with the babies and Barbies, but all else is excised. Was Depp in the picture in the moments before, when the kids may have been tired, cranky, and not yet changed? We don't know. When producer Jerry Bruckheimer comes calling, does Daddy Depp pack up the Barbies and the babies and take them with him, or does he kiss them good-bye and head to the States for as long as it takes to make *Pirates*? We don't know that, either.

Notice, also, how each of the details of Depp's life has been interpreted by the reporter to fit the script of the good and decent family man, when other frames would have been equally plausible. The hugely significant career decision to make the leap from offbeat films to summer blockbusters? Well, the kids "should get a kick out of" a pirate movie. Those outlandishly expensive bottles of wine that he orders? They are not suggestive of liking the spirits a bit too much, nor even of self-centered splurges (those are bachelor issues), but a symbol of a man who has arrived. Depp's voracious reading, though, didn't quite fit into the family album. The magazine called it "a habit he can't shake," as if it, too, should have been left in the dust with Depp's strong, soulful renderings of poignant and quirky characters.

In the current quest to valorize men who play with babies, there is an admirable corrective. A few generations back, the only dolls that dads got caught playing with were the ones from the office. At home they did not need to have a soft, communicative side. In fact, many who fit the role of the strong, silent type were revered for it. If they seemed a bit too driven to succeed at work, well, that, too, could be construed as dedication to the breadwinner role.

So it is laudable that many men care more than they did before about the important people in their lives, including the tiniest ones. But I do not think they honor their partners, their children, themselves, or anyone else when they disown everything that lies beyond the family circle. Depp was once part of a fine tradition of filmmaking that thrives outside of the major studios. Why can't he be proud of the work that he did back then, and respectful of that community of artists? And why can't the magazine express admiration, rather than exasperation, for Depp's love of books?

Perhaps *USA Weekend* should be forgiven for predicting that Johnny Depp would have led a drunken and wanton life had he not met the woman of his dreams and had a couple of kids. Bachelors have long been regarded that way, and not just in the popular press. When I first started searching for academic writings on bachelors, I found a 1977 article in a sociology journal titled "Working Without a Net: The Bachelor as a Social Problem." The "net" that bachelors lack is marriage. Without wives to keep them in check, they are at risk of spinning out of control. With no restraints, who knows what they might do with their time? Therein lies the "social problem": Bachelors may be up to no good.

More than two decades later Linda Waite and Maggie Gallagher—you may remember them from Chapter 2—were hawking the same wares. They, too, described bachelors as behaving badly. In a section of their book called "The Wild Lives of Single Men," they claimed that the health benefits of marriage for men can be summarized with a snappy slogan:

fewer stupid bachelor tricks. Married men are healthier, Waite and Gallagher insist, because wives "discourage drinking, smoking, and speeding" and also cook with less fat and cholesterol and serve more vegetables and fruit. (Yes, this book in which the women's place is in the kitchen really was published in the year 2000.) Single men, in contrast, go on living their "warped lives."

Already there are problems with the Waite and Gallagher analysis. First, as I show in Chapter 2, getting married does not generally make men (or women) healthier. Second, if married men are getting fed fruits, vegetables, and low-fat and low-cholesterol meals, and single men are not, then why did the CDC study (also from Chapter 2) show that the married men are fatter?

But it made for a good story. "Wedded life boosts husbands' health," declared MSNBC on its website. Next to the heading was a picture of a grinning groom and his veiled bride. Then came the story, including this: "Researchers have long documented that marriage is good for health, particularly for men's. Left on our own, we eat poorly, carouse too much, drive too fast."

Waite and Gallagher seem especially enamored with their proclamation that single men are alcohol abusers. They noted, for example, that, compared to married men, "single men drink almost twice as much." In Chapter 2, I presented the data collected by the CDC at just one point in time. Four percent of the currently married Americans were heavy drinkers, as were 5 percent of the people who were currently widowed or had always been single, and 8 percent of the people who were divorced or separated. Drinking, though, is more a guy thing—and single men, much more so than single women, are likely to be characterized as drunken fools—so it could be instructive to look at the numbers separately for men and for women. In a 2002 paper Robin Simon did just that. Better still, she got back in touch with the 8,161 Americans five years later and found out whether their marital status had changed.

Look at the table to see what she found. The numbers show the percentage of people in each category who had a drinking problem. The first thing to notice is how low all these numbers are. No matter whether they are men or women, married or single, no group ever reaches double digits in problem drinking. (The CDC found that, too.) And in every marital status category, women report fewer drinking problems than men do.

Percentage of People with a Drinking Problem		
Current and Future Marital Status	Men	Women
Married, will stay married	2.3	.3
Widowed, will stay widowed	2.9	.6
Has always been single, will stay single	3.7	1.1
Single, but will marry within five years	3.7	1.4
Married, but will divorce within five years	4.1	1.0
Divorced or separated, will stay that way	8.2	1.1

From Simon (2002). A total of 8,161 Americans participated.

Let's focus on the men and their marital status. At first glance, marriage looks good for sobriety. Men who were married when first asked and were still married five years later were the least likely to report having a drinking problem. Was it because, as Waite and Gallagher believe, they had wives in place who would "discourage drinking"? The men who were widowed for all five years had no wives, but their rate was almost as low as the men who were married the whole time. But they were older, too, so maybe that's why they were so sober.

A better comparison is the men who stayed single the whole time: 3.7 percent of them had drinking problems, compared with 2.3 percent of the men who stayed married. You could say, as do Waite and Gallagher, that "single men drink almost twice as much as married men." But look at those numbers: just over 2 percent, compared with just under 4 percent. That's what "almost twice as much" drinking means. Both scholarly and popular writings delight in this sleight of mind. Start with a bad or sad state of affairs, characteristic of very few people, such as problem drinking or severe mental illness or even murdering people. Show that one group is badder or sadder than another. Note that the problematic group is twice or three times or ten times badder or sadder than the good group. If the base rate is low enough, even a tenfold difference may not be that big at all. With regard to the specific problem of drinking too much, even in the group of men most likely to be inebriated, more than 90 percent of them did not have a drinking problem.

Let's look more closely at the wife theory. Another group of men who had a wife in place were those who were currently married but headed toward divorce. Their rate of problem drinking was a tad higher than that of men who never did have a wife (4.1 percent, as opposed to 3.7 percent). The men with the highest rate of problem drinking were not those who never had a wife, but those who once had a wife and then divorced. Of the men who were divorced when the study began and were still divorced five years later, 8.2 percent had a drinking problem.

Waite and Gallagher would have you believe that the divorced men were drinking because they had no wife to keep them on the wagon. But then why were they more likely to have a drinking problem than the men who never had a wife? Maybe because they were different people, and neither marriage nor divorce has anything to do with drinking.

Here's another possibility. Perhaps wives really do pressure men to drink less. Maybe some husbands take to the new norm just fine. They get used to drinking less, and it takes no special effort to continue to do so. They could be the men who account for the drop in problem drinking from 3.7 percent for bachelors to 2.3 percent for married men. Other men, though, are chafing at the restraints. Maybe they manage to keep their drinking in check as long as they are married, but it is a struggle. Once divorced and released from the pressure to abstain, they do not simply go back to their bachelor levels (3.7 percent), but beyond (8.2 percent). It is similar to what happens when you have tried too long to stay on a diet that was intolerable. Once you let yourself off the hook, you do not go back to your ordinary eating habits, you pig out. Maybe you would have been better off never trying that diet at all.

I'll mention just one other alternative to the wifely watchdog point of view. It arose from an analysis of an extraordinary database—a collection of information on nearly sixteen thousand pairs of male twins who were born between 1917 and 1927 and subsequently served in the U.S. Army. In 1972 both members of nearly five thousand of those pairs responded to survey questions about their health habits and marital status. Twin studies are important in that they tell us something about genetic predisposition. What the veterans study showed was that marriage did not generally save men from behaving badly when it came to their own health. Instead, in some ways, marriage magnified men's genetic tendencies. Men who were predisposed to becoming a smoker were even more likely to smoke if they were married than if they were unmarried. Similarly, men who were genetically predisposed not to smoke were even less likely to smoke if they were married than if they were not. The same was true for eating fruits and vegetables. Marriage magnified whatever direction the men were already headed. Once again, the bottom line is more complex (and, I think, more interesting) than Waite and Gallagher's simplistic "get married, get healthy" mantra.

As Bill Clinton settled into his second term as president of the United States, it was not at all clear that the person who would emerge from the other side of the aisle to vie for the presidency in the year 2000 would be George W. Bush. A far more intriguing prospect for the Republican nomination was General Colin Powell.

As chairman of the Joint Chiefs of Staff for the first President Bush during the Gulf War of 1991, Powell had achieved national and international prominence and respect. A few years later he took a step that often signals an intention to run for the highest office in the land: He wrote his autobiography. *My American Journey* soared to the number one spot on national bestseller lists. As Bob Woodward would note years later, Powell "was poised at the epicenter of American politics, with stratospheric poll ratings, the Republican nomination nearly his for the asking, and the presidency within reach."

Then suddenly the music stopped. On November 12, 1997, Colin Powell declared definitively that he would not run for president in 2000.

What happened? There is probably never just one accounting for such a momentous decision. There was, however, one piece of the explanation that was never denied, not even by Powell. Alma Powell would not stand for it. Woodward claims that Mrs. Powell issued her husband an ultimatum: "If you run, I'm gone."

Colin Powell, had he run in 2000, was in a position to be the ultimate uniter. He was a Republican embraced by Democrats, and an African American adored across the lines of color and creed. In a nation never quite at peace with issues of race, the mere presence of an African American atop the Republican ticket could have offered hope for a better and less fractious country. Instead, the 2000 election split the electorate nearly down the middle, and the candidate with the short end of the popular vote took the White House. Four years later even more Americans were passionate about politics, but as many seemed driven to the polls by scorn for the opposing candidate as by unmitigated devotion to their own.

Alma Powell alone did not change the history of the nation or the world. It is possible, though, that she had some small role in the events that unfolded at the turn of the twenty-first century.

When I hear scholars and pundits claim that single men lead "warped lives" until they marry and become magically transformed; when I read that bachelors "eat poorly, carouse too much, drive too fast"; and when I am treated to the thousandth rendition of the morality tale of how a young and foolish George W. Bush was saved from a life of alcoholism and recklessness by the firm admonitions of wife Laura, I remember Colin and Alma Powell. I think about what might have been, had it not been for the restraint of a spouse.

Speeding, drinking, smoking, and eating all the wrong things are among the most popular features of the wanton bachelor caricature. They anchor the middle range of ridicule. Over on the more innocuous end of the scale are the notions that single men are either slovenly and undomesticated or soft and mushy mama's boys. On the more sinister side is the expectation that if there is a scary criminal out there, he is probably single. All the problems that are pinned on the tails of bachelors have one thing in common: They can all be solved by getting married. I'll begin with the innocuous.

In *The New Yorker* in March 2004, Christopher Caldwell reviewed a book called *The Paradox of Choice*. The book argues that too much choice is not always a good thing. The paradox, Caldwell suggests, helps explain

> why so many marriageable singles wind up alone. You await a spouse who combines the kindness of your mom, the wit of the smartest person you met in grad school, and the looks of someone you dated in 1983 (as she was in 1983) . . . and you wind up spending middle age by yourself, watching the Sports Channel at 2 A.M. in a studio apartment strewn with pizza boxes.

What I really care about here are those strewn pizza boxes. After all, I did promise to start with the silly stuff. But first a word about the weightier nonsense. A man who was in graduate school in 1983 is probably in his late forties by 2004. A man who was in graduate school has a graduate education. What is he doing in a studio apartment? Can't he at least afford a separate bedroom, not to even mention a house? And didn't his advanced degree land him a job? If so, what's he still doing up watching racing reruns at 2 A.M.? And did we really need a whole new book to generate the suggestion that a person who is single in middle age is probably just too picky?

Okay, on to the pizza boxes. Which guy is more likely to be living among strewn pizza boxes: A middle-aged bachelor with a graduate education, or a married man with a house full of kids? Logic, though, has little to do with this. Bachelors are deemed disgusting slobs almost by definition.

For a story posted on the website msnbc.com, a reporter collected complaints that married and single people had about each other. She was especially enamored of a married man who had this to say: "Sorry, but belching guys with barbecue sauce on their fingers are no match for a glass of wine and a wife in a silky red teddy." The reporter wondered wistfully whether the guy had any brothers.

Maybe the man who lodged the complaint was himself a grimy burping pig back when he was a bachelor. But he has had a magical marital transformation. Now he has wine, a wife, sensuality, and sex.

A different story on the same website explains why marriage is (supposedly) so good for men: "There's the security of a refrigerator with actual food in it, and the promise of regular sex."

The foodless refrigerator is a staple in the parody of the lives of single men. Remember the story about the census worker appearing at the door of a solo dweller, and all the resident would have to offer would be a beer or a sip of sour milk?

So what's it all about? A nearly empty refrigerator suggests a transitory existence. Its owner is not settled down. He can cut and run anytime. He needs a wife to fill it up and weigh it down, so it won't move—and neither will the guy who raids it. (And, of course, she will fill it with fruits and vegetables.) The mindless melding of foodlessness and sexlessness is also telling. Single men, it seems to suggest, simply have no sustenance.

In 2005 "lost another loan to Ditech" became one of those refrains repeated ad nauseam on a series of interrelated television commercials. The poor guy who loses one home loan after another to his competitor is an unnamed doughy boy-man. His suits are ill fitting, his voice is singsongy, and his pudgy fingers are clearly ringless. In some of the ads, his mother appears, as he calls her or visits her.

In one version, a neat and trim couple comes to see Dough Boy. They sit in swivel chairs in front of his desk, facing a window with the blinds pulled down. Dough Boy raises the blinds to let in a little light, and lo and behold, a huge billboard advertising great rates from Ditech appears in the window. When he turns away from the window, he sees the two chairs spinning, with no one left sitting in them. The respectable twosome has hightailed it toward the couples-friendly arms of Ditech.

In another variant, Dough Boy is lying on a couch in his therapist's office, whining about losing another loan to Ditech. His therapist tiptoes over to his computer and goes to the Ditech website to get his own loan there. Still another ad ends with Dough Boy plaintively wailing, "Mommm!!" Even his own mother has gone to Ditech for her home loan.

A real adult man, who is lean, handsome, and successful, can have only one woman in his life. That woman is not Mom.

Some serial killers take a very long time to catch. One such person was Dennis Rader, who was not arrested until thirty-one years after he had murdered the first of his ten victims. Rader christened himself the BTK killer, because he bound, tortured, and killed his victims. Days after he was apprehended in February 2005, *Newsweek* remarked that "Rader would seem an unlikely serial-killer suspect. Far from a shadowy loner, he is married with two grown children and was active in his church." The *Los Angeles Times* noted that "BTK's habit of collecting souvenirs from his victims led some investigators to suspect he was single because they thought he would be unlikely to keep macabre trophies in a home where a wife or children could stumble across them."

On one side is a churchgoing married man with a house full of kids; on the other is a shadowy murderous loner whose doorstep is never darkened by any other human. The juxtaposition is an entrenched favorite among reporters and pundits. Three years earlier television host Nancy Grace asked criminologist Jack Levin to speculate about the characteristics of the person or persons who were then terrifying the residents of the Washington, D.C., area with their apparently random shooting spree. Levin mentioned the possibility of a wife. Grace was flabbergasted. "How many serial killers actually go home to a wife and a family and a dog and a white picket fence?" she asked incredulously. "You're stretching even my vivid imagination with the wife mention."

Levin reminded Grace of John Wayne Gacy, the married man who murdered thirty-three men and buried many of them in the crawl space under his home while his wife remained clueless. He could have mentioned other high-profile married serial murderers as well, such as the Hillside Strangler, Kenneth Bianchi. Even more compellingly, Levin could have informed Grace and the television audience of a chapter he had coauthored several years before. It was called "Serial Murderers: Popular Myths and Empirical Realities." Myth #2 is "serial killers are unusual in appearance and lifestyle." The empirical reality is that many "hold full-time jobs, are married or involved in some other stable relationship, and are members of various local community groups."

Serial murderers are among the most terrifying criminals believed to be bachelors. But all manner of male miscreants come under suspicion if they are not married, and they are protected from innuendo if they are. Take Arnold Schwarzenegger, for example. In the fall of 2003 he was best known as a brawny action hero on the silver screen. What he really wanted, though, was a whole new role as governor of California. He was a candidate in a historic recall election in which dozens of hopefuls were vying to unseat the current governor. There was, at the time, one looming obstacle. Actually, fifteen of them. That's how many women claimed that Arnold had behaved inappropriately toward them—groping them, fondling them, and spanking them. Television reporters tossed the topic around, and some trolled the streets to see what ordinary citizens thought of the allegations. Said one unnamed man, "He's married. He's got a wife. I don't think he's a pervert or anything."

Even the really small stuff has different meanings if it comes from the mouth of a man who is married rather than from one who is not. A friend who was having renovations done in her home regaled a table of dinner guests with stories of the carpenter. Whenever the tiniest thing went wrong, he would spew forth a string of expletives. Were you afraid of him? someone asked. "Oh, no!" she replied. "He's married and has kids."

I have been describing specific men such as the carpenter, the governor, and the BTK killer. Seeing single men more darkly than married men, though, seems to be a pervasive phenomenon. In a nationally representative sample of three thousand adults, single men were more likely than married or cohabiting men to say that in their everyday lives other people act as if they are afraid of them.

Decades after sociologists described bachelors as "a social problem," evolutionary psychologists outlined their understanding of the link between marriage and mayhem. Like the sociologists, they believed that single men might run amok and needed to marry in order to be pacified. To this thesis, scholars such as Robert Wright have added a potent motive. Single men are murderous, Wright claims, because they are fighting for their genetic lives.

What men really want, according to Wright, is access to women—fertile ones, specifically. Married men already have that access, so their genes have ample opportunities to skip merrily into successive generations. To seize similar potentialities for themselves and their genes, single men kill the competition. Literally. Wright notes that "an unmarried man between the ages of twenty-four and thirty-five years of age is about three times as likely to murder another male as is a married man the same age."

A single man does not stop at killing other men, says Wright.

He is also more likely to incur various risks—committing robbery, for example—to gain the resources that may attract women. He is more likely to rape. More diffusely, a high-risk, criminal life often entails the abuse of drugs and alcohol, which may then compound the problem by further diminishing his chances of ever earning enough money to attract women by legitimate means.

So what are the implications?

It is not crazy to think that there are homeless alcoholics and rapists who, had they come of age in a pre-1960s social climate, amid more equally distributed female resources, would have early on found a wife and adopted a lower-risk, less destructive lifestyle.

One reason "female resources" are not being distributed more equally these days, Wright believes, is the high rate of divorce. According to his analysis, when a high-status man first marries, he monopolizes the fertile years of his young wife. If he then divorces, he moves on to another young woman. By then he has monopolized more than his share of female fertility and has left a less fortunate man wifeless.

Therefore, claims Wright, "a drop in the divorce rate, by making more young women accessible to low-income men, might keep an appreciable number of men from falling into crime, drug addiction, and sometimes homelessness."

It is easy to make fun of the notion that a man can walk up the aisle a homeless, alcoholic, drug-addicted, woman-groping thief, rapist, and murderer; pause at the altar long enough to say, "I do"; and return an upstanding citizen and CEO. Maybe too easy. So I had better put a few disclaimers up front.

I'm not challenging the evolutionary perspective on human behavior. It is not as if I think some intelligent omnipotent creator put the world together in a matter of days, then sat back to admire the design. Instead, I want to point out some of the ways in which single men have been subtly disparaged in Wright's analysis and probably in others like it.

Let's start with the murder statistic: "An unmarried man between the ages of twenty-four and thirty-five years of age is about three times as likely to murder another male as is a married man the same age." Murder is, fortunately, a very rare event. Far rarer than, say, problem drinking. Annual rates vary over time, but for the United States, one homicide for every ten thousand citizens would not be a bad guess. If single men really were three times as likely as married men to commit homicide, the difference in real raw numbers would not be all that big. Ultimately, no matter how you frame it, very few single (or married) men are murderers.

Notice, though, that Wright's claim is not that single men are three times more likely than married men to murder people. It is far more specific. One particular age range is selected: twenty-four to thirty-five. And only male victims are included. Wright is arguing that men are killing the competition for fertile women, and other men are the competition, so the sex restriction is appropriate as far as it goes.

But by the time Wright offers up his parting prediction, that "making more young women accessible" to men "might keep an appreciable number of [them] from falling into crime," he no longer seems to be limiting the lawlessness to crimes against men.

So, let's look at crimes against women. In November 2000 the National Institute of Justice released the findings from the National Violence

Against Women Survey. Here is the key finding, based on responses from eight thousand American women and a comparison group of eight thousand men:

> Violence against women is primarily intimate partner violence: 64.0 percent of the women who reported being raped, physically assaulted, and/or stalked since age 18 were victimized by a current or former husband, cohabiting partner, boyfriend, or date.

In any given year, that amounts to about 1.8 million American women who experience violence at the hands of intimate partners. (Among men, 16.2 percent who were targets of violence were victimized by an intimate partner. That's about one million per year.)

Remember that scare story from the 1980s about how women who reached the age of forty and had not yet married were more likely to be killed by a terrorist than to find a husband? It was false. But perhaps a different version is true. Once a woman does find an intimate partner, she is more likely to be harmed by him than by a terrorist.

Of course, not all intimate partners are partners in marriage. Maybe the high rates of intimate partner violence can get pinned on partners who are not officially married. Rates of violence are in fact higher among cohabitors than among married spouses. Perhaps that is because cohabiting partners who are violent are especially unlikely to go on to marry—which to me sounds wise.

When intimate-partner violence is compared across different marital status categories at one point in time, the results are similar to what we have seen for problem drinking and health and happiness. Violence is most common among those who were once married and are now separated and divorced, not among those who have always been single. A woman who leaves her husband to live elsewhere is especially at risk. She is far more likely to be tracked down and murdered by her husband than her husband is to be slain by her if he leaves. Again, though, overall rates of homicide are low.

The most compelling approach to the study of the pacifying effect of marriage on men is to follow men over time as they transition out of bachelorhood and into marriage. For twenty-five years, starting in 1940, a team of researchers did just that. They started with a group of five hundred delinquent fourteen-year-old boys, and a comparison group of five hundred same-age nondelinquents. Did the delinquent boys who married become less lawless? Actually, they did, gradually. But only if their marriages were good ones, meaning that their relationship "evolves into a strong attachment." The delinquents whose marriages were not as good often got into even more trouble than they had as bachelors.

I have one more bone to pick with Wright. (Well, actually, I have lots, but I shall limit myself to just one.) It concerns his claim that single men are more likely to commit robbery "to gain the resources that may attract women." I don't understand this. Is robbery supposed to make a man more attractive? Or is Wright assuming that women are too stupid to recognize when they are being wooed with stolen goods?

Author Katha Pollitt has a name for the arrangement that Wright and others describe, in which women are expected to step in and deliver a man from delinquency by marrying him. She calls it a "barbarian-adoption program." She has a question, too: What's in it for the women?

I'll say this for Robert Wright: He had his thesis and he stuck to it. All the data, the arguments, and the examples he summoned were at least superficially consistent with his wives-as-pacifiers point of view.

Not so for E. Mavis Hetherington. She is the psychologist, introduced earlier, who devoted her decades-long professional career to the study of people who had divorced. In *For Better or for Worse*, she (with coauthor John Kelly) looked back at what she had learned after all that time, and set out to dispel some myths. "The biggest myth about divorce," she believes, is that "men are the big winners."

They are not. Most often it is the wife, not the husband, who calls an end to the marriage. Then, in their post-divorce lives, women do better than men emotionally and socially. Women stop pining for their ex sooner and spend more time with people they value. Though it is true that men still fare better than women economically after a marriage ends, even that advantage is not as formidable as it once was.

Hetherington's style throughout the book is to describe the results of her research in general terms, then bring the conclusions to life with stories from the people she interviewed. That's the model she follows in the chapter in which she discusses the lives of men and women who were single twenty years after they divorced.

There are separate sections on single women and single men. The section on the single women begins with the bottom line: "At the end of the study, as at its beginning, single women were leading more satisfying, meaningful lives than single men." Hetherington then describes in general terms the contours of these women's lives—spending time with friends, traveling, caring for one another and for relatives, and participating in church activities.

But, she notes, scattered among the successes were "some dark spots." (There's the dark aura again.) To illustrate, she recounts her last interview with Betty Ann, a woman whose marriage had ended violently. To wit, Roger pummeled Betty Ann until she had two broken ribs and two black eyes. She, in turn, whacked Roger on the head with a poker.

After an initial acknowledgment that Betty Ann was managing a store (apparently successfully and on her own), Hetherington lights into her:

> She was leading an almost pitifully stripped-down life. . . . There was no new man in her life. . . . she was smoking two packs of cigarettes a day and consuming a six-pack of beer each evening as she sat watching television alone. . . . Stocky when I first met her, she weighed almost 270 pounds when the study ended. . . . and drove people off with her sullen, sarcastic demeanor.

That was the end of the section on single women and their meaningful lives.

Now on to the single men. The opening line is "Some of our single men ended the study in states ranging from melancholy to despair." Hetherington then talks generally about some of the factors that landed these divorced men in their now sorry single state. Some never did develop networks of friends, and some who had children were estranged from them. Others were hampered by age-related illnesses.

Health problems, though, Hetherington is quick to add, were not unique to the single men. One of the single women in the study talked about an elderly neighbor who seemed to have few visitors other than a nurse: "Her whole life is sitting on the front porch and watching soap operas. Every time I see her, I think, Is that going to be me in thirty years?"

Back to the single men. Not all were having a difficult time after their divorce. Some were doing quite well, and to illustrate, Hetherington tells the stories of two of them.

The first is James Pennybaker. He had "an extremely successful career, a satisfying social life, and close relationships with his two children." By the time of the twenty-year interview, he had "matured and mellowed. [He] moved and smiled with the easy grace and confidence of a man who had always been considered handsome and accomplished."

Next up, Simon Russell. "His thick curly hair had turned gray, but his face was unlined, and his manner more lively and responsive." Simon described his enthusiasm for the trip he had planned, and for the time he could devote to his family and to his community during his retirement. He summed up his life as a single man quite succinctly: "I've never been happier."

Hetherington's treatment of single women and single men beautifully illustrates the paradox that so stumped me when I first started studying singles. In the scientific literature differences between single men and single women—when there were any—more often favored the single women. The women seemed to take to singlehood with greater gusto than did the men, especially as they strode into their middle and later adult years. Yet the men seemed to be cut more slack. Here, in *For Better or for Worse,* is a great example of just how that happens. Hetherington found, as have others, that single women do better than single men. She admits that. Yet the stories she tells are of the fat and surly Betty Ann versus the suave and successful James and Simon. And adding the crowning ironic jewel, Hetherington does so under the guise of dispelling what she calls the biggest myth about divorce, that men are the winners.

In the same month when the short story "The Disappearance of Elaine Coleman" appeared in *The New Yorker,* another story about a single protagonist was also published there. This one is about a single man.

William Trevor's story "The Hill Bachelors" begins as twenty-nine-year-old Paulie heads home from the midlands of Ireland to the farmhouse where he grew up. He is going to his father's funeral. His mother is relieved that Paulie has come, as he and his father had an uneasy relationship. Paulie's four married siblings also come home. "Paulie knew that an assumption had already been made. . . . He was the bachelor of the family, the employment he had wasn't much. His mother couldn't manage on her own." Paulie feels no resentment about this. He only regrets that the woman back in the midlands he so loves has no interest in moving with him to the farm.

Paulie dates other women, but none of those relationships endure. The townspeople know that the men who stay on the hills "found it difficult to attract a wife to the modest farms they inherited." A neighbor Paulie has known since his childhood offers to buy his fields. His mother says she could move in with one of Paulie's sisters. Paulie, though, declines.

Day after day, Paulie tends to the fields, the fences, and the feed for the cattle, just as his father had. It becomes apparent that "while his presence was so often overlooked he had watched his father at work more conscientiously than his brothers had." Paulie's mother "realized that although it was her widowhood that had brought him back it wasn't her widowhood that made him now insist he must remain."

After Paulie's mother dies, Paulie stays on the farm. "Enduring, unchanging, the hills had waited for him, claiming one of their own."

The story of Paulie suggests that there is a place for single men that I have not yet acknowledged. They are not all slovenly or scary or gay. They can, like Paulie, be just fine.

Elaine Coleman, you may remember, is of so little significance that she literally vanishes. Paulie, in contrast, leaves the woman of his dreams but finds his soul. He returns to the land that he loves more than any human. He is grounded and complete.

Elaine and Paulie are fictional creations. We can read their stories, savor the graceful writing, and regard them as plucked arbitrarily from a magazine filled with great literature. But suppose those two stories do point to something more. Suppose they teach the same lesson that Hetherington seems to favor when she contrasts the sullen Betty Ann with the debonair James and Simon. What if women truly believe that unless they marry and have children, they will disappear into the woodwork, or be doomed to despair, regardless of the level of richness or celebrity they might achieve? And what if men feel no such pressure but believe that they, like the Paulies of the world, could be happily married to a woman or equally happily wedded to the land? Men would have the basis for power and privilege: They would have a choice.

CHAPTER NINE

Myth #7 Attention, Single Parents

Your Kids Are Doomed

Parents who are single get pummeled in the public discourse—especially if they are poor. President Ronald Reagan seared a scathing image onto the national psyche when he described the Welfare Queen in her welfare Cadillac, who only pretended to have an array of dead husbands so she could bilk the public assistance system for even more ill-gotten gains. The queen had a short life—not because she was single but because she never existed. She was fabricated. Her legacy, though, has been enduring.

As insulting as single parents must find such apocryphal morality tales, they seethe even more, I think, when it is their children who are chided. True, their kids are rarely branded as bastards anymore, but often they are still described as illegitimate or as products of "broken" homes. Then there are those ominous prognostications of lives filled with delinquency, failure, and despair, emanating like black smoke from the labs of evil scientists.

There was a time when the disparagement of children was not the American way. In the civil rights era of the 1960s and 1970s, the march toward social justice for all improved the lives of even the smallest Americans. Before that time children of single parents were second-class citizens by law. They could even be taken from their mothers and put up for adoption. In a series of decisions beginning in 1968, the Supreme Court ruled it illegal to single out children for lesser treatment simply because they did not have married parents. Instead, the court declared that all the nation's children were guaranteed equal protection under the law. As an unassailable legal category, illegitimacy was history.

The rulings were in step with the times. More and more people seemed to believe that the moral standing of the nation was honored, not compromised, when the human dignity of all its citizens was acknowledged and respected.

In the opening decade of the twenty-first century, though, the shaming of single parents and their children made a comeback. Writing for the *National Review* in 2002, Kate O'Beirne opined that our society needs to "stigmatize unmarried sex and the irresponsibility of single mothers who risk damaging their children by failing to marry before giving birth"; otherwise, it is unlikely that "the number of illegitimate (whoops!) children will be significantly reduced. If single mothers bore the social stigma of smokers, children would be far better off."

Under the guise of concern, Waite and Gallagher included a prescriptive statement in the final chapter of their *Case for Marriage*. The children of single parents, they claimed, "need teachers, schools, counselors, and other caring adults to acknowledge, rather than deny, their suffering."

O'Beirne, Waite, and Gallagher are just a few of the voices of the emerging "marriage movement." Backed by think tanks with undisguised political agendas, select segments of the scientific community, and genuinely concerned citizens of many stripes, the marriage movement had a simple three-point message. First, there is too much bad stuff in society. Too much poverty, too much crime, too much "illegitimacy," too few high school graduates. Second, there is a clear cause of all this moral and human decay: too much single parenting—a result of too many out-of-wedlock births and too much divorce. Finally, there is an equally clear solution. Get married first, then have your kids, then stay married.

President George W. Bush signed on. He proposed an allocation of $1.5 billion in federal funds to get the pro-marriage message out. With marriage-education classes, billboards, and married-couple "ambassadors" roaming from city to city with their teachings, the news would reach those believed to be most in need of hearing it: the poor.

About the same time, public television was being pelted with accusations of liberal bias and threatened with take-backs of federal funding. With regard to the marriage movement, though, they were pretty much onboard. That became evident when the PBS show *Frontline* aired an hour-long documentary, "Let's Get Married." Cowritten by the correspondent and award-winning author Alex Kotlowitz, the program took a serious look at the movement and its claims. I'll describe some of the highlights of the show first.

Kotlowitz opens "Let's Get Married" with this question: "Is this simply a moral crusade, or is the marriage movement onto something bigger?"

We learn that in America, rates of divorce are highest in the Bible Belt. Statewide, Oklahoma comes in second. Governor Frank Keating is not pleased. But at least he knows what he is up against: "too much divorce, too many out-of-wedlock births, too much drug abuse and violence." He seems convinced that the first two moral lapses cause the latter two scourges in his state. Channeling Kate O'Beirne, he declares, "You need to be judgmental and say that."

Mike McManus, head of a group called Marriage Savers, claims to have the statistics to make good on Keating's word. "Children of divorced or children of never-married parents are twice as likely to drop out of school," he begins. "They're three times as likely to get pregnant themselves as teenagers." The list goes on. He ends his litany with this conclusion: "So we're creating the next generation of monsters."

At the rate of about once every fifteen minutes, someone else appears to make the same kind of claim. Says President Bush:

Children from two-parent families are less likely to end up in poverty, drop out of school, become addicted to drugs, have a child out of wedlock. You see, strong marriages and stable families should be the central goal of American welfare policy.

Pennsylvania senator Rick Santorum also has a turn:

Every statistic that I'm aware of—and I'd be anxious to hear if there's one on the other side—says that marriage is better for children—every one—and usually by a very large margin.

What might the marriage movement do for the people it touches? Kotlowitz spends time with several such people and tells their stories. One is a woman I'll call Janny. Her first marriage, to a preacher's son, did not last. Then along came Eugene. Janny was smitten with this cowboy. "He had the Wranglers and the boots and the spurs and the hat." They planned a wedding. But Janny was getting anxious and uncertain. She confided in her friend Annie, who assured her that she need not follow through with the nuptials. Janny still wasn't sure. Annie tried again to reassure her. Ultimately, though, Janny chalked up her reservations to cold feet and married her man.

Eugene was not all swagger. As Janny tells it, "He had threatened me. He had hit me hard enough to knock me down while I was holding Cassidy in my arms, so I fell with her. He then started in with the girls—'You're stupid. You're ignorant like your mama.'" That marriage, too, ended in divorce.

Janny was on welfare, where the marriage movement had succeeded in installing a relationships training class as a requirement for receiving aid. Kotlowitz observes as Janny, twelve other women, and one man pursue the twelve-hour curriculum. The instructor asks Janny to role-play her end of a conversation she might have with her husband, using the speaker-listener techniques she learned in class. Said Janny: "I feel like I have been working really hard, while you sit at home and do nothing but watch TV. And you don't even get out and try to find another job."

Kotlowitz asks Janny if she thought the lessons could have saved her marriages. With the first marriage, she muses, maybe it would have helped. But not with the second. Not with the husband who had heaped emotional and physical abuse upon her and her child.

In another class the instructor urges the women to get married if they get pregnant, and to exhort their daughters to do the same. Afterward, Janny and her friend Kelle exchange their own views on the matter. They think it isn't quite so simple. The man could be dangerous. He could be the wrong person for lots of reasons. Neither Janny nor Kelle would be so quick to leap to the altar, and they would not want their daughters to be, either.

Another single woman who tells her story on "Let's Get Married" is Ashaki, who has seven children by three fathers. Her mother moved in with her to help raise them. Kotlowitz asks Ashaki if she considered marrying any of the fathers. Ashaki says there was one she thought she would marry, but he turned out to be violent. Currently, things are great with Steven, the father of her youngest child. He adores Ashaki, and the kids love him. Ashaki calls Steven her soulmate. They plan to marry.

When Kotlowitz catches up with Ashaki and Steven some time later, though, their plans have changed. Out of work, Steven has taken to the streets to sell drugs. He needs the money to buy milk and Pampers for the kids. He is arrested and sent to boot camp for three months.

Kotlowitz then turns to economist Ronald Mincy, who has studied men who live in poverty. Mincy notes that men like Steven make up the pool of possible marriage partners for the poor single women who want to wed. Poor men arrive at the job market with less education and fewer skills than the men sitting atop them on the socioeconomic ladder. When the economy heads south, their employment prospects plummet fastest. Some also have problems with addiction. Too many are incarcerated. The men who are nonwhite as well as poor can sometimes add discrimination to their list of challenges.

Sociologist Kathryn Edin, who spent years living in run-down neighborhoods and talking in depth with 162 poor women, found that their assessments aligned with Mincy's. They had serious reservations about the men who were available to them as marriage partners. They did, though, very much want to marry.

One more set of people get a say on "Let's Get Married"—a group of grandmothers whose children and grandchildren have been the recipients of the marriage movement's largesse. What do they think of the government's point of view? Kotlowitz wants to know.

Here are a few of their answers:

- "I'm really insulted by it. Who is the government to tell us, because we poor, we need to get married?"
- "Marriage does not take you out of poverty. It really doesn't. You can be married, and you still can't get a job."
- "When you got to worry about how you're going to eat, live, and go to the bathroom, marriage is way down on the bottom of that list."

None of them seem to think that the government is onto something big. They do not see marriage as their ticket to mobility.

Kotlowitz speaks with Janny and Ashaki one last time before bringing the program to a close. Janny is with her friend Annie and both sets of kids. One of the kids has Janny's enthusiastic attention: "You pulled your tooth! Oh! Let me see. How cool! Tooth Fairy's going to visit you."

Janny, Kotlowitz explains, "was sharing the burdens of raising two young families with her friend, Annie. She still hangs onto the dream of a happy marriage."

"I think there's somebody out there," Janny says. "My sister is married to a wonderful man. You know, he's really been good to her. They are really happy, and there has to be one out there somewhere. And if not, then I'll grow old alone."

Over at Ashaki's place, one of the children has drawn a picture of a ring. Kotlowitz believes the drawing was "a child's plea for [Ashaki] and Steven to stay together." He concludes, "At least on this, the experts now agree: It would probably be better for the children if they did."

Sometimes the wordfare waged against single people is subtle. You really need to be alert to notice it. Not so when it comes to single parents and their children. The blaming and shaming is flaunted. When Mike Mc-Manus looked into the camera and declared that single parents were "creating the next generation of monsters," he seemed almost pleased with his pronouncement. As Governor Keating said, "You need to be judgmental."

Here's another word I found interesting: *burdens*. I'm referring to Kotlowitz's comment that Janny "was sharing the burdens of raising two young families with her friend, Annie." If Annie were Danny and married to Janny, I bet Kotlowitz would have picked out a different descriptor: *joys*.

One more word whine. This one is not at all specific to the *Frontline* show. It is standard nomenclature: *single parents*. Anyone who has a child is a parent; that's the definition. We would not call Janny and Danny "married parents." They would just be "parents." So why do we call anyone a single parent?

Now let's look at the targets of the pro-marriage programs. Janny is the one who was knocked around by Eugene, but it is she—together with twelve other women and just one man—who is in the class on relationship skills. Remember the little kid who was so excited about her missing tooth? She is a member of McManus's prophesied "generation of monsters." What did she do to deserve that? And why bother grumbling about the free pass given to Rush Limbaugh with his three divorces or Larry King with his six marriages? The marriage movement is quite up-front about whose morals need fixing—just poor people's.

Time to talk solutions. The name of the *Frontline* show neatly captures the proposed cure for poverty, crime, addiction, and just about any other ill: "Let's Get Married." For a poor woman who is not yet married and wants children, a husband is the answer. With marriage, she will become magically transformed and morally worthy of bearing children. A poor single woman who already has children needs redemption. A husband can provide that, too. President Reagan's trickle-down economics has been replaced by President Bush's trickle-down dignity. Take one single woman and her kids, add a man, and stir. That's the recipe for redemption by nuclear family.

I'm making fun of the marriage movement shtick, but not everything about it is dopey. A two-paycheck household is less likely to be mired in poverty than a home kept afloat by the earnings of just one adult. Children who can bask in the time, love, and attention of two adults, instead of just one, should be better protected from the lures of drugs and delinquency.

So, how does this lesson play out in the lives of the two single women we met on *Frontline*? Should Janny have stayed married to her first husband? We are never told much about him, so it is hard to know. As for Eugene the batterer, it seems clear to me that Janny's gut feelings, and Annie's advice, were right on target; Janny should have stayed far, far away from that man.

With regard to Ashaki and Steven, Kotlowitz thinks the answer is obvious and that all experts agree with him: It would be better for the children if the two of them wed. Really? All experts agree that kids are better off if Mom marries a man who sells drugs and is put away for months at a time than if Mom stays single?

Personally, I think the grandmothers are right. Adding a flat-broke man to a flat-broke woman does not lift anyone out of poverty. The marriage of a poor woman to an abusive man does not fail because she lacked the proper relationship skills, nor should it be papered together with government meddling.

Enough with the opinions. I want some numbers. Don't worry, I'm not going to plow through every study linking the fate of children to whether they live with one or both parents. I'm just going to choose one. And since I'm going to present just one, it had better be good, and it is. First, it documents drug use, one of the most widely heralded "risks" of growing up with just one parent. Second, the results are drawn from "the principal source of data about drug use in the United States." I'll call it the National Drug Abuse Survey. The people who were sampled for the research represent the population of the United States, ages twelve and older. The report focused on the subgroup often believed to be the most worrisome—adolescents ages twelve to seventeen. More than 22,000 participated.

The fear for the children of single parents is not just that they will try drugs or alcohol but that the use will become a problem. The substance abuse might result in symptoms such as anxiety, irritability, or depression. The abusers might be unable to use less often, even if they try, and may need more and more of the substance to achieve the same high. Abusers might also get less work done than they had before they became so taken with the alcohol or the drug. To be classified as having a problem with drugs or alcohol, the adolescent had to report at least two such troublesome experiences in the past year.

The numbers in the table show the percentage of adolescents in each family type who had a substance-abuse problem. The family types included single-mother and single-father families, mother-and-father families, and two other two-parent families: mother and stepfather, and father and stepmother.

Substance-Abuse Problems Among Twelve- to Seventeen-Year-Olds	
%	Family Type
4.5	Mother plus father
5.3	Mother plus stepfather
5.7	Mother only
11.0	Father only
11.8	Father plus stepmother

The first thing to notice is the overall rates of substance abuse. In every type of family, at least 88 percent of the adolescents do *not* have a problem with drugs or alcohol. Second, what the pro-marriage advocates have claimed all along is that kids raised by their own mom and dad should do better than all the others. They do. And not because two is a magic number. Adolescents living with a father and stepmother had more drug-abuse problems than all the rest.

The most important comparison, I think, is the one the culture has obsessed about the most: How do the kids raised by a single mom compare with the kids raised by their mother and father? Again, the adolescents living with their own two parents do better: 4.5 percent of them have substance-abuse problems, compared with 5.7 percent of the adolescents living with only their mom. It is a difference, but not much of one.

In the table, I list only some of the family types included in the National Drug Abuse Survey. I wanted to highlight the single-parent and two-parent homes, since those are the ones that have most often been subject to debate. But Ashaki's kids do not fit into any of the categories in the table. Remember, they were living with their mother and grandmother. So, here now is the full list of family types described in the report, and the corresponding rates of substance-abuse problems.

%	Family Type
3.4	Mother plus father plus other relative
4.5	Mother plus father
5.3	Mother plus stepfather
5.7	Mother only
6.0	Mother plus other relative
7.2	Other relative only
8.1	Other family type
11.0	Father only
11.8	Father plus stepmother

Substance-Abuse Problems Among Twelve- to Seventeen-Year-Olds

"Other relative" included relatives other than a mother or father. Typically, they were grandparents, aunts, or uncles.

"Other family types" included miscellaneous combinations of adults, including adults to whom the children were not related.

The mom-plus-dad family has been knocked off its perch. Kids are even less likely to have substance-abuse problems if they live with Mom, Dad, and another relative—typically a grandparent, aunt, or uncle. Notice also that there are two new family types that do not include Mom or Dad: other relatives only, and other family types. (In the latter, the kids live with miscellaneous combinations of people, including adults to whom they are not related.) The rate of substance abuse is only a few percentage points higher in the families in which neither a mother nor a father is present than in the families that include both Mom and Dad.

There is more to say about these numbers. But before continuing, here are a few disclaimers.

First, none of the numbers from the National Drug Abuse Survey, or any other study for that matter, prove that growing up in a particular type of family *causes* substance-abuse problems (or any other problems). Maybe, for instance, children in father-stepmother families have higher rates of abuse not because of anything about stepmothers but because when kids have serious problems in their families of origin, fathers are more likely to divorce and remarry. Or maybe it is a matter of genetics. The kinds of men who marry, divorce, and then remarry may be more genetically predisposed to substance abuse than are men who marry just once, so their children may be similarly predisposed, too.

The second caveat, which should also sound familiar, is that the results of scientific studies are averages. There are always exceptions—usually lots of them. Plenty of adolescents who live with their father and a stepmother, for example, do as well or better at resisting addictive substances than do the kids next door who are living with Mom and Dad.

Third, I am not saying that none of these differences is big enough to matter. I'd like to wipe out all the differences, preferably by reducing the level of substance abuse to exactly zero in every family.

Finally, the results describe the way things were at the time of the survey, not necessarily the way they should be or the way they always will be. One thing that jumps out at me from the expanded table is that the five family forms associated with the lowest rates of adolescent substance abuse have one thing in common: Mom was living with the kids. If fathers are becoming more involved with their children than they were at the time of the survey (1991–93), then perhaps that pattern is already changing.

I want to return now to the two family types that set off so much of the sound and fury about mothers who need to be stigmatized, children who need to have their suffering acknowledged, and monsters in the making. They are the single-mother families, in which 5.7 percent of the kids had substance-abuse problems, and the mom-plus-dad families, in which

4.5 percent did. Here's the question that bothers me: Why is this difference so small?

Think about it this way. If you had a town with a hundred adolescents living with their mother and father, and another hundred living just with their mothers, there would be four or five substance-abusing kids in the former group, and maybe six in the latter. Think about all the advantages that adolescents supposedly have when they live with Mom and Dad rather than just Mom. There are two adults in the home to help them, care about them, and spend time with them. The adults can also support each other, and that, too, can redound to the benefit of the kids. There are two sources of income. And there is no source of stigma or shame attached to growing up in a home with your own mother and father.

For double the money, time, love, and attention, the kids of mom-plus-dad families did not seem to be doing all that much better than the kids of single moms. There must be something wrong with my blather about all that emotional goodness that kids in nuclear families get that children living with just their moms do not.

If it really were true that the children of single mothers had only one adult in their lives to care for them, love them, spend time with them, and contribute to their well-being and that their moms had no adults in their lives to help them, and if it were also true that the children in nuclear families had two fully devoted adults in their lives, loving them and each other—well, then it would be astounding that there could be so little difference in the problem behaviors of the two sets of adolescents.

I think there are several ways around this dilemma. The first is to let go of the fantasy that all children living in nuclear families have two totally engaged parents who lavish their love and attention on all their children, and on each other, in a home free of anger, conflict, or recriminations. The second is to grab onto a different sort of possibility—that many children living with single mothers have other important adults in their lives, too. I don't mean (just) kids like Ashaki's, who have Grandma living with them. I also mean all the kids who have grandparents, aunts, uncles, neighbors, teachers, family friends, and others who care about them and make sure they know it.

It is true that the other important adults in the lives of the children of single parents do not always live in the same home as the children. That means that they are not always on the scene to help with homework or cover for Mom while she runs to the store. Again, though, it is important to remember that two-parent homes are not always homes with two continually available parents. And something else is important: Although mutual love and support is what adults hope to enjoy when they live together and raise children, sometimes what they get instead is chaos, strife, and even abuse.

Frankly, I don't like Senator Rick Santorum's views. But I'm going to grant his wish. Santorum, you may remember, said, "Every statistic that I'm aware of—and I'd be anxious to hear if there's one on the other side—says that marriage is better for children—every one—and usually by a very large margin." So, here, in the spirit of magnanimity, is not just one but a whole array of findings you did not hear about on *Frontline*.

Let's start with that "very large margin." In the National Drug Abuse Survey the difference in abuse between adolescents in mother-plus-father homes and mother-only homes was 1.2 percent. Hardly "a very large margin." Moreover, on average, marriage was the worst possible outcome for kids when the marriage was between a father and a stepmother.

When studies find that children of single-parent households do worse in some way or another than children of married parents, there is often a critical difference in the two kinds of households: The single-family households have less income, less in savings, and fewer assets. That means that the married parents are more likely to be able to afford health insurance, safe neighborhoods, and SAT prep courses for their kids. The issue, in short, is not (just) having too few parents, it is having too little money.

Here's something else Senator Santorum does not seem to know: Sometimes the number of parents, their marital status, and their biological links to the children just do not matter at all. That's what a quartet of sociologists discovered when they looked closely at a nationally representative sample of different kinds of households. Two-parent biological households, adoptive households, stepmother, stepfather, and single- (divorced-) mother households were all part of their study. The researchers asked about the children's relationships with their siblings and with their friends, as well as their grades. They looked for different points of view, asking mothers and fathers about their lives and the children's, and asking the children, too. The type of household made no difference whatsoever. But here are some things that did

matter, and not in a good way: conflict within families, disagreements between parents, and arguments between parents and kids. As the authors
conclude, "Our findings suggest that adoption, divorce, and remarriage are
not necessarily associated with the host of adjustment problems that have at
times been reported in the clinical literature. . . . It is not enough to know
that an individual lives within a particular family structure without also
knowing what takes place in that structure."

Of course, some degree of conflict is commonplace in all families, even
in the most loving and cohesive ones. So, it is not the low level of everyday
sniping that matters but the loud drone of relentless dissent. There is little
doubt that the latter atmosphere is bad for kids. A study of thirty-nine nations found that children were emotionally better off around the globe if
they were raised by a single mother than if they stayed in a home with two
married parents who couldn't stop fighting. Kids also did better in that
cross-national study if they were raised by one divorced parent than by remarried parents, even if the remarriages were not marked by particularly
high levels of turmoil.

To understand how children really are faring in single-parent homes,
watch how they do year after year as their living situation changes. Divorce
is a great example, as there is often a clear "before" and "after" set of living
arrangements. If you look at children after a divorce has occurred—let's say
when they are living with only their mother—some may have behavioral
problems, substance-abuse problems, self-esteem issues, and other troubles.
But if you had been following those children for many years before the divorce ever occurred, you would have found something interesting. For some
kids, the problems began to materialize as early as twelve years before the divorce. The difficulties, then, did not spring from the soil of single motherhood, they developed under the roof of two married biological parents.

In their everyday lives, the emotional experiences of children in single-
parent and married-parent homes are similar. In one study 396 children on
the cusp of adolescence (ten to fourteen years old) agreed to carry pagers
every day for a week. During their waking hours the pager went off at random intervals about five times a day. As soon as it did, the children recorded
whom they were with, what they were doing, how they felt, and how friendly
the other person seemed. The main difference was not in how the children
felt but in how the parents behaved toward them. Parents in single-parent
homes were friendlier to their kids than were the married parents.

I do think that Senator Santorum and I agree on one thing: Stability is important to children. I think he locates stability primarily within the homes of continuously married parents. Single parents, though, can provide stability, too. When they settle in with their kids, maintain a good connection with them, and do not jump from one marriage to another, they are probably going to have children who are as healthy and secure as anyone else's.

Stability does not come from parents alone. Other people in children's lives, such as siblings, cousins, friends, grandparents, aunts, uncles, and parents' friends, can contribute, too. In the pager study, the children from single-parent homes spent more time with their extended families than did the children living with married parents.

All of which brings me back to Janny. Alex Kotlowitz was so busy worrying about what Janny did not have—a husband—and whether she would find one that he seemed completely oblivious to what she did have. Janny was already living with someone whom she and her children had known for years. The coparent in Janny's home was Annie, her longtime friend whom she trusted with her most dreaded fears. Janny and Annie had each other to cover some of the household expenses and run some of the errands, to watch each other's kids now and then, or just hang out. Apparently, neither parent was hot-tempered or abusive. They enjoyed each other and each other's children. No thanks to the government-sponsored relationship classes or to the team of PBS reporters, Janny and Annie came up with their own solution for living their lives with kids but no husband. I think it is brilliant.

I know. Janny wasn't totally thrilled with the arrangement. She was still holding out hope for a conventional soulmate. That's okay as far as it goes, but I wish she—and Kotlowitz and everyone else—would recognize the value of what she already has.

I'm concerned that I might seem to be pooh-poohing the possible pain of divorce, the likely challenges of solo parenting, or even the true incidence of very real problems among the nation's children. I'm not. I'm protesting the campaign to stigmatize single parents—not just because it is cruel and ineffective but because it is wrong.

There really are too many children and adolescents who have emotional and health problems, who abuse drugs and alcohol and engage in risky sexual behaviors, who can't seem to get along with other people and fail badly in school. If you want to find those kids, banging on the doors of single-parent homes is going to be an inefficient way to go about it. A more effective search strategy (if you are intent on locating problems within households) is to look for families that are "characterized by conflict and aggression and by relationships that are cold, unsupportive, and neglectful." Those are the truly risky families. That's what three UCLA social scientists concluded after they reviewed every single study they could find on the matter.

Want a shortcut? Follow the money. As the scholars noted, "Both sustained poverty and descent into poverty appear to move parenting in more harsh, punitive, irritable, inconsistent, and coercive directions." The descent part is especially revealing. The parents were not characteristically cold, cruel, and neglectful. They became that way (or at least some did) as they lost their toehold on dignity.

The shortcut is not flawless. Lots of wealthy mothers and fathers are icy, contentious, and derelict in their parenting. And many children are resilient and will do just fine even if their parents are pathetic. Still, it is a decent heuristic. If you really want to help children, go after poverty, not single parenting.

There's another reason I'm lashing out against the smearing of single parents. Those solo parents who really do care about their kids (just about all of them) sometimes find the cultural condemnation and innuendo hard to ignore. What if the slimeballs are right? they worry. Maybe I should go soulmate seeking, they think, for the sake of the children.

Whenever the latest census figures roll around, so does the blame. "Disturbing," intone the interpreters of the trends as the line tracking the number of single parents climbs up the charts. "Alarming," others add. Then the backlash begins. Single mom Amy Dickinson pointed this out to me and to all the other readers of *Time* magazine in an essay she wrote in 2001. She did not appreciate the predictable name-calling that followed the announcement of the latest uptick in single parenting. She kept hearing words like *dysfunctional, broken, risky,* and *vulnerable* applied to her family, but she did not think they fit.

Sometimes, Dickinson said, she forced herself to go out on dates. But she enjoyed her time with her daughter a lot more. And they both loved getting together with another single mom and her two kids. They had dinner together every Sunday and often watched movies and went to the kids' games in between. "We watch each other's back, lend each other money and love each other's kids." And "we don't feel alone."

Sociologist E. Kay Trimberger talked in depth to thirteen single mothers over the course of nearly a decade. Those mothers also reported that the drumbeat of blame unnerved them, and they tried to make it stop. Gamely, many tried to pursue relationships with men, thinking their kids needed a father figure in the house. Typically, they came to the same conclusions as did Amy Dickinson. Their kids already had important adults in their lives. They were the men and women who had known and cared about them for years. None were Mom's soulmate. They were her long-standing friends, lifelong family members, and trusted neighbors.

I especially liked the preparations my friend Marilyn made when she adopted Maria. Marilyn asked the dozen people closest to her to be Maria's godparents. They all agreed, and all have been an important part of the child's life ever since.

Single mothers have their limitations, just like any other parents. I'm not trying to romanticize them, but rather take them seriously. The families and social networks they form are part of the evolving face of the nation. As much as Kate O'Beirne or Maggie Gallagher or Mike McManus or anyone else might like to round up all citizens, corral them into nuclear-family homes, and lock all the windows and doors so they can never escape, that's just not going to happen. The tidy unit of Mom, Dad, and the kids is today's American minority group. It will be tomorrow's, too.

CHAPTER
TEN
Myth #8 Too Bad You're Incomplete

You Don't Have Anyone and You Don't Have a Life

After I moved from the East Coast to the West, there was a time when I knew I wanted to stay out west but was not yet sure whether I could make it happen. Would I be able to sell my home in Virginia? Would anyone hire me for only as many hours as it took to pay my bills so I could devote the rest of my time, and all of my heart and soul, to the study of singles? What about all the rest of it—would it all work out? Then one day I got a phone call, and I knew that it had happened. I hung up and sat in quiet stunned amazement for a moment. Then I thought to myself, I can have it all.

It took a second for me to realize just how bizarre that thought was—at least by the prevailing standards. There I was, stepping into a life in which I had no husband, no children, no full-time job, and, for the first time in more than a decade, no home that I owned. Yet to me, I was about to have it all.

I doubt that I would have thought of my life that way many years before. I loved my friends, my family, my job, and my home, but I would not have spontaneously appropriated a cultural catchphrase, nor refashioned it so thoroughly.

Here in this chapter are some of my favorite "what's wrong with this picture" puzzles and word games. Thinking about them has helped me understand how Myth #8 gets perpetuated. It is one of the boldest, broadest scams of them all, claiming as it does that single people do not have anyone and do not have a life. Yet the stories that have this canard at their core rarely sound overtly hostile or dismissive. Sometimes they don't even sound that dumb.

I'll begin with a word game.

Do you have a family?" Tim Russert asked the guest of his television interview show in July of 2002. Maya Lin, the acclaimed architect who designed the Vietnam Memorial, indicated that she did, and described her husband and children.

There was nothing special about the question. The same question is asked on many shows and in countless informal conversations, and has been for as long as I can remember. There was nothing unusual about the answer, either.

The exchange, and so many others like it, seems unremarkable because singlism is so routinely practiced and so rarely recognized. We know that the family in Russert's question is the one that is regarded as traditional, the one that Americans "start" as adults, together with their partner in marriage. Russert was asking Lin whether she had the kind of family that counts. Lin responded with the predictable, and valued, response. The conversation was seamless. Both were speaking the same language, the language of singlism that recognizes just one sort of family as the real thing.

There are, of course, other meanings of family. Lin could have replied, "Oh, yes, I have a family: I have a mother and a father." Or she could have answered, "Yes, I have a brother, a sister, three cousins, a grandmother, an uncle, and two aunts." She could have even offered this response: "Terri and I have been friends since kindergarten. We went to different high schools, but now she and I, and my two best friends from high school, and her best friend from work, and her three kids all share our lives with one another." Any of those answers, however, may have left Russert befuddled, if only for a moment, as he realized that Lin was speaking a different and less familiar language.

The overvaluing of couples places one meaning of the word *family* at the tips of our tongues, when other meanings are at least as deserving of that place of honor. Why, for example, do we not immediately think of the meaning of family that excludes no one: the family of origin? And why is the question about "family" so much more likely to be asked than one that, to me, is far more interesting: Who are the important people in your life? If you were asked that question and you had a spouse and children, you would be free to name them. But you, and everyone else, would also have an open invitation to acknowledge any person who had been important to you in your lifetime.

The seemingly innocent question about having a family does important work. People such as Lin who can respond with the approved answer feel valued and validated. People who answer, "No, I do not have a family," may instead feel shamed. That's what singlism does—it separates people into categories and designates some categories as more valuable and more worthy than others.

In the summer of 1999 John F. Kennedy Jr., son of the late president, set out in a plane he was piloting to attend a wedding at the family compound in Hyannis Port. His wife, Carolyn Bessette Kennedy, who was thirty-three, was with him, as was Carolyn's sister Lauren Bessette, who was thirty-four and single. They never made it to the wedding. Tragically, the plane crashed and all three died.

A few days later the Bessette family released a statement that ended on this note: "John and Carolyn were true soulmates and we hope to honor them in death in the simple manner in which they chose to live their lives. We take solace in the thought that together they will comfort Lauren for eternity."

I empathized with the many expressions of grief that I heard during those doleful days, but something about the Bessette family statement puzzled me. Lauren was the older sister. Why was she being comforted by her younger sister and John? Why wasn't she comforting them? On second thought, they were all adults; why weren't they all comforting one another?

Lauren was comforted by Carolyn and John, I thought, because Lauren was single and they were married. The adult who remains single when a younger sibling has married often becomes the de facto baby of the family, in perpetual need of comfort and consolation.

But the statement about Lauren was released by her own family. Why would the people who loved Lauren so deeply read to the public a statement that diminished her? Even knowing nothing at all about the family, I could not imagine that they intended to say anything disrespectful, especially at a moment of such sorrow. I learned later that Lauren had a high-powered job and had traveled the world. Surely her family did not regard her as childlike in her talents or accomplishments.

So, why did the family describe Lauren as the person in need of comfort from Carolyn and John? I asked lots of people this question, and those who had an answer thought it was obvious: Lauren was comforted by the couple not because she was single but because she was alone.

If you imagine a snapshot of Lauren, Carolyn, and John as they were about to board the plane on that fateful evening, it seems evident that Lauren was indeed alone. Maybe you picture Carolyn and John nestled together, with Lauren off a bit to the side. In that photo there is just one relationship, and Lauren is not in it.

The life stories of the three adults, though, did not begin with the 1999 snapshot. Among the three, there was just one relationship for most of the first three decades of their lives. The two people who had spent their lives together, who knew just about everything there was to know about each other, who shared family and personal histories, were not John and Carolyn. They were, of course, Carolyn and Lauren. Lauren was not alone.

Suppose, though, that the threesome had not met such a tragic fate. Take the snapshot, turn it into a moving picture, and play it forward for the next couple of years. What do you see? It is easy to imagine what John and Carolyn's life might hold. Like so many other couples, they might work during the day, have dinner together in the evening, maybe run some errands on weekend afternoons and socialize with other couples at night. They might have children and find shows about singing dinosaurs competing with the theater for their attention.

But what about Lauren? How do you see her life unfolding? Do you see her returning home every night to an apartment that is empty except for some cats? That's not how I live my single life. There is no obvious script for the life of a singleton, not even one that is specific to a particular race or class.

In our cultural imagination, Carolyn and John have each other. They have full-bodied lives. Lauren does not have anyone, and her life is skeletal. She is alone.

I think that when we look at the expanse of our adult lives, as we imagine them unfurled in their entirety, we see marriage as the long red carpet, with a few inches of shiny hardwood at the beginning (the youthful single lives we lead until we settle into marriage) and then perhaps a few more inches of scuffed floor at the end (that short segment of widowhood that befalls the spouse who outlasts the other). The sturdy realists among us may even allow for a rent in the rug somewhere along the line, to mark the place where one marriage has ended and the next has not yet begun. By that imagining, our married years are our adult years.

In the real-life stories of contemporary Americans, though, the section of shiny hardwood is expanding as the age at which people first step onto the marital rug slips further away. The rate of divorce is leaving more than just a little tear in the carpet. As life spans lengthen and widows stay widows longer, that scuffed floor becomes ever more noticeable. All told, the time that we spend single during our adult lives adds up to a conclusion stunning enough to pull that red rug right out from under our feet: The total is greater than the time we spend married. It is marriage, rather than singlehood, that is the transitional status, the interlude connecting the first singlehood to the second. Further, marriage merits interlude status only if it has any place at all; for the millions of life singles, it does not.

Now go back to that moving picture and project it forward not just a few years but ten or twenty years. Where would John and Carolyn be? Statistically, it's almost fifty/fifty whether they'd still be with each other. Where would Carolyn and Lauren be? They would still be sisters. Their relationship would likely be intact.

Suppose, though, that John and Carolyn really were the true soulmates the Bessette family portrayed them to be and that they stayed together until parted by death. Now who is in the picture? Again, statistically speaking, it is not John who is likely to be left standing. Women usually outlive men, and both Carolyn and Lauren were younger than John. Of the three people in the original picture, the two who were most likely to grow old together were Carolyn and Lauren. And if Lauren and Carolyn were like many sisters, they would become even closer as they aged.

Lauren was not alone.

It was two days after the terrorist attacks of September 11, 2001. For me, it was a day of long, intense phone calls. I had just hung up from the third in a row, when the phone rang still again. It was someone I was getting to know since moving to the West Coast the year before. "Hi," she said. "How are you doing? I wanted to call, since I figured you had no one to talk to."

May of 2003 was not a good month for The New York Times. The Times is perhaps the most prestigious newspaper in the world, but it had done the unthinkable—it had printed quotes that were never said, scenes that were imagined rather than witnessed, and stories that were simply untrue. Reporter Jayson Blair was the culprit, but executive editor Howell Raines was in big trouble, too. How could this have happened on his watch? *Newsweek* did some reporting of its own.

"At the time, the feeling in the *Times*'s newsroom was that Raines was looking for young, unmarried reporters . . . who were just as comfortable in a Holiday Inn as they were in their own beds."

Why, I asked myself, would anyone assume that single people would be just as comfortable in a hotel bed as they would in their own bed? Is the idea the stereotypical one that singles are not "settled"? That their own beds are no more their own than the beds in hotels? Maybe singles, when they are not on the road, are presumed to sleep in whatever bed happened to be left at their place by the last tenant or on some mattress they found on the sidewalk.

Or is the assumption here that singles spend so much time having affairs in hotel rooms that they are more comfortable there than married people are? If so, then I have a question: With whom, I wonder, are single people having their affairs?

I'm taking the quote too literally as a way of making fun of it. I understand the true meaning: Single people "don't have anyone," and married people do. You already know that I don't believe this. But I shall grant one small slice of it: On any given evening married people are more likely to have someone else in the same bed with them than are single people. That's why I think married people would be more comfortable in a Holiday Inn than they would in their own bed. On the road they won't have anyone next to them snoring, farting, and hogging the covers.

In 1990 President George H. W. Bush had an opportunity to nominate a candidate for the Supreme Court, and he chose Judge David Souter. Before Souter stepped up to his Senate confirmation hearings, *Newsweek* tried to read the tea leaves of a court marked by his presence. Clues to Souter's position on issues such as abortion, civil rights, gay and lesbian rights, and gun control were tracked down. Questions were raised. Does Souter really believe in basing judicial decisions on what he believes to be the original intent of the framers of the Constitution? Would the senators succeed in wrangling meaningful answers from the nominee, or would Souter evade with the best of them?

After two pages *Newsweek* ended the story with this conclusion:

> Souter has come to be known as a decent if drab ascetic: a 50-year-old man from rural, white New England who has never married, never had children, never really been part of the modern America that constitutional law must necessarily confront. Taking the measure of the man—does Souter's detachment show someone with a special capacity to judge or does it reflect a stale mind and a narrow heart?—is the Senate's challenge. Because more than abortion or any single issue that may not even be on the docket in five or 25 years, it is that perspective on life and law that will shape his decisions.

You have to hand it to *Newsweek*—at least it entertained the possibility that a single man without children could have a "special capacity to judge." Souter, though, was getting the singles treatment. It was there right from the outset. *Newsweek* failed to dig up any dirt on Souter, so it had to concede that he was "decent." One word later, though, that grudging concession was undone, twice: Souter was drab, and he was an ascetic. (Used in reference to a single man, *ascetic* is code for "As far as we know, he does not have regular sex." Recall that Chris Matthews said the same thing about Ralph Nader.) *Newsweek* takes a taste of this drab, ascetic Souter stew, made from a sallow, single, childless stock and a sprinkling of rural, white New England seasoning, and claims that it has no place in modern America.

So, does *Newsweek* think that Souter's detachment shows "a special capacity to judge" or "a stale mind and a narrow heart"? Hmm, I wonder. And come to think of it, why has *Newsweek* concluded that being single and childless is a recipe for detachment?

There is much to ponder in *Newsweek*'s three-sentence wrap-up of the Souter candidacy. Why exactly is Souter deemed not part of modern America? Considering the composition of the court then and historically, surely *Newsweek* was not disqualifying Souter on the grounds that he was white or male. Does *Newsweek* mean to imply that only people who are married with children are part of modern America? That would be odd, in that even in 1990 only 26 percent of American households were composed of married parents and their children.

Maybe the point is that only people who are married with children have the proper "perspective on life" that enables wise judgments on matters such as schools or obscenity. If so, then should it also follow that the court needs to be packed with women to weigh in on matters such as abortion or reproductive technologies, or with gay men, lesbians, African Americans, and Arab Americans to make richly informed decisions about matters pertaining to discrimination, due process, and civil rights?

I also wonder about that stale mind. Who is more likely to end up with a brain like a piece of day-old toast—the single man who can spend his weekends thinking and reading, attending professional conferences, and conversing with colleagues and friends, or the married dad who spends Saturdays at puppet shows and Sundays with the in-laws? Who has the narrower heart—the husband who has invested his entire emotional portfolio in his wife and his children, or the single man who can value the people he finds valuable, whether friends or kin or colleagues, and can evenhandedly weigh the health and well-being of all the world's children?

To me, there is a lot to think about here. To *Newsweek,* though, the lesson is the simple one that so many Americans have already learned so well. Single = no mind, no heart, no life.

With Souter, though, the American media was just warming up. By the end of 2002, when Condoleezza Rice walked into the spotlight, it was really hot. Rice was profiled in *The New Yorker* in October, she was on the cover of the December 16 issue of *Newsweek,* and she was a topic of discussion on *Larry King Live* on the evening of December 11, when journalist Bob Woodward was the featured guest. Her celebrity did not begin or end with those stories, but the three are sufficient to tell the pertinent cultural tale.

Rice's story is a compelling one. She is an African American woman, born in Birmingham, Alabama, in 1954, who by age thirty-five was named a member of President George H. W. Bush's National Security Council. Four years later she became the youngest person ever to serve as provost of Stanford University. At the time of all the media attention, Rice was President George W. Bush's national security advisor.

Most of the stories about Rice focused primarily on her role in the Bush administration. More interesting to me was the commentary about the other aspects of her life. *Newsweek,* in "The Quiet Power of Condi Rice," offers this description: "Rice begins her day at 5 A.M. to exercise. Her chief recreations are going to concerts at the Kennedy Center, watching football on TV, playing her grand piano, and shopping. . . . She dresses beautifully and agreed to pose for *Vogue*." *Newsweek* also notes that Rice is a concert pianist who is "accomplished enough to have performed with cellist Yo-Yo Ma before 2,000 people at Constitution Hall earlier this year." Picture captions add that Rice attends religious services and enjoys playing tennis and reading Dostoyevsky. Toward the end of the seven-page profile, *Newsweek* sums up Rice's life: "The fact is that her job is Rice's life. She doesn't socialize much, if at all. Rice told an avuncular friend that she preferred to go out with black men. On his own initiative, the friend, a prominent Washingtonian, says that he asked another well-known Washingtonian, who is black, to arrange some suitable dates. They were not a success, reports this source."

The New Yorker, in "Without a Doubt," also acknowledges Rice's musical talents by mentioning the Brahms sonata Rice played with Yo-Yo Ma at Constitution Hall. In a way *The New Yorker* seems impressed with Rice's personal ties to the Bush family: "In Washington, nothing matters more than closeness to the President, in terms of time logged in his presence. It isn't just that she briefs him every morning . . . it's also that she spends many weekends as the Bushes' guest at Camp David or at the Presidential ranch, in Crawford, Texas. Rice, who shares the President's passions for exercise and watching sports events . . . will often spend hours with him during non-working time when other staff members never see him."

In the end, though, Rice's time spent with the Bushes is just further evidence for the conclusion that Rice hardly has a life beyond her job: "For Rice—who has never married, has no siblings, and was orphaned just a few weeks before assuming her post—Bush and the job represent a very large part of her life, even by upper-level White House staff standards. She has a close circle of old friends and relatives, but most of them live down South or in California. She isn't on the Washington social circuit. Home is a sparsely furnished apartment in the Watergate complex. Entertaining means ordering take-out. Her primary off-hours companions seem to be George and Laura Bush."

Bob Woodward got right to the point. Asked by Larry King how important Rice was to the Bush administration, Woodward replied, "Probably the most key person. She has no personal life."

The three accounts of Rice's life tell one story: Outside of her job, Rice has no life. The consistency of this story line across these versions and many others may seem to suggest that it is the natural and true tale, an apt summary of what Rice's life is really like. In contrast, I think the accounts are scripted by singlism and hide an amazing multilayered life in plain view.

How does singlism ensure that Rice's life is so readily trivialized and dismissed? The first step is to set aside Rice's job. She is arguably one of the most influential women in the most powerful nation on earth. Previously she held one of the highest posts at one of the most prestigious universities in the world. Put all of that in brackets. Include in the same aside all her job-related activities outside of the White House, such as her frequent appearances on the Sunday morning talk shows and her travel to other lands.

What might count as worthy components of a life outside of work? What about the pursuit of other interests? Rice likes to read, shop, and watch sports on TV. What about staying fit? Rice works out every day and plays tennis. How about a spiritual life? Rice still practices the religion that her father preached, often attending services at the National Presbyterian Church in D.C.

Let's up the ante a bit. So what if she shops and watches TV? Has she really distinguished herself in any way other than her work? She has performed at Constitution Hall and modeled for *Vogue*.

What about her relationships? Does she have meaningful relationships with other people? Yes, "she has a close circle of old friends and relatives."

There are other reliable ways of trivializing the lives of people who are single. *The New Yorker* could have noted that Rice's residence is home to a Steinway piano; instead, we learn that "home is a sparsely furnished apartment." The author could have expressed awe at Rice's stamina, noting that after getting up at five A.M. to exercise, then engaging with the likes of Donald Rumsfeld, Dick Cheney, Colin Powell, and President Bush all day, she opts not to collapse on the couch but to head off to a concert at the Kennedy Center. Instead, we read that "entertaining means ordering take-out." Rice could easily have been praised for her commitment to the people in her life who are important to her, maintaining lifelong ties with friends and family, even though those people live far away. She could have been respected and admired for continuing to care about people whose names no one would recognize after she had forged a friendship with one of the most powerful couples in the country. But that is not the story that is told. *The New Yorker* instead discounts Rice's lifelong friends and relatives because they live so far away, notes that Rice is not part of the Washington social circuit, and sadly observes that "her primary off-hour companions seem to be George and Laura Bush." *Newsweek,* for its part, notes with feigned neutrality that Rice's arranged dates with black Washingtonians "were not a success."

What other story could have been written about Rice? How about this theme: If a person with such high-level responsibilities at such a crucial time in history prefers not to pursue unappealing dates, indeed if she prefers to pursue virtually nothing else but work during the duration of her service, perhaps it could be said that she is putting the needs of the country first.

The lesson of singlism is clear. As long as Condi Rice (or any other adult) does not have a mate, there is nothing she can do, nothing with which she can fill her days or her nights, that would qualify her to count as having a life.

How are powerful married people treated? Just a month or so after Rice graced the covers of so many magazines, *Time* ran a feature story, "Pentagon Warlord," about Defense Secretary Donald Rumsfeld. Here is the brief synopsis of a typical Rumsfeld day: "He arrives at his office each day at 6:30 A.M. and typically stays at his post for 12 hours before heading home and working several more hours." Someone who is at work by 6:30 A.M. has already been up for some time. Add that, plus twelve hours, plus the time to get from work to home, plus a few more hours of work at home, and it must be just about bedtime. This, it seems, is a man who could plausibly be portrayed as having no life outside of his work. But there is no intimation of anything of the sort anywhere in the profile. Rumsfeld, it turns out, is covered. As *Time* explains, before Rumsfeld was invited to serve as defense secretary, "he became rich, bought a gigantic spread in Taos, N.M., and was living quietly with Joyce, his high school sweetheart and wife of 48 years." He had his credentialing—his wife. It would matter little if Rumsfeld had hardly seen his wife in those forty-eight years. He wore the badge of that one truly important relationship, and no one would ever question whether he had a life outside of his work.

With that badge come other special privileges. Here, for example, is *Time*'s description of a friendship of Rumsfeld's: "Among those in the Bush inner circle, Rumsfeld is closest to Cheney philosophically and personally. Friends for 35 years, the two men talk about everything." This is clearly a work-related friendship, as much or more so than Rice's friendship with George and Laura Bush. But whereas Rice's friendship is bracketed—it goes with her job, not her life—Rumsfeld's friendship with Cheney counts.

Another powerful married person who was profiled a few months later was Tommy Franks, the general who was about to direct the war against Iraq. *Time,* in "Straight Shooter," tells us that Franks's day usually begins at four A.M. If the time of waking were a perfect indicator of time spent working, Franks might have even less of a life outside of work than Rice or Rumsfeld. Franks, however, holds the grand prize. Not only is he married, but he also has a daughter who is married and two grandchildren. That makes all the difference. Biographical facts that might otherwise seem disreputable can now be covered over with humor or sentimentality.

Franks, it seems, was not a distinguished student, either in high school or in his first attempt at college. (He dropped out.) *Time* describes a conversation between Franks and his high school principal many years later: "'You were not the brightest bulb in the socket,' the retired principal remarked to the general at a recent reunion. Replied Franks, 'Ain't this a great country?'"

Time also reports that Franks married "with a promise that he would soon be leaving the Army. He has been in uniform ever since." The tale seems to be told with the same softhearted whimsy as the one so often told about George W. Bush's promise to Laura that she would never have to make a speech. No harm done. Franks's wife still "kisses him goodbye each morning with a charge: 'Go make the world safe for democracy.'"

The tone could have become more serious as *Time* went on to describe allegations that Franks had permitted his wife to sit in on top-secret briefings for which she had no clearance. One such charge was upheld. That, however, can be treated dismissively. "It seems very petty," an unnamed officer is quoted as saying. The same paragraph continues: "Franks and his wife sit next to each other on his aging 707 command plane—there are four stars on his headrest and four hearts on hers. 'It's cute,' says a fellow passenger. 'When she doesn't travel, he likes to leave the seat empty.'"

In this heroic narrative, even luck becomes an achievement. Says *Time,* "Franks excelled at another mission of all rising stars: making your own luck."

Finally, here is the friendship tale in the Franks profile, an anecdote that provides the lead for the story: "When two soldiers under fire are thrown into the same foxhole, survival depends on putting any differences aside. Perhaps that explains why General Tommy Franks and Pentagon Chief Donald Rumsfeld left work one night recently for a stag dinner right out of a buddy movie. Back in January, their wives out of town, Franks and Rumsfeld hit a Georgetown sushi bar after the multimillionaire Pentagon chief decided to give the Oklahoma-born and Texas-reared artilleryman his first taste of raw fish."

This work-related friendship counts.

Single people whose lives are filled with friendship and passion and marvelously developed talents and stunning achievements can be chided as not having anyone and not having a life simply because they are not coupled. As for people who do have that one special person, and maybe also some kids, it is a whole different story. They are esteemed as having a life, and a wonderful one at that, if they make their own family the center of their lives and their highest priority—always. But for people in positions of staggering responsibility, is such intense and narrow devotion to one's own family really the wisest way to lead a life, or a nation? Here are a few examples of what I mean.

In the early months of 2001 the new residents of the White House prided themselves on not letting their work take over their lives. In March *Time* reported that

> our new President doesn't like to overtax himself. Bush routinely takes an hour or more each day for exercise, is out of the office by 6, keeps a light schedule on the road and starts the weekend early, on Friday afternoons.
>
> Said Andy Card, Bush's chief of staff, "He doesn't want our time to be White House time all the time. He wants people to have a life. This does not have to be all consuming."
>
> Senior staffer Mary Matalin agreed. "There is no guilt associated with making a respectable departure," she said.

In August, Bush headed to Crawford, Texas, for one of the longest absences from the White House in modern presidential history. Filing from the Bush family ranch, *USA Today* reported on August 25 that

President Bush, in grimy bluejeans and sweaty T-shirt, wielded his chain saw against a dead hackberry tree Saturday, determined to make his beloved ranch less "jungle-y" for a wife who had problems with the place at first.

Later, the country would learn that while the president and his people were spending relaxed family time, high-level officials had been trying desperately but unsuccessfully to be heard. Back in January, Richard Clarke, Bush's counterterrorism coordinator, had sent a memo to National Security Advisor Condoleezza Rice requesting an urgent cabinet-level meeting to address what he believed to be an impending al Qaeda attack. The word *urgent,* Clarke said, was underlined. The urgent meeting requested in January was not convened until September 4. The day in August when Bush led the *USA Today* reporter on a leisurely tour of his ranch came just a few weeks after the president had received a daily briefing memo that would later become infamous. It was titled "Bin Laden Determined to Strike in U.S." On September 11, of course, bin Laden did just that.

I'm picking on Bush, but on this issue I am not partisan. The other side of the aisle displays the same mentality. During the 2000 presidential campaign, for example, Democratic candidate Al Gore took his turn on *The Oprah Winfrey Show.* Oprah asked him what he would do if he were elected president and the job "was obviously toxic to your family." Gore did not hesitate. "I would change the job," he said.

To be there when your family needs you or just wants you around, to clear the brush because your spouse thinks it looks unkempt—all that is fine, maybe even admirable, if your responsibilities stop at the door of your own home. But the man or woman who would be president is entrusted with the care and safety of hundreds of millions of Americans. Studio audiences should not cheer, and White House reporters should not file fawning stories, when the leader of the free world claims that the one adult who is most important to him will always come before all others. They should gasp in horror.

CHAPTER ELEVEN

Myth #9 Poor Soul

You Will Grow Old Alone and You Will Die in a Room by Yourself Where No One Will Find You for Weeks

When little children are engaged in seemingly innocent pursuits, such as reading storybooks or playing simple card games, they are already learning about singlism and the dire fate that awaits them if they reach the twilight of their years uncoupled. In one of the card games that has remained popular for generations, almost everyone is a winner. Everyone, that is, except the one player who fails to pair off all cards and is stuck with the one remaining unpaired and unpairable card. That player is holding the losing card—the Old Maid.

Children's books, too, convey ominous messages about old people who are single. That's what a pair of scholars found when they looked closely at just those sorts of characters in more than a hundred children's books. The female characters who had been widowed, when not cast as simply boring, were portrayed as selfish, insensitive hermits, whiling away their time "knitting sweaters nobody needed." That last crack is kind, though, compared with the depictions of the old men who had always been single. They included "a crazed old man wielding a hatchet at people who approached him, a senile man who had talked to no one but his horse for as long as villagers could remember, [and] a man living in the woods who was so unsociable and pathetic that even the animals hesitated to befriend him."

If you are a single person of a certain age, the mythology has a place for you. First, you will grow old alone. That means that no one else will live with you, visit you, include you, or care about you. That's especially so if you never have any children. Then comes your finale. In the oft-quoted words from *Bridget Jones's Diary,* you will end up "dying alone and found three weeks later half-eaten by an Alsatian."

That quip seemed to stick. Of all the verbal volleys lobbed by *Bridget,* the one about dying alone is topped probably only by "smug marrieds" in the speed at which it penetrated the public discourse and stubbornness with which it stayed there. For me, it inspired a new and perhaps perverse addition to my singles collection: stories in the media about death scenarios. Here is an example:

> John Andrew Jamesley, 56, was a busy man who spent much of his time volunteering with agencies serving senior citizens in Carpinteria. He also liked to surf, bicycle and play basketball or golf. . . . That all changed Thursday when his body was found floating face-down in the waters off Carpinteria State Beach.
>
> Beachgoers tried unsuccessfully to revive him. About 30 children from a Camarillo day camp formed a circle, held hands and said prayers as he was carried away on a stretcher.
>
> No one was at the beach with Mr. Jamesley and he had no identification with him. Authorities did not know whom to contact about his death.

Although Jamesley's body was first sighted at noon that day, it was not identified until eight-thirty that evening.

That story appeared in my local newspaper in 2003. I changed the man's name, but otherwise it is a true story. It is a kinder, gentler version of the cautionary tale so often conjured up to frighten single people into getting married: If you stay single, you will die alone. John Jamesley's tale is kinder because it has its touching elements, such as the dozens of children who formed a circle and prayed for him. It is gentler because it admires him for his service and his zest for life.

Still, as far as it goes, the story makes its point. It scares singles into looking longingly toward an entirely different final curtain. In the fantasized version you have lived a long, meaningful, productive life. At the end you are not a dead body floating unidentified in the ocean. Instead, you are with people you have known and loved for decades and who have known and loved you. Maybe you can even count movie stars and international leaders among the friends who just happen to be with you on the day you die. Perhaps you imagine yourself in a bucolic setting, feasting on fine food. Your death is sudden and unexpected, and except for an initial jolt, it is painless. The suddenness is not especially unfortunate, as you did not wait for a sober warning of mortality to express your appreciation to the important people in your life. After you are gone, people from all walks of life remember you with deep love and great admiration.

That story may seem fanciful, but it, too, is true.

It befuddles me that the "dying alone" myth could have such staying power. To me, it seems even more blatantly preposterous than most of the other myths. How could marriage possibly provide insurance against dying alone? Unless both partners to the marriage die at the same instant, one is guaranteed to die without the other. And even the spouse who is the first to die cannot rest assured that his or her partner will be there when the time has come. In fact, even if the couple had children with whom they maintained a warm connection, there would still be no certainty that any of them would be there, either.

That very uncertainty is what drew me to the story of the man who drowned and was not identified until more than eight hours later. After I read past the first few paragraphs, I discovered that he actually was married and had two kids. The second story is about Katharine Graham, the brilliant and fearless publisher of *The Washington Post* who stood behind two young reporters as they pursued the story that would bring down the Nixon presidency. At the time of her death, she had been widowed for thirty-eight years (and had never remarried). As journalist Margaret Carlson tells the story, "At an elite retreat in Sun Valley, Idaho, after lunch with Tom Hanks and before dinner with Mexican President Vicente Fox, [Graham] fell and lost consciousness." Just weeks before, on her eighty-fourth birthday, she had told a gathering of friends how much they meant to her.

I also collect fictional death scenes, such as those portrayed on television. Back in Chapter 2, I took on the claim that single people are doomed to an early demise and insisted that it is greatly exaggerated. On TV, though, it may not be. There, if you are a woman in your thirties who has always been single, you just may end up on your deathbed—alone. This is a fate worse than growing old alone—it is not growing old at all.

On *Judging Amy* a woman with advanced breast cancer arrives at a hospital and is assigned to the care of a young single male doctor. Recognizing that her last days are near, he asks her if there is anyone he can call for her. She says no, there is no one. So the good doctor spends some time at her bedside. The woman confides her wish that she could be spending this moment with a drink and a great-looking guy. In the next scene the doctor returns to her side, drink in hand.

A year later on *CSI Miami,* a young, single Erin Brockovich–type character gets poisoned and has just a short time left to live. Horatio (David Caruso), the hip single man who is the crime scene investigator, asks the woman if there is anyone he can call for her. She names a few family members, but they never show up.

I am not denying the undeniable fact that some single women do die young, just as some single men and married men and married women do. And I'm only a tiny bit annoyed that on both shows a single man swooped in to comfort the dying damsel. (Ah, if only the two had met under more auspicious circumstances and had wed.) But I draw the line at the alone part. The premise that a thirty-something-year-old woman would have absolutely no one in her life who would come to her bedside as she lay dying? I don't buy it. Especially for the one who had dedicated her life to working tirelessly for the public good.

The last death story I relate goes beyond the circumstances of the old single woman's demise and offers a glimpse of the life that came before. That's important. Maybe the threat that if you are single, you will "die alone" is really just shorthand—a way of saying that you will live all by yourself, in nobody's home and in nobody's heart, until the day you die.

In this story a woman I'll call Margaret burned to death in her own home. Margaret was in her seventies and had been single all her life. The report, together with a picture of the charred remains of the home, appeared on the front page of my local newspaper, above the fold. Here are the first few lines:

> An elderly woman died in a fire early Monday in a small home that was
> so cluttered with stacks of newspapers and other belongings that it was

difficult to navigate the debris. . . . Neighbors said she had lived in the small cottage, decorated quaintly with pink shutters, for at least 3 decades.

That much is on page one. Inside, the story continues under the heading "Woman Apparently Had No Family, Visitors":

Some neighbors said "they periodically cut back brush from Margaret's driveway. . . . [Other neighbors] checked up on her regularly. They offered her assistance through Meals on Wheels." Margaret, though, "insisted on" cooking her own food.

Another neighbor who had kids describes visits in which Margaret would tell them all about growing up in Santa Barbara and teaching music. At the end, when Margaret's house was in flames, a frantic crowd of men, women, and children were all there attempting to help. One tried to get in through a window, another called 911, a teen woke his mother, and a man with a garden hose refused to get out of the way until the firefighters got their hoses going full blast, even though the authorities threatened to have him arrested if he didn't move.

The most telling line in this story is the heading printed above the continuation of the story on the inside of the paper: "Woman Apparently Had No Family, Visitors." The heading proclaimed, Here Is a Woman Who Is Completely and Totally Alone, even as the story beneath it tells of the neighbors who had visited her, helped with her yard, offered to help with meals, listened to her stories about her childhood and her livelihood, and, in the end, had to be fought off from trying to save her.

Personally, I don't know anything about Margaret other than what is presented in the story. But even sticking to just those facts, I would have told a different story than the newspaper does. My lead, for example, might have said something about a beloved teacher, lifetime Santa Barbara resident, and spirited septuagenarian. The newspaper instead starts with a description of clutter.

The newspaper wants to see this ever-single older woman as kind of cute rather than as independent, well informed, knowledgeable, and effective. So we hear about her quaint pink shutters instead of the amazing accomplishment of owning her own home on just one salary in one of the most expensive housing markets in the country. We hear about Margaret's stacks of newspapers rather than her continued interest in the world. The reporter may think Margaret is cute, but she also seems to see her as a stubborn old bird. So, instead of noting that Margaret still had the skill and the interest to cook for herself, the reporter instead repeats the neighbors' charge that Margaret "insisted on" cooking her own food.

Three days before the story on Margaret appeared, the same newspaper printed an interesting letter to Ann Landers. It starts like this:

> Dear Ann Landers: My husband is a "junk man." He saves magazines, newspapers, jars and anything else he finds on the ground. He is 55 years old and says he will get rid of his stuff when I get rid of mine. "Mine" consists of one box of Christmas ornaments.

Ann Landers did not attach real names to readers' letters, so I never will know how the first paragraph of Junk Man's obituary will read. I bet my autographed Mickey Mantle baseball glove, though, that it will not be about the clutter.

Judging from the account in the paper, I think the reporter felt sorry for Margaret. Not just because of her gruesome death but maybe also because she lived alone, didn't have any visitors (even though she did), and did not have any kids. So I want to consider those aspects of Margaret's life in the context of thinking about the lives of old people who are single.

First, is it sad that Margaret lived alone? Only if she wished that she hadn't. When I think about the matter of living alone in old age, I always remember one of the most renowned psychologists of the twentieth century. Mary Ainsworth was a much-loved woman who lived on her own for decades. As she approached retirement, she began to receive unsolicited invitations from friends and relatives who wanted her to move in with them for the rest of her life. As she described these extraordinary offers to me, she expressed neither gratitude nor relief but something more akin to indignation. She had no desire to move in with anyone. When the time came when she did need help, she moved into a retirement home where she could still have her own space and yet have others nearby. This was her choice. Mary Ainsworth was, by all measures, an exceptional woman. But the choice she made was not. The wish to live independently for as long as possible is now the normative one.

Well, then, is it sad that Margaret had no children? Again, only if she wished that she had. A sociologist who surveyed more than three thousand adults in middle and old age found three categories of people who were more likely than the others to be depressed: women who did not have children but thought that it would have been better if they had, and both mothers and fathers who had troubled relationships with their children.

A pair of psychologists reviewed 286 studies of the kinds of life circumstances that are linked to feelings of well-being in later life. They found that the people who had adult children did not necessarily feel more satisfied with their lives when they had more contact with their children. Instead, what mattered more was the quality of their interactions. Adult children can, of course, offer profound feelings of love. When that sentiment dominates the time they spend with their aging parents, then their parents do indeed benefit. But adult children may show up feeling more obligated than loving, dragging the family baggage along with them. Maybe that's why the authors conclude that many parents of adult children prefer to enjoy their intimacy at a distance: "Although older adults consider their relationships to their adult children as important, they do not wish to be in their immediate vicinity on an ongoing basis, for example, by living together."

There was a more reliable source of good feelings than the company of adult children: the company of friends. Older adults who spent more time with friends generally felt better about their lives than those who spent less.

If we cannot drown Margaret in our pity simply because she was old and living alone, and we cannot pity her just because she had no children, either, then can we at least assume that she was lonely and pity her for that? Well, no.

Social scientist Pearl Dykstra has been studying loneliness in older adults for more than a decade. The survey results she published in 1995 are based on the responses of 131 Dutch men and women, between sixty-five and seventy-five years old, who had always been single or were previously married (divorced or widowed). They rated their loneliness on a scale of 0 to 11, where 11 is the loneliest number. Here are the averages for each group:

	Previously Married	Always Single
Men	4.3	3.6
Women	3.4	2.0

The first thing to notice is how low the numbers are in every group. The scale midpoint is 5.5. They are all well below that. On the average, then, these old people were not very lonely. Second, the men were lonelier than the women, regardless of whether they had always been single or were once married. Third, people who were once married were lonelier than people who had always been single, regardless of whether they were men or women. And for the grand finale: The least lonely people of all of these sixty-five-to-seventy-five-year-olds were the women who had always been single. Their average loneliness rating is an extraordinarily low 2.0.

Still, the study was a fairly small one, and married people were not included. Nine years later, though, Dykstra reported a much larger study of 3,737 Dutch men and women between the ages of fifty-four and eighty-nine. This time married and remarried people were also surveyed, and the previously married people were separated into those who were divorced and those who were widowed.

For the people who were unmarried, the results were the same as before. All the groups had loneliness scores below the midpoint of the scale. The men were lonelier than the women (except for the divorced group, in which the men and women were equally lonely), and the previously married were lonelier than the people who had always been single. No one was less likely to be lonely than the women who had always been single.

The married and remarried people were not very lonely, either. In fact, the married and remarried men were less lonely than the unmarried men. But among the women, those who had always been single were again remarkable for how little loneliness they experienced. Only the women in their first marriage were as unlikely to be lonely as the women who had always been single.

A smaller study of several hundred American women (ages fifty and older) found the same thing. The women who had always been single and those who were currently married were least likely to be lonely. The formerly married were the loneliest, but even they, on average, were on the not-so-lonely end of the scale.

There are at least three reasons why I am awed by the amazingly low level of loneliness among older women who have always been single. First, they are old. Second, they are women. Third, they have always been single. If we were to believe the mythology, these are people who don't have anyone, who never have had anyone, and who are supposed to be most in need of someone. That should be a triple whammy. How can they be doing so well?

There is a reason that has been suggested now and then for why life singles sometimes do better than widowed or divorced singles in later life: They haven't suffered a loss. Of course, that does not explain why women in particular do so well, but set that aside for now. First we need to dig a hole; toss into it the idea that if you are single, you suffer no real losses; and bury it in scorn.

Back to the ever-single women in later life. Barbara Simon, a professor of social work, interviewed fifty ever-single women born near the turn of the twentieth century. At the time of the interview, they ranged in age from 65 to 105. Simon did find evidence of social isolation—among one of the fifty women. The other forty-nine described a total of forty-seven friends with whom they were in contact every day. Sixteen of those friendships had lasted more than forty years. The same forty-nine women described another ninety-eight people they were in touch with once or twice a week. Twenty of those less intense friendships had lasted more than forty years. None of these numbers includes equally close friendships with people who had died. The women Simon studied had also worked. After they retired, they spent even more time pursuing their interests and enjoying their friendships.

This study offers great big hints as to why ever-single women are so unlikely to be lonely in later life. They have close friendships—typically, more than one. Those relationships are extraordinarily stable, often lasting for decades. These were not women who put their friends on the back burner while they practiced intense romantic coupledom.

There is another reason ever-single women fare even better than previously married women in later life. They mastered the single life long ago. From structuring social events in a culture that caters to couples, to figuring out how to work and get all the tasks of everyday life accomplished when there may or may not be others readily available to do their unfair share, always-single women have been there, done that. It is not a new or daunting challenge. They are aging successfully because of their skills, strengths, and resilience, not because they have suffered no significant losses.

Single men—whether divorced, widowed, or always single—are often a bit lonelier than single women in later life. There have been far fewer studies of ever-single men than of ever-single women, so the explanation for the gender difference is not entirely clear. What is known, though, is that in contemporary American society, men are less likely than women to develop and maintain close same-sex friendships. That's not because of any intrinsic differences between men and women. At different times and in different places—most famously, in ancient Greece—men sustained intense friendships with other men. Today, though, the lingering homophobia that attaches itself more readily to men than to women makes it easier for a pair of women to meet for coffee or dinner or to just spend time together. Men more often seem to need the cover of a business or sporting event. By the time they get to their later years, ever-single women are more likely than always-single men to have the deep and enduring friendships that keep loneliness far away. If I am right about this, an interesting irony would seem to be in play: In old age, many of the men who are burdened by the fallout from homophobia are (and always have been) straight. Indeed, they may have even practiced some heterosexism themselves.

Among those who do marry, women are still more likely than men to attend to friends. When asked to name their best friend, married men typically name their wife, but married women are more inclined than their husbands to name a same-sex friend. In that sense, men practice coupling even more intensively than women do. When a marriage ends, women are more likely to have close same-sex friends in their lives than are men.

There is something else that men and women attend to differentially during marriage, and that's the housework. Typically, wives still do more of it than do husbands. That difference, too, seems to come back to bite men when the marriage ends. Research has shown that among those who are widowed in old age, the men are more likely to feel stressed and depressed by having to do housework than are the women.

From journalistic accounts, there appears to be a growing trend among Americans who are fast approaching, or even looking back at, their retirement age. In 2002 *Time* profiled groups of people—including men and women, single and married—who were "making their closest friends a priority in their retirement scheme." Some sets of friends had scattered geographically over the years but planned to move back to the same location for retirement. Others anticipated sharing homes or living in the same apartment building. Two years later *The New York Times* reported that a "friends-helping-friends model for aging is gaining momentum among single, widowed or divorced women of a certain age." An architect told the *Times* that he had designed a home specifically for two older single women who wanted to live together, and soon thereafter had half a dozen additional requests just like it.

When I read trend stories like the ones in *Time, The New York Times,* and all the others like them, and when I read books like Simon's about singles in later life, I think about all the single people who take the myths seriously and worry about growing old alone. There was Janny, for example, the woman who has probably never spent a day in her life without a friend. Yet in her parting words to the interviewer, she fretted about the possibility of growing old alone if she did not marry. There was also the woman who told psychologist E. Mavis Hetherington about watching the old woman across the street who seemed to have no visitors and wondering, "Is that going to be me in thirty years?" I have an answer for her: Could be. But she could also attend to her friends and plan her future with them. She could also become like the woman who wrote to *People* magazine after it published its cover story on "sexy, single, sizzling" men. That reader quipped, "The guys were great, but how about Sexy, Single, Sizzling Seniors?" Or she could fashion herself after the four single smart-talking women who, as of 2003, were still drawing 13 million viewers a week to watch them in reruns. No, not the *Sex and the City* women, silly! *The Golden Girls.*

CHAPTER TWELVE

Myth #10 Family Values

Let's Give All the Perks, Benefits, Gifts, and Cash to Couples and Call It Family Values

When I first decided to study singles scientifically, I had a particular theoretical model in mind. I called it the Developmental Life Tasks model. (Catchy, I know.) There are, I thought, particular life tasks that people in a given society are expected to accomplish, with a corresponding timetable. For example, by a certain age, you "should" be married. Then, before too long a married couple "should" start having children. Violate those cultural mandates, I theorized, and you get stigmatized.

My study of singlehood focused on the getting-married part of the model. I expected people who stayed single "too long" to be stereotyped in the ways I've been describing. Other people would begin to view them as immature, irresponsible, lonely, and miserable. They would wonder what was wrong. They would entertain hypotheses of uncommon predilections. I had lots of such expectations, but at first they were just guesses. To see if there was anything to them, I teamed up with some colleagues to do a series of studies.

Our notion was that we could create brief biographical sketches of people—let's say, forty-year-olds—with particular jobs and hometowns and interests, and ask adults to read the profiles and give us their impressions. All the people read the exact same sketches, with one exception: Half the time, the person in the sketch was described as single; the other half, the person was described as married.

The results were as expected. A hypothetical forty-year-old with the same hometown, same job, and same interests was judged as less socially mature, less well adjusted, and more self-centered when described as single than when described as married. To make sure that these stereotypes applied only to people who, culturally speaking, "should" have been married and not to much younger people, we also created identical sketches in which all the people were described as twenty-five-year-olds. That's where we were wrong. Even the twenty-five-year-olds were judged more harshly if they were single than if they were married. The twenty-five-year-old singles were not seen quite as negatively as the forty-year-old singles; still, in our readers' minds, they did not measure up to the twenty-five-year-old married people.

That made us wonder whether twenty-something-year-olds might be disparaged for even flimsier reasons than not being married—for instance, for not being in a romantic relationship or not having been in such a relationship in the past. We did more studies similar to the first set, except this time all the people in the sketches were described as college students. Again, the stereotyping persisted. College students who were not in a romantic relationship or who had never been in such a relationship were deemed less socially mature, less well adjusted, and more self-centered than the students who did have romantic relationship experience.

By expecting singlism to kick in only when adults get to an age when they "should" be married, I was minimizing the reach of the stigma of being single. Thinking of getting married as a life "task" was also a bit too lighthearted. It was more like a long-term project with a goal at the end. Like, say, becoming a brain surgeon. You don't just step into the OR and start drilling. You need to get a great residency, and before that you need to get into a terrific med school, and before that you have to have great grades in college, and so on, back to listening to Beethoven in the womb. Same for getting married. By the time you can toddle, the grown-ups are already teasing you about whether you have a boyfriend.

There was something else wrong with my focus on the unkind labels stuck to singles. The labels are the soft side of singlism. They are the words. Other brands of discrimination, such as racism and heterosexism, include practices that can be bone-breakingly hurtful. Does singlism have its own sticks and stones?

Because I am approaching the issue of singlism at this point in history,

I should have lots of advantages. Before me came all the activists and scholars who put racism, sexism, heterosexism, agism, and so many other isms on the map. I don't need to figure out how to do this from scratch. I just need to follow their example.

Heart-stopping discrimination is the kind that constrains the course of a person's life. It limits opportunities and offers fewer rewards for the same amount and quality of work. Big D discrimination means that you can't get the education you need to get the job you want. When and if you do get a job, you won't get the pay you deserve. Hard-core discrimination means you can't live where you want. It means that you cannot afford decent health care, or you won't get the best of it even if you can afford it. In the retail market, discrimination amounts to paying more and getting less. In the criminal justice system, it means more criminal convictions and less justice.

Can I really make such bold claims about the discriminatory treatment of singles? No, for two reasons. First, I do not think that single people really are subject to all forms of discrimination, or the most extreme versions of discrimination, that stymie certain other socially devalued groups. For example, I doubt that singles are disadvantaged at all in their pursuit of higher education.

Second, there is very little relevant research. That, in itself, is telling. Why don't I know for sure whether singles face discrimination in their attempts to further their education?

I wonder whether the defendant whose spouse shows up in the courtroom every day gets more forgiving verdicts and gentler sentencing than a single defendant charged with the exact same crime. I wonder whether single people are accorded the same respect and spiritual support in their places of worship. I wonder whether the doors to fertility clinics open as widely to single women as to married ones. The academic journals are not stuffed with studies on these matters, and reporters do not seem to be poking around looking for answers.

When it comes to singlism, most Americans just don't get it. Either they don't think that single and married people are treated any differently, or if they do notice married people getting the better deal, it doesn't occur to them that there is anything wrong with that. Mostly, though, they just don't think about the matter at all.

No Shelter for Singles

When I was in Virginia and had just started talking about my interest in singles, some students told me about their experiences looking for rental housing. In one instance, a man and a woman who were platonic friends went looking together and did not get such a warm reception from the landlords. About the same time, a married couple was also looking for rental housing and encountered no resistance at all. I shook my head in dismay, but I wasn't totally surprised. In many states—Virginia included—housing discrimination on the basis of marital status is perfectly legal. Perhaps the pair of friends just happened to come up against old-fashioned landlords who believed that cohabitation was tantamount to living in sin, even though the two actually were not romantically involved.

Then a friend told me about a single man who tried to rent a place and was turned down. The landlord explained, without apology, that he wanted to rent the place to a married couple or a family.

Next, a single woman who was a college professor tried to rent an apartment, and she was turned down, too. The landlord said it was because in the past she had not always paid her phone bill on time. She offered to pay an extra month's rent up front. No deal. She had her father write a letter promising to cover the rent anytime she failed to pay it. Still no deal.

That was the third strike. It was time to collect some data. My colleagues Wendy Morris and Stacey Sinclair took the lead. They recruited fifty-four rental agents to participate in a simple study. All the agents had to do was read about three pairs of people who were interested in a particular property, then indicate the pair to whom they would most prefer to rent and why. The three pairs of applicants were all composed of a man and a woman. One was a married couple, another a cohabiting couple, and the third a pair of platonic friends. If the rental agents were evenhanded in their selections, they would have chosen each pair an equal percentage of the time—about 33 percent each. Instead, they favored the married couple 61 percent of the time. The cohabitors came in a distant second at 24 percent, and the friends were left with just 15 percent. We repeated the same study with 107 college students, asking them to play the role of rental agents. They were even more brutal. Eighty percent of them chose the married couple, compared with 12 percent who chose the cohabitors and 8 percent who chose the friends.

Maybe the students assumed that the married couple was especially likely to be stable. To counter that, we conducted a new study in which we purposely made the cohabitors seem more stable. We said that they had been together for six years, whereas the married couple had been together for only six months. It didn't matter. The students still favored the married couple 71 percent of the time, and the cohabitors only 29 percent.

We tried one more version of the study, in which the choices were a married couple, a single woman, and a single man. Again, the married couple was favored overwhelmingly (70 percent), with both the single woman (18 percent) and the single man (12 percent) lagging in the rear.

In each study we asked the participants to justify their choices. They offered lots of different reasons for their selections, but one in particular came up again and again. Both the students and the rental agents said that they chose the married couple because they were married. If you don't see anything wrong with that, imagine that the choice had been between a black renter and a white one, and the rental agents stated flatly that they chose the white renter because she was white.

That gave us the idea to design another study involving a (hypothetical) landlord who really did practice blatant discrimination. The landlord, we said, was trying to rent a house and had two interested tenants. Both had steady jobs and good recommendations from their current landlords. One was single and the other was married. The single person offered to pay more for the house than the married person did. The landlord, though, preferred to lease houses to married people and decided to accept the married person as the tenant. Why, we asked, did the landlord make that decision? And was it legitimate?

We also conducted another version of the study, in which one tenant was black and the other was white. The black tenant offered to pay more, but the landlord chose to lease to the white person. When asked why the landlord chose the white person, participants' responses were unambiguous: The landlord was racist and prejudiced. The decision was unfair and illegitimate. Not so when it was a single person whose offer of more rent was rejected in favor of a married person. To many participants, that decision was just fine. They generated reasons in support of the landlord's decision—maybe the single person would not stay as long as the married person, maybe the single person would not care for the property as well as the married person would. It was as if they were answering the question,

What's wrong with single people? Maybe half a century ago Americans would have headed down the same mental road in thinking about the landlord who favored the white person. Today, though, many adults know blatant racism when they see it.

Handouts for Husbands

I complained earlier that there is very little research on the differential treatment of single and married people. There is one important exception, though. There have been several studies of differences in pay. For women, marital status does not map onto pay in any consistent way from one study to the next. For men, though, it's a different story.

It is a simple story, too. Married men get paid more than single men. Sociologist Steven Nock, who studies marriage in men's lives, has this to say about men's "marriage premium": "Employers value marriage and reward it." Maybe. But if the single men and the married men are doing the same work at the same level of competence and seniority, then I'd have a different take on the matter. I'd call it blatant discrimination.

The "if" is a big one. If married men really did work longer or harder or more productively or more creatively than single men, then the pay difference would amount to just rewards rather than unfair practices. So, which is it?

The only studies that have a prayer of answering the question are the ones that compare married and single men who are similar in their accomplishments. Virtually all the studies do so. That in itself suggests that single men are probably wrongfully underpaid. My next question is, By just how much? Estimates of the marriage premium vary from about 4 percent to about 50 percent. The best estimate is probably 26 percent. That's how much difference in pay there is for pairs of men who are, in many ways, as similar to each other as two men can be (they are identical twins), except that one is married and the other is single.

How substantial is a 26 percent pay differential? Assume that a single man and a married man each works for forty years at the same job. The single man earns an average annual salary of $50,000. The married man earns 26 percent more, or $63,000. Over the course of the forty years, the married man has been paid $520,000 more than the single man. That half-million-dollar spread is the most conservative estimate imaginable—the difference that would result if the married man stuffed the difference under his mattress and never earned a cent of interest and if higher salary were not pegged to other perks such as greater retirement benefits.

And speaking of benefits—even if single workers were paid exactly the same salaries as married workers, their total compensation package may still end up way less than that of their married coworkers. That would happen in workplaces in which married employees could add their spouse to a health-care plan or any other benefit program at a reduced rate, when single employees had no such option to add an adult to their plans. Married workers can easily end up with total compensation packages worth 25 percent more than the ones their single colleagues get. This is an inequity that is not limited to men; married women can add their spouse to their plans, too.

But if the single workers are getting health-care coverage and the married workers are, too, then why should the single workers care if the married workers' spouses are also covered? Maybe they shouldn't—if they can add an adult of their choosing, such as a parent, other relative, or friend, to their plans. If that's forbidden, then they should care because the money used to offer discounted health care to coworkers' spouses is coming from somewhere and it is headed selectively only to workers who are married. The practice amounts to unequal compensation for the same work.

Workers who have children can sometimes add them to their health-care plans at a reasonable rate, when workers without children have no comparable option. I don't mind this, for two reasons. The first is the one I've tried to keep in mind all along: Whether people have spouses is a whole different issue from whether they have kids. Some married people have no kids, and some single people do. Second, to me, kids are in a special category that includes anyone of any age who needs the care of others. New considerations apply. I'll offer some suggestions when I get to the final chapter.

A Matrimaniacal Work Environment?

Pay and benefits are two workplace inequities I can nail down with data. I wonder if there are others. For example, are single applicants less likely to be hired than married applicants who are no better qualified? Are they less likely to be promoted? More likely to be laid off?

Apart from issues of compensation, I don't know for sure whether singles are treated less fairly than married people in the workplace. But I have heard plenty of stories from singles and read about many others. Remember Myth #8? That's the one that maintains that as a single person, "you don't have anyone and you don't have a life." The scores of stories I've collected indicate that many bosses and married coworkers act as if they really believe that myth. The assumption that single workers have no life seems to account nicely for the expectations that single people can stay at work later or come back at night, show up on the weekends and holidays, do more work and more traveling, and settle for whatever vacation weeks are left after the married workers stake out their preferences.

One evening I invited some singles over for dinner at my place so we could compare notes on workplace issues. One person who wanted to come had a competing commitment. She had been asked by her department chairperson to entertain a visiting scholar and his spouse.

Although the extra time that singles are presumed to have may seem like a boon to bosses, it may be threatening to married coworkers who fear that single people might use that time to work hard and get ahead. A married professor addressed this issue in an essay he wrote. Trying to get tenure is challenging, he said, "when you have other things to devote your life to," such as family obligations. In contrast, "single faculty have so much time to spend on work, like they're still grad students." (Note the implication of immaturity.) He cautioned his fellow "family faculty" not to envy their single colleagues. When family faculty "get a few precious hours to focus on research, they are more likely to use those hours to move their current project forward, rather than pursue daydreams." Family faculty "pursue a steady trajectory," while "single faculty are more easily buffeted and sent off course." Single faculty may well be "bright, hardworking people," but come tenure time, their superiors may realize that they have fallen "victim to distraction." Their bids for promotion may prove "unsuccessful," while married faculty "navigate successfully in academia."

The essay was published by the university's Teaching Resource Center and distributed to all faculty, married and single.

When single employees are greatly outnumbered by married coworkers, they may be at special risk for ribbing and ridicule. One such single worker told me about his married colleagues who clipped newspaper and magazine stories about the supposed superiority of married people and brought them in to work to show him. "Hey, look, single people jump off bridges while married people cavort merrily in the park," they taunted.

The end of the workday is not always the end of the workplace slights for people who are single. Many companies sponsor parties and other social events. Sometimes married workers are encouraged to bring their spouse. Uncoupled single workers are often not allowed to invite anyone. A single man looking for work was told about such practices at his job interview and was asked how he would feel about being single at company outings when his coworkers would be accompanied by their spouses. (It could have been a coincidence that he did not get the job.)

Family Doctors

On Amazon, Dr. Cathy Goodwin, a business and career consultant, comments on a book about single people and adds some of her own observations. "The medical world tends to stereotype singles," she says. "I've had firsthand experience with prejudices directed against those who are single and childless. The whole system is based on the assumption that every patient comes with a family."

What happens to patients who do not have close family members at their side? A team of psychologists decided to find out. They contacted a nationwide sample of physicians in frequent contact with patients over fifty-five years of age. Here is their conclusion:

> The results were clear: Physicians reported not only that they themselves provided better or more complete medical care to patients who had supportive families than to patients who appeared to be socially isolated, but also that, in their experience, other doctors, nurses, and ancillary staff did the same.

Most single people are not socially isolated. But when the important people in their lives are friends rather than family, it is not clear that they will be treated with the highest standards of care. The implications are significant. As long as the prejudice against patients without traditional families persists, then even comparable access to health insurance and to the health-care system for all citizens would not guarantee comparable care.

The Command Team Wears Wedding Bands

A year or two into the war in Iraq, during the holiday season, I was asked to sponsor "morale calls" for soldiers who were away from home. This seemed a cause with no downside, so I agreed. A few months later, though, when I was interviewing single service members about their experiences in the military, some of them complained that morale calls were awarded preferentially to soldiers who were married. That made me wonder whether the married service members are also favored in other ways.

Many examples of unfair treatment described to me by single service members sound just like the ones that come out of any other workplace. Single soldiers believe that they work longer hours, get assigned to more than their share of holiday duty, and are constantly covering for their married buddies when something comes up.

In other ways, though, military discrimination stands out above all the rest. Take pay, for example. Since World War I married service members have been paid more than single members at the same rank. This disparity has grown over time, and by 2006 had reached an average advantage to married members of 25 percent.

Married personnel are also eligible for a whole array of special allowances that are off-limits to single people. One of them is the Family Separation Allowance. Under certain conditions, two soldiers who are married to each other can be eligible for an extra allotment of several hundred dollars a month if they are separated for more than thirty days.

Now consider two soldiers who are similar in all the following ways: They have no children or siblings, and their parents are deceased. They are equal in rank and in all other matters relevant to competence, achievement, and deployment. Finally, they both die in the same firefight. If one is single and the other is married, only the married soldier is considered to have a legal survivor. The spouse of the married soldier, but no one in the life of the single soldier, can make a claim for insurance. Only the spouse can get reimbursed for personal property that was destroyed during the deployment.

There is still segregated housing in the military. Not by race, of course—President Harry Truman decreed that a disgrace by executive order in 1948. If you are married, though, often you can still live apart from soldiers who are single. As the army.com website explains, "if you are married and living with your spouse and/or minor dependents, you will either live in on-base housing, or be given a monetary allowance called BAH (Basic Allowance for Housing) to live off-base." And if you are single with no kids? If you want to live off base and your base allows it, you can—but at your own expense. You will get no housing allowance, nor even a food allowance. Consequently, most single service members live in barracks or dormitories. That means that whereas your married friends can head home to a whole different place, where they can have some privacy and space for their dirt bikes, your workplace is your home. Whereas married soldiers with the same rank as you may be able to build up equity in a house, you get to tend to your little room and keep it in tip-top shape so it will pass inspections, some of which are unannounced.

Before I started studying singles, I didn't know what a "command team" was. Or if I had heard the term, I probably thought I already knew what it meant. A team of commanders, right? Actually, a command team is traditionally an officer and his wife. (Yes, there are female officers now, but they are still the exception.) The officer does what officers do, and gets paid for it (extra for being married). The wife ("first lady") plays hostess, booster of morale among the families of the soldiers, and supervisor of support groups. For free. That's up-front. An army captain who had always been single told *Salon* that behind the scenes, officers' wives "socialize, politicize [in order to] help the husband's career."

Officially, the "voluntary" contributions of wives cannot be used in officers' performance appraisals; Department of Defense policy prohibits it. But mentions of wonderful wives are still pervasive in letters of recommendation. And statistically, higher-ranking military men are especially likely to be married men. In 2002 only about 9 percent of new recruits (ages eighteen to twenty-four) were married. Among enlisted men, the number was 50 percent, and for active-duty or reserve officers, it was 71 percent and 77 percent, respectively. (Relative to comparable civilians, new recruits were less likely to be married, enlisted men and active-duty officers were about as likely to be married, and reserve officers were more likely to be married.) Service members draw their own conclusions as to what these statistics mean. As another army captain told *Salon*, "acquiring a first lady [is] more or less a job requirement—advisable by captain, essential by lieutenant colonel."

The lower pay, the stingier benefits, and the third-rate housing, together with the command team culture and the "up or out" ethic, sends a clear message to single soldiers. Get married or get out.

Cheaper by the Couple

I love living in Summerland, but I don't much like driving to the Los Angeles airport. Luckily for me, there is a convenient shuttle with a stop just a few miles from my home. For sixty-eight dollars, I can book a round-trip fare. The couple next door can board the same shuttle together for just fifty-eight dollars each.

The owners of the shuttle service don't really care about my marital status. They just want more people to sign up for their rides. They think they are pursuing a wise business practice. I think they are practicing discrimination against me and everyone else—single or otherwise—who travels solo. Of course, it is not the kind of discrimination that can get them into any legal trouble. Still, why don't they just charge me—and every other customer—less money the more often I sign up for their rides?

I buy lots of books. I have a line item in my budget that never gets vetoed. From Amazon alone, I'm sure I have bought literally hundreds of books. The company would like me to sign up for Amazon Prime for seventy-nine dollars and get free express shipping on qualifying purchases. A household made up of five people could split the bill so that each of them would pay less than sixteen dollars. I don't think that's a very good return on my loyalty.

Free lunch! Free dinner! My local papers are filled with ads flaunting such offers in bold typeface. In the small print is the qualifier: Buy one meal and the second is free. Maybe I'll ask if they will give me the second meal to go.

If I wanted to sign up for the elite level of the US Airways Club, it would cost me 30 percent more than it would cost each member of a couple. My annual auto club membership costs 33 percent more. Private health insurance is cheaper by the couple, and often auto insurance is, too. I don't have pets, but in Virginia I came across a bright pink flyer from the local SPCA. That's how I learned that married people can get their cats neutered for a special low price available only to them. At a Harvard reunion in 2001 classmates who were married to each other could register for half the price of everyone else. Which just goes to show, subsidies for married people extend even to households headed by two Harvard graduates.

My father liked golf, and when I was in high school he thought I might, too. So one evening after dinner we set out for the driving range. He thought I swung the club like a baseball bat. I liked the night air but not much else. Good thing. If I were smitten by the sport and wanted to pursue it, say, by joining the Bernardo Heights Country Club in San Diego in 2004, it would have cost me. Memberships were $9,500. Married people could tuck their spouse and all their kids under that one fee. Single people, though, could only bring a guest if the guest paid seventy dollars each time. Even then, the guest could be invited only six times a year.

The travel industry seems to thrive on extracting exorbitant fees from single people. Some of the most egregious examples come from the cruise lines; they charge as much as three times the per-person double-occupancy rate for a single person traveling sans roommate. Charging double would be somewhat understandable: If the cruise line could book two people to a room, for every room, for every cruise, then it would lose by charging singles any less. But triple? That's supposedly to make up for the money a second person would have shelled out on sundry items not included in the tour package. Well, maybe. What I do know is that some cruise lines, hotels, adventure trips, and vacation destinations are offering friendlier fares. Perhaps every adult who is single, ever was single, may be single in the future, or knows someone who is single should favor those places with their travel dollars.

There is another way that single people living by themselves lose out, relative to couples living together. The concept, in the jargon, is known as economies of scale. A married couple living together has one rent or mortgage, one utility bill, one set of living-room furniture, and one of just about everything else. A single person living alone has that same one mortgage, utility bill, and so forth, to be paid from just one person's source of income. I recognize this disparity, but I don't object to it. I want to live by myself, and I'm willing to pay for it.

Welfare for Wealthy People Who Have Married

In the chapter on single parents, I ranted about President Ronald Reagan's story about the Welfare Queen who drove a welfare Cadillac and filed claims for still more ill-gotten benefits by fabricating four dead husbands. I thought it was nasty of him to stoke hostility toward the poorest people in the country, based on just one person. It was mean of him to taint the reputations of qualified recipients when their legitimate benefits were so paltry. And it was lazy and dishonest of him to make up this story of a welfare cheat who never really existed, and present it as true. If he thought there were scads of welfare cheats, why didn't he go out and find some real ones?

At the same time I do understand the resentment of citizens who suspect that the money they earned, then paid back in taxes, is being handed over to undeserving recipients. So here are my stories of unworthy beneficiaries of government largesse. In a tip of the hat to the twenty-first century, I have updated their vehicles and included men as well as women. Plus my stories are extrapolations from a column called "Social Security Q&A," prepared by the Social Security Administration and distributed by Knight Ridder News Service. The questions answered in the column were submitted by people who really do exist. The category names, though, are my own.

In my first category are married people who drive BMWs. I'll call them the Eager Beamers. They lead lives of luxury and decadence, frequenting spas and country clubs and trendy restaurants and treating themselves to spectacular vacations. They have no children or dependent elderly relatives and never worked a day in their lives. When they (and their spouse) reach "retirement" age, though, they apply for and receive government checks from that day forward. Hey, why not? Their spouse worked.

The next category includes formerly married people who have four spouses they divorced after hanging around for a decade or so each time. Like the people in the first category, they lived the good life while they were married, never had kids, and never did any paid work themselves. When they nuzzle up to their golden age, the government lines up four different payout options (one for each ex), and they are free to choose the most generous one. Their checks also keep coming until the day they die. In my book, they are the Richly Re-Divorced.

In the third category are people who did work for many years. They also married. Then divorced. Then remarried. Then divorced and remarried again. Then did the same thing still again. When these people retire, the government sends them checks for the rest of their lives. It also sends checks to their current spouse and to all their unmarried exes. I'll call them the Magnanimous Remarriers, though that is a bit too kind. After all, it is not their money that is being awarded to a lifetime of spouses.

The three sets of people I have described are today's Welfare Queens and Kings. Like Reagan's fake queen, these real people receive government handouts. The payments are not called welfare but entitlements—Social Security, to be exact. What's more, none of the people receiving the checks are cheats. All these government handouts are considered perfectly legitimate.

Who is subsidizing these handouts? I am. So is every other citizen who pays taxes and is not among the Eager Beamers, the Richly Re-Divorced, or the exes of the Magnanimous Remarriers. This is not my idea of family values.

I am not assailing people who have no children (I don't have any, either), nor am I objecting to lawfully attained wealth. Moreover, I value the Social Security program and do not think it should be dismantled or privatized. I just don't think I should have to subsidize able-bodied and fully competent grown-ups who are not doing any care work, simply because they are married. I don't think that, on my dime, people who have divorced repeatedly should be able to line up the Social Security checks due them from each of their exes and choose the biggest one. And I'm not sure that I want to subsidize the Social Security checks of a whole array of ex-spouses, based on the earnings of just one worker who did all that remarrying.

Oh, and one other thing. When the Magnanimous Remarriers die, the Social Security checks continue to make their way to all the ex-spouses. When I die, my account is closed and no one is entitled to the benefits I worked my whole life to earn.

Sam Snubs Singles

That's Uncle Sam, of course, who is doing the snubbing of singles. In January 2004, in response to a request from the U.S. Senate, the General Accounting Office searched the books for all the federal provisions "in which marital status is a factor in determining or receiving benefits, rights, and privileges." The grand total was 1,138. There are untold numbers of state-granted legal marriage rights, too.

When you get married, you get the equivalent of a government-issued two-for-one coupon pack. If one spouse is eligible for Medicare or Medicaid, the other probably is, too. If you immigrate legally and you are married, your spouse can probably join you. If you are in the military, you have commissary privileges; if you are married, so does your spouse. If one spouse is a veteran, both spouses get plots in veterans' cemeteries.

If bad things happen to you and you are married, sometimes your spouse is entitled to special consideration on the basis of your misfortune. When bad things happen to single people, forget about it—often no one qualifies for compensation. Let's start with the gravest of bad things, death. I've already mentioned Social Security benefits for the surviving spouses and ex-spouses of workers who were married. There are also special survivor benefits for the spouses of railroad workers, longshoremen, harbor workers, coal miners who died of black lung disease, veterans, public safety officers killed on the job, and federal employees.

If you are killed as a result of negligence, then regardless of your marital status, your parents or children can sue in state court for wrongful death. If you are married, then one more person is qualified to complain—your surviving spouse. Legally speaking, it is as if the death of a single person is not quite as wrongful as the death of a married person.

The federal government seems to have a special fondness for married people who are rich and have homes, properties, and big-time estates. When wedded people die, they can pass along any amount of money or property to their spouse, totally tax-free.

The bad things the government frets about if you are married do not have to be as bad as death. If you are seriously ill, your spouse may qualify to take time off from work to care for you under the Family and Medical Leave Act. If you are single, no one in your generation is eligible to do the same for you. Sometimes married people get relocated; if their spouses leave jobs to join them, they can collect unemployment.

As a married person, you even have special privileges if the bad thing that happens to you is your own fault—let's say you commit murder. Your spouse might know you did it but need not testify against you in court. Spousal communications are "privileged." There are no such privileges for a close friend, nor even for parents or children. If you are imprisoned for your crime, your spouse is more likely to be allowed to visit you than is the most important peer in the life of a prisoner who is single.

I won't even try to describe all the other legal perks for married people. In fairness, though, I will say this. When the General Accounting Office said that the list of 1,138 provisions described "benefits, rights, and privileges," I don't think that was quite accurate. Some of the laws stipulate responsibilities or burdens rather than rewards. For example, if one spouse wants to apply for certain loans, the other spouse's income and assets may be figured into the calculations.

The obligation to mention a spouse's financial resources on a loan application is not the married person's burden that is best known throughout the land. The marital hardship that gets the most press and the most congressional hand-wringing is, of course, the so-called marriage penalty in the tax code.

"Marriage Penalty"? No Such Thing

Once upon a time, the U.S. Congress rewrote the tax code so that it would be more fair to single people. This is not a fairy tale. It really did happen, and it wasn't eons ago, either. The time was the sixties, and single woman Vivien Kellems was fed up with paying more than her fair share of taxes. She organized a group called War Widows of America and held a press conference. Because so many men had died in war, she claimed, the country was teeming with widows and other single women who never would be able to find husbands. Why should they pay for the crushing consequences of war, not only with their spinsterhood but also with extra taxes?

I can't say I liked Kellems's "poor me, I don't have a husband" appeal, but it did succeed. At least for a while. She mobilized enough single women to ensure the passage of the Tax Reform Act of 1969.

Before I started writing this chapter, I thought I understood, at least in general terms, the basics of the so-called marriage penalty as of the year 2005. First, I recognized that the "marriage penalty" was one of those monikers like the "Blue Skies Initiative," in which the reality is exactly the opposite of what the name implies. More married people get a marriage bonus than are hit with a marriage penalty. Second, I thought I understood the condition under which married people would be penalized—when both spouses made a lot of money.

I wanted to see what the discrepancies really amount to, so I started making a table, which you can see on the next page. My question was, If a single person's taxable income were exactly the same as that of a married couple filing jointly, how much more—or less—would the single person pay in federal taxes? I started at $25,000. That's not much money, so I did not expect the marriage penalty to kick in yet, and it did not. The single person was penalized by owing more in taxes than the married couple who listed the same total taxable income on their joint return. The single person was penalized at $50,000, too, paying $2,395 more in federal taxes than the married couple; that's 35 percent more. I tried $75,000. Singles still paid more. Then $100,000. Then $200,000, then $300,000. The single person was still paying more. I skipped up to a million dollars, then 2 million. By then it seemed clear that at the very high incomes, the single person was always going to pay $6,407 more in federal taxes than the married couple. That's a singles penalty.

The Singles Penalty in the Federal Tax Code: 2005

| Taxable Income | TAXES OWED | | EXTRA PAID BY SINGLE PERSON | |
	Single Person	Married Couple (filing jointly)	%	$$
$25,000	$3,385	$3,020	12.1	$365
$50,000	$9,165	$6,770	35.4	$2,395
$75,000	$15,507	$12,080	28.4	$3,427
$100,000	$22,501	$18,330	22.8	$4,171
$200,000	$52,999	$46,592	13.8	$6,407
$300,000	$85,999	$79,592	8.0	$6,407
$1,000,000	$330,470	$324,063	2.0	$6,407
$2,000,000	$680,470	$674,063	1.0	$6,407

I went back to my collection of clippings about the marriage penalty and read more closely. The "marriage penalty," it turned out, is not about comparing the taxes paid by a single person to those paid by a married couple on the same taxable income. It is, instead, a matter of comparing two different kinds of couples—those who are married and those who pool their income but are not married. At a combined taxable income of $100,000 ($50,000 for each member of the couple)—which seems like a decent amount of money to me—the tax bill is the same ($18,330) regardless of whether the two people are married or unmarried. At $200,000, alas, there is a difference. The married couple owe $46,592. For the unmarried couple, with two incomes of $100,000 each, the combined tax bill is $45,002. So, yes, the married couple with an income of $200,00 pays $1,590 more in taxes than the unmarried couple with the same income. Meanwhile, the single person is still paying more than anyone else ($52,999) on that same $200,000.

What Is the Life of a Single Person Worth?

After the terrorist attacks of September 11, 2001, the U.S. government created a fund to compensate the families of the victims. Compensation was calculated separately for each victim, based in part on projected lifetime earnings and other sources of money. In addition, each family was paid a standard $250,000 for pain and suffering. The final component was an extra $50,000 for spouses and for each child. According to these calculations, the lives of single victims are automatically worth less than those of married victims. The $50,000 that would go to a married victim's spouse would not go to any living person who cared about the victim who was single.

The Victim Compensation Fund declared in cold, hard numbers that in contemporary American society, the life of a single person is worth less than the life of someone who is married. That's only one of the reasons I find it interesting. The fund also makes another set of values unusually clear: A relationship with a spouse is considered worthier than any other adult relationship, including even ties to parents or siblings. Said the mother of one of the 9/11 victims, "When they did this formula, why didn't they consider the parents? My daughter-in-law was married for five years. We had Jonathan for 33 years."

The person in charge of the excruciating task of assigning a dollar value to victims' lives, attorney Kenneth Feinberg, had second thoughts about the matter after the job was completed. In the book he wrote about his experiences, he concludes that if Congress ever decides to create such a fund again, all victims should be valued equally.

Does It Really Matter?

Singlism seems to seep into way too many of the nooks and crannies of a person's life and leave its stain. A job applicant shows up for an interview and is asked how he will feel at company social events when he is the only one without a spouse. Single faculty members open the pages of the latest university publication and read that they are regarded as idle daydreamers buffeted about by this distraction or that and, with nothing else to devote their lives to other than their work, more like flighty graduate students than their grounded and focused married colleagues. Accomplished singles show up at social events and find their achievements ignored but their dating life scrutinized. Condoleezza Rice turns on the television after a long day in one of the most powerful positions an American woman has ever commanded and hears Bob Woodward intone to Larry King on national television that she "has no personal life."

Each individual instance of singlism considered by itself may seem utterly trivial. But is it really? And if each particular experience of singlism seems lightweight and inconsequential, then what about the cumulative impact of those slights over the course of a lifetime? Can singles be bruised by a ton of feathers?

I don't know. Social scientists have mostly ignored singles in their study of the effects of stereotyping and discrimination. But they have taken other marginalized groups, such as women and African Americans, very seriously. Research on the implications of stigma for groups other than singles may provide hints of how singlism may get under the skin of the people who are its targets.

In a study of everyday sexism, participants kept diaries, every day for two weeks, of all the instances of sexism they experienced. They kept a running record of their moods and emotions, as well as their feelings of self-esteem. The kinds of experiences they recorded include sexist jokes and language, sexual innuendo, and garden-variety gender prejudice (as, for instance, from the man who told a woman, "It's not my job to wash dishes"). The everyday hassles left a smudge. When women experienced sexism (and to a lesser extent, when men did, too), they felt more uncomfortable, depressed, and angry than they did when sexism did not intrude upon their lives. Their self-esteem was battered a bit, too.

Suppose other people really do believe the stereotypes about you and expect you to behave in accord with them? Imagine, for example, that a person you just met assumes that because you are single, you must "have issues." She thinks there must be something wrong with you and expects you to behave in a socially awkward way. Will her expectations matter? Will you actually end up acting more awkwardly than you would with someone who did not make such assumptions? No one has conducted this particular study with single people, so we don't know the answer. But there are lots of studies of the power of interpersonal expectations in other domains.

The most famous study demonstrates the impact of positive (rather than negative) expectations. Schoolteachers were led to believe that some of their students had been identified by a Harvard test as intellectual bloomers. Over the course of the next year, the bloomers were likely to do especially well in school. In fact, however, the "bloomers" were no more talented than the other students; on the average, the only differences between the two sets of students were the expectations created in their teachers' minds. Yet those expectations shaped the teachers' interactions with the students; for example, they were warmer to the bloomers than to the other students, called on them more often, and gave them more time to answer. By the end of the year, the students who were expected to do better—and who had started the year no smarter or more diligent than anyone else—actually did do better than the students who were not expected to excel.

What if you just think that other people expect you to behave in accord with a stereotype? Can your own fear of confirming other people's worst stereotypes about you undermine your performance? Again, with regard to singles, we don't know. But there is quite a lot of research on the implications of "stereotype threat" for other groups. For example, African Americans presented with a test of intellectual ability may fear that they will live down to the stereotype of being not quite as bright as whites. And, in fact, when a difficult test is described as a test of intellectual ability, African Americans do much worse at it than when the exact same test is described as completely irrelevant to the test taker's intelligence.

Stereotype threat literally gets under your skin. Physiological reactivity changes when people worry about behaving in ways that confirm other people's prejudices. For example, when African Americans are taking the test described as a measure of intellectual ability, their blood pressure is dramatically higher than it is when they are taking the exact same test while thinking that it is not a measure of intelligence. Any one instance of stereotype threat, with its concomitant spike in blood pressure, may or may not be all that important, but what about a lifetime of such experiences? Maybe an accumulation of blood-pressure-raising experiences contributes to another documented difference between stigmatized groups such as African

Americans and other nonstigmatized groups: The stigmatized groups are more likely to experience hypertension, stroke, and heart disease.

What about getting excluded—does that matter? Is it any more than a mere annoyance to people who are single when couples from their workplace or their social circles go off with one another and exclude them? We don't know. But we do know that ostracism matters a great deal to every other group that has ever been studied. The repeated and dramatic instances of ostracism obviously matter—as, for example, when certain high school students are shunned and ignored, day after miserable day. Social scientists have now uncovered something much more surprising—even the most minimal forms of exclusion can hurt. If three people are connected to one another in cyberspace, with no identifying information, and play a virtual ball-tossing game, the players care about getting their fair share of tosses. If two of the players begin tossing mostly only to each other, the excluded player feels devalued and disliked, anxious and sad. These negative reactions occur even though, as the authors note, the players "were accessing the internet in their own private environments [and were therefore] insulated from public embarrassment and ridicule. In fact, they had no idea who the ostracizing sources were and certainly would not be expecting any future contact with them."

Getting stereotyped, stigmatized, and excluded is all part of singlism, the self-evidently nasty side of the singles treatment. What about the other side of being single—making your way through a culture that glorifies couples? Other than the irritation factor, is there any threat to single people of having images of blissful coupled people constantly paraded all around them?

Take, for example, one particular version of the marital mythology—the fantasy of the Knight in Shining Armor. He of wealth and royalty whisks away the poor bedraggled maiden and converts her into his princess, who lives happily ever after. You can ask women if they believe that these myths apply to their own lives, but they would know how dumb it would sound to say yes. It is possible, though, to find out in a more indirect and nonobvious way whether some women really do associate a romantic partner with a White Knight or a Prince Charming. Just ask them to press one button when the word *boyfriend* is paired on their computer screen with another word or phrase like *hero* or *Prince Charming,* and to press a different button when the word *boyfriend* is instead paired with words or phrases like *kind* or *Average Joe*. The actual procedure is a bit more complicated, but I've said enough to explain the bottom line. Some women push the relevant button much more quickly when *boyfriend* is paired with heroic words than when it is paired with ordinary ones. More important, the same women who are especially likely to associate boyfriends with rescue heroes "showed less interest in high-status occupations, the economic rewards that accompany them, and the educational commitment they require." Who needs a great job or a superb education when you can just step into the glass slipper and live happily ever after?

So far, I've focused on the psychological implications of singlism and matrimania and have left many questions dangling unanswered. It is much easier to pin down the economic implications. As with the social slights, many of the individual economic disadvantages do not seem all that consequential when considered one at a time. When I walk into a supermarket and pay a higher price per unit for the smaller package, I am subsidizing all my fellow shoppers who are buying the more reasonably priced jumbo packs. In any one instance, though, I'm probably talking about cents rather than dollars. But what am I talking about over the course of a lifetime?

If I stopped for dinner by myself on my way home, I could not use the two-for-one coupon, so I'd end up subsidizing all the couples in the restaurant who did get their discounted meals. Maybe I drove to the restaurant in a car for which I paid higher insurance than the married couples. If I wanted to stop at the gym after dinner, I'd probably be paying more for my membership than each member of a couple would. Same for hotels, cruises, and so much else.

The groceries and the gym memberships are just the small stuff. Add the extra salary for married men, the discounted health benefits for many spouses, the greater Social Security options that currently married and ever-married people often have when they reach retirement, and the lower tax bill that married people pay, and the economic disadvantages of being single in contemporary American society no longer seem trivial. In fact, it seems inconceivable that people who are single could, at least on the average, do as well as married people financially over the course of a lifetime. And, indeed, they do not.

People who are single for life never do get any of the money and prizes awarded other people simply because they are married. A nationally representative survey of nearly ten thousand preretirement adults (ages fifty-one to sixty-one) included an assessment of each person's total wealth, including stocks and bonds, cars, homes, businesses, and everything else, minus any debt. Men who had always been single had 61 percent less wealth than men who had been continuously married (never divorced or widowed). Ever-single women had 86 percent less wealth than continuously married women.

Divorced people end up disadvantaged, too. Adults who reach their fifties divorced from their first marriage and not remarried have spent some of the years of their adult lives collecting marital manna, but they have spent other years losing it on the expenses and sequelae of the breakup. Divorced men end up with 64 percent less wealth than their ever-married age-mates, and women with 79 percent less. Up to at least age sixty-one, then, financial fortunes are more closely tied to marriage for women than they are for men. People who are already widowed (and not remarried) by then, though, are the exceptions—both the men and women have about 53 percent less wealth than continuously married people.

The Social Security system has been remarkably successful in reducing the overall rate of poverty among the elderly. Because women typically out-live men, most old people are women. Even with their pensions, though, widows are not always protected from poverty; some have spent down their savings in caring for a dying spouse. Past the age of seventy, about a quarter of unmarried women of every variety (widowed, divorced, and ever single) are living in poverty.

People who have fewer financial resources, such as people who are single, are less likely to purchase health insurance. Single people also do not have the option of getting coverage under a spouse's plan. As a result, they may be more likely to put off visiting a doctor for a troubling problem, perhaps waiting until the condition worsens and becomes even more expensive to treat. Then, once singles do access the health-care system, they may be less likely than married people to receive the highest quality of care.

Considering all the financial and psychological benefits that come with getting married, people who have crossed the marital threshold really should be much happier and healthier than people who have been single and stig-matized all their lives. But as I showed in Chapter 2, getting married does not seem to have dramatic implications for health or well-being. Instead, people who are single—especially women who have always been single—often do just fine. There is an intriguing juxtaposition here: Single people are stereotyped, stigmatized, marginalized, and ignored, yet they often live hap-pily ever after. Single people start out as targets of discrimination, but they do not end up as hapless victims. Their lives, in many instances, are instead sparkling examples of psychological strength and resilience.

CHAPTER
THIRTEEN

It Is Perfectly Understandable That You Thought Singles Were Miserable and Lonely: Here's Why

I have to admit it. For far too long when I opened a scientific journal to read a study comparing single people and married people, I expected the worst. Typically, I was sent scurrying to the original report of the research after watching a cutesy segment on TV or reading a snappy story in a newspaper or magazine. The gist of the media reports was always the same: Single people are faring far more poorly in life than people who have gotten married. Even after chasing down hundreds of such headlines and finding each one to be just another son of Shamster, I'd still rush to check out each fresh claim, filled with the familiar sense of trepidation.

My fear was not that the media had gotten the results all wrong but that they, and the social scientists they were interviewing, had gotten the findings exactly right. I worried that the latest study actually had shown that marriage transforms miserable single people into blissfully married couples. Now, many years later, I know what I shall really find when I look up studies of health or happiness or longevity or satisfaction with life or just about any other emotional or physical or interpersonal characteristic. Single and married people are always far more similar than they are different. Often if there is one group that is having a more difficult time than the others, it is a group of people who were once married, and not the people who had always been single. Still, even the previously married are not so different from everyone else, and as they stride further away from the end of their marriage, they typically fare better and better.

It seems odd that I needed so much reassurance. I've never been one to pine away for a soulmate. I love being single. Did I think I was the only one?

If so, I should have known better. There is a genre of books about singles that I think of as the collected life stories. Typically, a journalist, a social scientist, or a practitioner interviews single people in great detail, sometimes over the course of many years, and then relates their individual life stories. The books are almost always about single women. An example of one I already mentioned is Barbara Simon's account of the fifty ever-single older women who were born about 1900. Simon found that only one of those women was socially isolated. The authors of the more recent books mostly come to the same conclusion: If there is a miserable and lonely woman among the interviewees, she's the exception.

Some of the women who were interviewed, though, seem nearly as oblivious as I was. I'm especially fond of a woman named Carrie, who told her story to Lee Reilly, author of *Women Living Single.* Carrie's final words to Reilly were "I'm sorry if I've thrown off your sample. But the truth is, I'm happy." I wonder how many of the other single women, in describing full and fulfilling lives, believed their experience of singlehood to be unusual. I wonder how many single people have hesitated to tell another person that they are not longing to become unsingle, fearing that they will be dismissed as defensive and insincere. I have a guess about this: I think there are untold numbers of singles leading secret lives of undisclosed joy.

Why had Carrie and I, and probably many other silent singles, been so sure that we were the only single people living happy and contented lives? The short answer is that singlism slipped by us undetected and the mythology of marital superiority prevailed. The narrative structured by singlism and fueled by matrimania is the only story that has been told of our lives. Or it is the only one that has stuck stubbornly in our minds, even though we must have known on some level that it is not really true. It is time for a more accurate rendering of our lives.

Richard Roeper tried once to tell a different tale. He didn't succeed, but I think his attempt, together with the reaction he triggered, provides an interesting case study of what singles are up against.

In January 2004 Roeper wrote an essay, published in the *Chicago Sun-Times,* about two handwritten notes he had received over the holiday season. Each was from a longtime friend who was married. The two friends did not know each other, but they both expressed the same wish for the coming year—that Roeper would "find the right person" and get married.

Here's how Roeper describes his reaction:

> I wasn't the least bit offended, because I know my friends want what they believe is best for me—but can you imagine how insulting it would have been if I had penned similar notes advocating my particular worldview? "To my dear, dear friend: I know you've been married for the last 12 years and you CLAIM to be happy, but for 2004 my greatest wish for you is that you open your eyes to the possibility of a commitment-free existence! Dump your husband and get back in the game! I don't want you to wake up at 60 one day and wonder why you didn't live the single life."
>
> I do wish married people would understand that a lot of singles actually WANT to be single. Why does that bother you? . . . It is like the story my (happily married) friend Neil Steinberg likes to tell about meeting the late Ann Landers, who said, "You tell that Richard Roeper to figure out what's keeping him from getting married and to fix it!"

Roeper's message is simple: I'm single. I like being single. Why is that so hard to understand? He was beginning to articulate a different point of view about the single life, and he was doing so without presumptuousness or rancor.

Three days later Steinberg replied. He wanted Roeper and everyone else to know why married people should indeed pressure single people to marry, even if the singles are happily single. Here is some of what he said:

> The short answer is: Because they don't know what they're missing. Being married is better. . . . Married people are more plugged into life, their shoulders are to the struggle of moving civilization. Single people keep the cosmetic surgery industry alive and that's about it.
>
> Of course single people are happy. I'd have been happy staying in kindergarten. But life requires you to move on.
>
> The social swirl is a fantasy, at least after age 30 or so, when all the normal people get married.
>
> . . . We are trying to help our single friends salvage what's left of their lives before the years pass, irretrievable. Single people are cowards and it

pains us to see them strut around in their narrow boxes, declaring them the whole wide world.

Married people risk their entire lives, and while things do go spectacularly wrong, they tend to go right and either way they are actually building something real, which is more than single people can say.

Married people are better. I can't imagine the monster I'd have become if I didn't have my sainted wife pulling me in the opposite direction. . . . That's why so many old people, deprived of their mates, reduce down into these bitter, vinegary distillates of their former selves.

. . . The years clock by, and the married people reap the rewards, while the single people buy cats and tell themselves they haven't missed anything. But they have.

Steinberg's statement is perhaps a bit more crass than most, but at its core it is the party line about the differences between single people and married people. Steinberg has rounded up just about every caricature in the book, planted them throughout his essay, and unabashedly signed his name.

By now I probably don't have to redline all the claptrap, so I'll make this quick. Single people, Steinberg insists, are not "really" happy; they are just happy in the way that five-year-olds are happy. It is an immature and dopey happiness. The life of the singleton is insignificant. Singles buy cats and "keep the cosmetic surgery industry alive and that's about it." They've already wasted too many years of their lives, so their married friends need to swoop in to help them "salvage" what's left before those years pass by "irretrievable." Singles are pathological; if they were "normal," they would be married by age thirty. Singles may think they have friends and relatives and people who matter to them, but all they really have is a "social swirl," "a fantasy." What's more, old people who become single by outliving their spouse "reduce to bitter, vinegary distillates."

Steinberg does not stop at spreading singlism. He also flaunts his fetish for married people. Wives are saints who save erstwhile bachelors from turning into monsters. Married people are better than single people and are the foundation for civilization. They are morally untouchable. Even when marriages "go spectacularly wrong," they were worthy endeavors because they were "real."

As for Roeper, he was gracious to take no offense at his friends, but I think they were boors. Under the guise of holiday cheer, they sent him their self-important "marrieds know best" wishes. I know I'm supposed to speak only good of the dead, but I am even more appalled at Ann Landers. She was one of the most famous American advice columnists, and probably among the most influential. Yet there she was, suggesting that Roeper's single status was the result of some problem that needed to be diagnosed and then fixed.

What I've whined about so far are the parts that I hope are old hat. Here's something else that got to me about Steinberg's crude and insulting essay. It was published not in some obscure blog, but in a newspaper serving the third-largest city in the United States—a city in which the majority of adults are single. Even apart from all the prejudice and vitriol—aimed at a man who was a friend—the essay has nothing to recommend it. It is not insightful, not imaginative, not well written, and not funny.

And yet the essay was published in the twenty-first century. Imagine if Steinberg had written the same kinds of things about, say, people who are Christians or African Americans or cancer patients. Would the *Chicago Sun-Times* allow a columnist to say that Christians are cowards strutting around in narrow boxes and that he could not imagine the monster he would have become if he were Christian?

The publication of the Steinberg essay proclaims that singles are fair game. Slurs that would be considered unconscionable when slung at most any other group are just fine when hurled at singles. I don't think the editors of the paper discussed Steinberg's sentiments and found them nonprejudicial. I doubt it ever even occurred to them to question the matter.

That, I think, explains the glue that makes all the silly stereotypes of singles stick in our heads. To peel a grimy label off a person to whom it should not be affixed, you first need to realize that it is a label, that it is grimy, and that it should never have been stuck on the person in the first place. If the label seems like a natural part of the person, growing from within like eyelashes rather than something that is attached from the outside, then it won't be recognized as problematic at all.

In our thinking about singles, Americans seem to be about where we were in the 1950s and early 1960s in our thinking about women. Then, women could be described in newspapers and magazines as gentle, flinching, and fragile, and no one would cry "sexist"—not even the women who were themselves described as shrinking violets. The concept of sexism, for the most part, did not yet exist. In children's storybooks, women were snugly ensconced in the kitchen. In the math books, girls were measuring the flour for brownies. No one thought to complain that in the real world, women were not represented on the boards of the most powerful companies in America. They were hardly anywhere in those companies, except maybe at the typewriters and the telephones, or cleaning the offices at night.

What changed over the succeeding years is that other points of view began to emerge. There was an awakening of the American psyche, a dawning awareness that the place of women in society was not what it should be. Increasingly, when people spoke as if all the world were men or only men really mattered, others noticed and protested.

With regard to singles today, there is little notice of singlism, and still less protest. Even among the critical and intellectual vanguard of society, singles are blithely bespattered. I love the smart edgy commentary on most other matters in places like *The New Yorker* and *The Washington Post*. That's why I make fun of the singlism that mucks up their pages much more often than I mock the prejudices printed in places like *People*. When singlism lurks along the entire spectrum of arts, literature, science, and entertainment, we are not talking about an isolated blind spot but a deep, dark cultural black hole.

The prevailing view of single people is straightforward. They are missing out on the one truly important peer relationship—the one that makes people whole and happy and their lives meaningful and complete. Because that relationship is so important, single people are consumed by the search for it. Because singles do not have that relationship, they don't have anyone, they are miserable and lonely, and their life is insignificant. If they never do find that one special person, they will grow old alone and die alone. Married people are better people—more important and more worthy. If they receive more, it is because they deserve more—as, for example, when married men work harder and more responsibly than single men. Moreover, all these tenets are self-evident truths. They are timeless and universal.

My take on single people is entirely different. It goes something like this. Adults qualify as single by just one criterion: They do not have a serious coupled relationship. Most other beliefs about singlehood are misconceptions. For starters, singlehood cannot be equated with living alone or feeling alone. Many singles live with other people, such as friends, roommates, children, or other relatives. Many who do live alone are living exactly as they wish. By definition, people who are currently single do not have a serious sexual partnership; typically, though, they do have close and enduring relationships—usually several of them. This is especially so for single women. Being single does not necessarily mean having no sex, having a great deal of sex, wanting a great deal of sex, or having sex with lots of different partners. Not all singletons are seeking a mate or wishing they had one. Rather than leading empty, boring, or meaningless lives, singles who have the means and the motivation to do so can go where their talents and interests take them. When singles are rewarded less generously than married people, discrimination is often the explanation.

My myth-busting story about single people comes packaged with a parallel story about people who are coupled. That one goes like this: Having a serious coupled relationship does not guarantee that you will not live alone or feel alone. It does not ensure that your relationship will be monogamous, that you will enjoy exactly the amount and kind of sex that you prefer, or that sex will never be an issue in your life. It does not mean that neither you nor your mate is looking for another partner. Although the official form of coupling known as marriage is honored as a commitment, the commitment need not be honored by those who practice it. Government rewards and social recognition are not often contingent on good behavior.

The mythological view of singlehood and coupledom has been propped up by chicanery. Think about how people talk about their marriages that did not work out. "I was too young," they say. Or "I had bad judgment. I read people better now." Or maybe "I married for all the wrong reasons back then. This time I'll get it right." These talking points, and many more like them, all have one thing in common: They keep the special place of marriage safe and protected. When individual marriages prove disappointing, the crestfallen spouses do not blame the institution of marriage, nor the intensive and insular way that marriage is practiced these days. Instead, they and their fellow Americans look for something much more fixable, like flawed choices, that can be pinned on imperfect individuals rather than on a faulty institution.

The reigning marital mythology tries to goad us all into following the same life path: Get married, have children, stay married. But when it comes to humans, one size never fits all. The intensive coupling that works for some would be stifling to those who thrive on generous portions of solitude.

Family life can be boring or distracting to those whose passion is the single-minded pursuit of scientific discovery or social justice. People who would like to have a spouse as well as passionate friendships might wish they lived in a time when the two were considered more compatible.

The mythology of singlehood has its own set of slick supports. There are, of course, the predictable verbal tricks. If you have siblings, colleagues, mentors, and lifelong friends, you are "alone." If you have no one but a partner in coupledom, you "have someone." Are you generous to friends, family, or the community? Maybe you are just trying to make yourself feel better. There are also the "gotcha" traps. If you are a young man who is single, you need to settle down. If you are an older man who is single and have a stable, satisfying life, you are set in your ways. The entire web of myths works the same way. If you can disentangle yourself from the insinuation that your life is dark and dreary, then you need to step gingerly around the next suggestion—that all you have is a wisp of a life, incredibly light and insignificant. If you insist that your life has meaning, the mythology will stalk you to the end of your days with the threat that you will die alone.

The changes in the American landscape that have made singlehood a place of great promise—especially for women—are fairly recent. Wages that more closely approximate those paid to men, the availability of reliable birth control, and advances in reproductive technology are among the significant societal shifts that date back just decades, not centuries. Our perceptions of singles have not yet caught up with the new and potentially powerful place of singles on the cultural map.

Cultural lag is one important explanation for why the mythological difference between single and married people is so vast, while the actual difference in the quality of their life experiences is so small. But I don't think it is the only explanation. I think there is something deeper at stake.

Think again about Steinberg's essay. It is a rant. Steinberg's friend Richard Roeper poses a fair question in a nonconfrontational way: "Why does [it] bother you" that a lot of singles actually want to be single? Steinberg, in response, spins out of control, sputtering insults and banalities. What's more, he never does answer Roeper's question: Why was he (Steinberg) so bothered by a single person who wanted to be single?

For that matter, what was eating Princess Anne? She's the one who impugned single people as "just plain selfish" when she heard that more and more of them were living alone. Why was the Japanese scholar so upset with single people who were enjoying their lives that he stooped to calling them parasites? Why was Chris Matthews so disturbed by the thought of an unmarried man serving as president of the United States? Why has it been so easy for me to find a whole book full of examples of people who have come undone by the mere intimation that singles might actually like their lives just the way they are?

What gives?

To Be or Not to Be Single:
Why Does Anyone Care?

In my experience as a public speaker, there are good days and bad. One day in May 2003 I had a very good day. At the meeting of the Midwestern Psychological Association, I gave a talk titled "Marginalized, Derogated, Happy, and Effective: The Untold Success Story of People Who Are Single." Hundreds of people were in the audience, the biggest crowd yet for any talk I had ever given on singles. It was also the most simpatico group I had ever addressed. After a while the group started to anticipate what was to come and to react in all the ways I hoped they would. After I finished speaking, audience members raised dozens of thoughtful and challenging questions.

The next day in a cab back to the airport, I was still on a high. When the driver asked what I had been doing in Chicago, I was delighted to tell him. He then had quite a few questions for me.

"So, you're single?"

"Um-hmm."

"Have you ever been married?"

"No, never."

"Why not?"

"I love being single."

"Some guy treat you badly? They're not all like that, you know."

"No, no, nothing like that."

"Maybe it's not guys you like. Nothing wrong with that."

"What I like is being single."

"I bet some guy was too controlling. Wouldn't let you have your freedom. They're not all like that, either."

"No, it is not that at all. I'm not running away from anything. I just love my life just the way it is."

"You're being so negative!"

I was speechless.

Negative? The accusation shocked the smile off my face. All along, I thought I had been brimming with enthusiasm. In my mind, I had not answered any question in any but the most positive way. Yet the person who posed all the questions insisted that I was being negative. Plus he seemed incredulous that I could have such a "negative" attitude.

When I got to my gate, I pulled out a notebook and wrote down as much of the conversation as I could remember. Once I figured it out, it seemed obvious: The cabdriver interpreted my positivity about singlehood as negativity about marriage. I don't think it bothered him that I was single; I think it bothered him that I was happily single.

The conversation and the way it followed me around afterward captured a lot about what it has been like to study singles. Just when I think I have some issue all figured out, something fresh and new and perplexing pops up. By now I have a few favorite approaches for trying to solve singles puzzles. One is to rewrite the relevant script substituting a married person for the single person. In the case of the conversation with the cabdriver, I'm married and have just given a well-received talk on married people. If the cabdriver treated the married me the same way he treated the single me, here's what his side of the conversation may have sounded like:

"So, you're married?"

"Have you always been married to the same person?"

"Why is that?"

"Are you afraid to live alone? It's not that bad, you know."

"Do you see yourself as incomplete without a mate? Nothing wrong with that."

"Do you think you need someone else to validate you and make you happy?"

"Maybe you are just not very imaginative. Lots of people think that they should get married, so you just assumed the same thing applied to you."

"What! You love being married? Why are you being so negative!"

That conversation would not happen. That's telling. Married people are rarely asked to justify their decision to marry.

Here's another heuristic I use. I ask myself about the questions that were not asked and the comments that were not made. In polite conversations between strangers, often there is a search for common ground. For example, the cabdriver might have said but didn't: "Yeah, I loved being single, too." Or, "My sister is single and doesn't seem to be in any hurry to change that."

If he had wanted to pursue something he considered strange, I think I gave him far better material than my love of singlehood. For instance, he could have asked why I spent all that time in a windowless hotel ballroom when I could have walked out the door and found my way to the waterfront, the shops, the ballparks, or the Frontera Grill.

The cabdriver example only hints at something else I've discovered in the time I've spent studying and talking about singles: It can get personal rather quickly. I mean nasty-personal. One time I was doing a radio interview about singles, and before the segment even ended, an e-mail message appeared in my mailbox. It was from someone whose name I did not recognize (probably fake): "I love your ideas, but with a mug like that I beg of you not to reproduce. Please remain single and consider a tubal ligation just to be safe. Thanks, Jill." I wish it were the only one like that.

I'm not entirely new to the world of radio and television, and I have not shied away from discussing hot topics. When I was studying deception, for example, I had a thing or two to say about the sex and lies of an American president. That, too, was controversial, but no one ever asked me to go sterilize myself.

At first, it was easy to think that it was something about me that provoked such hostility—and that may well be true. But now I'm quite sure that when it comes to the topic of singles, I'm not the only one whose claims of contentment elicit something akin to rage. In 2000 a cover story in *Time* noted that "more women are saying no to marriage and embracing the single life" and asked, "Are they happy?" Some said they were. That did not sit well with the reader who wrote that "as long as women bounce around kidding themselves that life is full when alone, they are putting their hedonistic, selfish desires ahead of what's best for children and society." He signed it with his full name and hometown, and submitted it for publication to a magazine with a readership of about four million.

Perhaps he thought it was selfish of those single women not to be mothers. A different story in the same issue reported on the experiences of single women who wanted to raise children, and went ahead and did so, without the help of a husband. That didn't work, either. Another reader scolded, "It is sadly typical of our narcissistic age that so many women are opting to have children and raise them 'on their own.'"

What I found interesting about the snide letter writers is that they were complaining about single women who were not complaining about their lives. The women in the first story were embracing their lives as singles, and the women in the second were pursuing their dream of loving and nurturing the next generation. Plus the women in the stories were strangers to the letter writers. It was not as if the men had some obvious personal investment in the way those particular women lived their lives. It made me wonder what single women (or single men) could do, short of marrying, that would not provoke the ire of others. I think the answer is, nothing. If you are single and you do not have kids, you're selfish. If you are single and you do raise kids, well then, you're selfish, too. That's the power of the set of myths—taken together, they wipe out the entirety of a person's life. There is nothing a single person can do that cannot be denied, dismissed, or belittled.

It used to amaze me when tremendously successful singles such as Condoleezza Rice or Ralph Nader got the singles treatment. Now, though, it seems to fit the developing pattern. Singles who excel at their careers, like those who are so dedicated to their parenting, are not raising hackles despite their success or their fulfillment, but because of it. They are making a mockery of the marital mythology.

I think that most Americans—including most single Americans—want the marital mythology to be true. They passionately want to believe that if only they find their soulmate, they will live happily ever after. They seem to find comfort in the promise that there is a predictable path through adult life and that the most important step along the way is to marry. They are invested in the thought that married people are better than single people—worthier and more valuable—and that they personally will be better after marrying. Single people who are happy, successful, and fulfilled challenge all that.

As much as I find the soulmate concept sappy and silly, I also understand its appeal. The soulmate promises an all-in-one solution. Find that one perfect person and you have—for starters—your best friend, your sexual partner, your comforter and caretaker, your cheerleader, your escort to every social function, your consultant on matters large and small, and the one and only teammate you will ever need in home management, money management, and vacation planning. And that list doesn't even include any of the potential coparenting possibilities. The soulmate mythology is the ultimate seduction: Find that one right person and all of your wishes will come true. Find that one perfect person, your All-Purpose Partner, and your path through the rest of your adult life is set. And it will be a happy path, indeed.

The soulmate mythology is so powerful that it keeps other nuggets of hard-won wisdom from enlightening the rest of our lives. In money matters, for example, Americans have become increasingly sophisticated. More citizens than ever before have their own little bundle nestled in the stock market. When the Enron bubble burst, thousands of employees lost the retirement money they had been saving for years; many had invested it exclusively in just one stock, the stock of the company they worked for, trusted, and believed in. More to the point, millions of other Americans learned a vicarious lesson. Diversify. Don't risk putting all your financial eggs into just one basket. How, then, did they keep their newfound financial savvy tucked tightly away in the economic compartment of their minds, never to sneak out at night and knock on the door of their hearts?

I'm not talking sex or infidelity here. I'm talking people, emotions, relationships—in the big, wide, openhearted sense of the word. That's what the marital mythology needs to be mighty enough to conquer. The mythology takes a relationship that is deeply valuable and deserves to be valued, and turns it into the only relationship worth valuing at all. What stays hidden is the risk. If you really do look to your partner to be your everything, then if your partner disappears, whether through death or divorce, you have lost everything. Now you have no best friend, no comforter, no caretaker, no cheerleader, no social escort, and no consultant. Moreover, the mythology may be mucking things up even while your partnership is alive and thriving. It is not wise to relegate all the other important kinds of people—close friends, valued colleagues, mentors, and kin—to the dustbin of human relationships. Ironically, it is also unfair to the one relationship partner who is mythologized. No mere mortal should be expected to fulfill every need, wish, whim, and dream of another human.

All that has to be kept under wraps. If a panoply of people are welcomed into our lives in a deep and meaningful way, then what's lost is the magical seductive simplicity of the all-in-one soulmate solution.

It is not just a thousand relationships that must be kept from blooming in order for the mythology to survive. The worth of all the other components of our lives must be mowed down, too. That's why women are warned that their jobs won't love them back. That's why men are cautioned that without a wife, they face lifelong confinement in a studio apartment strewn with pizza boxes. It is why mythmaking about singlehood is so often suffused with the specter of loneliness and so rarely filled with the beckoning of solitude. All these sentiments are ways of registering the same plea: "Please let it be true that marriage is the only answer, the only rewarding path through adult life. Let it be true that if only I find that one special person, then all the other pieces of my life will fall into place." Surely, that sounds simpler than creating and sustaining a village, dedicating yourself to a career or a cause, or tending to all the different parts of your life. It is simpler. If only it were true.

There is something else about the marital mythology that has great appeal to the American imagination. It seems so democratic. Mythologically, just about anyone from any life station can marry anyone else from any other place in life, as long as they fall in love. And just about all can find that one special person as long as they work at it—make themselves attractive, put themselves out there.

The work component is important. In our minds, it sits right alongside the other, more familiar work ethic. In that mythology, good fortune comes to those who work hard and take personal responsibility for their lives. If some people have more than others—more money, better health, bigger and more comfortable homes—it is because they earned it. Social class differences are legitimate and fair.

In the parallel marital mythology, in which all is fair in love and marriage, singlism is fair, too. If some people have found a mate, it is because they worked at it. If they have kept their mate, it is because they worked at their relationship. Because they did all the work, they deserve all the rewards.

To anyone who is married or ever was, the mythological story line has far greater appeal than the one I'm trying to draw. I think that when singles receive less bountiful helpings of perks, benefits, or other good things in life, it is often because of practices that are discriminatory, illegitimate, and unfair. And if that's true, then maybe the special privileges of married people are actually ill-gotten gains. Now, there's a threat.

Americans reach for the soulmate solution because it promises so much and seems so simple. They sign up for marriage because it seems so expected and so natural to do so and because the institution seems so democratic and so fair. But what keeps people holding so tightly to the whole mythological package? It is the sense that what they really have in their hands is the moral high ground.

In the mythology, marriage is not just one among many ways to lead your life; it is the good and moral way. If we all can agree to that, then we have a metric by which to measure our lives. People who marry can feel good about themselves and confident that they have earned universal respect and admiration. They can, mythologically, feel morally superior to people who are single.

What happy and successful single people are threatening is not the institution of marriage but the cultural consensus on its special value. Same-sex marriage does not threaten the institution of marriage, either. The sticking point (or at least one of them) is that large numbers of Americans remain unconvinced that gay men and lesbians are the moral equivalent of straight people. To them, keeping marriage pure and sacred means keeping same-sex partners out.

The consensus that makes marriage into a uniquely powerful and self-affirming experience is not something that needs to be newly assembled brick by brick. It is already built into the structure of religion, politics, and the law. But maybe not permanently. When a single woman refuses to keep her happiness to herself, she has pulled a brick out of the edifice. When another single woman raises happy and healthy children, she has dislodged another. When a man stays single his entire life and then is nominated to the Supreme Court, the embracers of the marital mythology begin to perk their ears at the rumbling they think they hear in the distance. What they are really hearing is fear—fear that it will all come tumbling down. One reaction to fear is to hold on ever more tightly to whatever it is that seems to be falling apart.

On September 10, 2001, most Americans were patriotic citizens who loved their country. But few flew flags on their front porches or on their cars. After 9/11 flags were everywhere. The 2001 attacks did not mark the first assault on the World Trade Center. In 1993 six people died there. Six tragedies. But the attempted attack seemed mostly a failure. Few Americans felt truly threatened, and few flags went up. The post-9/11 flag raising represented not a feeling of security but of fear. Citizens were clinging to a familiar and potent symbol, in hopes of finding courage and comfort and solidarity. When the flags came down, Americans were not becoming less patriotic. They were just less scared. They had accommodated to a new normal.

The contemporary American scene is papered with matrimonial flags. Each airing of a show like *The Bachelor*, every television series that ends with a wedding, and each mate-trap manual is a flag of fear. There are so many of them right now not because we are so certain that marriage is the royal road to a life well lived but because we are so afraid it might not be.

Consider American society in the couple of decades starting with the 1950s. The percentage of Americans who wed during that era was just a few points shy of 100. Americans were marrying at a younger age than they ever had before, and the rate of divorce was fairly low, too. As marriage historian Stephanie Coontz noted, "As late as 1963 nothing seemed more obvious to most family experts and to the general public than the preeminence of marriage in people's life."

In a milieu in which the place of marriage was so safe, there was no need for a relentless trumpeting of its joys and benefits. No one was writing books with titles like *The Case for Marriage*. The case was already obvious. On television *Leave It to Beaver* did not build to a "Wally's Wedding" crescendo, with June Cleaver fretting about the guest list in the episodes leading up to the big day and Ward Cleaver and the Beaver bravely choking back tears as Wally says, "I do." In fact, there was no wedding episode at all. On *Lassie*, the loving and dutiful dog was at Timmy's side for many an adventure, but Timmy's wedding was not one of them. Lassie never was subjected to the indignities of donning a cummerbund and big white bow as she wagged her tail for the cameras. That's because there was no "Timmy's Wedding" episode, either. There were reality shows back then, but the prizes were often different than they are now. In the wildly popular *Queen for a Day*, for example, the contestant applauded most fervently by the studio audience was not rewarded with a king but with a sturdy appliance such as a washing machine. In the mid-twentieth century, neither books nor television dramas nor reality shows needed to stir up matrimania. The place of marriage in society and in the cultural imagination seemed secure.

People who want most desperately to believe in marriage as the place where they can feel morally superior to people who are single, and where all their dreams can come true, are in big trouble. The social forces that have been nipping at marriage are not going away. Maybe a few points can be shaved off the divorce rate, and maybe there will be a time when adults marry younger than they do today. But birth control and sexual freedom outside of marriage are here to stay, and so are working women. I have a hunch about why, in the opening decade of the twenty-first century, so many Americans raced to the polls to slam shut the gates of marriage on people who are gay. It was one of the few remaining ways that they could put a legal stop to the social changes that were rocking their world.

I don't think that the marriage movement is fueled only by fear. Genuine religious convictions are also in the mix. So is serious commitment to the welfare of children, paired with the belief that a home with a married mother and father is the best place for them. But I become skeptical of "for the children" arguments when they focus too single-mindedly on marriage as the answer. Even if divorce could be ended and all single women could be forever dissuaded from ever bearing children, there would still be children with just one parent. Death happens. Plus more than a few married parents fail to provide their children even the most rudimentary levels of care, protection, and affection. There have to be other ways to ensure the well-being of children beyond telling their parents to "just get married."

CHAPTER
FIFTEEN

The Way We Could Be

In 1999 the *Chicago Tribune* began printing an occasional series on relationships that continued for years. The relationship partners who were interviewed described how they met, what they valued about each other, and what sealed the relationship. They said the predictable things: "We fell in love." "We are planning a future together." "We use the exact same expressions, sighs, and body language without realizing it, often at the same time." Many experts were consulted. Some of their observations were predictable, too. "They [the partners] are memory banks for each other," one of them said. Not all the series was about relationships that lasted. Breakups were described, too. Several people told the reporter that they continued to dream about their partner for years after they split.

In other words, it was just the kind of series that qualifies as utterly ordinary. Except for one thing. The relationships were friendships.

Friendship is rarely taken quite that seriously. It should be. So should solitude and work and kin and the pursuit of great causes and most everything else that makes life meaningful and even magical. If couples and weddings did not fill up so much of the cultural space, maybe we would not have arrived at the strange place we are right now.

The closing decades of the twentieth century and the opening years of the twenty-first have been a time of exquisite sensitivity to all sorts of injustices. Racism, sexism, ageism, heterosexism, and classism have all made their mark on the cultural consciousness. So many identity groups have emerged to stake their claim and object to the way they have been labeled that citizens have begun complaining about the language police. Yet oddly, singlism has sneaked by mostly undetected.

This is also a time when the gay-marriage debate has created a populace more conversant with the legal, social, and political advantages of official full-fledged marriage than ever before. One of the fundamental arguments of the same-sex marriage advocates is this: You should not have to be a heterosexual couple to pass along your Social Security benefits to the person you care about the most, or to transfer your home and worldly possessions, tax-free, or . . . well, you know the list. Every major newspaper in the land, every television network, armloads of magazines, and baskets full of books have weighed in on the issue. Yet only a few scattered voices, barely perceptible amid the drone, have raised the question that, to me, should have been obvious. Why should you have to be any kind of couple to qualify for the cornucopia of perks, privileges, and benefits that are currently available exclusively to couples who are married?

I would like to live in a society that is equally respectful and supportive of all its citizens, regardless of whether they are single or married, uncoupled or coupled. Here are some basic principles that could become the foundation of such a society.

First, fairness. Every citizen is equal under the law. In some ways American society already implements this principle. For example, every citizen of voting age gets exactly one vote. You don't get two just because you are married.

Second, more fairness. As a starting point, every citizen gets exactly the same amount of everything that government has to offer. If the government hands out two-for-one coupons, everyone gets them. (No cheating, though; recipients of the freebie cannot be restricted to people with whom you are having sex.) Taxes should be based on the earnings of individual citizens, not couples. That's already how it is done in the vast majority of industrialized nations.

I'm not fixated on twosomes. If four siblings want to will their property to one another, tax-free, they should be able to do so. If three lifelong friends want to trust one another with emergency medical decisions, they should be able to arrange for that as easily and inexpensively as could a couple.

Fairness isn't just for the government. Businesses should not charge married people less than single people for the same product, just as they would not charge whites less than people of color. Same for pay. If two men—one married and one single—do the same job for the same amount of time at the same level of competence, they should get paid the same. And get the same benefits package.

Now I admit that my principles do allow for privilege. Not everyone ends up getting the same amount of everything. There are people who really are dependent on other people. Children, obviously. But plenty of adults, too, including many who are seriously ill or disabled as well as the frail elderly. They should all receive what they need to lead a dignified life. The rest of us should subsidize them and the people who care for them.

The privileging of people in special need of help, together with the people who care for them, is of special importance to many single people, including those who outlive their friends and relatives. But my principles are designed not to favor single people but to accord them the same considerations as married people—no more and no less. Married people whose serious illnesses, disabilities, or frailties make them dependent on others deserve society's support, too, as do the people who take care of them.

No cheating on this principle, either. You don't get subsidized for caring for a fully competent, healthy, able-bodied adult partner. That, you do for love. You do, though, get subsidized for caring for adults who need care, even if you do not happen to be their sexual partner. I mean all adults—aging parents, friends in need, neighbors and strangers. If you are willing to do the intense and challenging work of caring for people who cannot care for themselves, your efforts should be valued and rewarded. If I could rewrite the laws of the land, I would expand the Family and Medical Leave Act to accommodate all the caregivers I just described, and I'd give the law a new and more inclusive name.

All that was principle number three. Here's four. There are some things that are so basic to a decent life that no one should be denied them. Too many single people go without health insurance or health care, and too many singles spend their later years living dangerously close to the financial edge. No one—single or married—should needlessly live in sickness or in poverty. The health and well-being of the nation's citizens are too important to be left to individual employers. We should have a universal health-care system and a minimum standard of living that is dignified.

In the meantime, the workplace should be about work. Marital status should not be a factor in allocating benefits. A cafeteria-style plan, in which all employees get the same dollar amount to spend as they wish, is one possibility that seems fair. Flextime should be equally flexible for all employees. All workers should cover their fair share of holidays and unwanted travel. Furthermore, workers should never be required or even asked to justify the time off that they have already earned by doing their job. I want to under-score this because many single people have told me that they get last dibs on vacation time, travel options, and choice of assignments because the ob-ligations and interests that make their lives meaningful are deemed less im-portant than the outside-of-work commitments of married people.

Again, though, fairness should accrue to all workers, regardless of marital (or parental) status. As sociologist E. Kay Trimberger has explained, "Many fathers, and some mothers, now do not take advantage of family leave policies because they fear they will be stigmatized as not serious and passed over for more desirable positions and for promotion. Family leave is linked to marginalization at work. Personal leaves for all employees, where no questions are asked, along with the ability to reject overtime work with-out giving reasons, benefit all members of the workforce."

Am I asking the government to do too much? I can make up for that. I think it should get out of the marriage business. I like how Michael Kinsley described this option on *Slate*:

> Let churches and other religious institutions continue to offer marriage ceremonies. Let department stores and casinos get into the act if they want. Let each organization decide for itself what kinds of couples it wants to offer marriage to. Let couples celebrate their union in any way they choose and consider themselves married whenever they want. Let others be free to consider them not married, under rules these others may prefer.

Under this arrangement, religious groups and other organizations that want to regard marriage as sacred are free to do so, but others who disagree are not required to comply. Church is kept separate from state.

The End of Civilization?

There sure has been a lot of bedrock talk of late, as when marriage is described as the bedrock of society or the foundation of civilization. Such proclamations seem to imply that if society were to implement the dis-mantling of marital privileges, plank by plank, as I have suggested, all of civilization would collapse. If that were truly so, I might reconsider my sug-gestions.

So what is all the bedrock talk really about? Typically it is summoned in fear and panic over the prospect of the coming together of two loving humans of the same sex. Consider, for example, the 2004 State of the Union address in which President George W. Bush threatened a constitutional amendment banning gay marriage if the country—especially those uppity "activist judges"—didn't shape up. "Our nation must defend the sanctity of marriage," he said. We need to "take a principled stand for one of the most fundamental, enduring institutions of our civilization."

Now I know that the cynics out there among you might dismiss such talk as mere pandering to a particular political base, but I have decided to take it seriously. What exactly is this threat posed by same-sex marriage? Bush never said. Best as I could figure on my own, the reasoning is that two same-sex persons could not create children with each other, and with no more children, there would be no more society. Fair enough, except that even without gay marriage, children would continue to be born and raised. The constitutional ban would not outlaw children-making among the heterosexuals. Nor would it stop the conception of children by lesbians. It could not legislate out of existence, even if it wanted to, the lifelong devotion to children that does not seem to come packaged solely in heterosexual clothing. Moreover, an adult who is deeply attached to a child—whether biological or adoptive—is not going to be any less protective of that child if there is no other official parent in the picture or if there is a coparent who subsequently leaves or dies.

But I'm just trying to think my way through this. I'm still a scientist at heart, though, so I'm partial to fact-based answers. The bedrock claim is that the marriage of one man to one woman is at the very heart of society. Is there any evidence for this? Has any civilization ever survived that did not have such a marriage at its core?

To find out, I went to the website of the American Anthropological Association, which is the world's largest organization of anthropologists. There I found a statement issued in response to the president's proposed ban on gay marriage. My own interest is not specifically in gay marriage. I want to know more broadly whether family forms other than Mom-plus-Dad have succeeded in raising children and sustaining societies at other times and in other places. Here's the heart of the statement. (Italics added.)

The results of more than a century of anthropological research on households, kinship relationships, and families, across cultures and through time, provide no support whatsoever for the view that either civilization or viable social orders depend on marriage as an exclusively heterosexual institution. Rather, anthropological research supports the conclusion that *a vast array of family types,* including families built upon same-sex partnerships, *can contribute to stable and humane societies.*

I think that when government supports marriages, however defined, what it is really trying to do is ensure the raising of healthy and happy children, and the nurturing of their talents, so they grow up to be educated, thoughtful, and productive adults. That's a noble goal, but the one-way marriage-only route to achieving it seems too restrictive and indirect. My principles go straight to the caretaking and to the consistency of care by the same person or persons over time. It is the bond between a child and an adult that needs to be protected. That attachment can seem to happen nearly instantaneously, even with no assist from biology. We see it in the relationships between parents and the children they adopted as infants, which are often "indistinguishable from those of mothers and offspring they gave birth to" (in the words of anthropologist Sarah Blaffer Hrdy, author of *Mother Nature*). The government's role, in my opinion, is to make sure that every child has access to health care and decent schools, safe neighborhoods and fresh air, dedicated caretakers when parents are at work, and freedom from poverty. With those safeguards in place, parents of all marital statuses can do their parenting more effectively.

There Goes the Neighborhood?

Another argument for favoring married people is that it is marriage that fosters connection and community. From this perspective, people who marry link to each other and to each other's families. Then when they have kids, they develop still more ties to other families and community members. Law professor Mary Ann Glendon, commenting on trends such as the declining birth rate, expressed her fear that America's "rampant individualism is about to get a whole lot worse."

Is the marriage-as-communal-glue argument really valid? Is it really married couples and the families they form who are holding us all together? Is the rising tide of single people, if left unchecked, likely to wash us all away, leaving only isolated pebbles and shells scattered from shore to shore?

To begin with, I don't think the United States is an individualistic society. Rather, I think it is a society that is based on couples. True, individual happiness is a much-touted American aspiration. But the celebrated route to happiness is through coupling. People who are unhappily married can point to their despair as a reason for leaving the union, but they are then urged to recapture their good feelings by recoupling with someone new.

America, in its own fantasies, is a nation of rugged individualists and daring adventurers. In reality, though, countless adults are so stuck on coupling that they seem reluctant to venture into safe and comfortable places, such as restaurants and movie theaters, unless they have another human at their side. Preferably, one of the opposite sex.

According to its own ideals, America is also a nation of nuclear families. When couples have children, they often settle into the comfort and privacy of their own home. They might slip out now and then for a baseball game or a pizza, but like the cliché says, the home is their castle. With a moat around it. They practice what I see as intensive nuclearity. They act as a tight, self-contained unit.

Of course, couples—or at least the happy ones—care for each other. So do the members of happy nuclear families. But their caring can be very constrained. I'm thinking of Angela, the wife and mother who for decades was neighbor to Claire. When Claire needed help, Angela protested that Claire wasn't her "job" and that she had already taken care of her own family. I'm thinking of the men regarded by sociologist Steve Nock as transformed by marriage into "better men." He said that they became "devoted to improving communities." Only they didn't. They actually spent less time in the community of coworkers in professional societies or labor organizations. They spent no more time in service clubs, fraternal organizations, or political groups than they had when they were single. They were less generous to their friends than they had been before they married and spent less time with them. They may well have been devoted to their wives and nuclear families, but that, to me, is a rather small measure of devotion. So when Nock lectures us on how the married men he has studied deserve "our respect and thanks," it is he who is undermining community.

I'm also thinking about Robert Putnam, who wrote the book on the need to revive American communities, but then urged Bob and Rosemary to try starting a PTA, because at a minimum, they will meet "another couple or two with whom they can catch a movie on Friday nights." His vision of community seems to be a community of couples.

If the mythology were true and singles really were people who "don't have anyone" and therefore spend all their time home alone, then yes, even intensive coupling and intensive nuclearity would be better for community-building than living single would. But the mythology is not true. Most single people—especially single women—have whole networks of people who are important to them. My guess is that single people, compared with coupled people, are more likely to be linked to the members of their social networks by bonds of affection. Unlike couples, who socialize primarily with other couples, single people are not tethered to friends-in-law, nor do they feel as obligated to socialize with a person they dislike, just because that person comes packaged with another person they do like. The networks of single people, I think, are more likely to be intentional communities rather than collections of matched sets of couples.

At their best, urban tribes are examples of (mostly) single people creating community ties that connect people to one another through work and leisure, holidays and crises. The communities that materialized during the AIDS crisis are another example. The people who stepped forward to help men who needed help most desperately were not their immediate family members and were not married couples. Many who did such challenging care work were total strangers to the people they were helping.

I don't think that people who are single are intrinsically more generous or caring than people who are married. But I do think they are more likely to think about human connectedness in a way that is further-reaching and less predictable. Consider single parents, for example. They do not have built-in coparents for their children. Partly as a result, I think, they build communities of people who care about their children, if at all possible. I learned this from sociologists Rosanna Hertz and Faith Ferguson, who studied fifty single mothers of different races and educational backgrounds, including heterosexuals and lesbians, with jobs ranging from waitresses to attorneys. These single parents differed markedly from parents in dual-earner married couples, who relied primarily on each other. Rather than raising their children single-handedly, the single parents had assembled a whole ensemble of friends, neighbors, and relatives who traded favors, cared for the children, and encouraged and helped one another. The adults in the ensemble were not paid babysitters who were available only during predetermined hours, but loving participants in the children's lives. The single mothers were not dependent on the network but interdependent with the people in it.

Cross-cultural research is also in sync with the suggestion that children do especially well if they have layers of people who care for them. For example, the results of a study of thirty-nine nations on six continents showed that after a high-conflict marriage breaks up, children do better if they live in collectivist societies than in individualistic ones. The conflict that sometimes comes with remarriage is also more bearable for children in collectivist countries.

I'm not saying that married couples and nuclear families cannot consist of wonderful people who help create and sustain community life. But if they wanted to define their community of caring as reaching no further than their own immediate family, they would incur little disapproval for doing so.

Parting Ode to Singlehood

The essayist Vivian Gornick once described her reflections upon turning the last page of a novel she had been reading:

> I'd thought it a fine piece of work, resonant with years of observation about something profound, but it struck me as a small good thing, and I remember sitting with the book on my lap wondering, Why only a small good thing? Why am I not stirred to a sense of larger doings here?

The novelist, Gornick concluded, sold herself and her characters short by accepting unquestioningly the transformative power of romantic love. When the married woman in the novel faces that "crucial moment when she's up against all that she has, and has not, done with her life," she believes that love is the answer. The character's quest for erotic passion, her "yearning to dive down into feeling and come up magically changed," is what made the novel a small good thing instead of something truly big and bold and beautiful and new. The woman in the story seeks romance in an affair, but the novel would have been just as diminished if she had looked to a first love or a second marriage as the way to understand her life, redeem it, or fill it with meaning.

Novels that are constructed around romantic love, Gornick believes, lean on convention and nostalgia rather than stand upright on the sturdier and more ennobling ground of reality and discovery. I think that too uncritical an embrace of the mythology of marriage and singlehood is similarly limiting of the real lives we lead, regardless of whether we are, or wish to be, single or coupled. If we take seriously the notion that the only good adult life is the one that begins with marriage and continues with children, if we focus so intensively on our sexual partner and our children that we fail to appreciate all the other people and pursuits that might otherwise brighten our lives, then we have let the mythology of romantic love ask far too little of us.

Fortunately, there are people who have resisted the lure of the mythical. They are the people who have stared down stigma and glided by all of the glittering matrimania, unfazed and unscathed. Here are some examples.

Oprah Winfrey is one of the most influential women in the world. She has fame, fortune, celebrity, and power. In an interview, she described as the greatest moment of her life the time when she brought thousands of gifts to South African children, many of whom had been orphaned by AIDS. At one point, 183 of the children all opened presents at once. "The joy in that room was so thick you could physically feel it," Winfrey said. The interviewer, thinking inside the mythological box, asked a conventional question: "But why not have it all?" Oprah Winfrey is not one to be boxed in. "If I were a wife and mother," she replied, "I wouldn't be open to this experience. I wouldn't have had the space in my life to embrace the world's children, because I would be taking care of my own."

A colleague and her sister shrugged off singlism and matrimania by valuing each other. When one of them was offered a position on the West Coast, they both packed up their Midwestern homes and moved in together in California. The mythologically minded found this puzzling. Why did both sisters move when only one of them had a job offer? As one of the sisters noted with sly satisfaction, that sort of question would never have been asked if the person who had accompanied her across the country were a romantic partner she had known for just a few months.

The mythology asks too little of us when it dismisses our passions and our talents and our commitment to anything but a spouse and the children we are raising with a spouse. I've described people whose lives are diminished like this as getting the singles treatment. But the mythology is powerful and can claim even married people as its victims. Or rather it can try. It does not always succeed.

The actress Felicity Huffman gets credit for this inspiring act of resistance to the mythological tug. The moment was captured by the blogger Mona Gable, who described it like this:

> Lesley Stahl was interviewing the 40-something actress, the hook being Huffman's astonishing rise from anonymity to fame. And what did Stahl career girl extraordinaire focus on? Huffman as Happy Mommy. Huffman, to my undying gratitude, was having none of it. When Stahl asked the mother of two little girls and accomplished actress if motherhood wasn't the best experience of her life, Huffman looked at Stahl as if she'd channeled Pat Robertson. And then—bless her wicked heart—Huffman said, "No, no, and I resent that question. Because I think it puts women in an untenable position, because unless I say to you—Oh, Lesley, it is the best thing I've ever done with my whole life—I'm considered a bad mother."

Here's something else the mythology wants us all to value: sex. Especially the sex that is ensconced in a serious coupled relationship or could lead to such a relationship. Surely that should trump other less fleshy pursuits.

Not for singer and songwriter John Mayer. He said, "I really might just be the guy who loves playing music so much that [even] if I'm on a date with somebody, I can't wait to go home and play guitar. If I even seal the deal, I can't wait for them to leave so I can play the guitar."

Here is my final example of the kind of experience that the mythology fails utterly to acknowledge and appreciate. Author Cheryl Jarvis penned this description of the appeal of working alone in her office at home:

> There I am drawn to the warm southern exposure, the familiarity of my papers strewn everywhere, piles on the bed, the floor, the desk. Mostly, I'm drawn to the stillness. The only sound is the muted hum of the computer. I've dreamed of a room like this for years but never imagined how comforting it would feel to walk in each day.

The excerpt was from the opening paragraph of the chapter called "Motivations." Jarvis was married but craved a sabbatical from her marriage. She wanted long stretches of solitude, where she could bask, uninterrupted, in her thoughts and in her work, in her own special place. What she really wanted—at least for a while—was to be single.

N O T E S

1. Singlism: The Twenty-First-Century Problem That Has No Name

1 **twenty-first-century problem that has no name** Betty Friedan famously used the phrase "the problem that has no name" to refer to *The Feminine Mystique*, the title of her 1963 book on the topic.

1 **list of offensive examples** Adapted from DePaulo and Morris, "Should Singles," 145–146.

6 **Your money goes back into the system** UnmarriedAmerica.org, "Some Laws."

6 **Social Security funeral allowance** *Social Security Survivor Benefits*, 5.

6 **regardless of "race, color, religion"** U.S. Commission on Civil Rights, "Mission."

6 **protections in the workplace** U.S. Equal Employment Opportunity Commission, "Discrimination by Type."

7 **87 million single adults** In most Census Bureau tables, marital status is reported for people ages fifteen and older. In some tables, people who are separated are included in estimates of the total number of unmarried adults. I report the more conservative figure—based on ages eighteen and older, and excluding people who are separated—whenever that figure is available. The Census Bureau reported that in 2003 there were 87.5 million adults eighteen and older who were divorced, were widowed, or had always been single. Adding separated people eighteen and older would increase that number to 92.2 million. Counting all adults fifteen and older and excluding separated people would produce a 2003 total of 100 million single people. Adding separated people would increase the total to 104.7 million. The 2003 figures are from the U.S. Census Bureau, "Current Population Survey, 2003."

Of the 87.5 million single people in 2003, 21.6 million were divorced, 14 million were widowed, and 51.9 million had always been single. The total adult population, eighteen and older, in 2003 was 212.4 million.

In 2004 the number of Americans ages eighteen and older who were divorced, were widowed, or had always been single increased to more than 88.7 million. However, as of the time of this writing (Fall 2005), there were no published reports of the number of those singles who were living as unmarried same-sex or opposite-sex partners. The 2004 figures are from the U.S. Census Bureau, "Current Population Survey, 2004."

7   **11 million cohabiting**   Elliott and Dye, "Unmarried-Partner Households." The authors report both opposite-sex unmarried partner households (4.87 million) and same-sex unmarried partner households (701,674). The 2003 U.S. Census Bureau report "America's Families" includes figures only for opposite-sex unmarried households. The number reported is slightly lower than Elliott and Dye's 4.6 million households (or 9.2 million opposite-sex cohabitors).

7   **more households with single person living alone**   The change has been dramatic. In 1970, 40 percent of all households included a married couple and their children, compared with just 17 percent one-person households. By 2003 the percentage of married-with-children households slipped to 23 percent while the number of one-person households jumped to 26 percent. U.S. Census Bureau, "America's Families," 4.

7   **most single people don't live alone**   In 2003 there were 87.5 million adults who were divorced, were widowed, or had always been single, and 29.6 million one-person households. U.S. Census Bureau, "America's Families," 4; U.S. Census Bureau, "Current Population Survey, 2003."

7   **more years single than married**   Kreider and Fields, "Number, Timing," 15.

7   **40 percent of the workforce**   In 2004 there were 54.6 million people in the workforce who were divorced, were widowed, or had always been single, out of a total workforce of 139.25 million. That amounts to 39.2 percent of the workforce. The most recent figures, seasonally adjusted, were for December 2005, when 43.7 percent of the workforce was not married. However, in that report, separated workers were not included in the category of married workers, so the actual percentage of unmarried workers is smaller than 43.7 percent by an amount that is not indicated. The 2004 statistics were reported by the U.S. Bureau of Labor Statistics, "Employment Status," at www.bls.gov/cps/wlf-table4-2005.pdf, and the December 2005 data, "Selected Employment Indicators," were at www.bls.gov/web/cpseea8.pdf.

7   **40 percent of all homes**   The SMR Research Corporation reported that in 2002, 46.7 percent of all home-purchase loans were made to single applicants rather than to co-applicants. SMR president Stuart A. Feldstein believes that the 46.7 percent figure underestimates the number of unmarried home buyers because there are more co-applicants who are not married (for example, mothers and daughters) than there are single applicants who are actually married. Feldstein, "Single People." Also, in a 2001 annual report the Census Bureau noted that since 1995 more than half of all one-person householders have been homeowners. U.S. Census Bureau, "Homeownership Rates," at www.census.gov/hhes/www/housing/hvs/annual01/ann01t15.html.

7   **contributed about $1.6 trillion**   U.S. Bureau of Labor Statistics, "Composition," at www.bls.gov/cex/2004/Standard/cucomp.pdf.

7   **presidential election of 2000 or 2004**   Pollster Celinda Lake told *The Christian Science Monitor* that single women voters "are 3½ times the [number] of NASCAR dads and double the [number] of soccer moms." Cook, "Celinda Lake." The Census Bureau reported in 2004 that there were approximately 82.5 million mothers in the United States (U.S. Census Bureau, "Facts for Features: Mother's Day"); even if all were "security moms," the total would still be less than the total number of single people.

10   **in the spirit of consciousness-raising**   For more on the implications of stigma awareness and consciousness-raising with regard to singles, see Morris, "Stigma Awareness," and Reynolds and Wetherell, "Discursive Climate of Singleness."

10   **women are still paid less than men**   U.S. Census Bureau, "Facts for Features: Women's History Month," at www.census.gov/Press-Release/www/releases/archives/cb05-ff.04.pdf.

11   **rights of children born to single mothers**   Coontz, *Marriage, a History,* 239, 257, 307; Fineman, *The Autonomy Myth,* 140, 335. The 1968 Supreme Court decision was *Levy v. Louisiana.*

11   **1956 newlyweds**   U.S. Census Bureau, "Estimated Median Age."

11   **twenty-seven-year-old man today**   Ibid.

11   **the promise is also the threat**   See, for example, the discussion in Koropeckyj-Cox, "Sociological Perspectives," of the threat that can be experienced by married people when other people stay single.

12   **realities were not nearly so serene**   As Stephanie Coontz has documented, Americans' beliefs about the way things used to be do not always correspond to the historical record. Coontz, *Way We Never Were.*

14   **Some women really do believe**   This set of attitudes has been described as "benevolent sexism" and is believed to inhibit gender equality just as hostile sexism does; however, benevolent sexist beliefs are more often endorsed by women than are hostile sexist beliefs. Glick and Fiske, "Ambivalent Alliance."

14   **close to 90 percent still do marry**   Kreider and Fields, "Number, Timing," 16–17.

14   **marriage on television**   For more details on the saturation of television, movies, magazine stories, and advertisements with wedding themes, see Freeman, *Wedding Complex,* and Ingraham, *White Weddings.*

15   **Cathy Guisewite**   Soukup, "Happily Ever After?" 12.

15   **dating advice books**   Marder, "Dating-Advice Books."

15   **brides in advertising**   Another list is described in Freeman, *Wedding Complex,* 1.

16   ***Judging Amy* poll**   CBS.com, www.cbs.com/primetime/judging_amy, accessed May 16, 2003.

17   **greater chance of getting hit by a terrorist**   Faludi, *Backlash,* 9–19.

18   **website for preparing wills**   Wilson, "In Brief," 88.

18   **home raffle**   Steepleton, "Raffle."

18   **"which bag is ours?"**   Magellan's catalog, heading at the top of a page of multicolored luggage straps and luggage tags.

18   **"lives of their spouses are changed forever"**   *Nightline,* "Coming Home."

19   **"will have [met] another couple or two"**   Putnam, *Bowling Alone,* 290.

19   **half of all service members are single**   U.S. Department of Defense, "Population Representation," at www.dod.mil/prhome/poprep2002.

19   **one in three children live in single-parent households**   U.S. Census Bureau. "All Parent/Child Situations."

20   **"She has no personal life"**   The transcript of the *Larry King Live* show is at www.cnn.com/transcripts/0212/11/1k1.00.html.

20   **Nader less responsible than Bush**   *Hardball with Chris Matthews,* February 23, 2004.

20   **"Do you ever sometimes lie in bed"**   *Nightline,* "Art of Conversation," September 16, 2004.

20   **"love was not expected to end well"**   Hatfield and Rapson, *Love & Sex,* 7.

20   **"marriage was not fundamentally about love"**   Coontz, *Marriage, a History,* 7.

21   **"the needs of the larger group"**   Ibid., 6.

21   **"propertied families consolidated wealth"**   Ibid.

21   **"concerns of commoners"**   Ibid.

21   **hardly ever washed anything**   Stone, *Family,* 304–8.

21   **sex as a mortal sin**   Hatfield and Rapson, *Love & Sex,* 7.

22   **"He who too ardently loves"**   Ibid.

22   **Protestant colonists and sex**   D'Emilio and Freedman, *Intimate Matters,* 4.

22   **modern theory of marriage takes hold**   Coontz, *Marriage, a History,* 7.

22   **more shameful to have sexual inhibitions**   D'Emilio and Freedman, *Intimate Matters.*

22   **unnerving practical considerations**   Cancian, *Love in America,* 35; Gillis, *Their Own Making,* 148.

22   **FDA approval of the pill**   D'Emilio and Freedman, *Intimate Matters,* 250.

22   **rather contemporary points of view**   In the words of scholar and sex therapist Lenore Tiefer, "The modern view of sexuality as a fundamental drive that is very individualized, deeply gendered, central to personality and intimate relationships, separate from reproduction, and lifelong (literally womb-to-tomb) would be quite unrecognizable to people living in different civilizations." Tiefer, *Not a Natural Act,* 17. See also Foucault, *History of Sexuality.*

22   **greatest love reserved for God**   Gillis, *Their Own Making,* 134.

22   **many deemed deserving of love**   Ibid., 133; Stone, *Family,* 247–48.

22   **"love developed slowly out of admiration"**   Coontz, *Marriage, a History,* 184.

23   **bonds between men**   Gillis, *Their Own Making,* 147.

23   **bonds between women**   Ibid., 148; Stone, *Family,* 252.

23   **big changes were afoot**   Cancian, *Love in America,* 32–35; D'Emilio and Freedman, *Intimate Matters,* 241; Gillis, *Their Own Making,* 148.

24   **Friendships got a demotion**   Coontz, *Marriage, a History,* 206.

24   **Aging parents were thrown out**   Ibid., 207–8.

24   **"intimacy and sexual relations between spouses"**   Cancian, *Love in America*, 31.

24   **"having children might weaken a family"**   Ibid., 34.

24   **exalted place of the insular couple**   Gillis, "Marriages of the Mind"; Langford, *Revolutions of the Heart*.

24   **"give priority to their relationship"**   Schwartz, *Peer Marriage*, 13.

24   **"interdependence becomes so deep"**   Ibid., 15.

25   **"We are just our own show"**   Ibid., 63.

25   **"the couple's isolation"**   Ibid., 194.

25   **"weekends with the family, not friends"**   Waite and Gallagher, *Case for Marriage*, 20.

25   **"Stop interacting with people"**   Greenwald, *Find a Husband*, 14.

26   **more unmarried parents, more childless marriages**   Teachman, Tedrow, and Crowder, "Changing Demography," 1239.

2. Science and the Single Person

28   **"Marriage is good for everyone"**   Marano, "Debunking."

28   **"marriage improves the health and longevity"**   Waite, "Importance of Marriage." Waite made her statements to *USA Today* and *The New York Times* in an attempt to refute claims made in 1972 by sociologist Jessie Bernard that men's marriages and women's were two different experiences and that men got more out of marriage than women did. Bernard, *Future of Marriage*.

28   **"impressive evidence"**   *Wall Street Journal*, "Marriage Bonus."

28   **"Social science research has established"**   Rauch, "Imperfect Unions."

29   **"oozes with disrespect"**   Sprey, "Book Reviews," 1199.

29   **"today married people," "Marriage itself adds something"**   Coontz, *Marriage, a History*, 309.

29   **nationwide survey of 1,300 American adults**   Thornton and Young-DeMarco, "Four Decades of Trends," 1036.

29   **"the means to health, happiness"**   Waite and Gallagher, *Case for Marriage*, 46.

33   **actual scientists more appropriately cautious**   Gove and Shin, "Psychological Well-Being."

34   **same table, with actual group names**   It could be argued that some people who divorce do so against their will, and in that respect are more like the no drug—withdrawn group than the no drug—intolerable group. However, the average happiness ratings are the same for both groups.

35   **Lifelines of Happiness Study**   Lucas et al., "Reexamining Adaptation."

37   **predictions of the 760 undergraduates**   The students originally reported their answers on a scale ranging from 1 to 9. The averages were 7.7 and 3.6. I converted those average scores to a 0 to 10 scale so that they would be comparable to the happiness scores reported by the participants in the Lifelines of Happiness Study. I did so using a "percent of maximum" score method. (The 1 through 9 scores were recoded to 0 to 8, then the resulting values, 6.7 and 2.6, were divided by the maximum

value—8 in each case—and the resulting values of 8.4 and 3.2 are shown on the graph.) The students made just one prediction, rather than one for each year; that is why the lines are flat.

38   **Divorce Graph**   Adapted from Lucas, "Time Does Not Heal," 947.

39   **Widowhood Graph**   Adapted from Lucas et al., "Reexamining Adaptation," 535.

40   **men's/women's happiness approching divorce**   Lucas, "Time Does Not Heal," 948.

40   **The line for widowhood**   Note that the line for the people who stayed single includes all such people. In that way, it is different from the line for the married people who did not divorce and had not yet become widowed. We can see from the line of the married people who did eventually divorce that they were less happy than the married people who did not divorce. We can also see that the married people who became widowed also became less happy than the other married people. People who stay single also experience the deaths of people who are important to them (more and more so as they grow older) and the dissolution of relationships that were once deeply important to them. However, there is no separate line, and no separate graph, for the single people who experienced the loss of one of the most important people in their lives (as there is for the people who married). Single people's sadness over their losses is incorporated into the one lifeline representing the average happiness they experience over the course of their adult lives.

41   **religious states with high divorce rates**   Coontz, *Marriage, a History,* 287; Kaplan, "Onward Christian Soldiers."

41   **"Virtually every study of happiness"**   Waite and Gallagher, *Case for Marriage,* 168.

41   **study of "every country"**   Stack and Eshleman, "17-Nation Study."

42   **in one country married people not happier**   The exception was Northern Ireland.

42   **what the study actually shows**   Waite and Gallagher also claim that the happiness advantage of married people is "very large." Even if just the currently married people (rather than all people who had ever gotten married) were compared with the always-single people, was the difference in happiness "very large"? The journal article cited by Waite and Gallagher (Stack and Eshleman, "17-Nation Study") did not report average levels of happiness for people of different marital statuses in the seventeen nations. However, elsewhere, Inglehart (*Culture Shift,* 451) reported the percentage of currently married people and the percentage of always-single people who described themselves using the most positive label available—"very happy." Across the seventeen nations, 25 percent of currently married people and 21 percent of always-single people described themselves as very happy. The difference between the currently married and the always-single was greatest in the United States (by 11 points, 37 percent to 26 percent) and Britain (by 10 points). In Belgium and Spain there was a difference of just one point favoring the currently married over the people who had always been single; in France there was no difference between the two groups; and in Portugal the one-point difference favored the people who had always been single. (Unfortunately, Inglehart did not report the percentages of married and single people who chose each of the less positive labels.)

42   **other life factors considered**   Richard Lucas and Portia Dyrenforth ("Myth of Marital Bliss") have argued that social scientists tend to overemphasize the importance of relationships to well-being and underestimate the importance of factors such as wealth or income. In a review in which they compared both sets of factors ("Does the Existence"), they found the same thing as did the authors of the seventeen-nation study: Income mattered more. In another review ("Frequent Positive Affect"), Sonja Lyubomirsky and her colleagues found that the links between social relationships and happiness were no stronger, and sometimes weaker, than the links between happiness and either health or work life.

42   **"threaten the health, wealth, and well-being"**   Waite and Gallagher, *Case for Marriage,* 188.

43   **CDC study**   Centers for Disease Control, *Married Adults.*

44   **differences not statistically meaningful**   Scientists use the term *statistical significance* to indicate whether the differences between groups can be regarded as reliable. One important factor in statistical significance is the degree of difference between the averages of the groups. Another factor is the size of the study. All else being equal, studies involving more people are more reliable than studies with fewer people. (The CDC study, with well over 100,000 participants, was a very big study.) A third factor is how variable the responses are in the different groups. Consider once again the Lifelines of Happiness Study. Imagine that the differences between the people who stayed married and the people who stayed single were bigger than they actually were. Suppose, for example, that the married people got a little happier every year and ended up with an average happiness score of 8 and that single people got a little less happy every year and ended up with an average happiness score of 5. Would that be a meaningful difference? It depends. If most of the single people rated their happiness as 4, 5, or 6 (so that the average score came out to 5) and most of the married people rated their happiness as 7, 8, or 9 (so that their average score came out to 8), the difference would be meaningful. The married people would be consistently describing themselves as happier than the single people. But suppose instead that the married people's scores were all over the scale and the single people's scores were, too. When some married people have very low happiness scores and some single people have very high ones, then the difference between the married people's average of 8 and the single people's average of 5 is less impressive. (See Rosnow and Rosenthal, *Beginning Behavioral Research,* for a more complete discussion of statistical significance and related issues.)

45   **currently married, always-single healthiest**   In a review of studies focused on physical health, Karen Rook and Laura Zettel ("Purported Benefits of Marriage") also conclude that the biggest differences are between the currently married and the previously married, and not between the stably married and the stably single.

45   **"Married Adults Are Healthiest"**   Centers for Disease Control, *Married Adults.*

46   **study comparing health at different times**   Williams and Umberson, "Marital Status, Marital Transitions."

48   **divorced people became healthier**   Unsurprisingly, people who were especially
likely to feel better (less stressed) after a marriage ends are those whose marriages
had many problems (Wheaton, "Life Transitions").

48   **divorced people did no worse than anyone else**   Another study followed 9,775
Canadians, ages twenty to sixty-four, as they transitioned into or out of marital or
cohabiting unions, or stayed in their current status (Wu and Hart, "Effects of Marital"). Health was assessed just twice, and only two years apart. When each of the
groups was compared with the people who stayed single over the two years, no
one's health was significantly better than the continuously single people's. Some
groups, such as the married people who stayed married, had significantly worse
health than the continuously single people.

48   **"it can literally save your life"**   Waite and Gallagher, *Case for Marriage,* 47.

49   **"more likely to die from all causes," shorten a woman's life span**   Ibid., 48.

49   **"one of the greatest risks"**   Cohen and Lee, "Catalog of Risks."

49   **important code word**   Roizen, *RealAge.*

49   **"equivalent of being one and a half years younger"**   Waite and Gallagher, *Case for
Marriage,* 48.

49   **"happily married couples are healthier, happier"**   Hetherington and Kelly, *Divorce Reconsidered,* 273.

49   **no one matches the unhappily married**   Gove, Hughes, and Style, "Does Marriage," 126; Ross, "Reconceptualizing Marital Status," 137.

50   **recommended review article**   Ross, Mirowsky, and Goldsteen, "Impact of the Family."

50   **mortality rates of married/widowed people**   Helsing, Szklo, and Comstock, "Factors Associated with Mortality."

50   **other two studies of death rates**   Berkman and Syme, "Social Networks, Host Resistance," and Litwak and Messeri, "Organizational Theory, Social Supports."

50   **the original study**   Lillard and Waite, "Marital Disruption and Mortality."

51   **"nine out of ten married men," "lose their lives when they lose their wives"**
Waite and Gallagher, *Case for Marriage,* 50.

51   **actual percentages in endnote**   Ibid., 212.

52   **Terman Life-Cycle Study**   Tucker et al., "Marital History at Midlife."

52   **more sex and better sex**   Waite and Gallagher, *Case for Marriage,* 79.

52   **cohabiting people have most sex**   Laumann et al., *Social Organization of Sexuality,*
88–89.

52   **"built around sex"**   Waite and Gallagher, *Case for Marriage,* 81.

52   **"don't seem to enjoy it quite as much"**   Ibid., 83.

53   **National Sex Survey**   Laumann et al., *Social Organization of Sexuality,* 117.

53   **being married beats shacking up**   Waite and Gallagher, *Case for Marriage,* 83.

54   **what they skip over**   Laumann et al., *Social Organization of Sexuality,* 370–71.

54   **"sex as a sacred union"**   Waite and Gallagher, *Case for Marriage,* 96.

54   **"an activist not a scholarly organization"**   Ibid., 218.

54   **"champions marriage and family"**   Family Research Council, www.frc.org, accessed April 30, 2005.

55   **"means to health, happiness"**   Waite and Gallagher, *Case for Marriage,* 46.

55   **"profound" benefits**   Ibid., 187.

57   **credible studies**   For the kinds of questions considered in this chapter, such as whether getting married makes people happier or healthier, studies in which the same people are followed over time are always more informative than studies in which people of different marital statuses are studied at just one point in time. For experiences such as getting married or getting divorced, to which people cannot be randomly assigned, following the same people over time helps shed light on the question of whether different marital statuses really do have anything to do with health or happiness. To answer other kinds of questions, though, people can be assigned at random to different experiences, and the implications can be compared. For example, suppose you wanted to know whether being marginalized by couples affects single people's mood or even their physiological responses. You could design a study in which single people interact with three other couples. Half of the single people who show up for the study are assigned (at random) to a group in which the couples include them in the conversation; the other half interact with couples who ignore them. The single people can be asked about their mood during the interaction, and their heart rate could be monitored, too. In studies such as these in which the experimenter can control the experiences of the various participants by randomly assigning them to different conditions, it is not necessary to follow the same people over time. Also, if the question addressed by the experiment is (for example) whether exclusion can affect a person's mood or blood pressure, then it is not necessary to study a large, nationally representative sample. (See Hoyle, Judd, and Harris, *Research Methods,* for a more detailed discussion.)

58   **marriage's protective powers for widows**   Waite and Gallagher, *Case for Marriage,* 51.

58   **range of numbers**   The variability of the scores of the people in the different groups is also important. See the note concerning statistical significance.

60   **singles and marrieds more similar than different**   Studies comparing people of different marital statuses probably number in the hundreds. I used several criteria in choosing the studies in this chapter. First, I looked for high-quality studies. The Lifelines of Happiness Study is unique in following so many people for so many years. It is also a very current study, one that is still ongoing. Because *Singled Out* is primarily about singles in American society, it would have been preferable to describe an American study, but there are none comparable to the Lifelines Study. One-time studies do not contribute as much to our understanding of marital status differences in outcomes such as health and happiness, but because so many one-time studies are conducted, I thought it important to describe some of them. (Also, with regard to sexual experiences, one-time studies are the only ones I found.) I selected studies that were based on large, nationally representative samples. I tried to find studies using statistics that most readers could understand—for example, average scores rather than regression coefficients. Importantly, I avoided studies reporting unusual results. (For example, there are studies in which people who have

always been single look better than people in all other groups, including the currently married.) I also looked closely at studies used by Waite and Gallagher to support their conclusions.

The four or five marital-status categories that are the usual focus of scientific research do not begin to capture all the complexities of individual lives. I tried to include some texture by mentioning gender differences, but there are many other important considerations as well. The experience of singlehood, for example, is different for the rich than for the poor, and for people of different races, ages, ethnicities, and sexual orientations. To be divorced is a different experience for people who were once married many years ago and have lived singly ever since than it is for people who were recently divorced for the third time. Similarly, a first marriage is a different experience from a fourth. No matter how multifaceted the results of research become, though, the basic scientific principles I have described still apply.

Finally, I have focused on experiences such as happiness, health, and longevity because they are favorite American aspirations. They have attracted the most research attention, and were the focus of Waite and Gallagher's book. They are, though, individualistic experiences and hardly represent all the kinds of experiences that make life important or meaningful. I hope that future research attends more to the contributions that people make to causes beyond their own health and well-being—causes such as social justice, scientific understanding, human understanding, caretaking, and the development of other people's potential.

3. Myth #1: The Wonder of Couples

62   *New York* **magazine reminiscences of JFK Jr.**   All quotes are from Roshan, "Prince."

63   **description of Tom Avery**   Shields, "Marriage Survivors," 66.

64   **"since Adam was alone"**   Amador and Kiersky, *Being Single,* 217.

64   **"You gotta love friends like that!"**   Ibid., 218.

65   **identity of Deep Throat**   Purdum, "Mystery Solved."

66   **Woodward told his wife**   Quinn, "The Secret."

66   **"Every time we were together"**   Ibid.

67   **clustering by common life paths**   McPherson, Smith-Lovin, and Cook, "Birds of a Feather"; Morgan, Carder, and Neal, "Are Some Relationships."

69   **"Now that you are married"**   MSN WomenCentral, "Friends."

70   **"tell him or her"**   Dee, "Instructions," 2o.

70   **"lunch . . . with the same person"**   Glass, NOT *"Just Friends,"* back matter.

4. Myth #2: Single-Minded

71   **"Are you single?"**   Single Gourmet, www.single-gourmet.com.

72   **"I am tired of these affairs"**   Kaganoff, "Other Uses," 37.

72   **"There's nothing like having a single friend"**   St. John, "Bob, Meet Jane."

74   *Time* feature story   Quotes are from Saporito, "New American Home," 56–75.

75   *Newsweek* feature story   Quotes are from Gordon, "Life as a House," 79–86.

75   **more households of single people**   U.S. Census Bureau, "America's Families," 4.

76   **39.8 million singles**   U.S. Census Bureau, "Current Population Survey, 2004."

76   **singles 40 percent of first-time buyers**   Albrecht, *Buying a Home,* 1; Chicago Title Insurance Company, "Who's Buying Homes," 5; Feldstein, "Single People"; Joint Center for Housing Studies, "Housing: 2004," 14.

76   **singles buying second homes**   Cohen, "A Home of Their Own"; Edwards, "Flying Solo," 48.

77   **"obvious" choices**   Albrecht, *Buying a Home,* 7.

77   **60 percent of single women were homeowners**   Edwards, "Flying Solo," 48.

78   **"If you are a single person"**   Orman, *Road to Wealth,* 133.

78   **about two-thirds voted for Gore**   Website for Women's Voices. Women Vote, www.wvwv.org.

78   **new demographic was great fun**   DePaulo, "Single Voter."

79   **"Pretend it's a hair appointment"**   Cho, "Nonvoting Bloc." Conway also volunteered her explanation for why married women vote more often than single women: "Women who have what we call the four magic M's—marriage, munchkins, mortgages, and mutual funds—are much more likely to vote than their unmarried, non-stake-holding, non-ownership counterparts." To Conway, responsible behaviors such as homeowning and saving (rather than spending) money are all part of the marital package. However, research suggests that when relevant factors such as income and assets are comparable, unmarried people save just as much as married people. Also, "home ownership is associated with an increase in Individual Development Account savings for unmarried but not married participants." (Both findings are from Grinstein-Weiss, Zhan, and Sherraden, "Saving Performance," 202–3.)

79   **"found time in their social schedules"**   Tierney, "Fall Affair."

79   **"Is it scary to think about politics?"**   Cho, "Nonvoting Bloc."

79   **PantyWare Party Kits**   Website for Axis of Eve, www.axisofeve.org, accessed July 1, 2004.

79   **"fun, fashionable, fed-up women"**   Website for Running in Heels, www.women-againstbush.org, accessed July 1, 2004.

79   **Code Pink**   Marinucci, "Courting."

79   **"help customers reach their ultimate goal"**   *Wall Street Journal,* "Voting Matters."

80   **issues concerning single women**   Abcarian, "Unmarried, Female"; Chaudhry, "New Swingers," 53–54; Pollitt, "Pull Over," 9. My description of the concerns of single women voters draws from the writings that were published in the months leading up to the 2004 election. In January 2006, a poll of 1,509 single Americans was conducted by Greenberg, Quinlan, Rosner Research, and the results were posted at the website of Women's Voices. Women Vote. The top five national issues of concern to single women were (in order of priority) the war in Iraq, health care, the economy and jobs, education, and retirement and Social Security. At the state

level, their top five concerns were education, health care, the economy and jobs, crime, and affordable housing. http://www.wvwv.org, accessed March 26, 2006.

81   **"Wife, parent, grandparent"**   www.governor.state.az.us, accessed in 1999.

81   **single men with lowest voting rate**   Abcarian, "Unmarried, Female"; website for Women's Voices. Women Vote, www.wvwv.org.

81   **American Association for Single People (AASP)**   As of 2005, AASP is called Unmarried America. The website, UnmarriedAmerica.org, describes Unmarried America as "an information service for unmarried and single Americans." Rights for singles are pursued by the Alternatives to Marriage Project, AtMP. The mission of AtMP, as described on its website, unmarried.org, is to advocate "for equality and fairness for unmarried people, including people who are single, choose not to marry, cannot marry, or live together before marriage."

81   **online AASP survey request**   E-mail message, October 31, 2004.

82   **I proceeded to the website**   Website of Single Syndrome: www.businessoflove.com.au, accessed October 30, 2004.

84   **Pew Internet & American Life Project survey**   Rainie and Madden, "Romance in America." Also, in 2003 AARP asked 3,501 single, divorced, and widowed adults between the ages of forty and sixty-nine about dating (Montenegro, "Lifestyles, Dating, and Romance"). Of those who said they were currently dating or would be interested in dating, very few said that they wanted to date in order to find someone to marry (8 percent), find someone to live with (9 percent), or fulfill their sexual needs (6 percent). Instead, the most common reason by far for wanting to date was to have someone to talk to or do things with (49 percent).

86   **"quirky art festival"**   Watters, *Urban Tribes,* 15.

86   **"jaw-droppingly bizarre"**   Ibid., 17.

86   **"it was about nothing"**   Ibid., 18.

86   **So what if he was happy?**   Ibid., 21.

86   **"talked in that compulsive way"**   Ibid., 136.

87   **"If things worked out"**   Ibid., 202.

87   **Hearing about the upcoming nuptials**   Ibid., 203.

87   **"I would not have grown"**   Ibid.

87   **"sincere hope that things work out"**   Ibid., 205.

87   **"I have faith"**   Ibid., 206.

87   **on his way to Hawaii**   Ibid., 211.

87   **two dozen or more newlyweds**   Ibid.

87   **"Having spent so many years"**   Ibid., 212.

87   **"The 'us' in my world"**   Ibid., 213.

88   **"of belonging"**   Ibid., 39.

88   **"the act of cooking"**   Ibid., 38.

89   **"yet-to-be-married"**   Ibid., 135, 213.

90   **"represent less a failure to mate"**   Ibid., 203.

93   **households were not so narrowly construed**   Coontz, *Marriage, a History,* 79; Gillis, *Their Own Making,* 10; Stone, *Family,* 28.

5. Myth #3: The Dark Aura of Singlehood

95 **"That's a lot of bowls of cereal"** Stuever, "Alone."

97 **undergraduates list thoughts on single people** DePaulo and Morris, "Singles in Society," 61. We asked 950 undergraduates to think about either married people or single people (we assigned them to think about one or the other) and list the characteristics that came to mind. Students who were thinking about married people were more likely to list traits such as mature, stable, happy, faithful, kind, and loving. Students thinking about single people were more likely to mention attributes such as immature, lonely, and self-centered (though also independent). The differences were sometimes huge. For example, 49 percent of the students described married people as kind, caring, or giving, whereas only 2 percent of the students described singles in those terms. Thirty-two percent described married people as loving; yet, of the hundreds of students describing single people, not even one listed "loving" as a characteristic that came to mind. Not one student, out of hundreds, described married people as lonely, but 17 percent described single people that way.

97 **"stunning explosion of solitary living"** Coontz, *Marriage, a History,* 276.

98 **"the dark aura of her singleness"** Merkin, "Country of Divorce," 186.

98 **"that dark zone that surrounds the cessation of love"** Shields, "Marriage Survivors," 63.

98 **"It's the most wonderful time of the year"** Christenson, "All I Want," 11.

99 **"I carry that label"** Ali, "The Crow," 51.

99 **"I ran into someone pretty well-known"** *Week,* "Why Crow."

99 **"regales her single friends"** Edwards, "Flying Solo," 52.

100 **"residue of mistrust and hurt"** Combe, "My Prince."

100 **"1, The loneliest number"** Hambly, "Numbers," 25.

101 **"that lonely number one"** *Honolulu Star-Bulletin,* "Problems of Single People."

101 **"Well-adjusted, self-sufficient, and socially skilled"** Hetherington and Kelly, *Divorce Reconsidered,* 105.

101 **"I have a dream"** White, "Marching," A45.

102 **"celebrated her victory alone"** Thomas, "The Pill," A35.

102 **Eudora Welty** Ford, "Eulogy," 19.

102 **"as a bachelor"** Pindell and Curley, "Candidates Meet."

102 **"king of the lonely hearts"** CNN.com, "Dennis Kucinich."

103 **"I, for instance, married a man"** Merkin, "Country of Divorce," 181.

103 **"Neil insisted on a punitive prenuptial agreement"** Barnett and Rivers, *Same Difference,* 64.

103 **Julia Roberts** *People,* August 27, 2001, 77.

104 **"Grealy's tremendous gift for friendship"** *The New Yorker,* "The Critics," 99.

104 **Being Single in a Couple's World** Amador and Kiersky, *Being Single.*

104 **Jennifer Frye tips** Borgenicht and Piven, "Valentine's Day," 13.

6. Myth #4: It Is All About You

106   **Sandals resorts**   All quotes are from www.sandals.com, accessed January 15, 2005.

106   **"we treat our girlfriends well"**   Tolbert, "Japan's New Material Girls."

107   **"most contented demographic group"**   Scanlon, "Japan's 'Parasite Singles.' "

107   **Masahiro Yamada book**   Yamada, *Parasite Single*.

107   **Not everyone agreed with Yamada**   The arguments of the critics, and the critics of the critics, are described in Ashby, "Problem or Victims?"; Genda, "Don't Blame the Unmarried"; Takahashi and Voss, "Uniquely Japanese?"; and Yamada, "Spoiled Singles."

109   **no more likely to be women than men**   Takahashi and Voss, "Uniquely Japanese?"

109   **"just plain selfish"**   Reuters, "Anne Slams 'Selfish' Singles."

111   **Beaches travel packages**   The information and quotes are from www.beaches.com.

111   **"the government is a partner"**   Kennedy, "Dems Need to Woo."

111   **"a nurturing Uncle Sam"**   Chaudhry, "Wooing the Single Women."

112   ***Judging Amy* episode**   *Judging Amy,* episode 54, "Surprised by Gravity," November 27, 2001.

113   **"he doesn't have his laundry done"**   Edwards, "Flying Solo," 52.

113   **"I take care of him"**   MSN Entertainment, "Parker Says."

115   **2002 median income**   U.S. Census Bureau, Table P-1, CPS Population and Per Capita Money Income, All Races, at www.census.gov/hhes/income/histinc/p01ar.html.

115   **average cost of a wedding**   Condé Nast Bridal Infobank, American Wedding Study, described at http://abc4.com/guides/wedding/default.aspx.

115   **cost of three years at University of Maryland**   Hopkins, "Soaring Cost."

115   **"wow factor at their nuptials"**   Mandell, "Over-the-Top," 22.

115   **average of 171 wedding gifts**   Otnes and Pleck, *Cinderella Dreams,* 76.

115   **average cost of wedding and shower gift**   CNNMoney, "Before Saying 'I Do.' "

115   **bridesmaids set aside $900**   *Wedding Gazette,* "The Costs."

115   **Macy's 5 percent reward back**   As advertised on WeddingChannel.com, http://weddingchannel.com/registry, accessed February 28, 2005.

116   **"Pay for us to go have sex"**   Sadin, "Till Death."

116   **"Dear Abby" column**   Van Buren, "Bridesmaid's Dress."

116   **weddings in previous centuries**   Pleck, *Celebrating the Family,* 207–32.

116   **relationship between the couple and their friends**   My discussion of this change draws from Freeman, *Wedding Complex;* Geller, *Here Comes the Bride;* Gillis, *Their Own Making,* 133–51; Pleck, *Celebrating the Family,* 207–32; and Rothman, *Hands and Hearts.*

116   **"each gift would be noted"**   Gillis, *Their Own Making,* 140.

117   **"the most dissatisfied guests"**   Otnes and Pleck, *Cinderella Dreams,* 74.

118   **singles table**   Jamieson, "Paired, Paired World."

120   **survey on men's giving**   Nock, *Marriage in Men's Lives.*

121 **"Might it be that any change"** Ibid., 117.

122 **"Marriage is also the engine"** Ibid., 63.

123 **"Husbands will be changed"** Ibid., 140.

123 **"a way to feel good about themselves"** Hetherington and Kelly, *Divorce Reconsidered*, 258.

124 **caregivers more likely single daughters** Connidis, *Family Ties*, 135.

124 **men get caretaker for parents** Ibid., 139.

124 **"In tears, I reach for the phone"** Jarvis, *Marriage Sabbatical*, 225.

124 **"all those nights in all those hotel rooms"** Wilgoren, "Wedding Candidate."

125 **"Nancy's Story"** Thomas and Clift, "Shadows Fell," 32.

126 **Bush biography** www.whitehouse.gov/president/gwbbio.html.

126 **Nader biography** Hertzberg, "Reckless Driver," 25; "In the Public Interest," at www.nader.org/blog/template.php?/categories/G-Biography, accessed May 12, 2006.

127 **"When I was young and irresponsible"** Schneider, "Style and Substance."

127 **Nader had read Upton Sinclair by fourteen** www.crashingtheparty.org/bio/html.

127 **Nader on *Hardball*** Quotes are from the transcript of the show, which aired February 23, 2004, at www.msnbc.msn.com/id/4361164.

129 **"Mrs. Smith is diagnosed"** Rauch, *Gay Marriage*, 25.

130 **Newt Gingrich** Berselli, "Newt Gingrich"; Blomquist, "Newt Knew."

131 **"My Turn" essay** Conrad, "Kindness of Strangers," 11.

7. Myth #5: Attention, Single Women

134 **"most professionally accomplished and independent generation"** www.randomhouse.com/catalog, accessed May 22, 2005.

134 **"This 42-year-old"** Whitehead, *No Good Men Left*, 122.

134 **more likely to be killed by terrorist** Faludi, *Backlash*, 9–19.

135 **"single men don't have as much need"** Whitehead, *No Good Men Left*, 123.

135 **"the exacting standards of educated women"** www.randomhouse.com/catalog, accessed May 22, 2005.

136 **"plenty of sexually conservative women"** Whitehead, *No Good Men Left*, 9.

136 **"upheaval in the mating system"** Ibid., 7.

136 **"epidemic of cohabitation"** www.randomhouse.com/catalog, accessed May 22, 2005.

136 **"new life pattern"** Whitehead, *No Good Men Left*, 9.

137 **most professional women "yearn for a child"** Hewlett, *Creating a Life*, front flap, dust jacket.

137 **"urgent priority to finding a partner"** Ibid., 301.

137 **"enormous regret"** Ibid., 302.

137 **"run out of eggs"** Ibid., 217.

137 **"avoiding professions with rigid career trajectories"** Ibid., 302.

137   **"Babies vs. Career"**   Gibbs, "Making Time."

137   **Boushey survey data**   Franke-Ruta, "Creating a Lie."

138   **"Man Shortages and Barren Wombs"**   Faludi, *Backlash,* 3.

138   *Elle* **review of Whitehead book**   Combe, "Prince Will Come."

139   **"Sure, they're rich and gorgeous"**   Schneider, "Everything But Love."

139   **"They seem to have it all"**   Ibid.

139   **"making historic strides"**   Cose, "Black Gender Gap."

139   **"a black woman can be anything"**   Ibid., 48.

140   **"accomplished but can't find a mate club"**   Ibid., 50.

140   **"they may end up on their own"**   Ibid., 49.

140   **"die in a room all by myself"**   Ibid., 51.

140   **"advancing faster than black men"**   Ibid., 3.

140   **"models of happiness"**   Ibid., 48.

140   **"Is this new black woman"**   Ibid., 48–49.

140   **"lives of success but also isolation"**   Ibid., 51.

140   **"weathering a period of transition"**   Ibid.

141   **always-single women least likely to be alone in old age**   Dykstra, "Loneliness"; Dykstra and de Jong Giervald, "Gender and Marital-History"; Essex and Nam, "Marital Status and Loneliness."

141   *Time* **magazine story**   Quotes are from Sachs, "Wedded to Work," A21.

143   **"You once said business is your life"**   *Larry King Live,* "Interview with Martha Stewart."

144   **"brought serious magazine journalism up against sitcoms"**   *Nightline,* "Art of Conversation," September 16, 2004.

146   **"You won't believe what she [Svetlana] has to say"**   Jersild, "More Olympic Ranting."

146   **"I think of the many conversations"**   Jarvis, *Marriage Sabbatical,* 225.

147   **"beautiful single woman in the neighborhood"**   Ibid., 103.

147   **no sex at all**   As bell hooks has noted, "The focus on 'sexual liberation' has always carried with it the assumption that the goal of such effort is to make it possible for individuals to engage in more and/or better sexual activity. Yet one aspect of sexual norms that many people find oppressive is the assumption that one 'should' be engaged in sexual activity. This 'should' is one expression of sexual coercion" (hooks, *Feminist Theory,* 149). Foucault's observation is also relevant: "We are often reminded of the countless procedures which Christianity once employed to make us detest the body; but let us ponder all of the rules that were employed for centuries to make us love sex, to make the knowledge of it desirable, and everything about it precious" (Foucault, *History of Sexuality,* 159).

147   **"The Disappearance of Elaine Coleman"**   Quotes are from Millhauser, "Disappearance."

8. Myth #6: Attention, Single Men

150   **"Oh, I don't know—seems longer"**   Chudacoff, *Age of the Bachelor,* 151.

150   SEXY, SINGLE, SIZZLING   *People,* July 2, 2001.

151   **"strong, offbeat movie roles"**   Katz, "American in Paris," 6.

151   **"soulfulness and strength"**   Maslin, "Johnny Depp."

151   **"depth beyond his years"**   Zacharek, "Not Just Another."

151   **"The early line on his career"**   This quote and the following quotes about Depp are from Katz, "American in Paris," 6–7.

153   **1977 sociology article**   Davis and Strong, "Working Without."

154   **fewer stupid bachelor tricks**   Waite and Gallagher, *Case for Marriage,* 53.

154   **wives "discourage drinking, smoking"**   Ibid., 55.

154   **"warped lives"**   Ibid., 164.

154   **"Researchers have long documented"**   Segell, "Wedded Life."

154   **"single men drink almost twice as much"**   Waite and Gallagher, *Case for Marriage,* 53.

154   **4 percent of married Americans heavy drinkers**   CDC 2004 news release.

154   **2002 Robin Simon paper**   Simon, "Revisiting the Relationships."

156   **Survey of U.S. Army twins**   Trumbetta, "Middle Age, Marriage."

157   **Powell autobiography**   Powell, *My American Journey.*

157   **"poised at the epicenter of American politics"**   Woodward, *Bush at War,* 4.

157   **Powell declines to run**   Berke, "Powell Says No."

157   **"If you run, I'm gone"**   Woodward, *Bush at War,* 5.

158   **"why so many marriageable singles wind up alone"**   Caldwell, "Select All," 92.

159   **"belching guys with barbecue sauce"**   www.msnbc.com.

159   **"security of a refrigerator"**   Segell, "Wedded Life."

160   **"an unlikely serial-killer suspect"**   Cloyd, "Bound, Tortured, Killed," 35.

160   **"BTK's habit of collecting souvenirs"**   Huffstutter and Simon, "Family Man Arrested."

161   **"stretching even my vivid imagination"**   *Larry King Live,* "Beltway Sniper," October 20, 2002, at http://transcripts.cnn.com/transcripts/0210/20/lklw.00.html.

161   **"serial killers are unusual in appearance"**   Fox and Levin, "Serial Murder," 167.

161   **Schwarzenegger's inappropriate behavior**   CBS News, "Arnold Grope."

162   **single men more likely to be feared**   Byrne and Carr, "Cultural Lag," 86–87. The single men were also more likely to say that they were treated with less courtesy and that other people acted as if they thought they were dishonest. Single women were more likely than cohabiting or married women to say that they were insulted and treated with less respect and that they received poorer service in restaurants. Both single men and women were more likely than cohabiting or married people to say that they had been threatened or harassed.

162   **Single men are murderous**   Wright, *Moral Animal.*

162   **"three times as likely to murder another male"**   Ibid., 100.

162   **"more likely to incur various risks"**   Ibid.

162   **"It is not crazy to think"**   Ibid., 101.

163   **"a drop in the divorce rate"**   Ibid., 102.

163   **annual U.S. murder rate**   *Newsweek,* "Numbers," 24.

164   **"primarily intimate partner violence"**   Tjaden and Thoennes, "Violence Against Women," 46.

164   **intimate-partner violence against men**   Ibid., 26.

164   **higher rate of violence among cohabitors**   Johnson and Ferraro, "Domestic Violence," 952.

164   **violent cohabitors unlikely to marry**   DeMaris, "Influence of Intimate Violence," 235.

164   **violence greatest among separated/divorced**   Centers for Disease Control, "Intimate Partner Violence," 559.

164   **women who leave more likely to be killed**   Wilson and Daly, "Spousal Homicide Risk," 3.

165   **"evolves into a strong attachment"**   Laub, Nagin, and Sampson, "Change in Criminal Offending," 227.

165   **"gain the resources that may attract women"**   Wright, *Moral Animal,* 100.

165   **"barbarian-adoption program"**   Pollitt, "Adam and Steve," 9.

165   **"biggest myth about divorce"**   Hetherington and Kelly, *Divorce Reconsidered,* 8.

166   **"more satisfying, meaningful lives"**   Ibid., 257.

166   **"some dark spots"**   Ibid., 258.

166   **whacked Roger on to the head with a poker**   Ibid.

166   **"almost pitifully stripped-down life"**   Ibid., 258–59.

166   **"states ranging from melancholy to despair"**   Ibid., 259.

166   **"Her whole life"**   Ibid., 260.

167   **James Pennybaker**   Ibid., 261.

167   **Simon Russell**   Ibid., 262.

167   **"The Hill Bachelors"**   Quotes are from Trevor, "Hill Bachelors," 80–87.

9. Myth #7: Attention, Single Parents

169   **Welfare Queen**   Reporters tried to find the Welfare Queen to interview her, but they never did find anyone who met Reagan's description. The closest they came was a woman from Chicago who was in fact charged with welfare fraud. Reagan claimed that the Welfare Queen used eighty names; the Chicago woman used four. Reagan also claimed that the queen had bilked the system for more than $150,000; the fraud alleged to have been committed by the Chicago woman amounted to $8,000. See *The New York Times,* " 'Welfare Queen' " and Zucchino, *The Myth of the Welfare Queen,* 65.

169 **Supreme Court protects children of unmarried parents**   Coontz, *Marriage, a History,* 239, 257, 307; Fineman, *The Autonomy Myth,* 140, 335. The 1968 Supreme Court decision was *Levy* v. *Louisiana.*

170 **"stigmatize unmarried sex"**   O'Beirne, "Altared States."

170 **"acknowledge, rather than deny, their suffering"**   Waite and Gallagher, *Case for Marriage,* 189.

170 **"marriage movement"**   See, for example, the talking points issued by the Heritage Foundation at www.issues-2004.org and www.heritage.org; reports from the Institute for American Values at www.americanvalues.org; or the report of the National Marriage Project, "The State of Our Unions 2003," at http://marriage.rutgers.edu/Publications/SOOU/SOOU2003.pdf.

170 **allocation of $1.5 billion**   Pear and Kirkpatrick, "Bush Plans $1.5 Billion."

170 *Frontline* **program**   Kotlowitz, "Let's Get Married."

175 **adding flat-broke man to flat-broke woman**   See, for example, Hays, *Flat Broke.* Also, encouraging ill-considered marriages is economically risky; low-income women who marry, and later divorce, experience higher rates of poverty than do comparable women who stay single (Lichter, Graefe, and Brown, "Is Marriage a Panacea?").

175 **National Drug Abuse Survey**   Hoffman and Johnson, "Adolescent Drug Use."

178 **lowest rates of adolescent substance abuse**   Biblarz and Raftery, "Rethinking the 'Pathology of Matriarchy,'" reports similar results from thirty years of research on the educational and occupational success of children raised in different family structures. Outcomes were better for children from mother-present families (single-mother families and two-biological-parent families) than for single-father families and stepfamilies. They interpret their findings from an evolutionary perspective, which suggests that "mothers have more of their reproductive investment tied up in their children than fathers" (356).

180 **issue is having too little money**   Entwisle and Alexander, "Parent's Economic Shadow"; Pong, Dronkers, and Hampden-Thompson, "Family Policies"; White and Rogers, "Economic Circumstances."

181 **"knowing what takes place in that structure"**   Lansford et al., "Does Family Structure Matter?" 850. See also Demo and Cox, "Families With Young Children," 886.

181 **kids better off with one divorced parent**   Gohm et al., "Culture, Parental Conflict." An American study followed children from different households (divorced or married parents, high and low conflict) into early adulthood (ages nineteen and older) to see whether they continued to feel caught in the middle between their parents. Here is the authors' summary of their findings: "Children with parents in high-conflict marriages were more likely than other children to feel caught between parents. These feelings were associated with lower subjective well-being and poorer quality parent-child relationships. Offspring with divorced parents were no more likely than offspring with continuously married parents to report feeling caught.

Feelings of being caught appeared to fade in the decade following parental divorce. These results suggest that, unlike children of divorce, children with parents in conflicted marriages (who do not divorce) may be unable to escape from their parents' marital problems—even into adulthood" (Amato and Afifi, "Feeling Caught," 222).

181 **difficulties began before divorce** Amato, "Consequences of Divorce"; Amato and Booth, "Prospective Study"; Cherlin, Chase-Lansdale, and McRae, "Effects of Parental Divorce."

181 **single parents friendlier** Asmussen and Larson, "Quality of Family Time."

183 **families "characterized by conflict and aggression"** Repetti, Taylor, and Seeman, "Risky Families," 330.

183 **"sustained poverty and descent into poverty"** Ibid., 355.

183 **shortcut not flawless** White and Rogers, "Economic Circumstances," 1045–46.

184 **"we don't feel alone"** Dickinson, "The Single Life," 92.

184 **long-standing friends, lifelong family members** Trimberger, *New Single Woman.*

10. Myth #8: Too Bad You're Incomplete

186 **possible Lin responses** The proposed answers are hypothetical; I do not know anything about Lin's actual relatives and friends.

187 **"John and Carolyn were true soulmates"** Associated Press, "Kennedys Speak."

187 **Lauren had a high-powered job** Leyden, "Peaceful Memorial."

188 **no obvious script for the life of a singleton** Marcelle Clements underscores the importance of this point in her book and in its title: *The Improvised Woman: Single Women Reinventing Single Life.*

190 **"Raines was looking for young, unmarried reporters"** Mnookin, "*Times* Bomb," 45.

191 **"Souter has come to be known as"** Kaplan and Cohn, "Presumed Competent?" 33.

192 **Rice in *The New Yorker*** Lemann, "Without a Doubt."

192 **Rice on cover of *Newsweek*** Thomas, "Quiet Power."

192 **Rice discussed on *Larry King Live*** The transcript of the *Larry King Live* show is at www.cnn.com/transcripts/0212/11/lkl.00.html.

192 **"Rice begins her day"** Thomas, "Quiet Power," 34.

193 **"performed with cellist Yo-Yo Ma"** Ibid., 30.

193 **"her job is Rice's life"** Ibid., 34.

193 **"nothing matters more than closeness to the President"** Lemann, "Without a Doubt," 167.

193 **"For Rice—who has never married"** Ibid., 177.

193 **"Probably the most key person"** www.cnn.com/transcripts/0212/11/lkl.00. html.

194 **"close circle of old friends"** Lemann, "Without a Doubt," 177.

194 **"sparsely furnished apartment"** Ibid.

194 **"entertaining means ordering take-out"** Ibid.

195 **"her primary off-hour companions"** Ibid.

195 **"were not a success"** Thomas, "Quiet Power," 34.

195 **"He arrives at his office"** Thompson and Duffy, "Pentagon Warlord."

195 **"he became rich"** Ibid.

195 **"Rumsfeld is closest to Cheney"** Ibid.

196 **Franks begins day at 4 A.M.** Duffy and Thompson, "Straight Shooter."

196 **"not the brightest bulb"** Ibid.

196 **"soon be leaving the Army"** Ibid.

196 **"Go make the world safe"** Ibid.

196 **"It seems very petty"** Ibid.

196 **"making your own luck"** Ibid.

197 **"When two soldiers under fire"** Ibid.

197 **"doesn't like to overtax himself"** Carney and Dickerson, "Easy Does It."

198 **"President Bush, in grimy bluejeans"** USAToday.com, "Bush Works."

198 **al Qaeda memo** Clarke, *Against All Enemies,* 26.

198 **"I would change the job"** Sack, "Oprah Show Lets Gore."

11. Myth #9: Poor Soul

199 **"knitting sweaters nobody needed"** Vraney and Barrett, "Marital Status," 492.

200 **"dying alone and found three weeks later"** Fielding, *Bridget Jones's Diary,* front flap.

200 **John Andrew Jamesly** Hobbs, "Carpinteria Loses."

201 **Katharine Graham death** Carlson, "Woman of Substance," 64.

202 **Judging Amy** *Judging Amy,* November 19, 2002.

202 **CSI: Miami** *CSI: Miami,* February 10, 2003.

202 **"An elderly woman died in a fire"** Hobbs, "Woman Dies."

204 **"Dear Ann Landers"** Landers, "Junk Man."

205 **wish to live independently for as long as possible** Krout and Wethington, *Residential Choices,* 3; Vartanian and McNamara, "Older Women in Poverty," 547. There is also evidence to suggest that older people living alone are less likely to feel lonely than they did in the mid-twentieth century. In Britain, studies of people age sixty-five and older showed that "reported loneliness amongst those living alone decreased from 32% in 1945 to 14% in 1999" (Victor et al., "Loneliness Amongst Older People," 585). Also, it is not the always-single people who become the most lonely as they age. A Finnish study of people who were sixty and older found that "over a 10-year period, loneliness increased most in those who, at baseline, were married and living alone with their spouse" (Jylha, "Old Age and Loneliness," 157).

205 **three groups more likely to be depressed** Koropeckyj-Cox, "Beyond Parental Status."

205 **"do not wish to be in their immediate vicinity"** Pinquart and Sorensen, "Socioeconomic Status," 190.

205 **older adults spending time with friends feel better** Ibid., 187.

205 **Pearl Dykstra survey** Dykstra, "Loneliness."

206   **second Dykstra survey**   Dykstra and de Jong Giervald, "Gender and Marital-History."

206   **smaller study of American women**   Essex and Nam, "Marital Status and Loneliness."

207   **They haven't suffered a loss**   See Keith, "Social Context," for a review.

207   **Barbara Simon interviews**   Simon, *Never Married Women.*

208   **men less likely to have same-sex friendships**   Sherrod, "Same-Sex Friendships," 165.

208   **same-sex relationships in ancient Greece**   Nardi, "Seamless Souls," 2.

208   **married women more likely to have same-sex best friend**   Tower and Kasl, "Depressive Symptoms."

208   **widowers more stressed by housework**   Umberson, Wortman, and Kessler, "Widowhood and Depression," 10.

209   **"closest friends a priority"**   Russo, "Buddy System," G1.

209   **"friends-helping-friends model"**   Gross, "Older Women Team Up."

209   **other trend stories**   Brown, "Growing Old Together"; Gross, "Aging at Home"; Gross, "Alone in Illness."

209   **"Sexy, Single, Sizzling Seniors"**   Accetta, "Mailbag," 3.

209   **13 million viewers a week**   *Santa Barbara News-Press,* "Before 'Sex.' "

12. Myth #10: Family Values

210   **teamed up with colleagues to do studies**   The studies are described in DePaulo and Morris, "Singles in Society." The colleagues were Wendy Morris, Janine Hertel, and Lindsay Ritter.

212   **no studies or reportage**   There are some statistics and studies here and there about the topics I mention. For example, a 2003 Census Bureau report on educational attainment in the United States includes a paragraph on marital status (Stoops, "Educational Attainment," 6). With regard to fertility services, there is also a brief essay in an alternative law journal (Millbank, "Every Sperm Is Sacred?"). What is missing is a substantial body of evidence on the topics, as there is, for instance, on sex and educational attainment, or race and criminal justice.

212   **they just don't think about the matter**   Morris, "Stigma Awareness."

213   **time to collect some data**   Morris, Sinclair, and DePaulo, "No Shelter for Singles."

214   **hypothetical landlord survey**   Ibid.

215   **married men paid more than single men**   Bellas, "Effects of Marital Status"; McCafferty, "Singles Discrimination"; Morin, "What's Marriage Worth?"; Toutkoushian, "Marital Status Differences"; Varian, "Marriage Gap."

215   **"Employers value marriage"**   Nock, *Marriage in Men's Lives,* 63.

215   **married/single twins study**   Varian, "Marriage Gap."

216   **compensation packages worth 25 percent more**   Conlin, "Unmarried America," 108.

217   **"family faculty" essay**   Martini, "Baggage vs. Ballast."

218   **"prejudices directed against those who are single"**   Goodwin, "Discussion of Single Life."

218 **"The results were clear"**   Cacioppo, Hawkley, and Berntson, "Anatomy of Loneliness," 71.

219 **married service members paid 25 percent more**   Philpott, "Pay Disparity"; see also Coleman, "Military Singles"; Meyer, "Quartered on Ship"; and Webb, "Myth of Military Poverty."

219 **Family Separation Allowance**   Philpott, "Pay Disparity."

219 **only spouses can make claims**   Personnel Claims Act 31 USC 3721.

219 **Truman's desegregation of army**   Katzenstein and Reppy, "Introduction," 5.

220 **Basic Allowance for Housing**   www.army.com/articles/article_030505_bah.html, accessed July 20, 2005; Military.com Forums, accessed July 20, 2005; *Military Report,* "Legally Speaking," March 16, 2000, at www.military.com, accessed July 20, 2005.

220 **unannounced inspections**   "Know Your On-Base Housing Options," at www.army.com/articles/article_020505_2.html, accessed February 18, 2006.

220 **"command team"**   Segal, "Military Culture," 259.

220 **"socialize, politicize"**   Cullen, "Don't Fall in Love."

220 **wives cited in letters of recommendation**   Segal, "Military Culture," 259.

220 **9 percent of new recruits married**   U.S. Department of Defense, "Population Representation," at www.dod.mil/prhome/poprep2002.

220 **"acquiring a first lady"**   Cullen, "Don't Fall in Love."

220 **clear message to single soldiers**   The families of single service members feel marginalized, too: Cullen, "Heartbreaking Decision"; Shane, "Researchers."

221 **Amazon Prime**   www.amazon.com/gp/subs/primeclub/signup/main.html, accessed July 12, 2005.

221 **US Airways Club**   www.secure.usairways.com/secure/club_application.htm, accessed July 20, 2005.

221 **auto club dues**   www.aaa-calif.com/members/membership.asp, accessed July 20, 2005.

221 **health insurance cheaper for couples**   Consider, for example, the rates described in an advertisement I received in the mail a few years ago. My estimated rate was $219. A husband and wife in the same age range as mine would pay less than $214 each. For parents in the same age range as mine, the rate for their entire family was $476. If the family included four people, the per-person rate would be $119. (The provider was Blue Cross of California, and the rates were for the Santa Barbara area, effective August 1, 2002.)

221 **auto insurance cheaper for couples**   Coleman, "Unmarried Drivers."

222 **Bernardo Heights Country Club**   Morgante, "Legal Fight."

223 **"Social Security Q&A"**   I read the columns that were printed in the *Santa Barbara News-Press* between 2003 and 2005. I also verified the accuracy of this section on Social Security in a phone call to the Social Security Administration, February 9, 2006.

224 **federal provisions "in which marital status is a factor"**   Shah, "Defense of Marriage Act." The benefits I review in this section are described in GAO-04-353R Defense of Marriage Act, especially Appendix A.

226   **Tax Reform Act of 1969**   Yoest, "Income Splitting," 6.

227   **"marriage penalty" table**   The numbers in the table are from the Federal Tax
Brackets section of MoneyChimp at www.moneychimp.com/features/tax_brackets
.htm, accessed July 22, 2005. The MoneyChimp figures are in accord with the IRS
figures as of April 2005 but do not reflect any changes to the tax codes after that
time.

227   **"marriage penalty" example**   In the examples I've used, the two members of a
couple each have the same taxable income. Of course, the two incomes often differ.
The degree to which married couples pay more or less than unmarried couples on
the same total taxable income also depends on relative amount contributed by each
member of the couple. Regardless of any differences within couples, though, the
singles penalty remains—single people still pay more taxes on the same total taxable income.

228   **Victim Compensation Fund**   Feinberg, *Life Worth,* 39.

228   **"When they did this formula"**   Ripley, "Life Worth," 27.

228   **all victims should be valued equally**   Feinberg, *Life Worth,* 183.

229   **study of everyday sexism**   Swim et al., "Everyday Sexism."

230   **teachers' expectations study**   Rosenthal, *Self-Fulfilling Prophecy.*

230   **African American test-taking study**   Steele, Spencer, and Aronson, "Contending
with Group Image."

230   **Physiological reactivity**   Blascovich et al., "Stereotype Threat."

231   **stigmatized groups more prone to hypertension**   Major and O'Brien, "Social Psychology of Stigma."

231   **ostracism matters a great deal**   Abrams, Marques, and Hogg, *Inclusion and Exclusion.*

231   **"were accessing the internet"**   Williams, Cheung, and Choi, "Cyberostracism," 753.

232   **"less interest in high-status occupations"**   Rudman and Heppen, "Glass Slipper
Effect," 1367. Another scholar, Julia T. Wood, believes there may be even more ominous implications of the romance fantasy. Wood listened to the stories of twenty
women who had stayed in emotionally and physically abusive romantic relationships
for an average of more than three years. All of the women initially viewed their ro-
mances as fairy tales, and their partners as princes. When the women later minimized
the abuse they endured, or discounted the violence as typical of most romantic relationships, they may have been doing so, Wood thinks, as a way of sustaining the fantasy. Many women also thought that they had to "have someone," and their partner,
though abusive, was their someone (Wood, "Normalization of Violence").

232   **survey of preretirement adults**   Wilmoth and Koso, "Marital Status and Wealth."
Importantly, differences in wealth cannot be explained by differences in propensi-
ties to put money into savings instead of just spending it. A study of more than two
thousand low-income participants (Grinstein-Weiss, Zhan, and Sherraden, "Saving
Performance," 202) found that when the proper statistical analyses—which take
into account, for example, how much people have in income and assets—were con-

ducted, there were no differences in savings between people who were married and people who were not.

233   **divorced disadvantaged financially**   People who are married and have never been divorced are also more likely to become affluent (i.e., to have an income that is at least ten times the poverty level for same-size households) than are people who were previously married or who have always been single (Hirschl, Altobelli, and Rank, "Odds of Affluence"). Marriage is especially likely to increase the odds of affluence for women.

233   **quarter of unmarried elderly women in poverty**   Vartanian and McNamara, "Older Women in Poverty." See also Carstensen and Pasupathi, "Women of a Certain Age."

13. It Is Perfectly Understandable That You Thought Singles Were Miserable and Lonely: Here's Why

235   **books about single women**   Adams, *Single Blessedness;* Anderson and Stewart, *Flying Solo;* Clements, *Improvised Woman;* Gordon, *Single Women;* Reilly, *Women Living Single;* Simon, *Never Married Women;* and Trimberger, *New Single Woman.* In another variation, single people write their own stories, which are collected in a thematic volume: for example, Ganahl, *Single Women,* and Kaganoff and Spano, *Women on Divorce.*

235   **"But the truth is, I'm happy"**   Reilly, *Women Living Single,* 163.

236   **"I wasn't the least bit offended"**   Roeper, "Lighten Up."

236   **"they don't know what they're missing"**   Steinberg, "Single Life."

238   **majority of Chicago adults single**   U.S. Census Bureau, Census 2000.

240   **imperfect individuals rather than faulty institution**   There are also indications that Americans dramatically underestimate the likelihood that their marriages will end in divorce, even if their own previous marriages ended that way (Fowers et al., "Positive Illusions").

241   **perceptions of singles not yet caught up**   Byrne and Carr, "Cultural Lag."

14. To Be or Not to Be Single: Why Does Anyone Care?

245   **"more women are saying no to marriage"**   Edwards, "Flying Solo."

245   **"what's best for children and society"**   Landsbaum, "Letters."

246   **single women who wanted to raise children**   Drummond, "Mom."

246   **"sadly typical of our narcissistic age"**   Witman, "Letters."

248   **they deserve all the rewards**   See also Cherlin, "Deinstitutionalization," who has argued that marriage has increasingly come to represent a personal achievement and that the symbolic significance of marriage has increased as its practical importance has decreased.

250   **marriage rate in the 1950s**   Kreider and Fields, "Number, Timing," 4.

250   **Americans were marrying younger**   U.S. Census Bureau, Table MS-2.

250   **divorce rate in the 1950s**   U.S. Census Bureau, "Mini-Historical Statistics."

250   **"nothing seemed more obvious"**   Coontz, *Marriage, a History,* 243.

251   **place of marriage secure in the 1950s**   See Coltrane and Adams, "Social Construction," for an analysis of anxiety about social change and its implications for attitudes and rhetoric about divorce.

251   **stop the social changes rocking their world**   Duggan and Kim, "Beyond Gay Marriage."

251   **"just get married"**   A related argument for stigmatizing singles and glorifying couples is that it is couples who produce children and thereby ensure that the species survives. I address this argument in the next chapter, so here I will offer just a few comments.

By the species-survival argument, even married couples who do not have children are subject to stigma—and I do think that they are. However, the argument also seems to assume that in order for people to have sex, have children, and then care for those children, they need extra pushes and pulls, such as the shame of singlism or the cultural celebration of married couples and nuclear families.

I don't think so. I don't think people need extra incentives to be prodded into having sex or children, nor do they need to be stigmatized, punished, or threatened with eternal damnation for failing to procreate. Try turning it around: What would it take to persuade huge segments of the population not to have sex, ever? What would it take to persuade that many people never to have children, or not to care for them once they did have them? On a vast scale, it is just not going to happen anytime soon.

I do think that an evolutionary perspective can help explain why people are so enduringly interested in sexual partnerships—their own and other people's. Yet, as evolutionary psychologists Pillsworth and Haselton have explained, there are important contemporary attitudes and practices that cannot be explained or justified by pointing to evolutionary arguments. Specifically, (1) "nothing from an evolutionary perspective suggests that all relationship roles can be collapsed into a single partner" (as the soulmate mythology seems to assume); (2) "the fact that humans have adaptations for coupling does not imply the moral superiority of coupled individuals"; (3) "the evolutionary perspective also does not suggest that coupling will result in a healthier or more satisfying life for any particular individual"; and (4) "in the modern world, coupling also does not guarantee an on-average fitness benefit to couple members or their children" (Pillsworth and Haselton, "Evolution of Coupling," 101–2).

See also DePaulo and Morris, "Another Problem," for a further discussion of why singles are stigmatized.

15. The Way We Could Be

252   *Chicago Tribune* **series**   Paul, "Series: Friendship."

253   **a few scattered voices**   Ackelsberg and Plaskow, "Against 'Coupledness' ";
Brown, "After Marriage"; Butler, "Can Marriage Be Saved?"; Card, "Against Mar-

riage"; Duggan, "Holy Matrimony!"; Easterbrook, "Single Entry"; Fineman, *Autonomy Myth;* Lehr, *Queer Family Values;* Nair, "Marriage and Immigration."

253   **tax earnings of individuals, not couples**   Yoest, "Income Splitting,"

255   **"do not take advantage of family leave policies"**   Trimberger, "Extending Benefits."

255   **"Let churches and other religious institutions"**   Kinsley, "Abolish Marriage." See also Fineman, *Neutered Mother.*

256   **"defend the sanctity of marriage"**   *New York Times,* "State of the Union."

256   **"more than a century of anthropological research"**   American Anthropological Association, "Statement on Marriage." See also Lancaster, *Trouble with Nature,* and Stacey, *In the Name.*

257   **"indistinguishable from those of mothers"**   Hrdy, *Mother Nature,* 159.

257   **"rampant individualism"**   Raspberry, "Having a Career."

258   **intensive nuclearity**   An important part of this is the practice of intensive mothering, as described, for example, by Hays, *Cultural Contradictions,* and by Douglas and Michaels, *Mommy Myth.*

259   **singles more linked to friends**   See Friedman, *What Are Friends For?* for a similar perspective on the importance of friendships. See also Allen, Blieszner, and Roberto, "Families," and Bengtson, "Beyond the Nuclear Family," for the increasing importance of close ties with people other than nuclear family members.

259   **people who helped AIDS patients**   Kayal, *Bearing Witness.*

259   **fifty single mothers survey**   Hertz and Ferguson. "Kinship Strategies."

260   **children of divorce in collectivist societies**   Gohm et al.

260   **define their own community**   Professor Mary Evans (*Love,* 123) framed the issue historically and sociologically. "Love has been personalized and sexualized in the past 200 years," she said. "When we started to think of love in terms of romance, of sexual desire and above all of a lifelong entitlement to both experiences, then we effectively turned away from engagement with the ultimate *social* question of the impact of our actions on others." See also Foucault, *History of Sexuality,* and Tiefer, *Not a Natural.*

260   **"I'd thought it a fine piece of work"**   Gornick, *The End,* 155.

260   **"crucial moment"**   Ibid., 158.

260   **"yearning to dive down"**   Ibid., 162.

261   **"embrace the world's children"**   Logan, "Power of One," 39.

262   **Felicity Huffman**   Gable, "Lesley Stahl."

262   **John Mayer**   Setoodeh, "John Mayer," 71.

262   **Jarvis working alone**   Jarvis, *Marriage Sabbatical,* 19.

BIBLIOGRAPHY

Abcarian, Robin. "Unmarried, Female and Turned Off by Politics." *Los Angeles Times,* May 10, 2004.

Abrams, Dominic, Jose Marques, and Michael Hogg, editors. *Social Psychology of Inclusion and Exclusion.* New York: Psychology Press, 2003.

Accetta, Patricia. "Mailbag," *People,* July 23, 2001.

Ackelsberg, Martha, and Judith Plaskow. "Gay and Committed, but Against 'Coupledness.'" www.womensenews.com, accessed July 21, 2004.

Adams, Margaret. *Single Blessedness: Observations on the Single Status in Married Society.* New York: Basic Books, 1976.

Albrecht, Donna G. *Buying a Home When You're Single.* New York: John Wiley, 2001.

Ali, Lorraine. "The Crow Must Go On." *Newsweek,* April 15, 2002.

Allen, Katherine R., Rosemary Blieszner, and Karen A. Roberto. "Families in the Middle and Later Years: A Review and Critique of Research in the 1990s." *Journal of Marriage and the Family* 62 (2000): 911–26.

Amador, Xavier, and Judith Kiersky. *Being Single in a Couple's World: How to Be Happily Single While Looking for Love.* New York: Free Press, 1998.

Amato, Paul R. "The Consequences of Divorce for Adults and Children." *Journal of Marriage and the Family* 62 (2000): 1269–87.

Amato, Paul R., and Tamara D. Afifi. "Feeling Caught Between Parents: Adult Children's Relations with Parents and Subjective Well-Being." *Journal of Marriage and Family* 68 (2006): 222–35.

Amato, Paul R., and Alan Booth. "A Prospective Study of Divorce and Parent-Child Relationships." *Journal of Marriage and the Family* 58 (1996): 356–65.

American Anthropological Association. "Statement on Marriage and the Family from the American Anthropological Association." www.aaanet.org/press/ma_stmt_marriage.htm.

Anderson, Carol M., and Susan Stewart. *Flying Solo: Single Women in Midlife.* New York: Norton, 1994.

Ashby, Janet. " 'Parasite Singles': Problem or Victims?" *Japan Times* online, April 7, 2000.

Asmussen, Linda, and Reed Larson. "The Quality of Family Time Among Young Adolescents in Single-Parent and Married-Parent Families." *Journal of Marriage and the Family* 53 (1991): 1021–30.

Associated Press, "Kennedys Speak of Their Grief," July 20, 1999.

Barnett, Rosalind, and Caryl Rivers. *Same Difference: How Gender Myths Are Hurting Our Relationships, Our Children, and Our Jobs.* New York: Basic Books, 2004.

Bellas, Marcia. "The Effects of Marital Status and Wives' Employment on the Salaries of Faculty Men: The (House) Wife Bonus." *Gender & Society* 6 (1992): 609–22.

Bengtson, Vern L. "Beyond the Nuclear Family: The Increasing Importance of Multigenerational Bonds." *Journal of Marriage and Family* 63 (2001): 1–16.

Berke, Richard L. "Powell Says No Once Again to Making a Run for the Presidency." *New York Times,* November 12, 1997, national desk.

Berkman, Lisa F., and S. Leonard Syme. "Social Networks, Host Resistance, and Mortality: A Nine-Year Follow-Up Study of Alameda County Residents." *American Journal of Epidemiology* 109 (1979): 186–204.

Bernard, Jessie. *The Future of Marriage.* New Haven, Conn.: Yale University Press, 1972.

Berselli, Beth. "Newt Gingrich, Dropping the Bombshell." *Washington Post,* August 14, 1999.

Biblarz, Timothy J., and Adrian E. Raftery. "Family Structure, Educational Attainment, and Socioeconomic Success: Rethinking the 'Pathology of Matriarchy.' " *American Journal of Sociology* 105 (1999): 321–65.

Blascovich, James, Steven J. Spencer, Diane M. Quinn, and Claude M. Steele. "Stereotype Threat and the Cardiovascular Reactivity of African-Americans." *Psychological Science* 12 (2001): 225–29.

Blomquist, Brian. "Ex-Wife: Newt Knew I Was Ailing." July 2000. www.mult-sclerosis.org/news/Jul2000/PWMSNewtsEx.html, accessed December 30, 2005.

Borgenicht, David, and Joshua Piven. "When Valentine's Day Doesn't Go Your Way." *USA Weekend,* February 7–9, 2003.

Brown, Patricia Leigh. "Growing Old Together, in New Kind of Commune." *New York Times,* February 27, 2006.

Brown, Wendy. "After Marriage." In *Just Marriage,* edited by Mary Lyndon Shanley. New York: Oxford University Press, 2004, 87–92.

Butler, Judith. "Can Marriage Be Saved? A Forum." *The Nation,* July 5, 2004.

Byrne, Anne, and Deborah Carr. "Caught in the Cultural Lag: The Stigma of Singlehood." *Psychological Inquiry* 16 (2005): 84–91.

Cacioppo, John T., Louise C. Hawkley, and Gary G. Berntson. "The Anatomy of Loneliness." *Current Directions in Psychological Science* 12 (2003): 71–74.

Caldwell, Christopher. "Select All." *The New Yorker,* March 1, 2004, 91–93.

Cancian, Francesca M. *Love in America: Gender and Self-Development.* Cambridge (England): Cambridge University Press, 1987.

Card, Claudia. "Against Marriage and Motherhood." *Hypatia* 11 (1996). www.indiana.edu/~iupress/journals/hypatia, accessed February 16, 2002.

Carlson, Margaret. "A Woman of Substance: Katharine Graham, 1917–2001." *Time,* July 30, 2001.

Carney, James, and John F. Dickerson. "Easy Does It." *Time,* March 19, 2001.

Carstensen, Laura L., and Monisha Pasupathi. "Women of a Certain Age." In *American Women in the Nineties: Today's Critical Issues,* edited by Sherri Mateo. Boston: Northeastern University Press, 1993, 66–78.

CBS News. "Arnold Grope Allegations Grow." October 5, 2003. www.cbsnews.com/stories/2003/10/06/politics/main576614.shtml.

Centers for Disease Control and Prevention. *Marital Status and Health: United States, 1999–2002.* Advance Data, Number 351. National Center for Health Statistics. Hyattsville, Md.: December 15, 2004.

———. *Married Adults Are Healthiest, New CDC Report Shows.* News Release. National Center for Health Statistics. Hyattsville, Md.: December 15, 2004. www.cdc.gov/nchs/pressroom/04facts/marriedadults.htm.

———. Morbidity and Mortality Weekly Report. "Prevalence of Intimate Partner Violence and Injuries—Washington, 1998." *Journal of the American Medical Association* 284 (2000): 559–60.

Chaudhry, Lakshmi. "The New Swingers." *Utne,* March–April 2004, 53–54. (Originally appeared on alternet.org, December 1, 2003.)

———. "Wooing the Single Women Vote," December 1, 2003. www.alternet.org/StoryID=17289.

Cherlin, Andrew J. "The Deinstitutionalization of American Marriage." *Journal of Marriage and Family* 66 (2004): 848–61.

Cherlin, Andrew J., P. Lindsay Chase-Lansdale, and Christine McRae. "The Effects of Parental Divorce on Mental Health Throughout the Life Course." *American Sociological Review* 63 (1998): 239–49.

Chicago Title Insurance Company. "Who's Buying Homes in America?" 24th Annual Survey of Recent Home Buyers. www.ctic.com/homesurvey/home.pdf.

Cho, Alina. "A Nonvoting Bloc with Potential." CNN, May 23, 2004.

Christenson, Elise. "All I Want for Christmas." *Newsweek,* November 11, 2002.

Chudacoff, Howard P. *The Age of the Bachelor: Creating an American Subculture.* Princeton, N.J.: Princeton University Press, 1999.

Clarke, Richard A. *Against All Enemies.* New York: Simon & Schuster, 2004.

Clements, Marcelle. *The Improvised Woman: Single Women Reinventing Single Life.* New York: Norton, 1998.

Cloyd, Courtney. "Bound, Tortured, Killed—and Captured." *Newsweek,* March 7, 2005, 35.

CNN.com. "Dennis Kucinich: Democrat, Candidate, Eligible Bachelor." November 10, 2004. www.cnn.com/2003/ALLPOLITICS/11/10/offbeat.kucinich.reut.

CNNMoney. "Before Saying 'I Do,' More Go to Target." March 23, 2005. http://money.cnn.com/2005/03/23/news/fortune500/npd_registry.reut/index.htm?cnn=yes.

Cohen, Bernard L., and I-Sing Lee. "Catalog of Risks." *Health Physics: The Radiation Safety Journal* 36 (1979): 707–22.

Cohen, Joyce. "A Home of Their Own." *New York Times,* September 19, 2003.

Coleman, Thomas F. "Military Singles Deserve Better Treatment." Unmarried America, December 19, 2005. www.unmarriedamerica.org/column-one/12-19-05-military-singles.htm, accessed December 30, 2005.

———. "Unmarried Drivers." Unmarried America, December 12, 2005. http://www.unmarriedamerica.org/column-one/12-12-05-shopping-for-car-insurance.htm, accessed December 31, 2005.

Coltrane, Scott, and Michele Adams. "The Social Construction of the Divorce 'Problem': Morality, Child Victims, and the Politics of Gender." *Family Relations* 52 (2003): 363–72.

Combe, Rachel. "My Prince Will Come." *Elle,* December 2002.

Conlin, Michelle. "Unmarried America." *Business Week,* October 20, 2003.

Connidis, Ingrid Arnet. *Family Ties & Aging.* Thousand Oaks, Calif.: Sage, 2001.

Conrad, Angela J. "Dependent on the Kindness of Strangers." *Newsweek,* January 31, 2005.

Cook, David T. "Stan Greenberg, Celinda Lake, and Anna Greenberg." *Christian Science Monitor,* April 21, 2004.

Coontz, Stephanie. *Marriage, a History: From Obedience to Intimacy, or How Love Conquered Marriage.* New York: Viking, 2005.

———. *The Way We Never Were: American Families and the Nostalgia Trap.* New York: Basic Books, 1992.

Cose, Ellis. "The Black Gender Gap." *Newsweek,* March 3, 2003.

Crittle, Simon. "No Decorating for a While." *Time,* July 26, 2004.

Cullen, Dave. "Don't Ask, Don't Tell, Don't Fall in Love." *Salon,* June 6, 2000.

———. "A Heartbreaking Decision." *Salon,* June 7, 2000.

Davis, Alan G., and Philip M. Strong. "Working Without a Net: The Bachelor as a Social Problem." *Sociological Review* 25 (1977): 109–29.

Dee, Dré. "Instructions for Living: How to Break Up (with a Single Friend)." *2: The Magazine for Couples,* Summer 2004.

DeMaris, Alfred. "The Influence of Intimate Violence on Transitions out of Cohabitation." *Journal of Marriage and Family* 63 (2001): 235–46.

D'Emilio, John, and Estelle B. Freedman. *Intimate Matters: A History of Sexuality in America.* New York: Harper & Row, 1988.

Demo, David H., and Martha J. Cox. "Families with Young Children: A Review of Research in the 1990s." *Journal of Marriage and the Family* 62 (2000): 876–95.

DePaulo, Bella M. "Sex and the Single Voter." *New York Times,* June 18, 2004.

DePaulo, Bella M., and Wendy L. Morris. "Another Problem That Has No Name— Singlism: The Unrecognized Stereotyping and Discrimination Against People Who Are Single." *Current Directions in Psychological Science* 15 (2006).

———. "Should Singles and the Scholars Who Study Them Make Their Mark or Stay in Their Place?" *Psychological Inquiry* 16 (2005): 142–49.

———. "Singles in Society and in Science." *Psychological Inquiry* 16 (2005): 57–83.

Dickinson, Amy. "The Single Life." *Time,* May 28, 2001.

Douglas, Susan J., and Meredith W. Michaels. *The Mommy Myth: The Idealization of Motherhood and How It Has Undermined All Women.* New York: Free Press, 2004.

Drummond, Tammerlin. "Mom on Her Own." *Time,* August 28, 2000.

Duffy, Michael, and Mark Thompson. "Straight Shooter." *Time,* March 17, 2003.

Duggan, Lisa. "Holy Matrimony!" *The Nation,* March 15, 2004.

Duggan, Lisa, and Richard Kim. "Beyond Gay Marriage." *The Nation,* July 18, 2005.

Dykstra, Pearl A. "Loneliness Among the Never and Formerly Married: The Importance of Supportive Friendships and Desire for Independence." *Journal of Gerontology: Social Sciences* 50B: S321–S329, 1995.

Dykstra, Pearl A., and Jenny de Jong Gierveld. "Gender and Marital-History Differences in Emotional and Social Loneliness Among Dutch Older Adults." *Canadian Journal on Aging* 23 (2004): 141–55.

Easterbrook, Gregg. "Single Entry." *New Republic,* May 24, 2004.

Edwards, Tamala M. "Flying Solo." *Time,* August 28, 2000.

Elliott, Diana B., and Jane Lawler Dye. "Unmarried-Partner Households in the United States: Descriptions and Trends, 2000 to 2003." Presented at the annual meeting of the Population Association of America, Philadelphia, Pa., March 31–April 2, 2005.

Entwisle, Doris R., and Karl L. Alexander. "A Parent's Economic Shadow: Family Structure Versus Family Resources as Influences on Early School Achievement." *Journal of Marriage and the Family* 57 (1995): 399–409.

Essex, Marilyn J., and Sunghee Nam. "Marital Status and Loneliness Among Older Women: The Differential Importance of Close Family and Friends." *Journal of Marriage and the Family* 49 (1987): 93–106.

Evans, Mary. *Love: An Unromantic Discussion.* Malden, Mass.: Polity Press, 2003.

Faludi, Susan. *Backlash: The Undeclared War Against American Women.* New York: Crown, 1991.

Family Research Council website, www.frc.org.

Feinberg, Kenneth R. *What Is Life Worth? The Unprecedented Effort to Compensate the Victims of 9/11.* New York: Public Affairs, 2005.

Feldstein, Stuart A. "Single People May Become a Majority of Home Buyers in 2004." SMR Press Release, March 11, 2004. www.smrresearch.com/gmi04release. html.

Fielding, Helen. *Bridget Jones's Diary.* New York: Viking, 1996.

Fineman, Martha Albertson. *The Autonomy Myth: A Theory of Dependence.* New York: New Press, 2004.

———. *The Neutered Mother, the Sexual Family, and Other Twentieth Century Tragedies.* New York: Routledge, 1995.

Ford, Richard. "Eulogy." *Time,* August 6, 2001.

Foucault, Michel. *The History of Sexuality: An Introduction.* Vol. 1. New York: Pantheon, 1978.

Fowers, Blaine J., Eileen Lyons, Kelly H. Montel, and Netta Shaked. "Positive Illusions About Marriage Among Married and Single Individuals." *Journal of Family Psychology* 15 (2001): 95–109.

Fox, John Alan, and Jack Levin. "Serial Murder: Popular Myths and Empirical Realities." In *Homicide: A Sourcebook of Social Research,* edited by M. Dwayne Smith and Margaret A. Zahn. Thousand Oaks, Calif.: Sage, 1999, 165–75.

Franke-Ruta, Garance. "Creating a Lie." *American Prospect Online,* June 30, 2002. www.prospect.org.

Freeman, Elizabeth. *The Wedding Complex: Forms of Belonging in Modern American Culture.* Durham, N.C.: Duke University Press, 2002.

Friedan, Betty. *The Feminine Mystique.* New York: Norton, 1963.

Friedman, Marilyn. *What Are Friends For? Feminist Perspectives on Personal Relationships and Moral Theory.* Ithaca, N.Y.: Cornell University Press, 1993.

Gable, Mona. "Is Lesley Stahl a Good Mother?" *Huffington Post,* January 18, 2006. www.huffingtonpost.com/mona-gable.

Ganahl, Jane, editor. *Single Women of a Certain Age.* Maui, Hawaii: Inner Ocean Publishing, 2005.

Geller, Jaclyn. *Here Comes the Bride: Women, Weddings, and the Marriage Mystique.* New York: Four Walls Eight Windows, 2001.

Genda, Yuji. "Don't Blame the Unmarried Breed." *Japan Echo* 27 (2000). Accessed online at http://japanecho.co.jp/sum/2000/270313.html on January 15, 2005.

Gibbs, Nancy. "Making Time for a Baby." *Time,* April 15, 2002.

Gillis, John R. "Marriages of the Mind." *Journal of Marriage and Family* 66 (2004): 988–91.

———. *A World of Their Own Making: Myth, Ritual, and the Quest for Family Values.* New York: Basic Books, 1996.

Glass, Shirley P. *NOT "Just Friends."* New York: Free Press, 2003.

Glick, Peter, and Susan T. Fiske. "An Ambivalent Alliance: Hostile and Benevolent Sexism as Complementary Justifications for Gender Inequality." *American Psychologist* 56 (2001): 109–18.

Gohm, Carol L., Shigehiro Oishi, Janet Darlington, and Ed Diener. "Culture, Parental Conflict, Parental Marital Status, and the Subjective Well-Being of Young Adults." *Journal of Marriage and the Family* 60 (1998): 319–34.

Goodwin, Cathy. "Begins a Discussion of Single Life." Reader review of *The New Single Woman,* amazon.com, November 24, 2005. Accessed December 3, 2005.

Gordon, Devin. "Our Life as a House." *Newsweek,* October 27, 2003.

Gordon, Tuula. *Single Women: On the Margins?* New York: New York University Press, 1994.

Gornick, Vivian. *The End of the Novel of Love.* Boston: Beacon Press, 1997.

Gove, Walter R., Michael Hughes, and Carolyn Briggs Style. "Does Marriage Have Positive Effects on the Psychological Well-Being of the Individual?" *Journal of Health and Social Behavior* 24 (1983): 122–31.

Gove, Walter R., and Hee-Choon Shin. "The Psychological Well-Being of Divorced and Widowed Men and Women." *Journal of Family Issues* 10 (1989): 122–44.

Greenwald, Rachel. *Find a Husband After 35 (Using What I Learned at Harvard Business School)*. New York: Ballantine, 2003.

Grinstein-Weiss, Michal, Min Zhan, and Michael Sherraden. "Saving Performance in Individual Development Accounts: Does Marital Status Matter?" *Journal of Marriage and Family* 68 (2006): 192–204.

Gross, Jane. "Aging at Home: For a Lucky Few, a Wish Come True." *New York Times*, February 9, 2006.

———. "Alone in Illness, Seeking Steady Arm to Lean On." *New York Times*, August 26, 2005.

———. "Older Women Team Up to Face Future Together." *New York Times*, February 27, 2004.

Hambly, Bob. "Numbers." *Time*, July 19, 1999.

Hatfield, Elaine, and Richard L. Rapson. *Love & Sex: Cross-Cultural Perspectives*. Boston: Allyn and Bacon, 1996.

Hays, Sharon. *The Cultural Contradictions of Motherhood*. New Haven, Conn.: Yale University Press, 1996.

———. *Flat Broke with Children: Women in the Age of Welfare Reform*. New York: Oxford University Press, 2003.

Helsing, Knud J., Moyes Szklo, and George W. Comstock. "Factors Associated with Mortality After Widowhood." *American Journal of Public Health* 71 (1981): 802–9.

Hertz, Rosanna, and Faith I. T. Ferguson. "Kinship Strategies and Self-Sufficiency Among Single Mothers by Choice: Postmodern Family Ties." *Qualitative Sociology* 20 (1997): 187–209.

Hertzberg, Hendrik. "Reckless Driver." *The New Yorker*, March 8, 2004.

Hetherington, E. Mavis, and John Kelly. *For Better or For Worse: Divorce Reconsidered*. New York: Norton, 2002.

Hewlett, Sylvia Ann. *Creating a Life: Professional Women and the Quest for Children*. New York: Hyperion, 2002.

Hirschl, Thomas A., Joyce Altobelli, and Mark R. Rank. "Does Marriage Increase the Odds of Affluence? Exploring the Life Course Probabilities." *Journal of Marriage and Family* 65 (2003): 927–38.

Hobbs, Dawn. "Carpinteria Loses a Dedicated Volunteer." *Santa Barbara News-Press*, August 30, 2003.

———. "Woman Dies in House Fire on the Mesa." *Santa Barbara News-Press*, January 1, 2002.

Hoffman, John P., and Robert A. Johnson. "A National Portrait of Family Structure and Adolescent Drug Use." *Journal of Marriage and the Family* 60 (1998): 633–45.

Honolulu Star-Bulletin. "Problems of Single People Should Be Taken Seriously." May 26, 2001.

hooks, bell. *Feminist Theory: From Margin to Center*. Boston: South End Press, 1984.

Hopkins, Jamie Smith. "The Soaring Cost of Love." *Baltimore Sun,* January 28, 2004.

Hoyle, Rick H., Charles M. Judd, and Monica J. Harris. *Research Methods in Social Psychology.* 7th ed. Stamford, Conn.: Wadsworth, 2001.

Hrdy, Sarah Blaffer. *Mother Nature: Maternal Instincts and How They Shape the Human Species.* New York: Ballantine, 1999.

Huffstutter, P. J., and Stephanie Simon. "Family Man Arrested in 10 Slayings." *Los Angeles Times,* February 27, 2005.

In the Public Interest website, www.nader.org/blog/template.php?/categories/ 6-Biography, accessed May 12, 2006.

Inglehart, Ronald. *Culture Shift in Advanced Industrial Society.* Princeton, N.J.: Princeton University Press, 1990.

Ingraham, Chrys. *White Weddings: Romancing Heterosexuality in Popular Culture.* New York: Routledge, 1999.

Jamieson, Paul. "It's a Paired, Paired, Paired, Paired World." *Washington Post,* April 6, 2003.

Jarvis, Cheryl. *The Marriage Sabbatical: The Journey That Brings You Home.* Cambridge, Mass.: Perseus, 2001.

Jersild, Sarah. "More Olympic Ranting." August 19, 2004. www.fiendishplot.com/ 2004_08_15_archive.htm, accessed June 8, 2005.

Johnson, Michael P., and Kathleen J. Ferraro. "Research on Domestic Violence in the 1990s: Making Distinctions." *Journal of Marriage and the Family* 62 (2000): 948–63.

Joint Center for Housing Studies. "The State of the Nation's Housing: 2004." Harvard University. www.jchs.harvard.edu/publications/markets/son2004.pdf.

Jylha, Marja. "Old Age and Loneliness: Cross-Sectional and Longitudinal Analyses in the Tampere Longitudinal Study on Aging." *Canadian Journal on Aging* 23 (2004): 157–68.

Kaganoff, Penny. "Other Uses for a Wedding Gown." In *Women on Divorce: A Bedside Companion,* edited by Penny Kaganoff and Susan Spano. New York: Harcourt Brace, 1995, 26–38.

Kaplan, David A., and Bob Cohn. "Presumed Competent?" *Newsweek,* September 17, 1990.

Kaplan, Esther. "Onward Christian Soldiers." *The Nation,* July 5, 2004.

Katz, Gregory. "An American in Paris." *USA Weekend,* July 4–6, 2003.

Katzenstein, Mary Fainsod, and Judith Reppy. "Introduction: Rethinking Military Culture." In *Beyond Zero Tolerance: Discrimination in Military Culture,* edited by Mary Fainsod Katzenstein and Judith Reppy. Lanham, Md.: Rowman & Littlefield, 1999, 1–21.

Kayal, Philip M. *Bearing Witness: Gay Men's Health Crisis and the Politics of AIDS.* Boulder, Colo.: Westview Press, 1993.

Keith, Pat M. "The Social Context and Resources of the Unmarried in Old Age." *International Journal of Aging and Human Development* 23 (1986): 81–96.

Kennedy, Helen. "Dems Need to Woo Singles." *New York Daily News,* July 27, 2003.

Kinsley, Michael. "Abolish Marriage." *Slate,* July 2, 2003.

Koropeckyj-Cox, Tanya. "Beyond Parental Status: Psychological Well-Being in Middle and Old Age." *Journal of Marriage and Family* 64 (2002): 957–71.

———. "Singles, Society, and Science: Sociological Perspectives." *Psychological Inquiry* 16 (2005): 91–97.

Kotlowitz, Alex. "Let's Get Married." PBS *Frontline,* November 14, 2002. From the transcript at pbs.org/wgbh/pages/frontline/shows/marriage/etc/script.html.

Kreider, Rose M., and Jason M. Fields. "Number, Timing, and Duration of Marriages and Divorces: 1996." U.S. Census Bureau, Current Population Reports, P70-80, issued February 2002.

Krout, John A., and Elaine Wethington. "Introduction." In *Residential Choices and Experiences of Older Adults: Pathways to Life Quality,* edited by John A. Krout and Elaine Wethington. New York: Springer, 2003, 3–25.

Kurtz, Howard. "Writer Backing Bush Plan Had Gotten Federal Contract." *Washington Post,* January 26, 2005, sec. C.

Lancaster, Roger N. *The Trouble with Nature: Sex in Science and Popular Culture.* Berkeley: University of California Press, 2003.

Landers, Ann. "My Husband Is a 'Junk Man.'" *Santa Barbara News-Press,* December 29, 2001.

Landsbaum, Mark. "Letters." *Time,* September 18, 2000.

Langford, Wendy. *Revolutions of the Heart: Gender, Power, and the Delusion of Love.* London: Routledge, 1999.

Lansford, Jennifer E., Rosario Ceballo, Antonia Abbey, and Abagail J. Stewart. "Does Family Structure Matter? A Comparison of Adoptive, Two-Parent Biological, Single-Mother, Stepfather, and Stepmother Households." *Journal of Marriage and Family* 63 (2001): 840–51.

Larry King Live. "Interview with Martha Stewart." CNN, July 19, 2004. http://transcripts.cnn.com/transcripts/0407/19/lk1.00.html.

———. "Panel Discusses Beltway Sniper." CNN, October 20, 2002. http://transcripts.cnn.com/transcripts/0210/20/lklw.00.html.

Laub, John H., Daniel S. Nagin, and Robert J. Sampson. "Trajectories of Change in Criminal Offending: Good Marriages and the Desistance Process." *American Sociological Review* 63 (1998): 225–38.

Laumann, Edward O., John H. Gagnon, Robert T. Michael, and Stuart Michaels. *The Social Organization of Sexuality: Sexual Practices in the United States.* Chicago: University of Chicago Press, 1994.

Lehr, Valerie. *Queer Family Values: Debunking the Myth of the Nuclear Family.* Philadelphia, Pa.: Temple University Press, 1999.

Lemann, Nicholas. "Without a Doubt." *The New Yorker,* October 14 & 21, 2002.

Leyden, Liz. "Peaceful Memorial Celebrates Bessettes." *Washington Post,* July 25, 1999.

Lichter, Daniel T., Deborah Roempke Graefe, and J. Brian Brown. "Is Marriage a Panacea? Union Formation Among Economically Disadvantaged Unwed Mothers." *Social Problems* 50 (2003): 60–86.

Lillard, Lee A., and Linda J. Waite. " 'Til Death Do Us Part: Marital Disruption and Mortality." *American Journal of Sociology* 100 (1995): 1131–56.

Litwak, Eugene, and Peter Messeri. "Organizational Theory, Social Supports, and Mortality Rates: A Theoretical Convergence." *American Sociological Review* 54 (1989): 49–66.

Logan, Michael. "The Power of One." *TV Guide,* October 4, 2003.

Lucas, Richard E. "Time Does Not Heal All Wounds: A Longitudinal Study of Reaction and Adaptation to Divorce." *Psychological Science* 16 (2005): 945–50.

Lucas, Richard E., Andrew E. Clark, Yannis Georgellis, and Ed Diener. "Reexamining Adaptation and the Set Point Model of Happiness: Reactions to Changes in Marital Status." *Journal of Personality and Social Psychology* 84 (2003): 527–39.

Lucas, Richard E., and Portia S. Dyrenforth. "Does the Existence of Social Relationships Matter for Subjective Well-Being?" In *Self and Relationships: Connecting Intrapersonal and Interpersonal Processes,* edited by Kathleen D. Vohs and Eli J. Finkel. New York: Guilford Press, 2006, 254–73.

———. "The Myth of Marital Bliss?" *Psychological Inquiry* 16 (2005): 111–15.

Lyubomirsky, Sonja, Laura King, and Ed Diener. "The Benefits of Frequent Positive Affect: Does Happiness Lead to Success?" *Psychological Bulletin* 131 (2005): 803–55.

Major, Brenda N., and Laurie T. O'Brien. "The Social Psychology of Stigma." *Annual Review of Psychology* 56 (2005): 393–421.

Mandell, Judy. "Over-the-Top Weddings." *USA Weekend,* September 10–12, 2004.

Marano, Hara Estroff. "Debunking the Marriage Myth: It Works for Women, Too." *New York Times,* August 4, 1998, science desk.

Marder, Dianna. "Dating-Advice Books Just Keep Coming to the Shelves." Knight Ridder News Service, in *Santa Barbara News-Press,* July 21, 2002.

Marinucci, Carla. "Courting the Single Female Voter." *San Francisco Chronicle,* May 23, 2004.

Marks, Nadine F. "Flying Solo at Midlife: Gender, Marital Status, and Psychological Well-Being." *Journal of Marriage and the Family* 58 (1996): 917–32.

Marks, Nadine F., Larry L. Bumpass, and Heyjung Jun. "Family Roles and Well-Being During the Middle Life Course." In *How Healthy Are We? A National Study of Well-Being at Midlife,* edited by Orville Gilbert Brim, Carol D. Ryff, and Ronald C. Kessler. Chicago: University of Chicago Press, 2004, 514–49.

Marks, Nadine F., and James David Lambert. "Marital Status Continuity and Change Among Young and Midlife Adults." *Journal of Family Issues* 19 (1998): 652–86.

Martini, Kirk. "Baggage vs. Ballast: Work and Family on the Tenure Track." www.trc.virginia.edu/Publications/OP_Balancing/Baggage.htm.

Maslin, Janet. "Johnny Depp as a Soulful Outsider," *New York Times,* December 17, 1993.

McCafferty, Dennis. "Singles Discrimination." MSN, August 21, 2001. http://content.careers.msn.com/WorkingLife/Workplace/gwp1070125.asp., accessed August 21, 2001.

McPherson, Miller, Lynn Smith-Lovin, and James M. Cook. "Birds of a Feather: Homophily in Social Networks." *Annual Review of Sociology* 27 (2001): 415–44.

Merkin, Daphne. "In the Country of Divorce." In *Women on Divorce: A Bedside Companion,* edited by Penny Kaganoff and Susan Spano. New York: Harcourt Brace, 1995, 178–89.

Meyer, Carlton. "Quartered on Ship." *G2Mil,* 2002. www.g2mil.com/sailors.htm, accessed December 31, 2005.

Millbank, Jenni. "Every Sperm Is Sacred?" *Alternative Law Journal* 22 (1997): 126–29.

Millhauser, Steven. "The Disappearance of Elaine Coleman." *The New Yorker,* November 22, 1999, 176–88.

Mnookin, Seth. "The *Times* Bomb." *Newsweek,* May 26, 2003.

Montenegro, Xenia P. "Lifestyles, Dating and Romance: A Study of Midlife Singles." Executive Summary Prepared for *AARP The Magazine,* September, 2003. Available at www.aarp.org.

Morgan, David, Paula Carder, and Margaret Neal. "Are Some Relationships More Useful than Others? The Value of Similar Others in the Networks of Recent Widows." *Journal of Social and Personal Relationships* 14 (1997): 745–59.

Morgante, Michelle. "Couple Find Legal Fight Puts Them in the Rough." *Santa Barbara News-Press,* July 4, 2004 (Associated Press story).

Morin, Richard. "What's Marriage Worth?" *Washington Post,* June 13, 2004.

Morris, Wendy L. "The Effects of Stigma Awareness on the Self-Esteem of Singles." Dissertation, University of Virginia, Charlottesville, May 2005.

Morris, Wendy L., Bella M. DePaulo, Janine Hertel, and Lindsay Ritter. "Perceptions of People Who Are Single: A Developmental Life Tasks Model." Manuscript submitted for publication, 2006.

Morris, Wendy L., Stacey Sinclair, and Bella M. DePaulo. "No Shelter for Singles: The Perceived Legitimacy of Civil Status Discrimination." Manuscript submitted for publication, 2006.

MSN Entertainment. "Parker Says She Takes Care of Broderick." May 19, 2003. http://entertainment.msn.com/celebs/article.aspx?news=158836, accessed May 19, 2004.

MSN WomenCentral. "Friends: Keeping Them After You Tie the Knot." The Knot, November 19, 2002. http://womencentral.msn.com/weddings/articles/friends.asp.

Nair, Yasmin. "Marriage and Immigration." *Identity,* March 1, 2006. www.windycitymediagroup.com, accessed March 3, 2006.

Nardi, Peter M. " 'Seamless Souls': An Introduction to Men's Friendships." In *Men's Friendships,* edited by Peter M. Nardi. Newbury Park, Calif.: Sage, 1992, 1–14.

Newsweek. "Numbers." October 31, 2005.

The New Yorker. "The Critics." July 12 & 19, 2004.

New York Times. "President's State of the Union Message to Congress and the Nation." January 21, 2004.

———. " 'Welfare Queen' Becomes Issue in Reagan Campaign." February 15, 1976.

Nightline. "The Art of Conversation: Celebrating Barbara Walters." ABC News, September 16, 2004. www.transcripts.net.

———. "Coming Home." ABC News, December 15, 2004. www.transcripts.net.

Nock, Steven L. *Marriage in Men's Lives.* New York: Oxford University Press, 1998.

O'Beirne, Kate. "Altared States." *National Review,* May 3, 2002.

Orman, Suze. *The Road to Wealth.* New York: Riverhead Books, 2001.

Otnes, Cele C., and Elizabeth H. Pleck. *Cinderella Dreams: The Allure of the Lavish Wedding.* Berkeley: University of California Press, 2003.

Patchett, Ann. *Truth and Beauty: A Friendship.* New York: HarperCollins, 2004.

Paul, Marla. "Series: Friendship." *Chicago Tribune,* 1999–2001.

Pear, Robert, and David D. Kirkpatrick. "Bush Plans $1.5 Billion Drive for Promotion of Marriage." *New York Times,* January 14, 2004.

Philipson, Ilene. *Married to the Job: Why We Live to Work and What We Can Do About It.* New York: Free Press, 2002.

Philpott, Tom. "End to Pay Disparity." February 17, 2006. www.military.com/features/0,15240,88118,00.html, accessed February 18, 2006.

Pillsworth, Elizabeth G., and Martie G. Haselton. "The Evolution of Coupling." *Psychological Inquiry* 16 (2005): 98–104.

Pindell, James W., and John Curley. "Candidates Meet for the First NH Forum." PoliticsNH.com, November 6, 2003.

Pinquart, Martin, and Silvia Sorensen. "Influences of Socioeconomic Status, Social Network, and Competence on Subjective Well-Being in Later Life: A Meta-Analysis." *Psychology and Aging* 15 (2000): 187–224.

Pleck, Elizabeth H. *Celebrating the Family: Ethnicity, Consumer Culture, and Family Rituals.* Cambridge: Harvard University Press, 2000.

Pollitt, Katha. "Adam and Steve—Together at Last." *The Nation,* December 15, 2003.

———. "Pull Over, NASCAR Dads." *The Nation,* April 12, 2004.

Pong, Suet-Ling, Jaap Dronkers, and Gillian Hampden-Thompson. "Family Policies and Children's School Achievement in Single- Versus Two-Parent Families." *Journal of Marriage and Family* 65 (2003): 681–99.

Powell, Colin L. *My American Journey: An Autobiography.* New York: Random House, 1995.

Purdum, Todd S. "Mystery Solved: The Overview: 'Deep Throat' Unmasks Himself: Ex–No. 2 at F.B.I." *New York Times,* June 1, 2005.

Putnam, Robert D. *Bowling Alone: The Collapse and Revival of American Community.* New York: Simon & Schuster, 2000.

Quinn, Sally. "The Secret That Didn't Reach Washington's Lips." *Washington Post,* June 3, 2005.

Rainie, Lee, and Mary Madden. "Romance in America." Pew Internet and American Life Program, February 13, 2006, www.pewinternet.org.

Raspberry, William. "Having a Career vs. a Family." *Charlottesville Daily Progress,* April 30, 2002.

Rauch, Jonathan. *Gay Marriage: Why It Is Good for Gays, Good for Straights, and Good for America*. New York: Times Books, 2004.

———. "Imperfect Unions." *New York Times*, August 15, 2004, opinion.

Reilly, Lee. *Women Living Single*. Boston: Faber and Faber, 1996.

Repetti, Rena L., Shelley E. Taylor, and Teresa E. Seeman. "Risky Families: Family Social Environments and the Mental and Physical Health of Offspring." *Psychological Bulletin* 128 (2002): 330–66.

Reuters. "Princess Anne Slams 'Selfish' Singles." London: April 4, 2000.

Reynolds, Jill, and Margaret Wetherell. "The Discursive Climate of Singleness: The Consequences for Women's Negotiation of a Single Identity." *Feminism & Psychology* 13 (2003): 489–510.

Ripley, Amanda. "What Is a Life Worth?" *Time,* February 11, 2002.

Roeper, Richard. "Lighten Up, Married Folks: Being Single Isn't So Bad." *Chicago Sun-Times,* January 20, 2004.

Roizen, Michael F. *RealAge: Are You as Young as You Can Be?* New York: Cliff Street Books, 1999.

Rook, Karen S., and Laura A. Zettel. "The Purported Benefits of Marriage Viewed Through the Lens of Physical Health." *Psychological Inquiry* 16 (2005): 116–21.

Rosenthal, Robert. *On the Social Psychology of the Self-Fulfilling Prophecy: Further Evidence for Pygmalion Effects and Their Mediating Mechanisms* (Module 53, pp. 1–28). New York: MSS Modular Publications, 1974.

Roshan, Maer. "Prince of the City." *New York,* August 2, 1999. http://newyorkmetro.com/nymetro/news/people/features/496.

Rosnow, Ralph L., and Robert Rosenthal. *Beginning Behavioral Research: A Conceptual Primer*. Englewood Cliffs, N.J.: Prentice-Hall, 2004.

Ross, Catherine E. "Reconceptualizing Marital Status as a Continuum of Social Attachment." *Journal of Marriage and the Family* 57 (1995): 129–40.

Ross, Catherine E., John Mirowsky, and Karen Goldsteen. "The Impact of the Family on Health: The Decade in Review." *Journal of Marriage and the Family* 52 (1990): 1059–78.

Rothman, Ellen K. *Hands and Hearts: A History of Courtship in America*. Cambridge: Harvard University Press, 1987.

Rudman, Laurie A., and Jessica B. Heppen. "Implicit Romantic Fantasies and Women's Interest in Personal Power: A Glass Slipper Effect?" *Personality and Social Psychology Bulletin* 29 (2003): 1357–70.

Russo, Francine. "Buddy System." *Time,* January 2002, G1.

Sachs, Andrea. "Wedded to Work." *Time,* September 2002, A21.

Sack, Kevin. "The 2000 Campaign: The Vice President; Oprah Show Lets Gore Reach Out to Women." *The New York Times,* September 12, 2000.

Sadin, Meredith. "Till Death or Kenya." *Newsweek,* June 23, 2003.

Salinger, Adrienne. *Living Solo*. Kansas City, Mo.: Andrews McMeel, 1998.

Santa Barbara News-Press. "Before 'Sex' There Were 'Golden Girls.' " June 25, 2003.

Sanz, Marie. "Democrats Seek Sex and the City Women." *Mail & Guardian Online,* October 19, 2004. www.mg.co.za.

Saporito, Bill. "Inside the New American Home." *Time,* October 14, 2002, 64–75.

Scanlon, Charles. "Japan's 'Parasite Singles.' " *BBC News,* May 31, 2001.

Schneider, Bill. "On Style and Substance, Heading Off Toward November." CNN.com, January 20, 2000.

Schneider, Karen S. "Everything But Love." *People,* August 27, 2001.

Schwartz, Pepper. *Peer Marriage: How Love Between Equals Really Works.* New York: Free Press, 1994.

Segal, Mady Wechsler. "Military Culture and Military Families." In *Beyond Zero Tolerance: Discrimination in Military Culture,* edited by Mary Fainsod Katzenstein and Judith Reppy. Lanham, Md.: Rowman & Littlefield, 1999, 251–61.

Segell, Michael. "Wedded Life Boosts Husbands' Health." www.msnbc.com/news/ 599521.asp, accessed August 21, 2002.

Setoodeh, Ramin. "John Mayer Q & A." *Newsweek,* December 20, 2004.

Shah, Danya K. "Defense of Marriage Act: Update to Prior Report." Letter from the Associate General Counsel of the United States General Accounting Office to Majority Leader Bill First, January 23, 2004. Available at www.gao.gov.

Shane, Leo, III. "Researchers: Alcohol Misuse, Divorce Rates Higher Among Returning Troops." *Stars and Stripes,* Mideast edition, December 9, 2005.

Sherrod, Drury. "The Influence of Gender on Same-Sex Friendships." In *Close Relationships,* edited by Clyde Hendrick. Newbury Park, Calif.: Sage, 1989, 164–86.

Shields, Carol. "The Marriage Survivors." In *Women on Divorce: A Bedside Companion,* edited by Penny Kaganoff and Susan Spano. New York: Harcourt Brace, 1995, 60–68.

Simenauer, Jacqueline, and Margaret Russell. *Single's Guide to Cruise Vacations.* Rocklin, Calif.: Prima Publishing, 1997.

Simon, Barbara Levy. *Never Married Women.* Philadelphia: Temple University Press, 1987.

Simon, Robin W. "Revisiting the Relationships Among Gender, Marital Status, and Mental Health." *American Journal of Sociology* 107 (2002): 1065–96.

Single Gourmet. www.single-gourmet.com., accessed February 16, 2002.

Social Security Survivor Benefits, SSA Publication No. 05-10084, May 2004.

Solot, Dorian, and Marshall Miller. *Unmarried to Each Other: The Essential Guide to Living Together as an Unmarried Couple.* New York: Marlowe, 2002.

Soukup, Elise. "Happily Ever After?" *Newsweek,* March 15, 2004.

Sprey, Jetse. "Book Reviews." *Journal of Marriage and Family* 63 (2001): 1199–1200.

Stacey, Judith. *In the Name of the Family: Rethinking Family Values in the Postmodern Age.* Boston: Beacon Press, 1996.

Stack, Steven, and J. Ross Eshleman. "Marital Status and Happiness: A 17-Nation Study." *Journal of Marriage and the Family* 60 (1998): 527–36.

Steele, Claude M., Steven J. Spencer, and Joshua Aronson. "Contending with Group Image: The Psychology of Stereotype and Social Identity Threat." *Advances in Experimental Social Psychology* 34 (2002): 379–440.

Steepleton, Scott. "Raffle Offers Allure of S. B. Home Ownership." *Santa Barbara News-Press,* July 4, 2004.

Steinberg, Neil. "Single Life Is Fine Until About 30, Then Normal People Marry." *Chicago Sun-Times,* January 23, 2004.

St. John, Warren. "Bob, Meet Jane. And Give Me the Details." *New York Times,* December 22, 2002.

Stone, Lawrence. *The Family, Sex, and Marriage in England 1500–1800.* New York: Harper & Row, 1977.

Stoops, Nicole. "Educational Attainment in the United States: 2003." U. S. Census Bureau, P20-550, issued June 2004. www.census.gov/population/www/socdemo/educ-attn.html.

Stuever, Hank. "Alone. Ahh. Sigh. 27 Million Singles Do Whatever They Want. All by Themselves." *Washington Post,* May 17, 2001.

Swim, Janet K., Lauri L. Hyers, Laurie L. Cohen, and Melissa J. Ferguson. "Everyday Sexism: Evidence for Its Incidence, Nature, and Psychological Impact from Three Daily Diary Studies." *Journal of Social Issues* 57 (2001): 31–53.

Takahashi, Hiroyuki, and Jeannette Voss. " 'Parasite Singles'—a Uniquely Japanese Phenomenon?" *National Association of Japan-America Societies.* www.us-japan.org/contemporary_society.html, accessed February 23, 2002.

Teachman, Jay D., Lucky M. Tedrow, and Kyle D. Crowder. "The Changing Demography of America's Families." *Journal of Marriage and the Family* 62 (2000): 1234–46.

Thomas, Cathy Booth. "The Pill That Unleashed Sex." *Time,* March 31, 2003.

Thomas, Evan. "The Quiet Power of Condi Rice." *Newsweek,* December 16, 2002.

Thomas, Evan, and Eleanor Clift. "As the Shadows Fell." *Newsweek,* June 21, 2004.

Thompson, Mark, and Michael Duffy. "Pentagon Warlord." *Time,* January 27, 2003.

Thornton, Arland, and Linda Young-DeMarco. "Four Decades of Trends in Attitudes Toward Family Issues in the United States: The 1960s Through the 1990s." *Journal of Marriage and Family* 63 (2001): 1009–37.

Tiefer, Lenore. *Sex Is Not a Natural Act.* 2nd ed. Boulder, Colo.: Westview Press, 2004.

Tierney, John. "W.M.'s Seek S.F.'s for Fall Affair." *New York Times,* June 6, 2004.

Tjaden, Patricia, and Nancy Thoennes. "Full Report of the Prevalence, Incidence, and Consequences of Violence Against Women." U.S. Department of Justice. Washington, DC: Office of Justice Programs, November 2000. www.ncirs.org/txtfiles1/nij/183781.txt.

Tolbert, Kathryn. "Japan's New Material Girls in No Hurry to Wed." *Washington Post,* February 10, 2000.

Toutkoushian, Robert K. "Racial and Marital Status Differences in Faculty Pay." *Journal of Higher Education* 69 (1998): 513–29.

Tower, Roni Beth, and Stanislav V. Kasl. "Depressive Symptoms Across Older Spouses: Longitudinal Influences." *Psychology and Aging* 11 (1996): 683–97.

Trevor, William. "The Hill Bachelors." *The New Yorker,* November 8, 1999, 80–87.

Trimberger, E. Kay. "Extending Benefits to Singles in Public Policy Initiatives." Paper presented to the XV World Congress of Sociology, Brisbane, Australia, July 10, 2002.

————. *The New Single Woman.* Boston: Beacon Press, 2005.

Trumbetta, Susan L. "Middle Age, Marriage, and Health Habits of America's Greatest Generation: Twins as Tools for Causal Analysis." In *Behavior Genetics Principles: Perspectives in Development, Personality, and Psychopathology,* edited by Lisabeth F. DiLalla. Washington, DC: American Psychological Association, 2004, 59–70.

Tucker, Joan S., Howard S. Friedman, Deborah L. Wingard, and Joseph E. Schwartz. "Marital History at Midlife as a Predictor of Longevity: Alternative Explanations to the Protective Effect of Marriage." *Health Psychology* 15 (1996): 94–101.

Umberson, Debra, Camille B. Wortman, and Ronald C. Kessler. "Widowhood and Depression: Explaining Long-Term Gender Differences in Vulnerability." *Journal of Health and Social Behavior* 33 (1992): 10–24.

USAToday.com. "Bush Works to Make His Ranch Less 'Jungle-y.'" August 25, 2001. www.usatoday.com/news/washington/august01/2001-08-25-ranch.htm.

U.S. Bureau of Labor Statistics. "Composition of Consumer Unit: Average Annual Expenditures and Characteristics, Consumer Expenditure Survey, 2003." www.bls.gov/cex/2004/Standard/cucomp.pdf.

————. "Employment Status by Marital Status and Sex, 2004 Annual Averages." Table 4. www.bls.gov/cps/wlf-table4-2005.pdf.

————. "Selected Employment Indicators." Table A-6. www.bls.gov/web/cpseea8.pdf.

U.S. Census Bureau. "All Parent/Child Situations, by Type, Race, and Hispanic Origin of Householder or Reference Person: 1970 to Present." Table FM-2. Current Population Survey, 2003. Annual Social and Economic Supplement. Internet release date: September 15, 2004.

————. "America's Families and Living Arrangements: 2003." Current Population Survey, P20-553, issued November 2004.

————. "Current Population Survey, 2003. Annual Social and Economic Supplement." Internet release date: September 15, 2004.

————. "Current Population Survey, 2004. Annual Social and Economic Supplement." Internet release date: June 29, 2005.

————. "Estimated Median Age at First Marriage, by Sex: 1890 to Present." Table MS-2. Internet release date: September 15, 2004. www.census.gov/population/socdemo/hh-fam/tabMS-2.pdf.

————. "Facts for Features: Mother's Day." April 19, 2004. www.census.gov/Press-Release/www/2004/cb04-ff08.pdf.

————. "Facts for Features: Women's History Month (March)." February 22, 2005. www.census.gov/Press-Release/www/releases/archives/cb05-ff.04.pdf.

————. "Homeownership Rates for the United States, by Age of Householder and by Family Status: 1982 to 2001." Table 15. Annual Statistics 2001, Housing and House-hold Economic Statistics Division. www.census.gov/hhes/www/housing/hvs/annual01/ann01t15.html.

————. "Mini-Historical Statistics." No. HS-11. Marital status of the population by sex: 1900 to 2002. Statistical Abstract of the United States: 2003.

U.S. Commission on Civil Rights. "Mission." www.usccr.gov/about/mission.htm, accessed June 1, 2005.

U.S. Department of Defense. "Population Representation in the Military Services, Fiscal Year 2002." www.dod.mil/prhome/poprep2002.

U.S. Equal Employment Opportunity Commission. "Discrimination by Type: Facts and Guidance." www.eeoc.gov.

Van Buren, Abigail. "Bridesmaid's Dress Alteration Is Not Gift Enough for Bride." ("Dear Abby" column.) *Santa Barbara News-Press,* February 29, 2004.

Varian, Hal R. "Analyzing the Marriage Gap." *New York Times,* July 29, 2004.

Vartanian, Thomas P., and Justine M. McNamara. "Older Women in Poverty: The Impact of Midlife Factors." *Journal of Marriage and Family* 64 (2002): 532–48.

Victor, Christina R., Sasha J. Scambler, Sunil Shah, Derek G. Cook, Tess Harris, Elizabeth Rink, and Stephen de Wilde. "Has Loneliness Amongst Older People Increased? An Investigation into Variations Between Cohorts." *Ageing & Society* 22 (2002): 585–97.

Vraney, Mary W., and Carol J. Barrett. "Marital Status: Its Effects on the Portrayal of Older Characters in Children's Literature." *Journal of Reading* 24 (1981): 487–93.

Waite, Linda J. "The Importance of Marriage Is Being Overlooked." *USA Today,* January 1, 1999, magazine.

Waite, Linda J., and Maggie Gallagher. *The Case for Marriage: Why Married People Are Happier, Healthier, and Better Off Financially.* New York: Doubleday, 2000.

Wall Street Journal. "The Marriage Bonus." September 1, 2000.

———. "Voting Matters: Every Single Vote Counts." June 3, 2004.

Watters, Ethan. *Urban Tribes: A Generation Redefines Friendship, Family, and Commitment.* New York: Bloomsbury, 2003.

Webb, Andrew. "The Myth of Military Poverty." *Washington Monthly,* April 2001.

Wedding Gazette. "The Costs of Being a Bridesmaid." www.weddinggazette.com/content/002494.shtml, accessed March 24, 2005.

Week. "Why Crow Is Alone." November 21, 2003.

Wellman, Barry, Ove Frank, Vincente Espinoza, Staffan Lundquist, and Craig Wilson. "Integrating Individual, Relational, and Structural Analysis." *Social Networks* 13 (1991): 223–49.

Wheaton, Blair. "Life Transitions, Role Histories, and Mental Health." *American Sociological Review* 55 (1990): 209–23.

White, Jack E. "Marching for a Dream." *Time,* March 31, 2003.

White, Lynn, and Stacy J. Rogers. "Economic Circumstances and Family Outcomes: A Review of the 1990s." *Journal of Marriage and the Family* 62 (2000): 1035–51.

Whitehead, Barbara Dafoe. *Why There Are No Good Men Left: The Romantic Plight of the New Single Woman.* New York: Broadway Books, 2003.

Wilgoren, Jodi. "The Wedding Candidate on the Trail." *New York Times,* October 24, 2004.

Williams, Kipling D., Christopher K. T. Cheung, and Wilma Choi. "Cyberostracism: Effects of Being Ignored over the Internet." *Journal of Personality and Social Psychology* 79 (2000): 748–62.

Williams, Kristi, and Debra Umberson. "Marital Status, Marital Transitions, and Health: A Gendered Life Course Perspective." *Journal of Health and Social Behavior* 45 (2004): 81–98.

Wilmoth, Janet, and Gregor Koso. "Does Marital History Matter? Marital Status and Wealth Outcomes Among Preretirement Adults." *Journal of Marriage and Family* 64 (2002): 254–68.

Wilson, Anamaria. "In Brief: Good Will." *Time,* May 1, 2000.

Wilson, Margo, and Martin Daly. "Spousal Homicide Risk and Estrangement." *Violence and Victims* 8 (1993): 3–15.

Witman, Edward P. "Letters." *Time,* September 18, 2000.

Wood, Julia T. "The Normalization of Violence in Heterosexual Romantic Relationships: Women's Narratives of Love and Violence." *Journal of Social and Personal Relationships* 18 (2001): 239–61.

Woodward, Bob. *Bush at War.* New York: Simon & Schuster, 2002.

Wright, Robert. *The Moral Animal.* New York: Pantheon, 1994.

Wu, Zheng, and Randy Hart. "The Effects of Marital and Nonmarital Union Transition on Health." *Journal of Marriage and Family* 64 (2002): 420–32.

www.UnmarriedAmerica.org. "Some Laws Affecting Single People." July 20, 2005. www.unmarriedamerica.org/laws-affecting.html.

Yamada, Masahiro. "The Growing Crop of Spoiled Singles." *Japan Echo* 27 (2000). http://japanecho.co.jp/sum/2000/270313.html, accessed January 15, 2005.

———. *Parasite Single no Jidai* (The Era of Parasite Singles). Tokyo: Chikuma Shinsho, 1999.

Yoest, Charmaine. "Income Splitting: A Solution to the Marriage Penalty?" n.d. www.people.virginia.edu/~ccy2c/income_splitting.html, accessed July 22, 2005.

Zacharek, Stephanie. "Not Just Another Pretty Face." *Salon,* April 19, 2001. http://dir.salon.com/ent/movies/feature/2001/04/19/johnny_depp/index.html.

Zucchino, David. *The Myth of the Welfare Queen.* New York: Simon & Schuster, 1999.

ACKNOWLEDGMENTS

Sometime in the 1990s, I slipped the first newspaper clipping into a file folder and called it the beginning of my singles collection. Since then, my accumulation of outrageous, telling, and ennobling stories from the front lines of singlehood has grown to fill boxes, drawers, file cabinets, and entire rooms. And now finally, this book. For that, I have many people to thank.

Here are the people who have my gratitude and affection. I'm listing them alphabetically, for the most part, because it made my head hurt to try to figure out some other way. (Not all of them agree with what I have said in *Singled Out*—special thanks to those who told me so.)

Mark Alicke. For fine dining, scintillating and hilarious conversation, and dead-on feedback on my chapter drafts.

Nichole Argyres, my editor. She "got it" about this book, instantly. She read my drafts, over and over again, and then revealed her uncanny connection with my inner voice. (When the voice asked in disbelief whether I was really going to go ahead and say what I just wrote, I often ignored it. Then Nichole would ever so politely and persuasively make the same point.) She knew a lot more than the voice, too, and *Singled Out* and I can hardly thank her enough.

Kathy Bell. A grounded, warm, and wonderful friend.

Tom Coleman. Thanks for putting singles advocacy on the map, for coaching and encouraging me, and for being such an indefatigable spokesperson for the cause.

My "baby" brother, Joseph DePaulo. He knew long before I did that it was time to walk away from the university where I worked for more than two decades, and he made sure that I could. I adore him, and I am eternally grateful.

My sister, Lisa DePaulo. She's the real writer in the family. I wish I had her masterful skills! I do get to draw on them, though, as, for example, when she saved me from submitting a query letter that would have sunk this entire project. She also helped craft the title of this book. For all that and more, thanks.

My brother Peter DePaulo. When we were little, we would take turns reading the same *Hardy Boys* book—fifteen minutes per turn. He always read many more pages in his fifteen minutes than I did in mine, but he never mentioned it. He beat me at checkers and chess, too. Still, with friends, he would always think of some one thing I was good at, and brag about how terrific I was. He still does.

Kathy Edwards. We've never met, but she found me online, and has sent me many smart and savvy missives about the single life, Australian style. She read chapter drafts, too, and made my work much better as a consequence.

Ralph Erber. For years of lively conversations everywhere from ball-fields to Duck U, and for offering me coveted opportunities to present my singles work at a conference and in a journal I love, *Psychological Inquiry*.

Robin Gilmour. Thanks for the long talks about singles on walks on just about every beach within driving distance of Summerland.

Pryor Hale. Eloquent, erudite, and wickedly funny, she's been a believer in *Singled Out* from the beginning. I've learned so much from her and have had great fun doing so.

Judy Harackiewicz. For more than three decades of friendship.

Sharon Hays. Once Sharon and I begin a conversation, I never want it to end. She is a profound thinker and a cherished friend.

Sara Hodges. For her inexhaustible supply of singles stories, served with side helpings of interpretive genius. And many thanks for the close and enthusiastic reading of chapter drafts.

Susan Hurt. There were so many questions that puzzled and stumped me as I tried to understand the places of singles in contemporary American society. In the end, though, they all had the same answer: Ask Susan. She always had the wisest and wittiest take. Susan read just about every draft of my book proposal and my chapters. She welcomed my impassioned reports of all the intrigue of the publication process and made fun of anyone who dared to criticize *Singled Out*. To a longtime cherished friend, thank you.

Ann Lane. My first introduction to Ann was at a talk she gave, which began with, "As every schoolgirl knows . . ." She brought together groups of women for lunches and dinners to listen to what I had to say about singles, and made it better every time.

Bob Lescher, my agent. I still cannot believe my great good fortune to have him as my representative. When I read fond and wistful tales of the good old days of publishing, when agents were lifelong guides and mentors to their authors, I realize I am living in those days. Thank you, Bob.

Richard Lucas. For his infinite patience and graciousness as I asked him for one graph after another, posed lists of questions, and then asked him to read the draft of what I wrote about his work. And many thanks to him for doing such important research.

Farzaneh Milani. She believed in this project long before I was sure I could make it happen. No matter how many of the latest rejections I laid at her doorstep, she would not be dissuaded from her confidence. Thanks to an amazing person and a great friend.

Wendy Morris. She provided the scholarly drive behind much of our collaborative research. For that, for her generous feedback on my chapter drafts, and for her friendship, I thank her.

Cathy Popp. When I first decided to pursue the study of singles in earnest, I had no grant money, no laboratory full of postdocs or graduate students, and no collection of books or journal articles. She offered to help, and did so for years.

Emilie Rissman. Longtime friend and foodie tutor.

Bob Rosenthal. Adviser, mentor, and friend, he modeled and taught the utter delight of discovering what social science data are really trying to say.

Stacey Sinclair. For good friendship, good ideas, and good values.

Bobbie Spellman. For years of friendship and singles stories, shared over the course of many adventures, culinary and otherwise.

Weylin Sternglanz. Spirited source of stories and tireless reader of my work.

Kay Trimberger. We submitted our book proposals to publishers at the same time, but she completed *The New Single Woman* long before I finished *Singled Out*. She offered advice, encouragement, and discerning commentary on every chapter of my book.

Per Wehn. We bonded as writers of serious, but not humorless, science-based nonfiction at a conference full of writers of novels and memoirs, poetry and plays. It is hard to think of anyone who has read more widely than Per, and what delightful conversation that inspires! Makes for welcome feedback on my chapter drafts, too.

Nancy Weinfield. For her understated brilliance and unflagging friendship. She improved my thinking, my writing, and my moods.

My nephews Brian, Mike, Kevin, and Danny, and my niece Natalie (DePaulos, all). They showed me that it is not only parents who fall instantly in love with children and stay fiercely attached to them forevermore.

So many people indulged me as I pursued the passion that would become this book. They mailed clippings or forwarded e-mails or critiqued sections or initiated conversations or asked how the book was coming along—and actually wanted to know the answer. Thanks to Rachana Bhide, Eileen Boris, Susan Brodt, Roger Brown (in spirit), Ray Chan, Marcelle Clements, Nancy Collins, Marlo Faulkner, Kit Filan, David Gies, Irv Gottesman, Annie Guichard, Martie Haselton, Janine Hertel, Dave Kenny, Debra Lieberman, Marian Lizzi, Brian Malone, Diane Mapes, Laurie O'Brien, Anne Peplau, Lindsay Piccotti, Harry Reis, Rebecca Robins, Karen Rook, Tom Scheff, Nicole Shelton, Carol Tavris, Prue Thorner, Jenny Tornqvist, and Molly Walker.

Others, too, were helpful and encouraging. They include Carolyn Ahlstrand, Eric Anderson, Gene Block, Kirsti Brandt, Dan Burke, Kathryn Carlin, Bettina Casad, Leslie Cole, Lerita Coleman, Sarah Corse, Carrie Cropley, Faye Crosby, Kristin Davis (no, not that Kristin Davis), Carrie Douglas, Maureen Erber, Maire Ford, Aspasia Dew Frederick, Jean Goddard, Kelly Griffin DePaulo, Carol Gottesman, Dave Hamilton, Merissa Hart Ferrara, Mary Hegarty, Rob Hofberg, Teresa Juarez, Heejung Kim, Bob Kleck, Neneh Kowai-Bell, Marianne LaFrance, Fran Lexcen, Nelson Lichtenstein, Judith Loftus, Brenda Major, Susan Marsnik, Susie McKinnon, Sue Milmoe, Denise Newman, Janna Olson, Maureen O'Sullivan, Seymour Rabinowitz, Suzanne Retzinger, Mary Lu Rosenthal, Zick Rubin, Joan Shelly, David Sherman, Lisa Silver, Roxanne Silver, Sandy Thompson, Carol Toris, Leslie Westbrook, and Rebecca Zwick.

Hundreds more people sent me e-mails, approached me at social events or after talks that I gave, and shared their singles stories. Thanks to all of you.

Many scholars whom I've never met were generous in sharing their wisdom and insights. They include Nancy Berke, Anne Byrne, Deborah Carr,

Ingrid Connidis, Stephanie Coontz, Tanya Koropeckyj-Cox, Shari Motro, Pat Palmieri, Jill Reynolds, and so many of the participants in the Scholars of Single Women Network.

I also offer my gratitude for the interest in my work expressed by students and colleagues at the University of California at Santa Barbara, members of the Social Psychology Network, and the Alternatives to Marriage Project. Thanks as well to the participants in my class on Singles in Society who engaged and challenged me as I tried to find my way around the science of marriage and singlehood.

A second round of thanks to Mark Alicke, Brian DePaulo, and Mike DePaulo. They came through for me with patience and graciousness, when I thought I was finished asking them for help on this project.

Thanks also to Aaron Belkin, who put me in touch with many service members; to Bridget Wilson, who answered questions about how marital status matters in the military; and to the many service members who spoke to me about their experiences. To Robert Sardis for his super-quick and helpful answers to my questions about the tax information on Money-Chimp.com. To the man at the Social Security administration who did not want to be thanked by name, but who listened as I read the section on the benefits available to people who have married, suggested changes, then listened as I read the revised version. To Jill Katz for designing my website.

Thanks to the Anthony Marchionne Foundation for funding scholarly work on singlehood, and especially for funding some of my earliest efforts; and to its able and dedicated director, Craig Parks. To Nicky Grist, Marshall Miller, and Dorian Solot, who have spearheaded the Alternatives to Marriage Project, for all that they do for unmarried Americans.

Thanks to Christie Casalino, Carol Fass, Courtney Fischer, and John Murphy for their commitment to getting this book into the hands of people beyond those mentioned on these pages. Thanks also to Jennifer Carrow and Susan Walsh for putting their great talents to work on the design of this book.

Thanks to Steve Lamont for his meticulous copy-editing. And for asking whether there was something meaningful about forgetting the letter *i* when I typed *married*. To Mark Lerner, who showed me that getting legal advice can be educational and great fun, too. Who knew? To production editor Meg Drislane and executive managing editor Amelie Littell, for their careful work on *Singled Out*. To St. Martin's Press for taking a chance on a book about singles in a matrimaniacal publishing environment. St. Martin's has been there for singles. In 1981, when Peter Stein looked for a publisher for what was probably the first collection of scholarly writings on singles in society, he found St. Martin's.

My parents, Josie and Joe, married in 1949, had four kids, and stayed married until my dad died in 1991. My mom then became an independent solo-dwelling singleton who stayed single from that day forward. She continued to welcome friends, neighbors, family, grown kids, and their friends and families into her home, where she filled them with smiles and ravioli until the day she died in 1998. Sadly, neither parent lived to see this book, but their spirit is on every page.

INDEX